Summary Guides

Maths 10

Mei Yi Tan

First published in 2024, reprinted in 2025.

Insight Publications Pty Ltd
3/350 Charman Road
Cheltenham Victoria 3192
Australia

Tel: +61 3 8571 4950
Email: books@insightpublications.com.au
www.insightpublications.com.au

Summary Guides – Maths 10 / Mei Yi Tan

ISBN: 9781923154575

Edited by Dr Geoffrey Marnell
Proofread by Sage Napthine-Morrison
Artwork by Artin Education
Layout by Aptara®, Inc.
Cover design by Melisa Paredes
Printed by Markono Print Media Pte Ltd

Table of contents

Introduction

The *Summary Guides – Maths* series has been written by practising teachers who are passionate about creating user-friendly, accessible guides on mathematics.

The explanations and exercises in these guides develop core numeracy skills for personal, work and civic life, and provide the base knowledge for professional applications of maths as well as for mathematical specialisations. Maths is part of your daily life no matter what you choose to do as an adult – it is important for thinking critically and making sense of the world.

This book summarises key concepts in a clear and comprehensive way. It includes examples with worked solutions and step-by-step explanations, as well as exercises for you to complete. The best way to use this book is to make a habit of it – regularly working through the exercises and examples, and comparing your answers with those provided. Whether you commit to a daily, weekly or fortnightly routine, consistent practice is the key to your success.

The content of this book is based on years of experience making maths comprehensible to students in the classroom. By working through this book you will be able to practise your skills, grow in confidence and reap the rewards that come from a solid understanding of maths.

Mei Yi Tan and Insight Publications

Mei Yi Tan PhD (Mathematics), GradDipEdu (Secondary) is a mathematics teacher at Helena College in Perth. She has taught in the secondary and tertiary sectors for a number of years, and is also a marker for WACE Mathematics Methods.

Chapter 1 – Algebra

1.1 Expanding algebraic expressions

To **expand** an expression, we multiply every term inside the brackets by the term(s) outside the brackets and then collect like terms. When expanding an expression, we follow the **distributive law**, illustrated below.

$$a(x+y) = ax + ay$$

An expression involving two sets of bracketed terms can also be expanded. This is known as binomial expansion and involves applying the distributive law multiple times. Each term inside one set of brackets is multiplied by each term in the other set of brackets. For example, the expression $(a + b)(x + y)$ can be expanded as:

$$(a+b)(x+y) = a(x+y) + b(x+y)$$

$$= ax + ay + bx + by$$

One way to remember to multiply all the terms is to think of the letters in the word '**FOIL**': **F** = first terms, **O** = outer terms, **I** = inner terms and **L** = last terms.

$$(a+b)(x+y) = ax + ay + bx + by$$

Note: remember to simplify the expression by adding like terms together.

Example

Expand the following expressions.

a. $4(a + 3b)$ **b.** $2y(6 - 2x)$ **c.** $3(x - 2) + 2(x + 1)$

✓ *Solution*

Working	Explanation
a. $4(a+3b)=4a+12b$	Multiply each pronumeral or number outside the brackets by each pronumeral or number inside the brackets. Collect like terms where they exist.
b. $2y(6-2x)=12y-4xy$	
c. $3(x-2)+2(x+1)=3x-6+2x+2$ $=5x-4$	

Example

Expand the following binomial expressions.

a. $(4a+3)(a-3)$ **b.** $(2-3c)(c+2)$ **c.** $(3x-2)(x-5)$

✓ *Solution*

Working	Explanation
a. $(4a+3)(a-3)$ $=(4a\times a)+(4a\times(-3))+(3\times a)+(3\times -3)$ $=4a^2-12a+3a-9$ $=4a^2-9a-9$	Using the FOIL method: 1. Multiply both first terms (F). 2. Multiply the first term of the first expression by the last term of the second expression (O). 3. Multiply the second term of the first expression by the first term of the second expression (I). 4. Multiply both second terms (L). 5. Collect like terms.
b. $(2-3c)(c+2)$ $=(2\times c)+(2\times 2)+((-3c)\times c)+((-3c)\times 2)$ $=2c+4-3c^2-6c$ $=-3c^2-4c+4$	
c. $(3x-2)(x-5)$ $=(3x\times x)+(3x\times(-5))+((-2)\times x)+((-2)\times(-5))$ $=3x^2-15x-2x+10$ $=3x^2-17x+10$	

Note:

- Pay attention to the sign of each term when multiplying terms.
- The product of two linear binomial expressions is known as a quadratic expression.

Exercise 1.1

Expand and simplify the following expressions.

a. $4(2y - 5)$

b. $7(2a + b - 3)$

c. $-5(2a - 3b) + 4(a + b)$

d. $2(3x + 4) - 3(2x - 5)$

e. $(3x + 2)(2x - 1)$

f. $(y - 4)(y + 3) - (y - 1)(y + 2)$

g. $(x^2 + 1)(x - 1)$

h. $(x + 2)^2 - (x - 3)^2$

i. $(x^2 + 2x + 1)(x^2 - 2x + 1)$

j. $(2x + 3)(2x - 3)$

k. $(1 - 4x)(4x - 1)$

l. $(2y - 1)^2 - (y + 2)^2$

1.2 Factorising algebraic expressions

Factorising is the process of converting an expression into its factors. You may have already learnt the following:

- factorising by taking out the highest common factor (HCF)
- factorising by grouping
- factorising monic quadratic expressions
- factorising non-monic quadratic expressions
- factorising perfect squares and the difference of two squares (DOTS).

Factorising by taking out the highest common factor (HCF)

To factorise by taking out the HCF, we work out the HCF of each term and separate it from the expression. The HCF of two or more numbers is the largest whole number that is a factor of each of the given numbers. For example, the HCF of 12 and 48 is 12.

Example

Factorise the following expressions by taking out the HCF.

a. $3x + 9$

b. $2a^2 - 4a$

c. $a(x - 4) + 6(x - 4)$

✓ *Solution*

Working	Explanation
a. HCF $= 3$ $3x + 9 = 3(x + 3)$	1. Identify the HCF in the expression (that is, the largest factor that is common to each term). 2. Place the HCF in front of a pair of brackets. 3. Inside the brackets, place the expression that results after dividing the original expression by the HCF.
b. HCF $= 2a$ $2a^2 - 4a = 2a(a - 2)$	
c. HCF $= (x - 4)$ $a(x - 4) + 6(x - 4) = (x - 4)(a + 6)$	

Factorising by grouping

To factorise by grouping, we collect terms that share a pronumeral and treat each group as a separate binomial expression.

Example

Factorise the following expressions by grouping.

a. $3ax - a + 12x - 4$

b. $gh - 6 + 2g - 3h$

✓ *Solution*

Working	Explanation
a. $3ax - a + 12x - 4 = (3ax - a) + (12x - 4)$ $= a(3x - 1) + 4(3x - 1)$ $= (3x - 1)(a + 4)$	**1.** Group the first two terms and the last two terms. **2.** Take out the HCF of each group (a and 4). We now have two factorised expressions. **3.** Fully factorise by taking out the HCF of the factorised expressions $(3x - 1)$.
b. $gh - 6 + 2g - 3h = gh + 2g - 3h - 6$ $= g(h + 2) - 3(h + 2)$ $= (h + 2)(g - 3)$	**1.** Rearrange the expression so that there are two groups, one with a HCF of g and the other with a HCF of -3. **2.** Factorise by taking out both HCFs. **3.** Fully factorise by taking out the HCF of both groups $(h + 2)$.

Factorising monic quadratic expressions

The product of two linear binomial expressions is a quadratic expression. It is usually written in the form $ax^2 + bx + c$ where a, b and c are real numbers. When $a = 1$, the equation is called a monic quadratic expression.

Note that

$$(x + p)(x + q) = x^2 + (p + q)x + pq$$

which can be rewritten as

$$x^2 + (p + q)x + pq = x^2 + bx + c$$

Hence, to factorise a monic quadratic equation of the form $ax^2 + bx + c$, look for two numbers (p and q) such that $p + q = b$ and $pq = c$.

Example

Factorise the following monic quadratic expressions.

a. $x^2 + 6x + 8$

b. $x^2 + x - 30$

✓ Solution

Working	Explanation
a. $x^2 + 6x + 8 = x^2 + 2x + 4x + 8$ $= x(x + 2) + 4(x + 2)$ $= (x + 2)(x + 4)$	**1.** Look for values of p and q that give $pq = 8$ and $p + q = 6$. Two values are $p = 2$ and $q = 4$. **2.** Rewrite $6x$ as $2x + 4x$. **3.** Factorise by grouping.
b. $x^2 + x - 30 = x^2 + 6x - 5x - 30$ $= x(x + 6) - 5(x + 6)$ $= (x + 6)(x - 5)$	**1.** Look for values of p and q that give $pq = -30$ and $p + q = 1$. Two values are $p = 6$ and $q = -5$. **2.** Rewrite x as $6x - 5x$. **3.** Factorise by grouping.

Factorising non-monic quadratic expressions

If $a > 1$ for an expression of the form $ax^2 + bx + c$, we have a non-monic quadratic expression.

To factorise a non-monic quadratic expression:

1. Factorise out the HCF, if there is one.
2. Find two numbers, p and q, such that $p \times q = ac$ and $p + q = b$.
3. Rewrite bx as $px + qx$.
4. Factorise by grouping.

Example

Factorise the following expressions.

a. $3x^2 - 2x - 8$

b. $4x^2 + 14x + 6$

✓ Solution

Working	Explanation
a. $3x^2 - 2x - 8 = 3x^2 - 6x + 4x - 8$ $= 3x(x - 2) + 4(x - 2)$ $= (x - 2)(3x + 4)$	**1.** There is no HCF to factorise out. **2.** Find two numbers, p and q, such that $p \times q = -24$ and $p + q = -2$. Two numbers are $p = -6$ and $q = 4$. **3.** Rewrite $-2x$ as $-6x + 4x$. **4.** Factorise by grouping.
b. $4x^2 + 14x + 6 = 2(2x^2 + 7x + 3)$ $= 2(2x^2 + x + 6x + 3)$ $= 2[x(2x + 1) + 3(2x + 1)]$ $= 2(2x + 1)(x + 3)$	**1.** Factorise out the HCF: 2. **2.** Find two numbers, p and q, such that $p \times q = 6$ and $p + q = 7$. Two numbers are $p = 1$ and $q = 6$. **3.** Rewrite $7x$ as $x + 6x$. **4.** Factorise by grouping.

Factorising a perfect square or a difference of two squares

A perfect square is an expression that results from multiplying two identical expressions. For example:

$$(a+b)^2 = a^2 + 2ab + b^2$$
$$(a-b)^2 = a^2 - 2ab + b^2$$

An expression is a perfect square if the constant term (b^2) is a square number (e.g. 4, 9, 16 etc.) and the coefficient of a ($2b$) is double the square root of the constant term.

A difference of two squares (DOTS) is one square expression minus another square expression.

$$(a+b)(a-b) = a^2 - ab + ab - b^2$$
$$= a^2 - b^2$$

To factorise a DOTS, recognise that the binomial is a difference of squares. Rewrite the binomial such that each term is written as a squared term. Hence the factors of a DOTS of the form $a^2 - b^2$ are $a \pm b$.

Example

Factorise the following expressions.

a. $x^2 + 8x + 16$ **b.** $3x^2 + 18x + 27$ **c.** $x^2 - 36$ **d.** $16x^2 - 25$

✓ *Solution*

Working	Explanation
a. $x^2 + 8x + 16 = x^2 + 2(4)(x) + 4^2$ $= (x+4)^2$	**1.** Note that 16 is 4^2 and $8 = 2 \times 4$. **2.** It follows that the quadratic is a perfect square and that the factorised form with identical factors can thus be obtained.
b. $3x^2 + 18x + 27 = 3(x^2 + 6x + 9)$ $= 3(x^2 + 2(3)(x) + 3^2)$ $= 3(x+3)^2$	**1.** The HCF for each term is 3. Therefore, factorise by taking out the HCF first. **2.** Note that 9 is 3^2 and $6 = 2 \times 3$. **3.** It follows that the quadratic is a perfect square and the factorised form can then be obtained.
c. $x^2 - 36 = (x-6)(x+6)$	**1.** Note that $36 = 6^2$ and hence the full expression is a difference of two squares (DOTS). **2.** Since the factors of a DOTS of the form $a^2 - b^2$ are $a \pm b$, the factorised form can be obtained.
d. $16x^2 - 25 = (4x-5)(4x+5)$	**1.** Note that $16x^2 = (4x)^2$ and $25 = 5^2$. Hence the full expression is a DOTS. **2.** Since the factors of a DOTS of the form $a^2 - b^2$ are $a \pm b$, the factorised form can be obtained.

Exercise 1.2

Factorise the following quadratic expressions.

a. $x^2 + 5x + 6$	**b.** $x^2 - x - 12$	**c.** $x^2 - 12x + 35$
d. $x^2 + 12x + 36$	**e.** $x^2 + 14x + 49$	**f.** $2x^2 - 20x + 50$
g. $x^2 - 144$	**h.** $1 - 49x^2$	**i.** $-3x^2 + 18x - 24$
j. $3x^2 + 11x + 6$	**k.** $8x^2 + 2x - 15$	**l.** $8x^2 + 28x - 60$

1.3 Algebraic fractions

Algebraic fractions are fractions with algebraic expressions as the numerator, denominator or both. For example:

$$\frac{3x}{5} \qquad \frac{5}{2x-3} \qquad \frac{x^2-2x}{4x+3}$$

Simplifying algebraic fractions

To simplify algebraic fractions:

1. Where possible, factorise by taking out the HCF from the numerator and from the denominator.
2. Where possible, factorise the numerator and the denominator.
3. Cancel out any common factors in the numerator and the denominator.

Example

Simplify the following algebraic fractions.

a. $\frac{9x-12}{3}$ **b.** $\frac{x^2+4x-12}{x^2+3x-18}$ **c.** $\frac{x^2-y^2}{x^2-xy}$

✓ Solution

Working	Explanation
a. $\frac{9x-12}{3} = \frac{3(3x-4)}{3}$ $= 3x - 4$	1. Factorise the HCF from the numerator. 2. Simplify the fraction.
b. $\frac{x^2+4x-12}{x^2+3x-18} = \frac{(x+6)(x-2)}{(x+6)(x-3)}$ $= \frac{x-2}{x-3}$	1. Factorise both the numerator and denominator. 2. Notice that the numerator and denominator share a common factor: $(x + 6)$. This can be cancelled thereby simplifying the fraction.
c. $\frac{x^2-y^2}{x^2-xy} = \frac{(x+y)(x-y)}{x(x-y)}$ $= \frac{x+y}{x}$	1. Factorise both the numerator and denominator. 2. Notice that the numerator and denominator share a common factor: $(x - y)$. This can be cancelled to simplify the fraction.

Exercise 1.3.1

Simply the following algebraic expressions.

a. $\dfrac{4x^2+6x}{2x}$

b. $\dfrac{24x^3y^2z-36x^2yz^2}{12xyz}$

c. $\dfrac{x^2+9x+14}{x+2}$

d. $\dfrac{2x^2+7x+3}{x+3}$

e. $\dfrac{2x^2+5x+2}{2x+1}$

f. $\dfrac{x^2-4}{x^2-2x-8}$

g. $\dfrac{2x^2-9x-5}{x^2-4x-5}$

h. $\dfrac{3x^2-8x-3}{x^2-6x+9}$

i. $\dfrac{4x^2-9}{2x^2+7x+6}$

Adding and subtracting algebraic fractions

To add or subtract an algebraic fraction, follow these steps.

1. Determine the lowest common denominator (LCD).
2. Express each fraction as an equivalent fraction with the LCD.
3. Add or subtract the numerators and simplify.

Example

Simplify the following algebraic fractions.

a. $\dfrac{3}{5x}+\dfrac{2}{3xy}$

b. $\dfrac{4}{3x}-\dfrac{2}{7}$

c. $\dfrac{x+3}{2}+\dfrac{x-2}{5}$

d. $\dfrac{3}{x-6}-\dfrac{2}{x+2}$

✓ *Solution*

Working	Explanation
a. $\dfrac{3}{5x}+\dfrac{2}{3xy}=\dfrac{3}{5x}\left(\dfrac{3y}{3y}\right)+\dfrac{2}{3xy}\left(\dfrac{5}{5}\right)$ $=\dfrac{9y}{15xy}+\dfrac{10}{15xy}$ $=\dfrac{9y+10}{15xy}$	1. Determine the lowest common denominator: LCD = $15xy$. 2. Express each fraction as an equivalent fraction with the LCD as the denominator. 3. Add the numerators together and simplify.
b. $\dfrac{4}{3x}-\dfrac{2}{7}=\dfrac{4}{3x}\left(\dfrac{7}{7}\right)-\dfrac{2}{7}\left(\dfrac{3x}{3x}\right)$ $=\dfrac{28}{21x}-\dfrac{6x}{21x}$ $=\dfrac{28-6x}{21x}$	1. Determine the lowest common denominator: LCD = $21x$. 2. Express each fraction as an equivalent fraction with the LCD as the denominator. 3. Subtract the numerators and simplify.

c. $\frac{x+3}{2}+\frac{x-2}{5}=\frac{x+3}{2}\left(\frac{5}{5}\right)+\frac{x-2}{5}\left(\frac{2}{2}\right)$ $=\frac{5(x+3)}{10}+\frac{2(x-2)}{10}$ $=\frac{5x+15+2x-4}{10}$ $=\frac{7x+11}{10}$	1. Determine the lowest common denominator: LCD = 10. 2. Express each fraction as an equivalent fraction with the LCD as the denominator. 3. Add the numerators together and simplify.
d. $\frac{3}{x-6}-\frac{2}{x+2}=\frac{3}{x-6}\left(\frac{x+2}{x+2}\right)-\frac{2}{x+2}\left(\frac{x-6}{x-6}\right)$ $=\frac{3(x+2)}{(x-6)(x+2)}-\frac{2(x-6)}{(x+2)(x-6)}$ $=\frac{3x+6-2x+12}{(x-6)(x+2)}$ $=\frac{x+18}{(x-6)(x+2)}$	1. Determine the lowest common denominator: LCD = $(x-6)(x+2)$. 2. Express each fraction as an equivalent fraction with the LCD as the denominator. 3. Subtract the numerators and simplify.

Exercise 1.3.2

Simply the following algebraic expressions.

a. $\frac{x+2}{3}+\frac{x}{2}$

b. $\frac{x+4}{3}-\frac{x}{6}$

c. $\frac{x+3}{5}+\frac{x+2}{4}$

d. $\frac{2x+3}{7}+\frac{x+1}{2}$

e. $\frac{x+1}{5}-\frac{x-2}{6}$

f. $\frac{x+4}{3}-\frac{2x-1}{8}$

g. $\frac{4}{x}+\frac{2}{3}$

h. $\frac{3}{2x}-\frac{7}{9}$

i. $\frac{5}{x}+\frac{2}{x+3}$

j. $\frac{4}{x-7}+\frac{3}{x+2}$

k. $\frac{4}{x-5}+\frac{2}{3x-4}$

l. $\frac{3}{x+2}-\frac{2}{x}$

m. $\frac{6}{x-1}-\frac{3}{x-4}$

n. $\frac{5}{x+7}-\frac{6}{2x-1}$

o. $\frac{3}{x+1}+\frac{2}{(x+1)^2}$

Multiplying and dividing algebraic fractions

The rules for multiplying and dividing algebraic fractions are the same as for multiplying and dividing numerical fractions. To multiply two fractions, we multiply the numerators and the denominators of each fraction. For example:

$$\frac{3x^2}{y}\times\frac{4x}{9y}=\frac{3x^2\times 4x}{y\times 9y}=\frac{12x^3}{9y^2}=\frac{4x^3}{3y^2}$$

Note: sometimes it may be easier to factorise the algebraic fractions before multiplying them.

To divide two fractions, we convert the fraction after the division sign to its reciprocal and then multiply the fractions together. For example:

$$\frac{4x}{3}\div\frac{7x^2}{y}=\frac{4x}{3}\times\frac{y}{7x^2}=\frac{4x\times y}{3\times 7x^2}=\frac{4xy}{21x^2}=\frac{4y}{21x}$$

Example

Simplify the following algebraic fractions.

a. $\frac{x}{x+1} \times \frac{x+2}{3x}$

b. $\frac{6x^2}{2x+3} \div \frac{2}{3x}$

c. $\frac{3x^2 - 7x + 2}{x^2 - x - 6} \times \frac{x^2 - 4}{6x - 2}$

d. $\frac{x^2 - 2x + 1}{x^2 + 3x + 2} \div \frac{x^2 - 1}{x^2 + 2x + 1}$

✓ Solution

Working	Explanation
a. $\frac{x}{x+1} \times \frac{x+2}{3x} = \frac{x \times (x+2)}{(x+1) \times 3x}$ $= \frac{x^2 + 2x}{3x^2 + 3x}$ $= \frac{x(x+2)}{x(3x+3)}$ $= \frac{x+2}{3x+3}$	1. Multiply the numerators together. 2. Multiply the denominators together. 3. Expand using the distributive law.
b. $\frac{6x^2}{2x+3} \div \frac{2}{3x} = \frac{6x^2}{2x+3} \times \frac{3x}{2}$ $= \frac{6x^2 \times 3x}{(2x+3) \times 2}$ $= \frac{18x^3}{2(2x+3)}$ $= \frac{9x^3}{2x+3}$	1. Since this is a division, we have to convert the fraction after the division sign to its reciprocal. 2. Multiply the two fractions. 3. Simplify where appropriate.
c. $\frac{3x^2 - 7x + 2}{x^2 - x - 6} \times \frac{x^2 - 4}{6x - 2}$ $= \frac{(3x-1)(x-2)}{(x+2)(x-3)} \times \frac{(x-2)(x+2)}{2(3x-1)}$ $= \frac{(x-2) \times (x-2)}{2(x-3)}$ or $= \frac{x^2 - 4x + 4}{2x - 6}$	1. Factorise the numerators and the denominators. 2. Cancel like terms. **Note:** you do not have to expand the numerator. 3. Multiply the terms in the numerator and denominator.

d. $\dfrac{x^2-2x+1}{x^2+3x+2} \div \dfrac{x^2-1}{x^2+2x+1}$ $=\dfrac{(x-1)(x-1)}{(x+2)(x+1)} \div \dfrac{(x-1)(x+1)}{(x+1)(x+1)}$	1. Factorise the numerators and the denominators.
$=\dfrac{(x-1)(x-1)}{(x+2)(x+1)} \times \dfrac{(x+1)(x+1)}{(x-1)(x+1)}$	2. Convert the algebraic fraction to the right of the division sign to its reciprocal and change the division to a multiplication.
$=\dfrac{x-1}{x+2}$	3. Cancel like terms.

Exercise 1.3.3

Simply the following algebraic expressions.

a. $\dfrac{x^2-x}{x-2} \times \dfrac{3x-6}{4x-4}$

b. $\dfrac{x^2-9}{x^2-1} \times \dfrac{2x+2}{x+3}$

c. $\dfrac{3x^2-6x}{x^2-4} \times \dfrac{x+2}{2x^2-2}$

d. $\dfrac{x^2+x-2}{x^2+4x-5} \times \dfrac{x^2+x-12}{x^2+6x+8}$

e. $\dfrac{2x^2+7x+3}{x^2-9} \times \dfrac{3x^2+17x+10}{2x^2+11x+5}$

f. $\dfrac{5x-20}{4} \div \dfrac{2x-8}{3}$

g. $\dfrac{4x^2-12x}{x^2-9} \div \dfrac{x^2-1}{3x-3}$

h. $\dfrac{6x^2+2x}{3x^2+7x+2} \div \dfrac{4x}{x^2+4x+4}$

i. $\dfrac{x^2-10x+25}{2x^2+5x+3} \div \dfrac{x^2-7x+10}{2x^2-x-6}$

j. $\dfrac{x^2+6x}{x^2+12x+36} \div \dfrac{x^2+5x}{3x-6} \times \dfrac{x^2-25}{6x^2-12x}$

k. $\dfrac{x^2-6x+9}{2x^2-4x-6} \times \dfrac{x^2-x-2}{2x} \div \dfrac{x^2+2x-8}{4x}$

Chapter 2 – Exponentials

2.1 Relations and functions

Relations

A **relation** is any set of ordered pairs (x, y) that connects two variables.

The **domain** of a relation is the set of possible values that x may take.

The **range** of a relation is the set of possible values that y may take.

The following table provides examples of various relations.

Graph	Relation	Domain and range
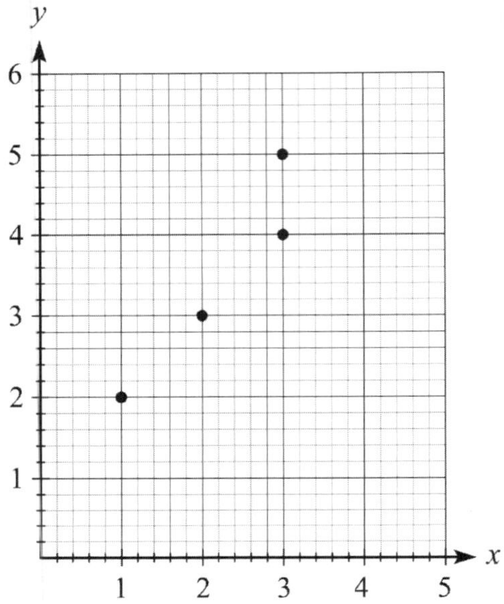	$A = \{(1,2), (2,3), (3,4), (3,5)\}$ For this relation there is no equation connecting x and y.	Domain: $\{1,2,3\}$ Range: $\{2,3,4,5\}$
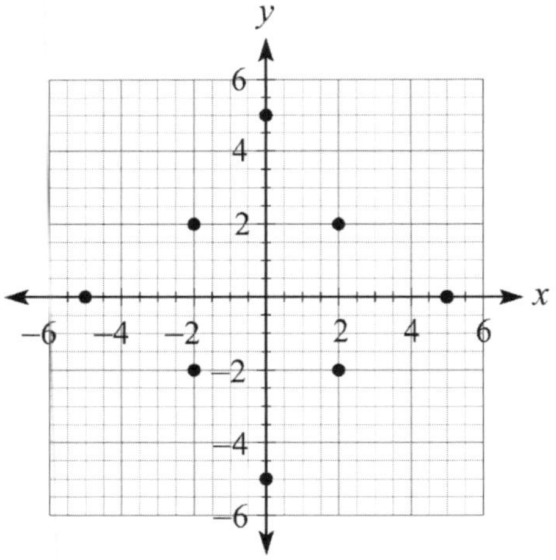	$B = \{(0, 5), (0, -5), (5, 0), (-5, 0), (-2, 2), (2, 2), (2, -2), (-2, -2)\}$ For this relation there is no equation connecting x and y.	Domain: $\{-5, -2, 0, 2, 5\}$ Range: $\{-5, -2, 0, 2, 5\}$

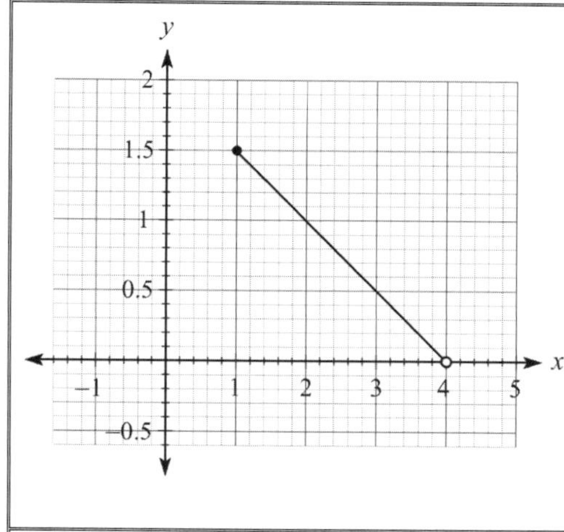	$y = -\frac{1}{2}x + 2$ The set of all points on the graph of this linear equation is a relation.	Domain: $\{x \in R, 1 \le x < 4\}$ Range: $= \{y \in R, 0 < y \le 1.5\}$ **Note:** • R represents all real numbers, that is, all numbers on the number line. • An open circle means that the number is not included, while a closed circle means that it is.
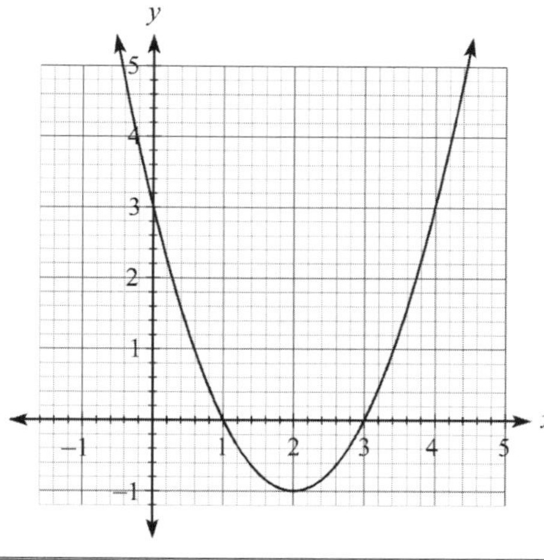	$y = x^2 - 4x + 3$ The set of all points on this parabola is a relation.	Domain: $\{x \in R\}$ Range: $\{y \in R, y \ge -1\}$

Functions

A function is a relation in which each x-value has only one corresponding y-value.

Example

Which of the following sets of ordered pairs could be the result of a function?

a. $\{(-3, -4), (-2, -2), (-6, 8), (1, 4)\}$

b. $\{(-3, 2), (-3, -2), (4, 1), (5, 2)\}$

✓ *Solution*

Working	Explanation
a. $\{(-3, -4), (-2, -2), (-6, 8), (1, 4)\}$ is a function.	For each x-value there is only one y-value.
b. $\{(-3, 2), (-3, -2), (4, 1), (5, 2)\}$ is not a function.	The relation contains two ordered pairs with the same x-value: $(-3, -2)$ and $(-3, 2)$.

The vertical line test is one way to determine whether a relation is also a function. If a vertical line can be drawn anywhere through the graph and it intersects the graph at most once, then the relation is a function.

Example

Which of these relations are functions?

a.

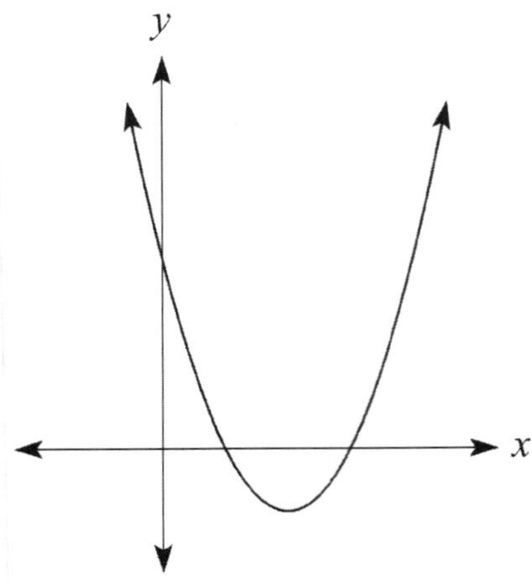

b.

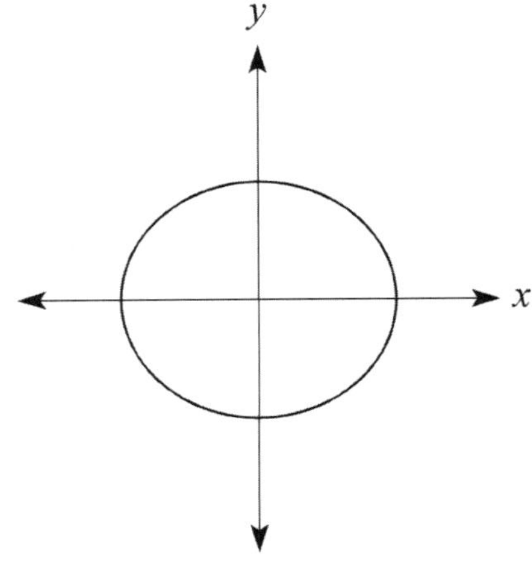

✓ *Solution*

Working	Explanation
a. The relation is a function.	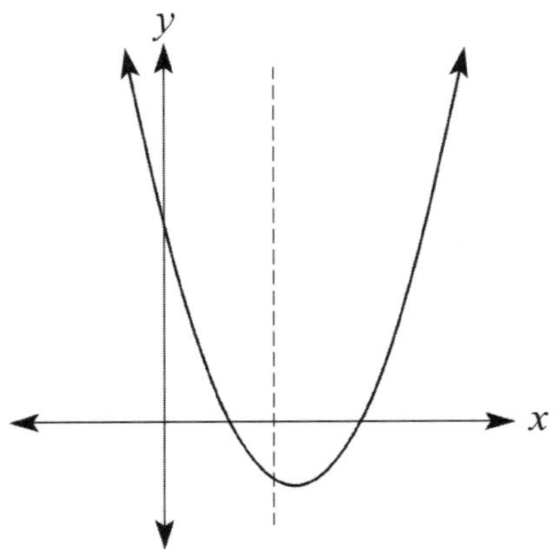 Every vertical line that can be drawn through the graph intersects the graph only once.
b. The relation is not a function.	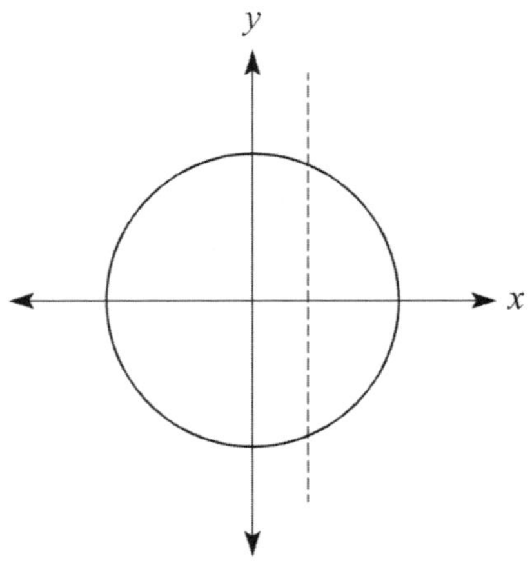 We can draw a vertical line that intersects the graph twice.

Exercise 2.1.1.1

State the domain and range of the following relations.

a. $\{(-3, -4), (-1, -1), (-6, 7), (1, 5)\}$

b. $\{(-4, 1), (-4, -1), (-6, 7), (-6, 8)\}$

c.

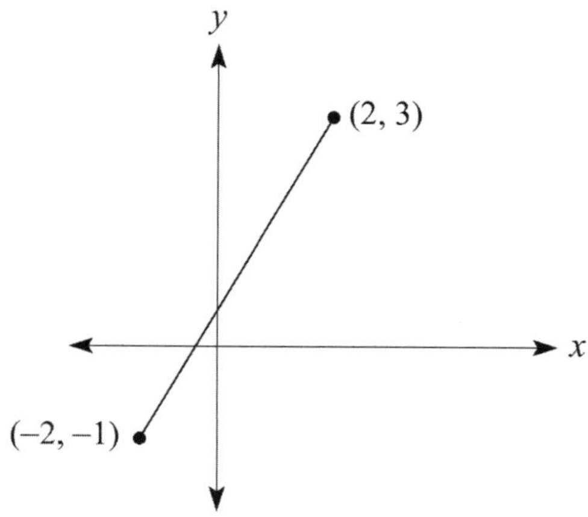

d.

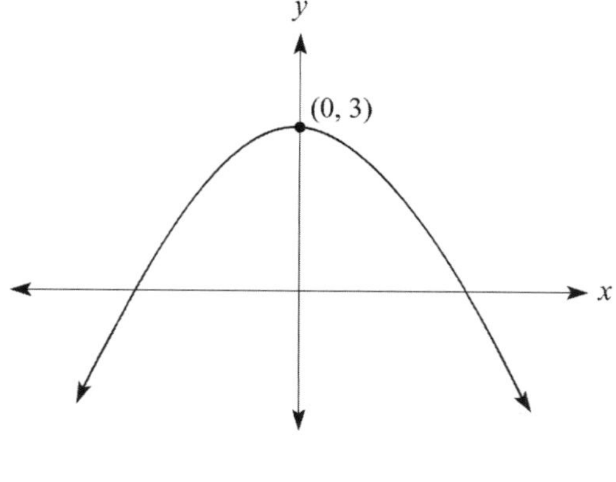

Exercise 2.1.1.2

Which of the following sets of ordered pairs are functions? Give reasons for your answers.

a. $\{(-1, 2), (-3, 2), (3, 2), (1, 2)\}$

b. $\{(3, -2), (3, 0), (3, 2), (3, 4)\}$

Exercise 2.1.1.3

Use the vertical line test to determine which of the following relations are functions.

a.

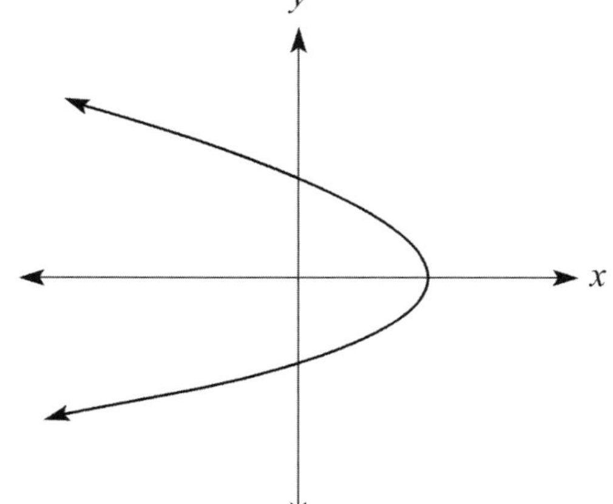

b.

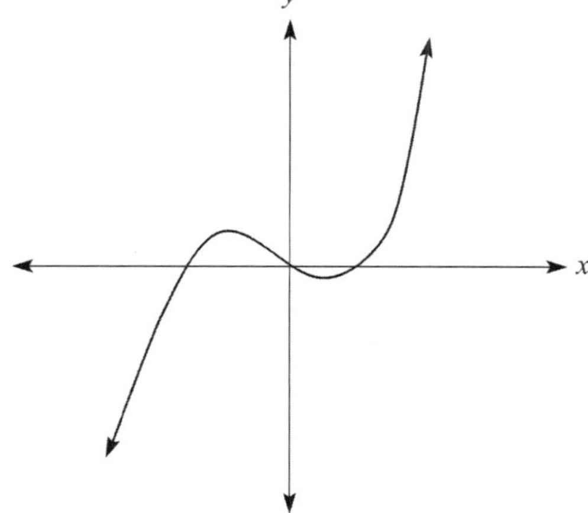

Function notation

Functions are usually denoted by lowercase letters, such as f, g, h etc.

We read $f(x)$ as 'f of x'. f is the function that relates an input to an output.

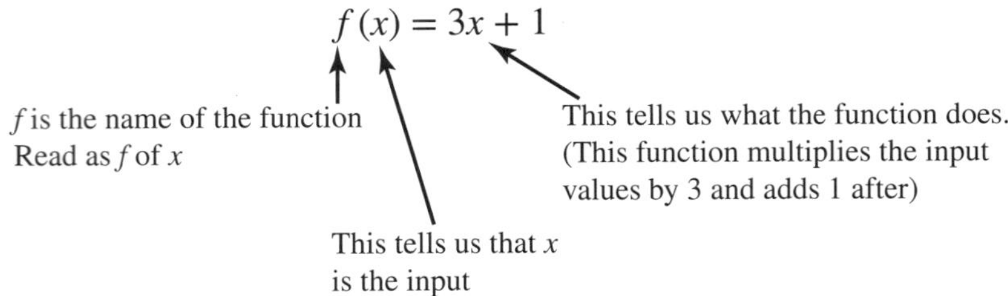

Instead of $y = 3x + 1$, we can write $f(x) = 3x + 1$. Then $f(2)$ means the y-value obtained when $x = 2$: $f(2) = 3(2) + 1 = 7$.

Example

For $f(x) = 2x^2 - 4x$, determine the value of the following.

a. $f(2)$ **b.** $f(-3)$ **c.** $f(p + 1)$

✓ *Solution*

Working	Explanation
a. $f(2) = 2(2)^2 - 4(2)$ $= 2(4) - 8$ $= 0$	Substitute $x = 2$ and simplify.
b. $f(-3) = 2(-3)^2 - 4(-3)$ $= 2(9) + 12$ $= 30$	Substitute $x = -3$ and simplify.
c. $f(p + 1) = 2(p + 1)^2 - 4(p + 1)$ $= 2(p^2 + 2p + 1) - 4p - 4$ $= 2p^2 + 4p + 2 - 4p - 4$ $= 2p^2 - 2$	Substitute $x = p + 1$ and simplify.

Exercise 2.1.2.1

For $f(x) = 2x + 3$, determine the following.

a. $f(0)$ **b.** $f(-3)$ **c.** $f\left(\frac{1}{2}\right)$ **d.** $f(a - 2)$ **e.** $f(2a)$

Exercise 2.1.2.2

For $f(x) = 3x^2 + 2x - 1$, determine the following.

a. $f(3)$ **b.** $f(-2)$ **c.** $f(-a)$ **d.** $f(a+1)$ **e.** $f\left(\frac{a}{2}\right)$

Transformation of functions

If functions $f(x)$ and $g(x)$ are similar, we can graph $g(x)$ by applying a transformation to $f(x)$.

The following table provides examples of various transformations.

Graph transformations	Explanation
y $y = f(x) + k$ k x $y = f(x)$	**$f(x) \rightarrow f(x) + k$** Graphs of $y = f(x) + k$ are found by translating the graph of $f(x)$ up or down by k units. In other words, the y-coordinates of $f(x)$ are translated by k units: $x, y \rightarrow (x, y + k)$. • If $k > 0$, the graph is translated upwards. • If $k < 0$, the graph is translated downwards.
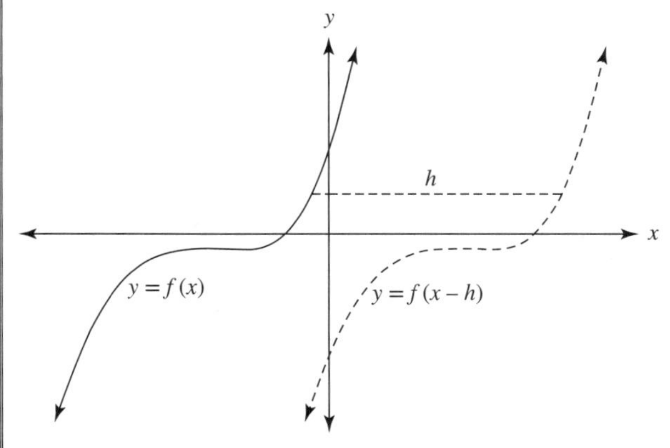	**$f(x) \rightarrow f(x - h)$** Graphs of $y = f(x - h)$ are found by translating the graph $f(x)$ left or right by h units. In other words, the x-coordinates of $f(x)$ are translated by h units: $x, y \rightarrow (x + h, y)$. • If $h > 0$, the graph is translated to the right. • If $h < 0$, the graph is translated to the left.
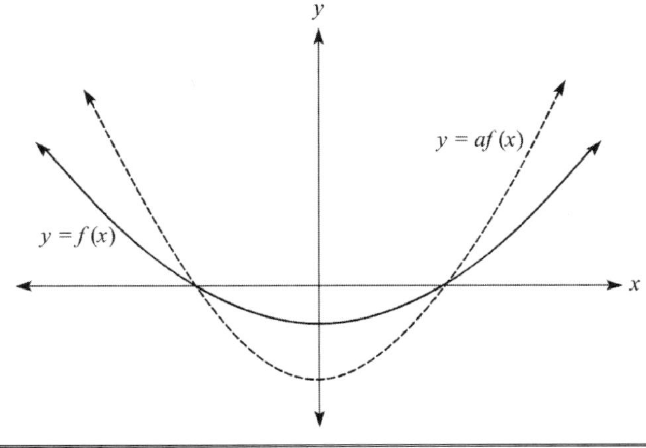	**$f(x) \rightarrow af(x)$** Graphs of $y = af(x)$ are found by dilating the graph $f(x)$ parallel to the y–axis by a scale factor of a. In other words, the y-coordinates of $f(x)$ are multiplied by a scale factor of a: $x, y \rightarrow (x, ay)$.

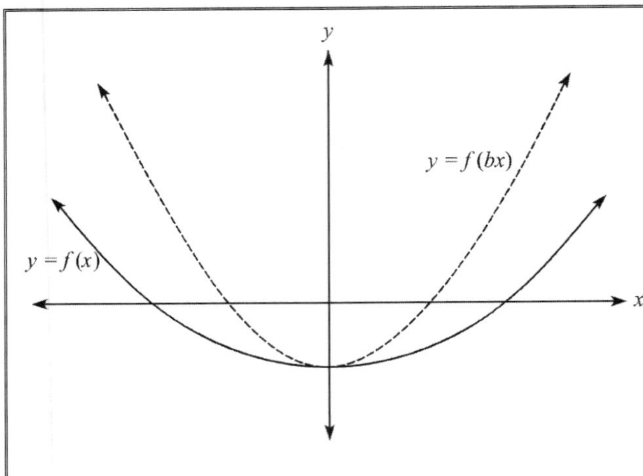	**$f(x) \rightarrow f(bx)$** Graphs of $y = f(bx)$ are found by dilating the graph $f(x)$ parallel to the x-axis by a scale factor of $\frac{1}{b}$. In other words, the x-coordinates of $f(x)$ are multiplied by a scale factor of $\frac{1}{b}$: $(x:y) \rightarrow \left(\frac{1}{b}x, y\right)$. **Note:** the graph is dilated by a scale factor of $\frac{1}{b}$ because it is being compressed horizontally. Therefore, the x-value only has to be $\frac{1}{b}$ times as big to reach the same y value.
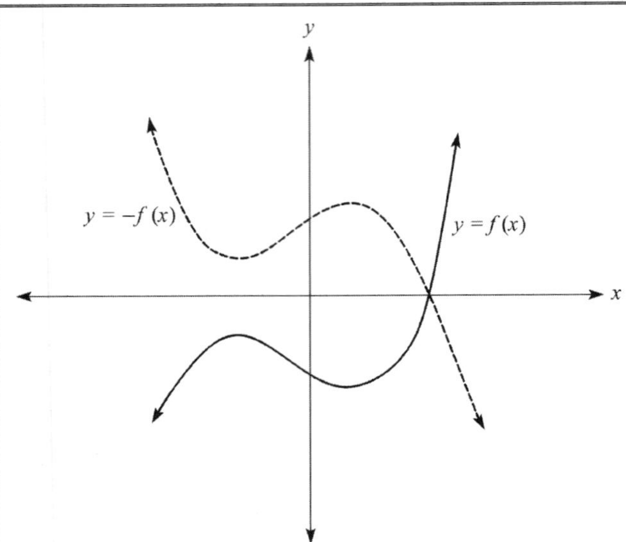	**$f(x) \rightarrow -f(x)$** Graphs of $y = -f(x)$ are found by reflecting the graph $f(x)$ about the x-axis. In other words, the y-coordinates of $f(x)$ are multiplied by a scale factor of -1: $x, y \rightarrow (x, -y)$.
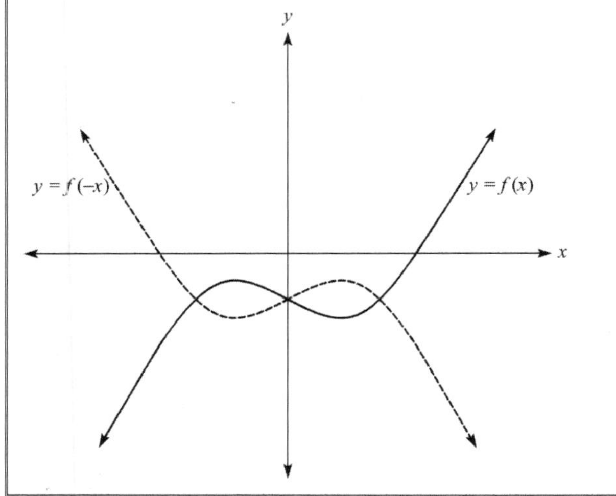	**$f(x) \rightarrow f(-x)$** Graphs of $y = f(-x)$ are found by reflecting the graph $f(x)$ about the y-axis. In other words, the x-coordinates of $f(x)$ are multiplied by a scale factor of -1: $(x, y) \rightarrow (-x, y)$.

Example

Consider the graph $y = f(x)$.

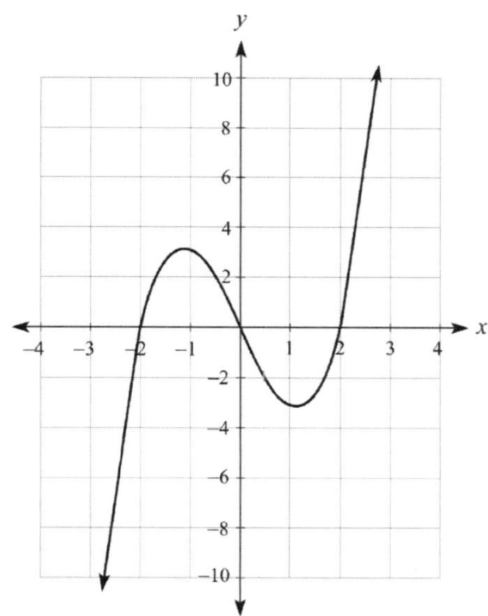

On separate axes, draw the graph of

a. $f(x) + 2$ **b.** $f(x - 1)$

✓ *Solution*

Working	Explanation
a. 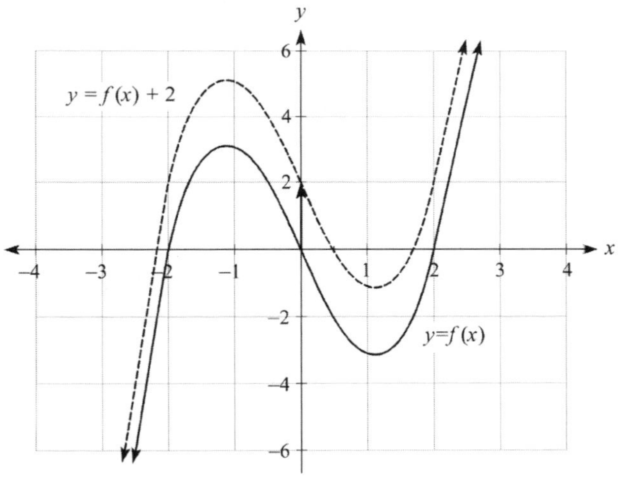	Translate the graph upwards by 2 units. $(x, y) \rightarrow (x, y + 2)$ Transforming the intercepts may help you draw the graph: $(2, 0) \rightarrow (2, 2)$ $(0, 0) \rightarrow (0, 2)$ $(-2, 0) \rightarrow (-2, 2)$

<table>
<tr>
<td>

b.

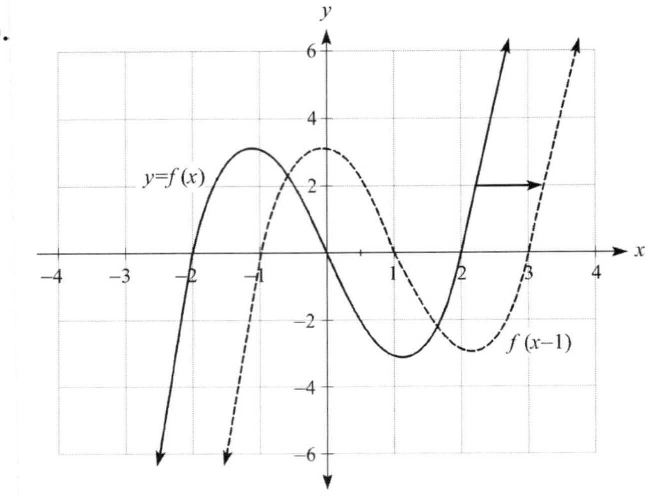

</td>
<td>

Translate the graph to the right by 1 unit.

$(x, y) \to (x+1, y)$

Transforming the intercepts may help you draw the graph:

$$(2,0) \to (3,0)$$
$$(0,0) \to (1,0)$$
$$(-2,0) \to (-1,0)$$

</td>
</tr>
</table>

Example

Consider the graph $y = f(x)$.

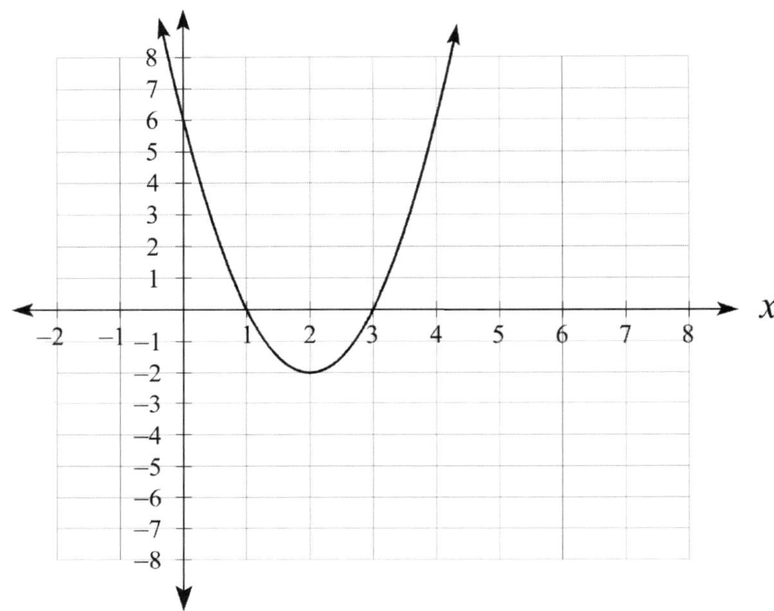

On separate axes, draw the graphs of the following expressions.

a. $\frac{1}{2}f(x)$

b. $f\left(\frac{1}{2}x\right)$

c. $-f(x)$

d. $f(-x)$

✓ *Solution*

Working	Explanation
a. 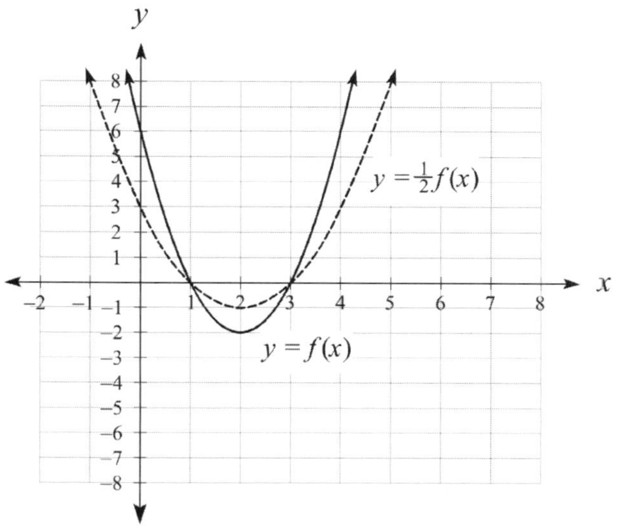 $y = \frac{1}{2}f(x)$, $y = f(x)$	Dilate the graph parallel to the y-axis by a scale factor of $\frac{1}{2}$ units: $(x, y) \rightarrow \left(x, \frac{1}{2}y\right)$ Consider the y-intercept and turning point: $(0, 6) \rightarrow (0, 3)$ $(2, -2) \rightarrow (2, -1)$
b. 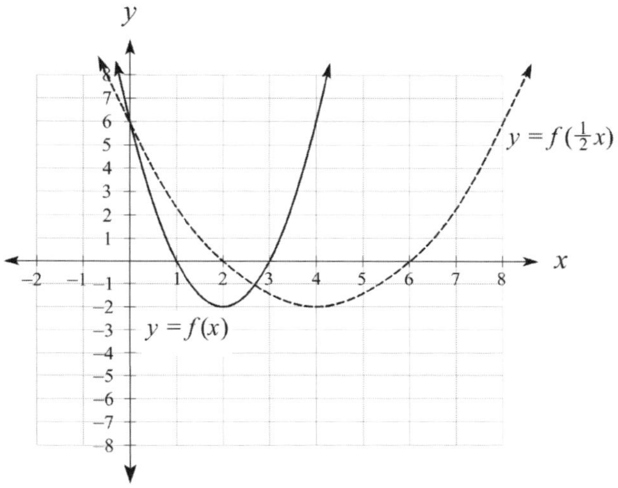 $y = f(\frac{1}{2}x)$, $y = f(x)$	Dilate the graph parallel to the x-axis by a scale factor of 2 units: $(x, y) \rightarrow (2x, y)$ Consider the x-intercepts and turning point: $(1, 0) \rightarrow (2, 0)$ $(3, 0) \rightarrow (6, 0)$ $(2, -2) \rightarrow (4, -2)$
c. 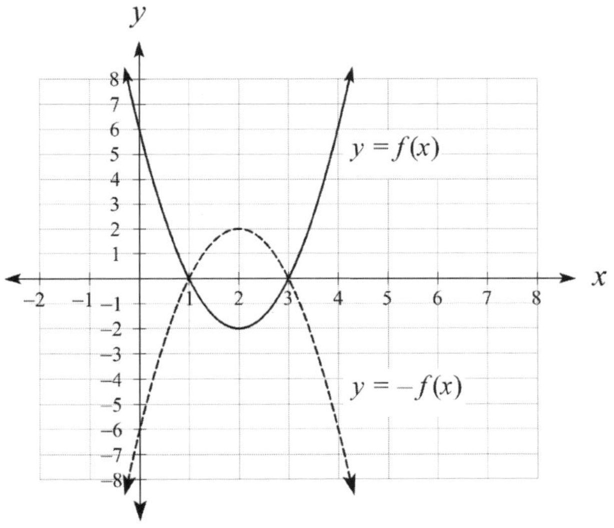 $y = f(x)$, $y = -f(x)$	Reflect the graph about the x-axis: $(x, y) \rightarrow (x, -y)$ Consider the y-intercepts and turning point: $(0, 6) \rightarrow (0, -6)$ $(2, -2) \rightarrow (2, 2)$

d. 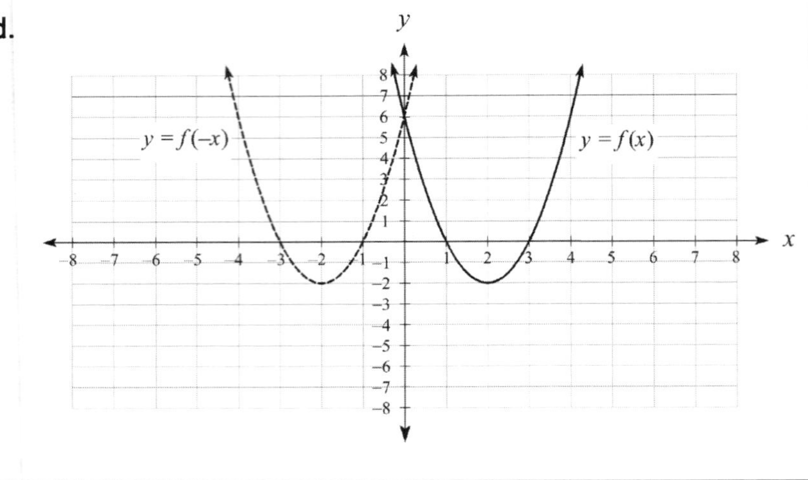	Reflect the graph about the y-axis: $(x, y) \to (-x, y)$ Consider the x-intercepts and turning point: $(1, 0) \to (-1, 0)$ $(3, 0) \to (-3, 0)$ $(2, -2) \to (-2, -2)$

Exercise 2.1.3

Consider the graph of $y = f(x)$.

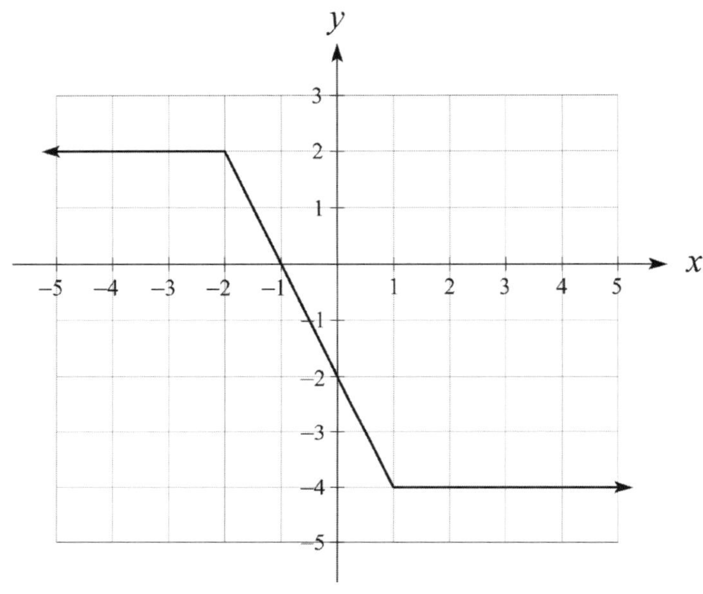

On separate axes, draw the graphs of

a. $f(x) - 3$ b. $f(x + 2)$ c. $f(x + 1) - 2$ d. $3f(x)$

e. $\frac{1}{2}f(x - 1)$ f. $f(2x)$ g. $f(-x) + 2$ h. $-f(x - 1)$

2.2 Exponential functions

An exponential function is a function of the form $f(x) = a^x$, where $a > 0,\ a \neq 1$.

Example

For the function $f(x) = 3^x$, determine the following.

a. $f(2)$ b. $f(-1)$ c. $f(2a)$

✓ Solution

Working	Explanation
a. $f(2) = 3^2 = 9$	Substitute $x = 2$ and simplify.
b. $f(-1) = 3^{-1} = \frac{1}{3}$	Substitute $x = -1$ and simplify.
c. $f(2a) = 3^{2a} = 9^a$	Substitute $x = 2a$ and simplify.

Example

For the function $f(x) = 1 - 2^{-x}$, determine the following.

a. $f(1)$

b. $f(-2)$

c. $f(-a)$

✓ Solution

Working	Explanation
a. $f(1) = 1 - 2^{-1}$ $= 1 - \frac{1}{2}$ $= \frac{1}{2}$	Substitute $x = 1$ and simplify.
b. $f(-2) = 1 - 2^{-(-2)}$ $= 1 - 2^2$ $= 1 - 4$ $= -3$	Substitute $x = -2$ and simplify.
c. $f(-a) = 1 - 2^{-(-a)}$ $= 1 - 2^a$	Substitute $x = -a$ and simplify.

To determine if a given table of values can be represented by an exponential function, we have to examine if the values are multiplied by a common factor over equal intervals. In other words, we have to ask: when the x-values change by the same increment, do the corresponding outputs have a common factor?

In the example below, as x increases by 1, $f(x)$ increases by a common factor: 2.

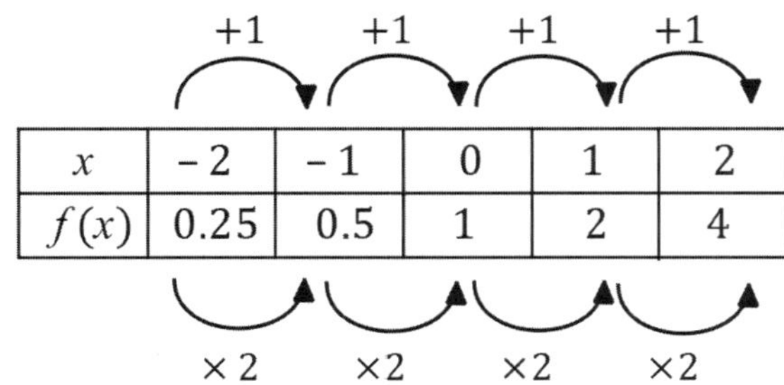

x	−2	−1	0	1	2
$f(x)$	0.25	0.5	1	2	4

Recall that an exponential function has the form $f(x) = a^x$, where a is the base. To determine the base, consider the common multiplier; that is, the ratio of consecutive values:

$$a = \frac{f(x_2)}{f(x_1)} = \frac{0.5}{0.25} = 2$$

$$\therefore f(x) = 2^x$$

Example

Determine which of the following tables of values can be represented by an exponential function, and provide the exponential function where appropriate.

a.

x	0	1	2	3	4
$f(x)$	5	7	9	11	13

b.

x	0	1	2	3	4
$f(x)$	1	0.5	0.25	0.125	0.0625

✓ *Solution*

Working	Explanation
a. x: 0, 1, 2, 3, 4 $f(x)$: 5, 7, 9, 11, 13 This table of values cannot be represented by an exponential function as the differences between consecutive y-values are constant.	As x increases by 1, y increases by a constant value of 2.
b. x: 0, 1, 2, 3, 4 $f(x)$: 1, 0.5, 0.25, 0.125, 0.0625 This table of values can be represented by an exponential function. $a = \frac{f(x_2)}{f(x_1)} = \frac{0.5}{1} = \frac{1}{2}$ $\therefore f(x) = \left(\frac{1}{2}\right)^x$	As x increases by 1, y is multiplied by $\frac{1}{2}$ each time.

Exercise 2.2.1

For $f(x) = 5^x + 1$, determine the following.

a. $f(0)$ b. $f(3)$ c. $f(-1)$ d. $f(2a)$

Exercise 2.2.2

For $f(x) = 2^{x-3}$, determine the following.

a. $f(0)$ b. $f(3)$ c. $f(5)$ d. $f(a+4)$

Exercise 2.2.3

Determine which of the following tables of values can be represented by an exponential function, and provide the function where appropriate.

a.

x	0	1	2	3	4
$f(x)$	1	3	9	27	81

b.

x	0	1	2	3	4
$f(x)$	4	1	0	1	4

2.3 Graphs of exponential functions

The graph of an exponential function, $f(x) = a^x$, is shown below.

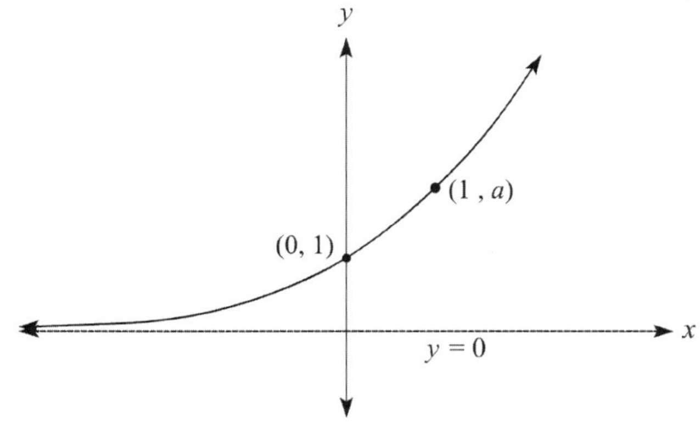

Note that:

- the y-intercept is always $(0, 1)$
- y-values are always greater than 0
- when $x = 1, f(1) = a$
- when $a \neq 1$ and $a > 0, y = 0$ is the horizontal asymptote, where the asymptote is a line that a curve approaches as it heads towards infinity or negative infinity.

The following graphs show how the value of a affects the shape of a graph.

If $a > 1$, the graph is increasing.

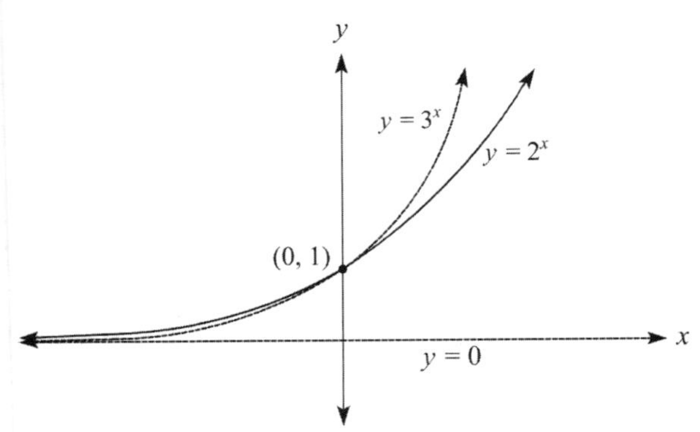

- as $x \to \infty,\ f(x) \to \infty$
- as $x \to -\infty, f(x) \to 0$

If $0 < a < 1$, the graph is decreasing.

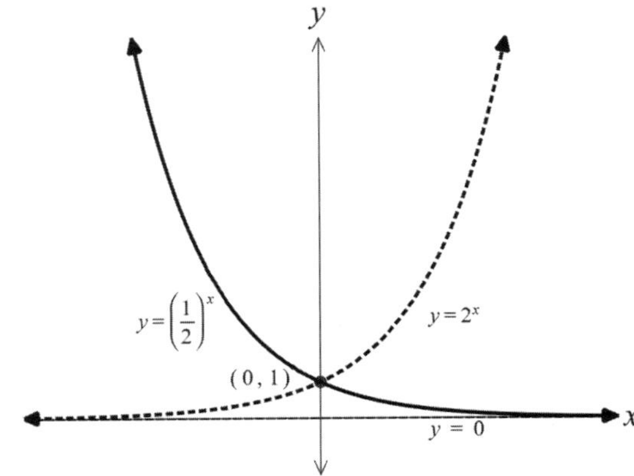

- as $x \to \infty,\ f(x) \to 0$
- as $x \to -\infty, f(x) \to \infty$

Example

Use a table of values from $x = -3$ to $x = 3$ to sketch the exponential function $f(x) = 2^x$.

✓ Solution

Working	Explanation
<table><tr><td>x</td><td>-3</td><td>-2</td><td>-1</td><td>0</td><td>1</td><td>2</td><td>3</td></tr><tr><td>$f(x)$</td><td>0.125</td><td>0.25</td><td>0.5</td><td>1</td><td>2</td><td>4</td><td>8</td></tr></table>	Complete the table of values.
y; $y = 2^x$; Asymptote: $y = 0$; $(0, 1)$; x	Plot the points in the table and sketch a smooth line through the points. Include the horizontal asymptote and label.

Example

Apply transformations to graph the following exponential functions.

a. $f(x) = 2^x - 1$ **b.** $f(x) = 2^{x-2}$ **c.** $f(x) = 3 \times 2^x$ **d.** $f(x) = 2^{\frac{x}{2}}$

✓ *Solution*

Working	Explanation
a. 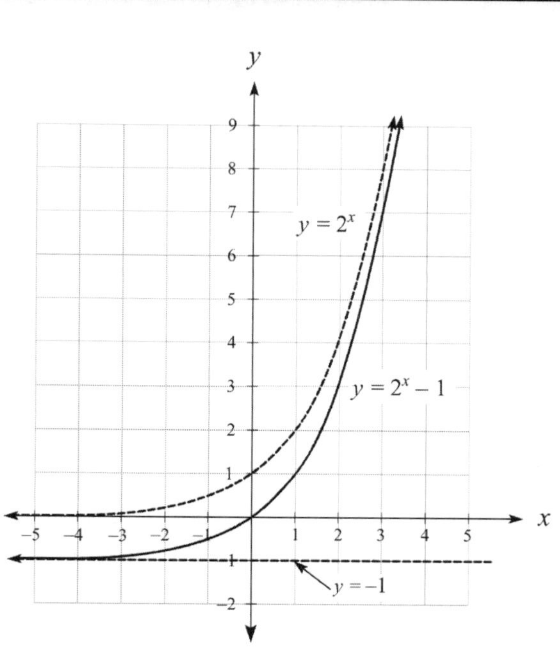	For $f(x) = 2^x - 1$, the graph of 2^x is translated downwards by 1 unit: $(x, y) \rightarrow (x, y - 1)$
b. 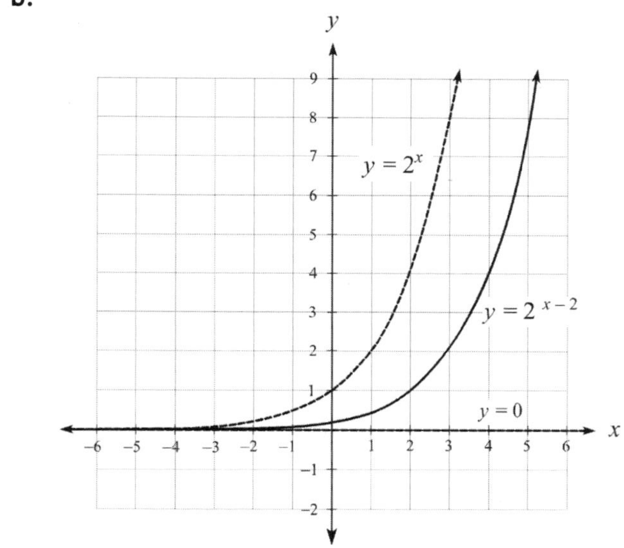	For $f(x) = 2^{x-2}$, the graph of 2^x is translated to the right by 2 units: $(x, y) \rightarrow (x + 2, y)$

Table for a.:

x	-2	-1	0	1	2
2^x	0.25	0.5	1	2	4
$2^x - 1$	-0.75	-0.5	0	1	3

Table for b.:

x	0	1	2	3	4
2^{x-2}	0.25	0.5	1	2	4

c.

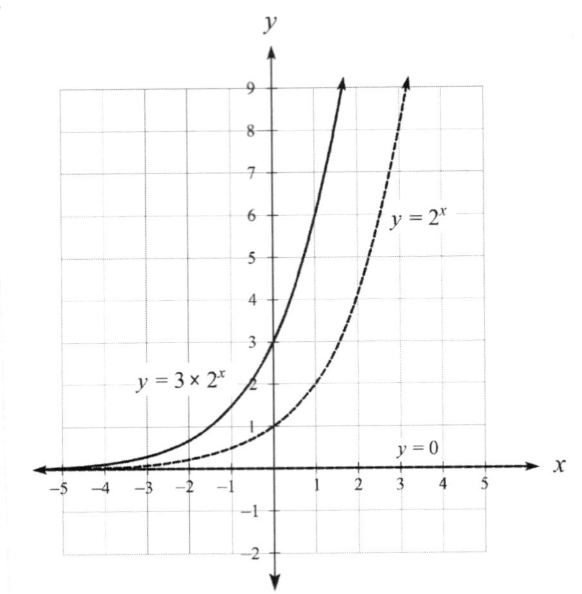

For $f(x) = 3 \times 2^x$, the graph of 2^x is dilated parallel to the y-axis by a scale factor of 3:

$$(x, y) \rightarrow (x, 3y)$$

x	-2	-1	0	1	2
2^x	0.25	0.5	1	2	4
3×2^x	0.75	1.5	3	6	12

d.

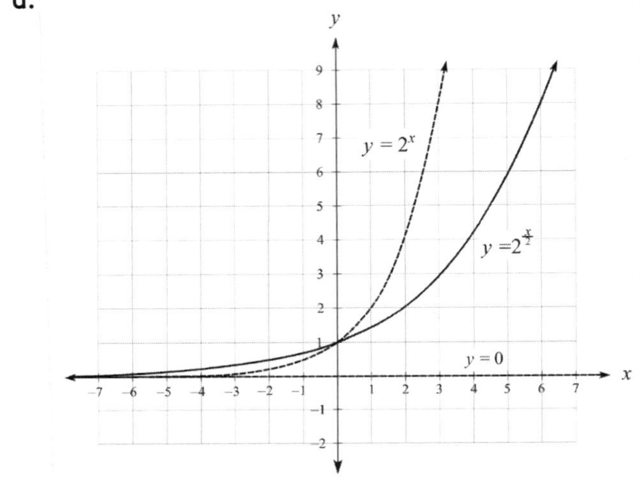

For $f(x) = 2^{\frac{x}{2}}$, the graph of 2^x is dilated parallel to the x-axis by a scale factor of 2:

$$(x, y) \rightarrow (2x, y)$$

x	-4	-2	0	2	4
$2^{\frac{x}{2}}$	0.25	0.5	1	2	4

Example

Apply transformations to graph the following exponential functions.

a. $f(x) = -2^x$

b. $f(x) = 2^{-x}$

✓ *Solution*

Working	Explanation
a. 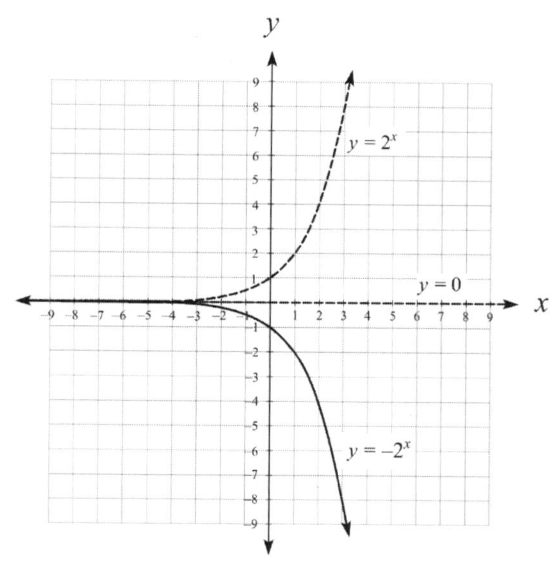	For $f(x) = -2^x$, the graph of 2^x is reflected about the x-axis: $(x,y) \rightarrow (x, -y)$
b. 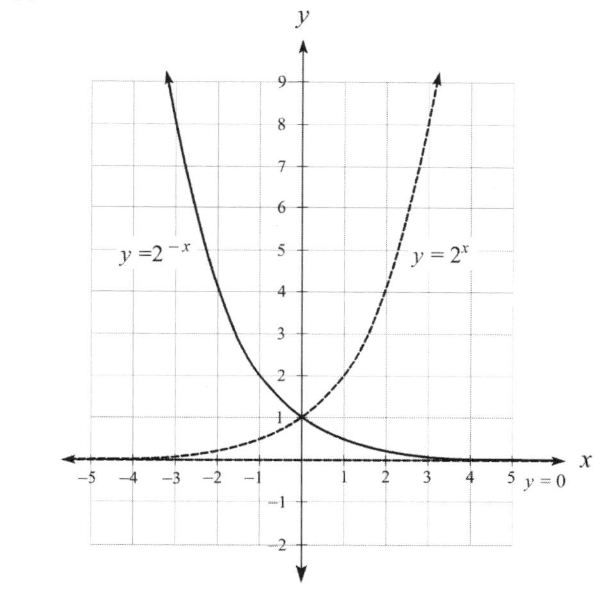	For $f(x) = 2^{-x}$, the graph of 2^x is reflected about the y-axis: $(x,y) \rightarrow (-x, y)$

Table for a.:

x	-2	-1	0	1	2
-2^x	-0.25	-0.5	-1	-2	-4

Table for b.:

x	2	1	0	-1	-2
2^x	0.25	0.5	1	2	4

✎ Exercise 2.3.1

Using a table of values from $x = -3$ to $x = 2$, sketch the graphs of the following exponential functions.

a. $f(x) = 5^x$ **b.** $f(x) = \left(\frac{1}{3}\right)^x$

✎ Exercise 2.3.2

Applying transformations to the graph of 3^x, sketch the following exponential functions.

a. $f(x) = 3^x + 2$ **b.** $f(x) = 3^{x-3}$ **c.** $f(x) = 2 \times 3^x$ **d.** $f(x) = 3^{\frac{x}{3}}$

Exercise 2.3.3

Sketch the graphs of the following exponential functions.

a. $f(x) = -5^x$

b. $f(x) = 5^{-x}$

c. $f(x) = 2 \times \left(\frac{1}{2}\right)^x - 1$

d. $f(x) = -\left(\frac{1}{2}\right)^{2x}$

2.4 Exponential equations

An exponential equation is an equation of the form $a^x = b$, where $a > 0$, $a \neq 1$, and $b > 0$. There is only one solution of x for an exponential equation.

If both sides of an exponential equation have the same base, we can solve it by equating the indices.

$$a^x = a^y \Rightarrow x = y$$

Example

Solve the following exponential equations for x.

a. $2^x = 32$

b. $6^x = \frac{1}{36}$

c. $3^{x-2} = \frac{1}{9}$

d. $4^{x-1} = \left(\frac{1}{2}\right)^{1-3x}$

✓ ***Solution***

Working	Explanation
a. $2^x = 32$ $2^x = 2^5$ $x = 5$	Express 32 as a power of 2. Equate the indices to determine x.
b. $6^x = \frac{1}{36}$ $6^x = \frac{1}{6^2}$ $6^x = 6^{-2}$ $x = -2$	Express 36 as a power of 6. Express the fraction as a whole number with a negative index. Equate the indices to determine x.
c. $3^{x-2} = \frac{1}{9}$ $3^{x-2} = \frac{1}{3^2}$ $3^{x-2} = 3^{-2}$ $x - 2 = -2$ $x = 0$	Express 9 as a power of 3. Express the fraction as a whole number with a negative index. Equate the indices and solve for x.

d. $4^{x-1} = \left(\frac{1}{2}\right)^{1-3x}$ $2^{2(x-1)} = 2^{-(1-3x)}$ $2(x-1) = -(1-3x)$ $2x - 2 = -1 + 3x$ $x = -1$	Express both sides as powers of 2. Equate the indices from both sides. Simplify to solve for x.

Exercise 2.4

Solve the following exponential equations for x.

a. $8^x = 1$ **b.** $5^x = \frac{1}{125}$ **c.** $3^x = 81$ **d.** $9^x = 27$

e. $8^x = 16$ **f.** $32^x = 2$ **g.** $7^{-x} = 49$ **h.** $2^{x+1} = 8$

i. $7^{x+5} = 49^{2x}$ **j.** $4^{2x+1} = \frac{1}{2}$ **k.** $\left(\frac{1}{2}\right)^{x-1} = \frac{1}{16}$ **l.** $27^{x+3} = 9^{2x}$

m. $5 \times 2^x = 40$ **n.** $3 \times \left(\frac{1}{2}\right)^x = 12$ **o.** $2^x \times 4^{2-x} = 8$ **p.** $2^{x^2-2x} = 8$

2.5 Exponential growth and decay

An exponential function is a function of the form $f(x) = A_0 \times a^x$, where A_0 is the initial value of $f(x)$ at $x = 0$.

Exponential growth occurs when $a > 1$.

Note that:

- $f(x)$ increases rapidly over time
- the graph exhibits an upwards curve.

Example

During a locust plague, the area of land eaten t weeks after the initial observation is given by $A = 6000 \times 1.6^t$ hectares (ha).

a. Determine the size of the area initially eaten.

b. Determine the size of the area eaten after 4 weeks.

✓ *Solution*

Working	Explanation
a. Initially $t = 0$. $A = 6000 \times 1.6^0$ $A = 6000$ ha	Substitute $t = 0$ to determine the area eaten at the initial observation.
b. When $t = 4$ $A = 6000 \times 1.6^4$ ≈ 39321 ha	Substitute $t = 4$ to determine the area eaten after 4 weeks.

Exponential decay occurs when $0 < a < 1$.

Note that:

- $f(x)$ decreases rapidly over time
- the graph exhibits a downwards curve.

Example

The current, I (in milliamps), flowing through an electric circuit in a fan t milliseconds after it is switched off is given by $I = 280 \times 0.8^t$ mA.

a. Determine the initial current in the circuit.

b. Determine the current after 12 milliseconds.

✓ *Solution*

Working	Explanation
a. Initially $t = 0$. $I = 280 \times 0.8^0$ $I = 280$ mA	Substitute $t = 0$ to determine initial current.
b. When $t = 12$ $I = 280 \times 0.8^{12}$ ≈ 19.24 mA (to 2 decimal places)	Substitute $t = 12$ to determine the current after 12 milliseconds.

Exercise 2.5.1

The weight of bacteria in a culture t hours after it has been established is given by $W = 2.5 \times 1.03^t$ grams.

a. Determine the initial weight of the bacteria.

b. Determine the weight of the bacteria after 5 hours.

c. Determine the weight of the bacteria after 8 hours.

Exercise 2.5.2

The number of people infected by a virus t days after an outbreak is given by $N = 18 \times 1.14^t$.

a. Determine the number of people initially infected.

b. Determine the number of people infected after 3 days.

c. Determine the number of people infected after a week.

d. Determine the percentage increase in the number of people infected during the first 4 days of the outbreak.

Exercise 2.5.3

Boiling water is left in a pot to cool. After t minutes its temperature is given by $T = 100 \times 0.78^t\ °C$.

a. Determine the initial temperature of the water.

b. Determine the water temperature after 1 minute.

c. Determine the water temperature after 30 minutes.

d. Comment on the validity of the formula after the pot has cooled for 30 minutes.

Exercise 2.5.4

The amount of a drug when it is injected into the bloodstream is modelled by the exponential decay function $A = 250 \times 0.8^t$, where A is the amount in milligrams and t is time in hours.

a. How much of the drug is in the bloodstream at $t = 0$?

b. How much of the drug is in the bloodstream after 30 minutes?

c. How much of the drug is in the bloodstream after 3 hours?

2.6 Compound interest

Compound interest differs from simple interest, which is calculated based only on the principal (the initial investment) and is paid at the end of the term of the investment or loan. Compound interest, on the other hand, is calculated and paid based on both the principal and the accumulated interest.

For example, suppose \$5000 is invested for 5 years at an interest rate of 2% per annum compounded annually. The following table shows how the interest earned increases each year.

After year	Interest earned	Account balance
0	\$0	\$5000
1	$5000 \times 0.02 \times 1 = \$100$	$5000 + 100 = \$5100$
2	$5100 \times 0.02 \times 1 = \$102$	$5100 + 102 = \$5202$
3	$5202 \times 0.02 \times 1 = \$104.04$	$5202 + 104.04 = \$5306.04$
4	$5306.04 \times 0.02 \times 1 = \$106.12$	$5306.04 + 106.12 = \$5412.16$
5	$5412.16 \times 0.02 \times 1 = \$108.24$	$5412.16 + 108.24 = \$5520.40$

Each year, the amount in the bank is increased by 2%, which corresponds to a multiplier of 1.02.

So the value after 5 years is

$$\$5000 \times 1.02 \times 1.02 \times 1.02 \times 1.02 \times 1.02$$
$$= \$5000 \times (1.02)^5$$
$$= \$5520.40$$

The compound interest formula is

$$A = P(1 + r)^t$$

where:

- A is the amount of the loan or investment after t years
- P is the principal (that is, the initial amount borrowed or invested)
- r is the interest rate charged or earned (as a decimal)
- t is the duration in years.

Example

\$4000 is invested for 5 years at 8% per annum compounded annually.

a. To the nearest cent, what will the value of the total investment be at the end of this period?

b. To the nearest cent, how much interest is earned?

✓ ***Solution***

Working	Explanation
a. $A = P(1 + r)^t$ $= 4000(1 + 0.08)^5$ $= 4000(1.08)^5$ $= \$5877.31$	Convert the interest rate from a percentage to a decimal: $r = 8\% = 0.08$. Substitute the given values into the compound interest formula: $P = 4000, r = 0.08, t = 5$ Simplify and evaluate.
b. Interest earned $= 5877.31 - 4000$ $= \$1877.31$	Subtract the principal from the total amount after 5 years to determine the interest earned.

Example

A savings account offers an interest rate of 5% compounded annually. How much must be invested now to have a total of \$8000 in 4 years?

✓ ***Solution***

Working	Explanation
$A = P(1+r)^t$ $8000 = P(1+0.05)^4$ $P = \frac{8000}{(1.05)^4} \approx \$6581.62$	Convert the interest rate from a percentage to a decimal: $r = 5\% = 0.05$. Substitute the given values into the compound interest formula: $A = 8000, r = 0.05, t = 4$ Simplify and evaluate.

Consider a loan at 12% per annum. The right-hand column in the table below shows interest rates for different periods.

If interest is compounded biannually (that is, every 6 months), there will be 2 time periods per annum.	$\frac{0.12}{2} = 0.06$
If interest is compounded quarterly, there will be 4 time periods per annum.	$\frac{0.12}{4} = 0.03$
If interest is compounded monthly, there will be 12 time periods per annum.	$\frac{0.12}{12} = 0.01$
If interest is compounded daily, there will be 365 time periods per annum (excluding leap years).	$\frac{0.12}{365} = 0.0033$

When the compounding period is not years, the formula for calculating compound interest is

$$\boldsymbol{A = P\left(1 + \frac{r}{n}\right)^{nt}}$$

where:

- A is the amount of the loan or investment after t years
- P is the principal (that is, the initial amount borrowed or invested)
- r is the interest rate charged or earned (as a decimal)
- n is the number of times interest is compounded each year
- t is the duration in years.

Example

\$30 000 is invested for 5 years at an interest rate of 7% per annum. If the interest is compounded monthly, find the following:

a. the total value of the investment after 5 years

b. the total amount of interest earned over the 5 years.

✓ *Solution*

Working	Explanation
a. $A = P\left(1 + \frac{r}{n}\right)^{nt}$ $= 30\,000\left(1 + \frac{0.07}{12}\right)^{12\times5}$ $= \$42\,528.76$	Convert the interest rate from a percentage to a decimal: $r = 7\% = 0.07$. Substitute the given values into the modified compound interest formula: $P = 30\,000, r = 0.07, n = 12, t = 5$
b. Interest $= 42\,528.76 - 30\,000$ $= \$12\,528.76$	Subtract the initial investment from the value after 5 years to determine the interest earned.

Exercise 2.6.1

Jack invests $4200 at an annual interest rate of 5.5% compounded annually for 8 years. Determine the interest earned over this period.

Exercise 2.6.2

Amie wants to have $10 000 after 8 years. She is considering an investment account that offers an annual interest rate of 4% compounded annually. What initial amount should Amie invest?

Exercise 2.6.3

Don invested $5000 at an annual interest rate of 6% compounded biannually. Calculate the total amount Don receives after 3 years.

Exercise 2.6.4

Calculate the total amount repaid on a loan of $10 000 taken out for 18 months at an annual interest rate of 8% compounded quarterly.

Exercise 2.6.5

How much needs to be invested to accumulate $9600 in 6 years if the interest rate is 8% per annum compounded every 6 months? Round your answer to the nearest dollar.

2.7 Comparing simple and compound interest

Simple interest is calculated on the original principal, while compound interest takes into account both the principal and accumulated interest, leading to greater growth over time.

Example

Jill invests $6000 over 3 years at an annual rate of 5% compounded annually. Jack invests the same amount for the same time, but at a simple interest rate of 5% per annum. How much more does Jill earn?

✓ *Solution*

Working	Explanation
Compound interest $A = P(1+r)^t$ $= 6000(1+0.05)^3$ $= \$6928.13$ Interest $= 6928.13 - 6000$ $= \$928.13$	Convert the interest rate from a percentage to a decimal: $r = 5\% = 0.05$ Substitute the given values into the compound interest formula to calculate the amount earned: $P = 6000, r = 0.05, t = 3$ Subtract the principal from the amount after 3 years to find the interest.
Simple interest $I = Prt$ $= 6000 \times 0.05 \times 3$ $= \$900$	Recall the simple interest formula. Substitute the given values into the simple interest formula: $P = 6000, r = 0.05, t = 3$
Conclusion Jill earns \$28.13 more than Jack.	Compound interest leads to higher returns compared to simple interest.

Exercise 2.7.1

Yannick wishes to invest \$5700 over 6 years. He is offered the following options.

- Option 1: simple interest of 16% per annum
- Option 2: compound interest of 14% per annum compounded annually
- Option 3: compound interest of 12% per annum compounded quarterly

Which is the best investment?

Exercise 2.7.2

Clive needs to borrow \$12 000 to buy a machine for his factory. He wants to pay back the loan in full within 3 years. Which of the three loans offered below should he pick?

- Quick Loans: simple interest of 6% per annum
- Zoom Loans: compound interest of 4.5% per annum compounded annually
- Magic Loans: compound interest of 4.45% per annum compounded quarterly

Exercise 2.7.3

Paula wants to borrow \$12 000 over 6 years. The bank offers her two options: 4.2% per annum compounded monthly or 5.3% per annum compounded biannually. Which loan option is best for Paula?

2.8 Exponential change and compound interest

The concept behind compound interest can be generalised to other situations involving exponential growth or decay, such as population growth. The general rule for exponential growth is very similar to the compound interest formula. The formula is

$$A = A_0(1 \pm r)^t$$

where:

- A is the final value
- A_0 is the initial value
- r is the rate of change (as a decimal)
- t is the time period.

Example

Formulate exponential rules that represent the following situations.

a. Jo invests her \$50 000 savings at a rate of 9% per annum.

b. The city's initial population of 100 000 is decreasing by 10% per year.

✓ *Solution*

Working	Explanation
a. Let A = amount of money at any time t = years the money is invested A_0 = initial amount invested	Define the variables in the general exponential rule.
$A = 50\ 000(1 + 0.09)^t$ $A = 50\ 000(1.09)^t$	Substitute the given value for each variable: $r = 0.09,\ A_0 = 50\ 000$ **Note:** since the exponential change is growth, we use '+' in the rule.
b. Let A = population at any time t = years passed A_0 = initial population	Define the variables in the general exponential rule.
$A = 100\ 000(1 - 0.10)^t$ $A = 100\ 000(0.9)^t$	Substitute the given value for each variable: $r = 0.1,\ A_0 = 100\ 000$ **Note:** since the exponential change is decay, we use '–' in the rule.

Exercise 2.8.1

Define variables and form exponential rules that represent the following situations.

a. the return on \$200 000 invested at 17% interest per annum

b. the value of a car bought for \$15 300 decreasing in value at 3% per annum

c. an initial population of 165 500 increasing at 12% per annum

d. a tank with 1200 litres of water suddenly leaking water at a rate of 8% per hour

Exercise 2.8.2

A tank that initially contained 12 000 litres of water leaks water at 6% per hour.

a. Formulate a rule for the volume of water (V) left after t hours.

b. Calculate, to the nearest litre, the amount of water left in the tank after 3 hours.

c. How much water is left after 2 days? (Round your answer to 2 decimal places.)

Exercise 2.8.3

Megan invests \$80 000 in an investment fund that has an annual return of 7.5%.

a. Formulate a rule for the value of her investment (V) after t years.

b. How much will Megan's investment be worth in 18 months?

c. How much will Megan's investment be worth in 6 years?

Chapter 3 – Linear relations

3.1 Solving linear equations

A linear equation is an algebraic equation in which each term is either a constant or the product of a constant and a single variable. **Its standard form is** $ax + b = c$, where a, b and c are constants, and x is the variable.

Some useful steps to take when solving a linear equation include:

- multiplying both sides of the equation by the lowest common denominator
- expanding brackets
- using inverse operations
- collecting like terms.

Example

Solve the following linear equations.

a. $\frac{x}{2} + 3 = 1$

b. $4(2x - 3) = 2x$

c. $2(x - 2) = 3(x + 4)$

d. $\frac{x}{2} = \frac{3 - 2x}{5}$

✓ *Solution*

Working	Explanation
a. $\frac{x}{2} + 3 = 1$ $\frac{x}{2} = -2$ $x = -4$	**1.** Subtract 3 from both sides. **2.** Multiply both sides by 2.
b. $4(2x - 3) = 2x$ $8x - 12 = 2x$ $6x - 12 = 0$ $6x = 12$ $x = 2$	**1.** Expand the brackets. **2.** Subtract $-2x$ on both sides. **3.** Add 12 on both sides. **4.** Divide both sides by 6.
c. $2(x - 2) = 3(x + 4)$ $2x - 4 = 3x + 12$ $-4 = x + 12$ $-16 = x$ $x = -16$	**1.** Expand the brackets. **2.** Gather like terms by subtracting $2x$ from both sides. **3.** Subtract 12 from both sides.

d. $\frac{x}{2} = \frac{3-2x}{5}$ $\frac{10x}{2} = \frac{10(3-2x)}{5}$ $5x = 2(3-2x)$ $5x = 6 - 4x$ $9x = 6$ $x = \frac{6}{9} = \frac{2}{3}$	1. Multiply both sides by the LCD of 2 and 5, which is 10. 2. Cancel common factors. 3. Expand the brackets. 4. Gather like terms by adding $4x$ to both sides. 5. Divide both sides by 9 and simplify the fraction.

Exercise 3.1

Solve the following linear equations.

a. $3x - 2 = 4x + 5$

b. $4(x-2) = 8(x-6)$

c. $4(x+1) - 2(x-4) = 5$

d. $\frac{5x}{3} + 1 = 6$

e. $2(x-3) + 4x = 10 - 3x$

f. $\frac{x+7}{4} = \frac{x+2}{2}$

g. $\frac{10-x}{2} = \frac{x+1}{3}$

h. $\frac{x-1}{2} + \frac{x+2}{5} = 2$

i. $\frac{x+2}{3} - \frac{x-1}{2} = 1$

3.2 Midpoints and the distance between points

Midpoint

The diagram to the right shows the midpoint, $M\ (x_m, y_m)$, between two points on the Cartesian plane with coordinates (x_1, y_1) and (x_2, y_2).

The coordinates of the midpoint can be found from the following equation.

$$(x_m, y_m) = \left(\frac{x_1 + x_2}{2}, \frac{y_1 + y_2}{2}\right)$$

If you know the coordinates of one point and the coordinates of the midpoint, you can rearrange the midpoint formula to find the coordinates of the unknown point.

$$(x_2, y_2) = (2x_m - x_1, 2y_m - y_1)$$

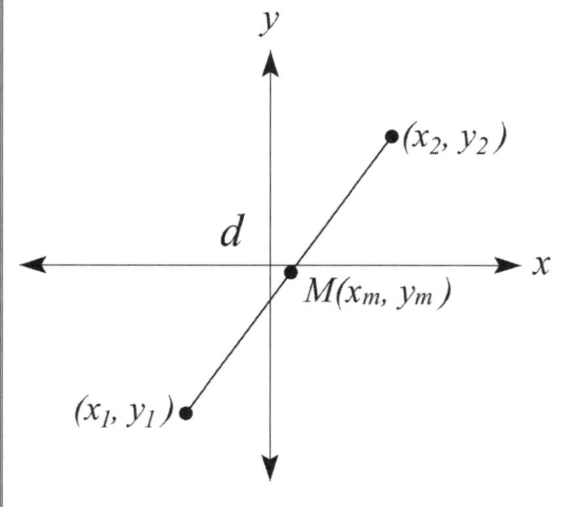

Example

Determine the coordinates of the midpoints between the following sets of points.

a. $(-2, 6)$ and $(4, 1)$

b. $(4, 7)$ and $(-4, -3)$

✓ *Solution*

Working	Explanation
a. $(x_m, y_m) = \left(\frac{(-2)+4}{2}, \frac{6+1}{2}\right)$ $= \left(\frac{2}{2}, \frac{7}{2}\right)$ $= \left(1, \frac{7}{2}\right)$	Substitute the coordinates into the midpoint equation. **Note:** • To avoid confusion, always enclose a negative number in brackets. • It is acceptable to leave the coordinates in fraction form.
b. $(x_m, y_m) = \left(\frac{4+(-4)}{2}, \frac{7+(-3)}{2}\right)$ $= \left(\frac{0}{2}, \frac{4}{2}\right)$ $= (0, 2)$	

Example

Given that the coordinates of the midpoint of a line are $(10, -2)$ and the coordinates of one endpoint are $(-2, 1)$, determine the coordinates of the other end point.

✓ *Solution*

Working	Explanation
$(x_2, y_2) = (2(10) - (-2), 2(-2) - 1)$ $= (22, -5)$	Substitute the coordinates into the equation to determine the coordinates of the other end point.

Distance

The distance, d, between two points with coordinates (x_1, y_1) and (x_2, y_2) is given by the equation

$$d = \sqrt{(x_2 - x_1)^2 + (y_2 - y_1)^2}$$

where $y_2 - y_1$ is the vertical distance and $x_2 - x_1$ is the horizontal distance between the two points.

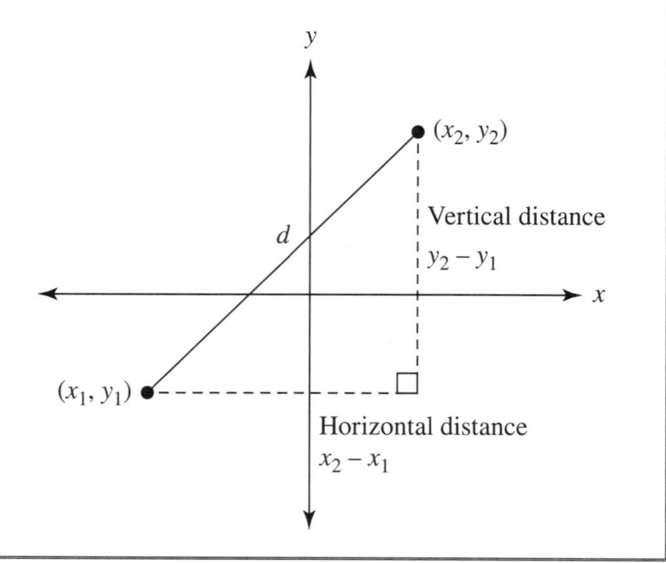

Example

Determine the distances between the following sets of points.

a. $(-2, 6)$ and $(4, 1)$

b. $(4, 7)$ and $(-4, -3)$

✓ ***Solution***

Working	Explanation
a. $d = \sqrt{((-2)-4)^2 + (6-1)^2}$ $= \sqrt{(-6)^2 + (5)^2}$ $= \sqrt{36+25}$ $= \sqrt{61}$ $= 7.81$ units	Substitute the values of the x- and y-coordinates into the equation to determine the distance between the two points. **Note:** calculate the distance to two decimal places, or as an exact value when appropriate.
b. $d = \sqrt{(4-(-4))^2 + (7-(-3))^2}$ $= \sqrt{(8)^2 + (10)^2}$ $= \sqrt{64+100}$ $= \sqrt{164}$ $= 12.81$ units	

Example

The distance between two points on the Cartesian plane is 10 units. One point has coordinates of $(2, 6)$ and the other point has coordinates of $(a, 12)$. Determine the possible value(s) of a.

✓ ***Solution***

Working	Explanation
$10 = \sqrt{(2-a)^2 + (6-12)^2}$ $100 = (2-a)^2 + (-6)^2$ $100 = (2-a)^2 + 36$ $64 = (2-a)^2$ $2 - a = \pm 8$ $a = -6$ or 10	Substitute the given information into the distance formula. Square both sides of the equation and collect like terms.

Exercise 3.2

a. Determine the coordinates of the midpoint between points $(-1, 10)$ and $(8, 5)$.

b. Given that the coordinates of the midpoint on a line are $(-3, 3)$ and the coordinates of an endpoint are $(-5, 7)$, determine the coordinates of the other endpoint.

c. Determine the distance between points $(-1, 10)$ and $(8, 5)$.

d. The distance between the two points $(2, a)$ and $(5, 1)$ is $\sqrt{13}$ units. Determine the possible values of a.

3.3 Sketching linear graphs

A straight-line graph can be described as a linear equation.

A linear equation can be expressed in three main forms, described in the table below.

gradient–intercept form	$y = mx + c$ where m = the gradient of the line and c = the y-coordinate of the y-intercept
point–slope form	$(y - y_1) = m(x - x_1)$ where m = the gradient of the line and (x_1, y_1) is a point on the line
general (or standard) form	$ax + by = c$ where a, b and c are constants

Gradient

The gradient, m, represents the constant rate of change. It describes the slope of the line, i.e. its steepness and direction.

The gradient can be derived from the coordinates of two points on the line.

Consider the diagram on the right. The gradient can be determined using

$$m = \frac{\text{rise}}{\text{run}} = \frac{y_2 - y_1}{x_2 - x_1}$$

Recall that $y_2 - y_1$ and $x_2 - x_1$ are the vertical and horizontal distances between two points respectively.

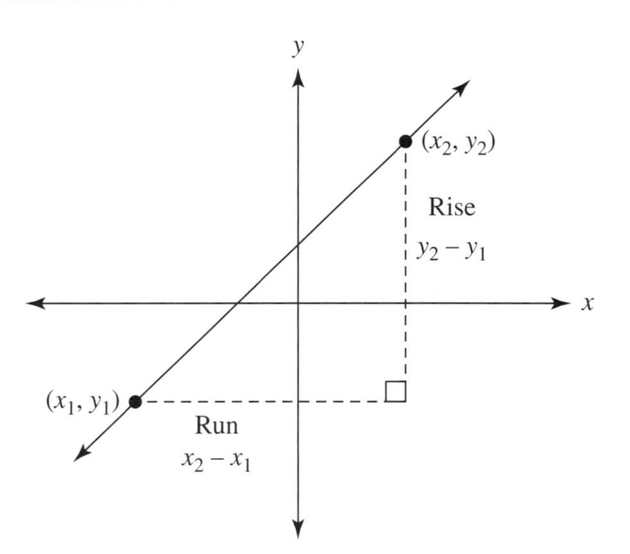

Note:

- If $m > 0$, the gradient of the slope is positive and the slope is increasing.
- If $m < 0$, the gradient of the slope is negative and the slope is decreasing.
- If $m = 0$, there is no change in the gradient (i.e. $y_2 - y_1 = 0$) and the line is horizontal.
- If m is undefined (i.e. $x_2 - x_1 = 0$), the line is vertical.

The four types of slope are illustrated in the diagrams below.

positive gradient

negative gradient

horizontal line
(gradient = 0)

vertical line
(undefined gradient)

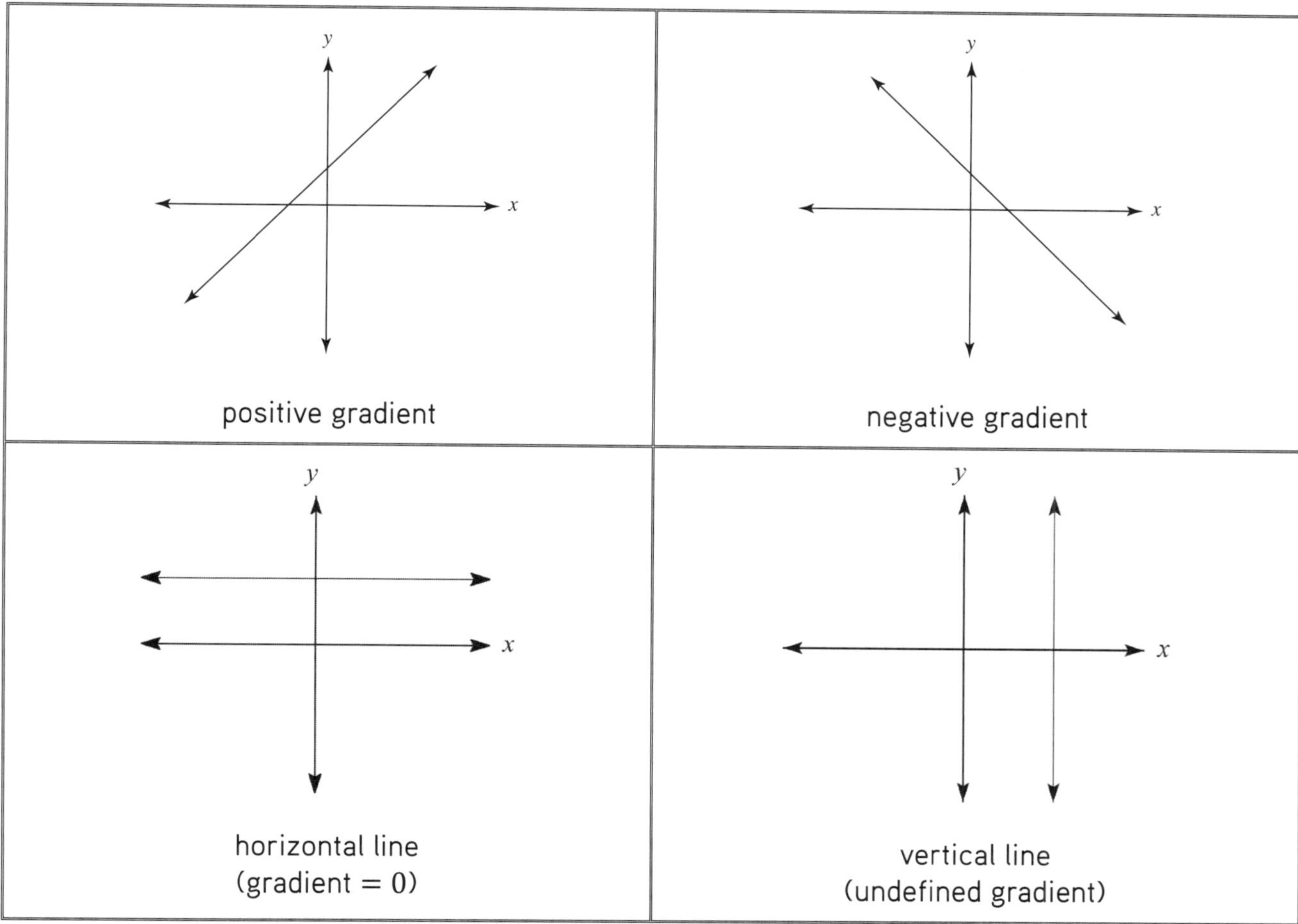

Sketching

Plotting a linear equation involves drawing a line on a grid that is labelled so that you can precisely pinpoint the points you are plotting. Sketching can be less precise, but still requires you to show the general form of the graph, such as the gradient, and the critical points (e.g. the x- and y-intercepts).

There are four ways of plotting or sketching a linear relationship on the Cartesian plane:

- from a table of values
- from the y-intercept and the gradient of the line
- from the coordinates of two points on the line
- from the two intercepts.

Example

Fill in the table of values below and use the values to sketch the graph of $y = 2x - 1$.

x	-2	-1	0	1	2
y					

✓ Solution

<table>
<tr><th>Working</th><th>Explanation</th></tr>
<tr><td>

x	-2	-1	0	1	2
y	-5	-3	-1	1	3

</td><td>1. Complete the table of values according to the rule $y = 2x - 1$.</td></tr>
<tr><td> 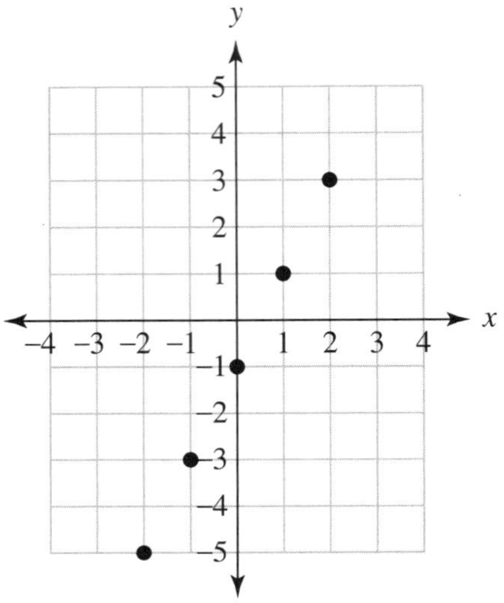</td><td>2. Draw and label the x-axis and y-axis.
3. Give the axes an appropriate scale.
4. Plot the points from the table of values.</td></tr>
<tr><td> 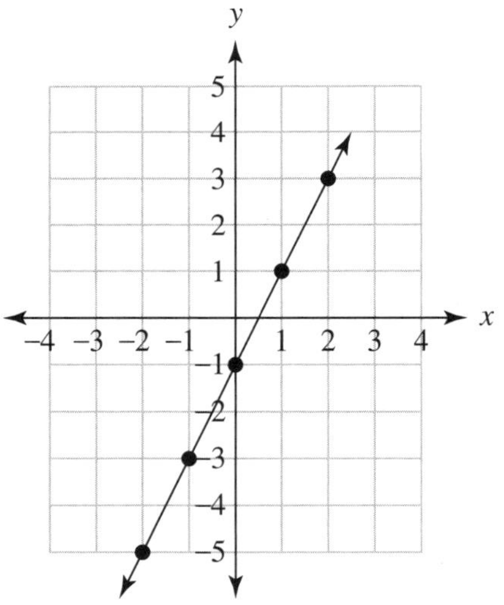</td><td>5. Join all the points with a straight line.
6. Draw arrows at both ends of the line.</td></tr>
</table>

Example

Using the gradient and the y-intercept, sketch the graph of $y = -2x + 1$.

✓ Solution

Working	Explanation
$y = -2x + 1$ y-intercept: $c = (0, 1)$ Gradient: $m = -2$	1. Identify the y-intercept from the equation, i.e. the value of c. 2. Identify the gradient from the equation, i.e. the value of m.
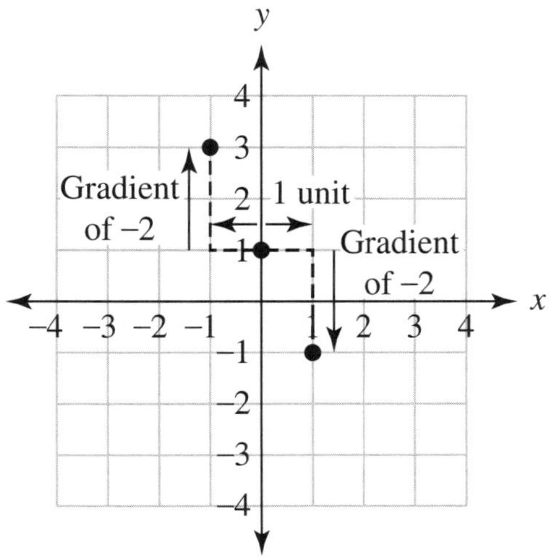	3. Plot the y-intercept. 4. From the y-intercept, use the gradient of -2 to locate another point. The gradient is 1 unit to the left and 2 units up, or 1 unit to the right and 2 units down. 5. Plot these points.
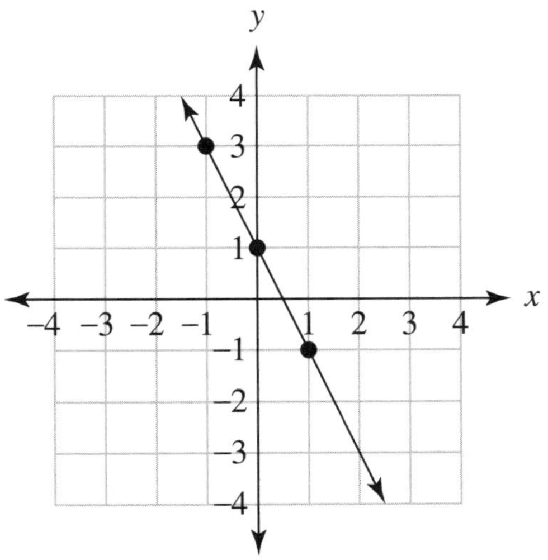	6. Draw a line through the y-intercept and the points. 7. Draw arrows at both ends of the line.

Example

Plot the graph of $y = 3x + 2$ by first determining the coordinates of any two points.

✓ Solution

Working	Explanation
$y = 3x + 2$ Substitute $x = -2$: $y = 3(-2) + 2 = -4$ One of the points is $(-2, -4)$. Substitute $x = 2$: $y = 3(2) + 2 = 8$ Another point is $(2, 8)$.	1. Select any two values for x. In this case, we have selected $x = -2$ and $x = 2$. 2. Substitute the values into the equation. This will give two points we can use to plot the graph.
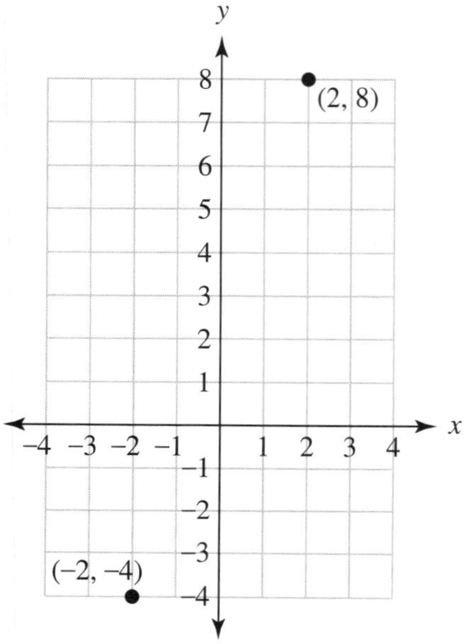	3. Plot the two points.
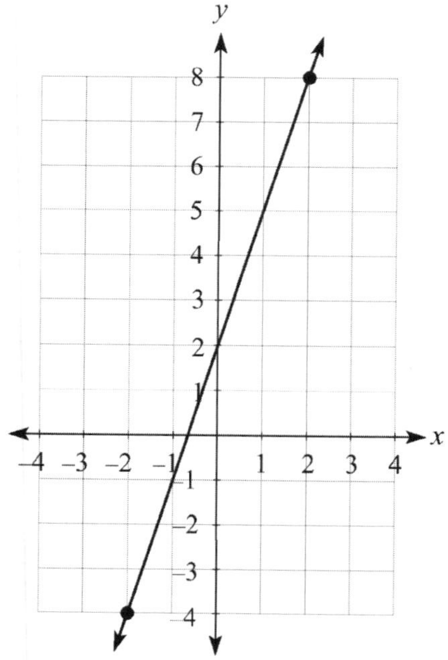	4. Connect the points with a straight line. Extend the line beyond the points. 5. Add arrows at both ends of the line.

Example

Plot the graph of $2y + x = 4$ by first determining the two intercepts.

✓ Solution

Working	Explanation
$2y + x = 4$ Substitute $x = 0$ to determine y-intercept. $2y + 0 = 4$ $y = 2$ y-intercept is $(0, 2)$	**1.** Determine the coordinates of the y-intercept.
Substitute $y = 0$ to determine x-intercept. $2(0) + x = 4$ $x = 4$ x-intercept is $(4, 0)$	**2.** Determine the coordinates of the x-intercept.
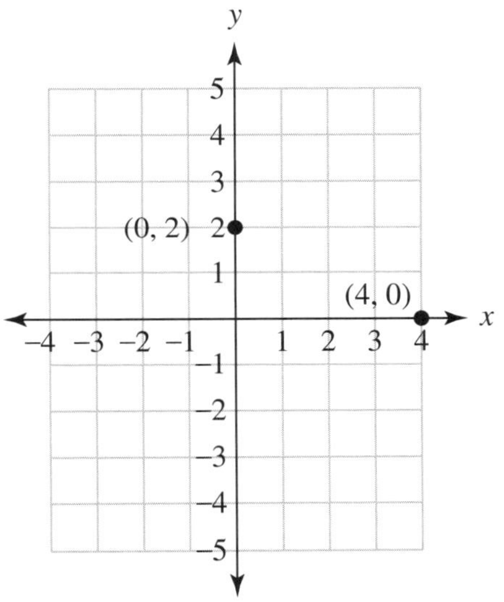 y 5 4 3 (0, 2) 2 1 (4, 0) x −4 −3 −2 −1 1 2 3 4 −1 −2 −3 −4 −5	**3.** Plot the two intercepts.
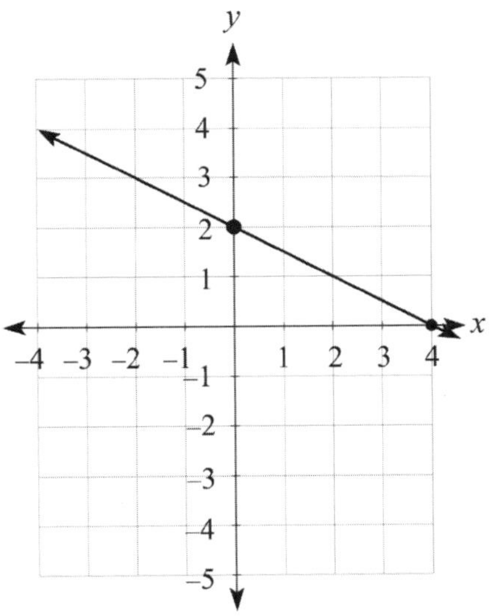 y 5 4 3 2 1 x −4 −3 −2 −1 1 2 3 4 −1 −2 −3 −4 −5	**4.** Connect the points with a straight line. Extend the line beyond the points. **5.** Add arrows at both ends of the line.

Exercise 3.3

a. Use the table of values below to sketch $y = -2x - 1$.

x	-2	-1	0	1	2
y	3	1	-1	-3	-5

b. Sketch the graph of $y = \frac{5}{2}x - 2$ by first identifying its gradient and y-intercept.

c. By substituting $x = -2$ and $x = 8$, determine two points that could be used to sketch $y = -\frac{1}{2}x + 4$.

d. Determine the x- and y-intercepts of $3y - 2x = 6$ and sketch the graph.

3.4 Finding the equation of a line

To determine if a table of values can be represented by a linear function, we have to examine the first-order differences, that is, the differences between the values of y when the values of x are increased or decreased by 1. If the values of the first-order differences are all the same, then the table of values represents a linear equation. An example is given below.

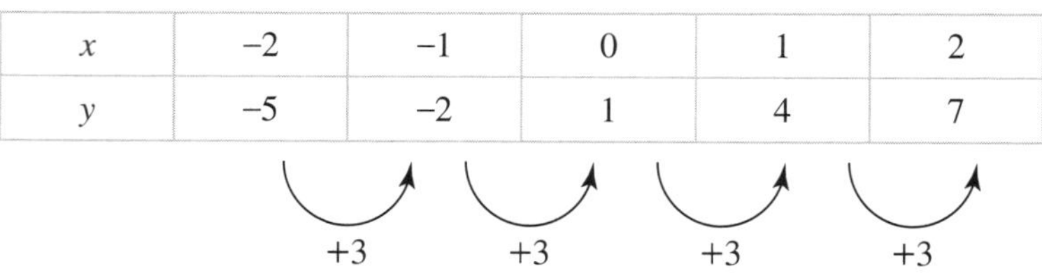

x	-2	-1	0	1	2
y	-5	-2	1	4	7

First-order differences are constant. For every 1 unit increase in x, y increases by 3 units.

Example

Determine which of the following tables of values can be represented by a linear function.

a.

x	-2	-1	0	1	2
y	5	7	9	11	13

b.

x	-2	-1	0	1	2
y	1	0.5	0.25	0.125	0.625

✓ *Solution*

<table>
<tr><th>Working</th><th>Explanation</th></tr>
<tr><td>a.
<table>
<tr><td>x</td><td>-2</td><td>-1</td><td>0</td><td>1</td><td>2</td></tr>
<tr><td>y</td><td>5</td><td>7</td><td>9</td><td>11</td><td>13</td></tr>
</table>
This table of values can be represented by a linear function.</td><td>As x increases by 1, y increases by a constant amount: 2.</td></tr>
<tr><td>b.
<table>
<tr><td>x</td><td>-2</td><td>-1</td><td>0</td><td>1</td><td>2</td></tr>
<tr><td>y</td><td>1</td><td>0.5</td><td>0.25</td><td>0.125</td><td>0.625</td></tr>
</table>
This table of values cannot be represented by a linear function.</td><td>As x increases by 1, y neither increases nor decreases by the same amount.</td></tr>
</table>

We can determine the equation of a line if we have certain information. The steps to follow are explained in the following table.

Information	Steps
gradient and y-intercept	Substitute the given information into the gradient–intercept form: $y = mx + c$.
gradient and the coordinates of a point that lies on the line	**1.** Substitute the given information into the point–slope form: $(y - y_1) = m(x - x_1)$. **2.** Rearrange the equation into the gradient–intercept form.
coordinates of two points that lie on the line	**1.** Determine the gradient of the line from the two coordinates. **2.** Substitute the given information into the point–slope form: $(y - y_1) = m(x - x_1)$. **3.** Rearrange the equation into the gradient–intercept form.

Example

a. Determine the equation of a straight line passing through the point (2, 3) with a gradient of -2.

b. Determine the equation of a straight line passing through points $(-2, 6)$ and $(3, 1)$.

✓ Solution

Working	Explanation
a. $(y-3)=-2(x-2)$ $y-3=-2x+4$ $y=-2x+7$	**1.** Substitute m and the given coordinates into $(y-y_1)=m(x-x_1)$. **2.** Rearrange the equation into the form $y=mx+c$.
b. $m=\dfrac{6-1}{-2-3}=\dfrac{5}{-5}=-1$ $(y-1)=-1(x-3)$ $y-1=-x+3$ $y=-x+4$	**1.** Determine the gradient of the line from the coordinates of the two points. **2.** Substitute m and one set of coordinates into $(y-y_1)=m(x-x_1)$. **3.** Rearrange the equation into the form $y=mx+c$.

Exercise 3.4

a. Determine the equation of the straight line with a gradient of 3 passing through the point $(-2, 3)$.

b. Determine the equation of the straight line that passes through points $(2, -3)$ and $(-4, -12)$.

c. Determine which of the following tables of values can be represented by a linear function. For those that can, construct the linear function.

i.

x	0	1	2	3	4
$f(x)$	-1	3	7	11	15

ii.

x	0	1	2	3	4
$f(x)$	-3	-1	0	-1	-3

3.5 Parallel and perpendicular lines

Let's explore when two lines are parallel or when they are perpendicular. Consider the following linear equations representing lines:

$$y=m_1x+c_1 \quad \text{(line 1)}$$
$$y=m_2x+c_2 \quad \text{(line 2)}$$

Parallel lines are lines that never intersect. Line 1 and line 2 would be parallel if they had the same gradient: $m_1=m_2$.

Perpendicular lines are lines that intersect at right angles. Line 1 and line 2 would be perpendicular if $m_1 \times m_2=-1$. If we know m_1, we can determine m_2 by taking the negative reciprocal of $m_1 \Rightarrow m_2=-\frac{1}{m_1}$.

To find the equation of a line that passes through the coordinates (a, b) and is parallel to a given line, we state the gradient of the new line and determine its equation using the point–slope form.

To find the equation of a line that passes through the coordinates (a, b) and is perpendicular to a given line, we take the negative reciprocal of the known gradient to be the gradient of the new line and then determine the equation of the new line using the point–slope form.

Example

a. Determine the equation of the line parallel to $y = 2x + 3$ that passes through the point $(1, -2)$.

b. Determine the equation of the line perpendicular to $y = 2x - 4$ that passes through the point $(1, 2)$.

✓ ***Solution***

Working	Explanation
a. $m = 2$ $(y - (-2)) = 2(x - 1)$ $y + 2 = 2x - 2$ $y = 2x - 4$	A line parallel to $y = 2x + 3$ has the same gradient: 2. Substitute $m = 2$ and the coordinates of the point into $(y - y_1) = m(x - x_1)$. Rearrange the equation into the form $y = mx + c$.
b. $m = -\frac{1}{2}$ $(y - 2) = -\frac{1}{2}(x - 1)$ $y - 2 = -\frac{1}{2}x + \frac{1}{2}$ $y = -\frac{1}{2}x + \frac{5}{2}$	A line perpendicular to a line with gradient m has a gradient of $-\frac{1}{m}$. Substitute $m = -\frac{1}{2}$ and the coordinates of the point into $(y - y_1) = m(x - x_1)$. Rearrange the equation into the form $y = mx + c$.

Exercise 3.5

a. Determine the equation of the line parallel to $y = 3x + 1$ that passes through the point $(4, -2)$.

b. Determine the equation of the line parallel to $2x - 3y = 4$ that passes through the point $(-1, 2)$.

c. Determine the equation of the line perpendicular to $y = 3x + 1$ that passes through the point $(4, -2)$.

d. Determine the equation of the line perpendicular to $2x - 3y = 4$ that passes through the point $(-1, 2)$.

3.6 Applying linear equations

Linear equations can be used to solve many problems in real life, including problems involving growth, costs or distance.

Follow the steps below when interpreting and solving practical problems involving linear equations.

- Define each unknown quantity by assigning a pronumeral to it.
- Translate the problem into a linear equation using each pronumeral.
- Solve the problem.
- Clearly state the solution to the problem.

Example

A tank initially holds 3 litres of water. More water is poured into the tank at a rate of 2 litres per minute. Determine the volume of water in the tank 5 minutes after the pouring begins.

✓ Solution

Working	Explanation
Let $t =$ time taken, in minutes. Let $V =$ volume of water in the container at time t.	1. Define the variables.
$V = 2t + 3$	2. Formulate the linear equation: • initial amount: when $t = 0$, $V = 3$ • rate: V increases at a constant rate of 2 litres every minute.
Substitute $t = 5$: $V = 2(5) + 3 = 13$ litres	3. Solve the question.
The volume of water in the container after 5 minutes is 13 litres.	4. State the solution.

Example

The weekly wage of a vacuum cleaner salesperson consists of a fixed sum of $280 plus $30 for each cleaner sold.

a. How much did the salesperson earn in a week when they sold 4 cleaners?

b. How many vacuum cleaners must the salesperson sell in a week to earn $550?

✓ Solution

Working	Explanation
Let $c =$ number of cleaners sold. Let $W =$ wage earned for the week.	1. Define the variables.
$W = 30c + 280$	2. Formulate the linear equation: • base pay: $280; rate: the wage increases at a constant rate of $30 for every cleaner sold.
a. Substitute $c = 4$: $W = 30(4) + 280 = \$400$	3. Solve the question.
The salesperson earns $400 in that week.	4. State the solution.
b. Substitute $W = 550$: $550 = 30c + 280$ $270 = 30c$ $c = 9$	1. Solve the question.
The salesperson must sell 9 cleaners in a week to earn $550.	2. State the solution.

Exercise 3.6

a. A plumber charges customers \$60 per hour in addition to a call-out fee of \$30. Determine the bill for a job that took 2 hours to complete.

b. A taxi charges an initial fee (also called a flag fall) of \$3.20 and then \$1.50 per kilometre travelled. What would it cost to travel 35 km?

c. An initially empty pool is filled with water at a rate of 25 litres per minute.

   i. Determine the volume of water in the pool after 30 minutes.

   ii. If the pool holds 15 000 litres, how long would it take to fill the whole pool?

d. A printing firm charges \$35 for printing 600 sheets of notepaper and \$47 for printing 800 sheets of notepaper.

   i. Determine the rule for the charge, C, in terms of number of sheets printed.

   ii. How much would the firm charge to print 1200 sheets?

3.7 Solving simultaneous equations

Simultaneous equations are a set of two or more algebraic equations that have a common solution – that is, there are values that satisfy all the equations.

Simultaneous equations can be solved graphically or algebraically. To solve simultaneous equations graphically, the equations are plotted on the Cartesian plane and the solution is the point of intersection. To solve simultaneous equations algebraically, the equations need to be manipulated to enable them to be solved by substitution or elimination.

Example

Graph and solve the pair of simultaneous equations $y = 2x + 3$ and $y = -x + 6$.

✓ *Solution*

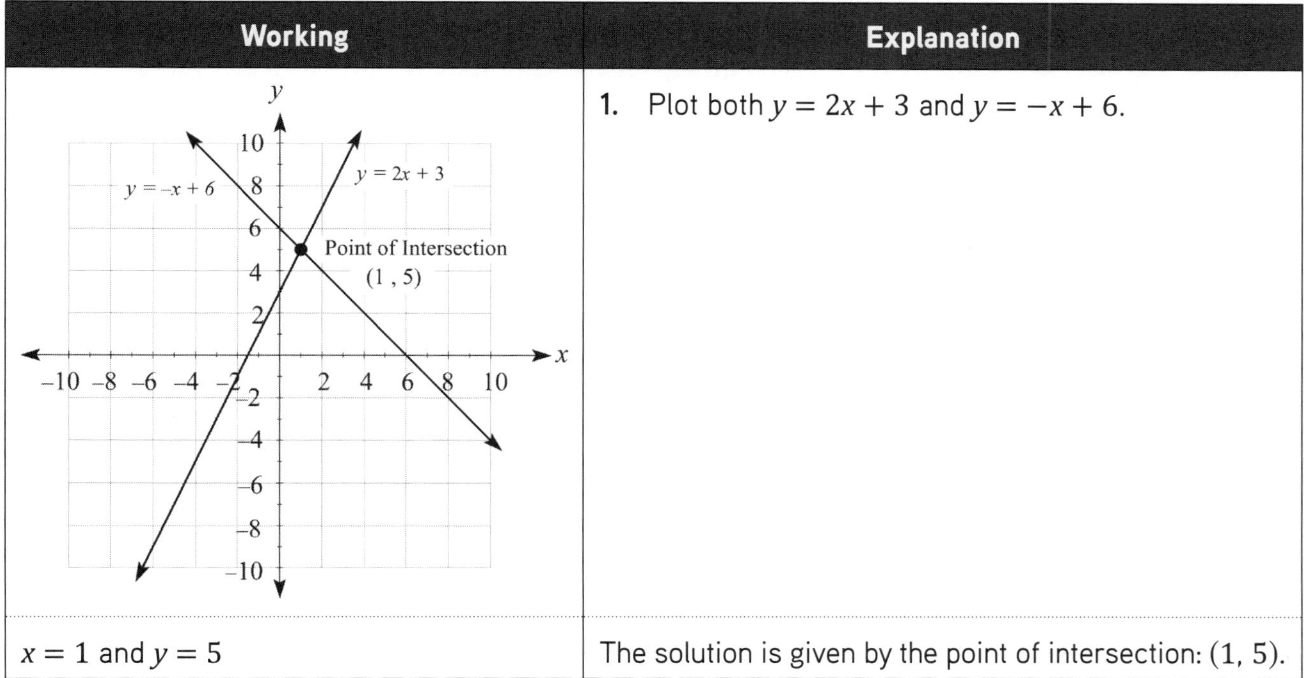

Working	Explanation
(graph)	1. Plot both $y = 2x + 3$ and $y = -x + 6$.
$x = 1$ and $y = 5$	The solution is given by the point of intersection: $(1, 5)$.

Example

Solve the simultaneous equations $5x - 2y = 17$ and $y = 2x - 7$ using substitution.

✓ ***Solution***

Working	Explanation
$5x - 2y = 17 \quad (1)$ $y = 2x - 7 \quad (2)$	1. Label the two equations.
Substitute (2) into (1): $5x - 2(2x - 7) = 17$ $5x - 4x + 14 = 17$ $x = 3$	2. Substitute equation (2) into equation (1). 3. Solve for x.
Substitute $x = 3$ into (2): $y = 2(3) - 7 = -1$	4. Substitute the value of x into one of the equations to obtain the value of y.
$x = 3$ and $y = -1$	5. State the solution.

Example

Solve the simultaneous equations $4x - 3y = 0$ and $3x + 4y = 25$ using elimination.

✓ ***Solution***

Working	Explanation
$4x - 3y = 0 \quad (1)$ $3x + 4y = 25 \quad (2)$ $4 \times (1) \quad 16x - 12y = 0 \quad (3)$ $3 \times (2) \quad 9x + 12y = 75 \quad (4)$	1. Label the two equations. 2. For the method of elimination, the coefficient of x or y in both equations must be the same. We can achieve this in this example by multiplying equation (1) by 4 and equation (2) by 3.
$(3) + (4) \quad 25x = 75$ $x = 3$	3. Since we have $-12y$ in equation (3) and $12y$ in equation (4), we add the equations to eliminate the terms with y. 4. Solve for x.
Substitute $x = 3$ into (1): $4(3) - 3y = 0$ $y = 4$	5. Substitute the value of x into one of the equations to obtain the value of y.
$x = 3$ and $y = 4$	6. State the solution.

Exercise 3.7

Solve the following simultaneous equations using the specified method.

a. Graphically: $y - 2x = 1$ and $4y + 3x = 15$

b. Substitution: $2x - y = 6$ and $3x + y = 10$

c. Elimination: $2 - 7x + 3y = 22$ and $3x - 6y = -11$

3.8 Applying simultaneous equations

Simultaneous equations also have various real-life applications. Follow the steps below when interpreting and solving practical problems involving simultaneous equations.

- Define each unknown quantity by assigning a pronumeral to it.
- Translate the problem into two linear equations using each pronumeral.
- Solve the problem.
- Clearly state the solution to the problem.

Example

3 kg of butter and 2 kg of marmalade cost $29, and 6 kg of butter and 3 kg of marmalade cost $54. Formulate a set of simultaneous equations to determine the cost per kilogram of butter and the cost per kilogram of marmalade.

✓ Solution

Working	Explanation
Let b = the cost of butter per kilogram and m = the cost of marmalade per kilogram.	1. Define the variables.
$3b + 2m = 29$ (1) $6b + 3m = 54$ (2)	2. Formulate the equations. • Equation (1) – cost of 3 kg of butter and 2 kg of marmalade • Equation (2) – cost of 6 kg of butter and 3 kg of marmalade
$2 \times (1)$ $6b + 4m = 58$ (3) $(3) - (2)$ $m = 4$ Substitute $m = 4$ into (1): $3b + 8 = 29$ $b = 7$	3. Solve using the method of elimination.
Butter costs $7 per kg and marmalade costs $4 per kg.	4. Answer the question.

Example

A volunteer decides to make cakes to sell at a charity fete. The fixed costs are \$400 and the cost of making each cake is \$1. Each cake sells for \$1.50.

a. How many cakes must the volunteer sell to break even?

b. If the volunteer only sold 700 cakes, would they make a loss or a profit? By how much?

✓ ***Solution***

Working	Explanation
Let x = number of cakes E = expense incurred I = income earned	**1.** Define the variables.
$E = 400 + x$ (1) $I = 1.5x$ (2)	**2.** Formulate the equations. • Equation (1) – expense of making a cake. • Equation (2) – income from selling a cake.
a. To break even, expense must equal income: $400 + x = 1.5x$ $x = 800$	**3.** Equate expense and income and solve for x.
800 cakes must be made and sold for the volunteer to break even.	**4.** Answer the question.
b. As 700 cakes is less than the break-even number, the volunteer would make a loss.	**5.** Compare the number of cakes to the break-even number.
$E = 400 + 700 = \$1200$ $I = 1.5\,(700) = \$1050$ $I - E = -\$150$	**6.** Calculate the expense and income in making and selling 700 cakes. Since difference is negative, a loss is made.
The loss is \$150	**7.** Answer the question.

Exercise 3.8.1

Formulate a set of simultaneous equations for the following problems and solve them.

a. In four years from now, a mother will be three times as old as her daughter. Four years ago, she was five times as old as her daughter. Find their current ages.

b. One-hundred-and-fifty tickets were sold for a basketball match and the total amount collected was \$560. Adult tickets were sold at \$4 each and child tickets were sold at \$1.50 each. How many adult tickets and child tickets were sold?

c. Jo has \$10 in 5-cent and 10-cent coins in her change jar. There are 157 coins in the jar. How many 5-cent coins does she have?

Exercise 3.8.2

In a city, electricity charges are calculated as follows:

- **Scheme A:** a fixed charge of \$30 plus 40 cents per unit of electricity used.
- **Scheme B:** a flat rate of 60 cents per unit of electricity used.

a. Find the cost of 50 units of electricity for each of the two schemes.

b. How many units of electricity would you need to use for the cost of both schemes to be the same?

3.9 Solving linear inequalities

A linear inequality is an expression that **compares** two values, by stating that one is greater than (or equal to) the other (written as $x > y$ or $x \geq y$). Unlike equations, inequalities do not use the equals sign. This means that the solution is not a specific number, but a range of numbers.

Solving inequalities is the same as solving linear equations, except that when you multiply (or divide) both sides by a negative number, you have to reverse the direction of the inequality symbol. For example, $-x > 2$ divided by -1 becomes $x < -2$.

Example

Solve the following inequalities.

a. $2x - 2 < 4$ b. $4 - 2x \leq 16$ c. $-6(x + 1) > 12$

✓ *Solution*

Working	Explanation
a. $2x - 2 < 4$ $2x < 6$ $x < 3$	1. Add 2 to both sides. 2. Divide both sides by 2.
b. $4 - 2x \leq 16$ $-2x \leq 12$ $x \geq 6$	1. Subtract 4 from both sides. 2. Divide both sides by -2. Note that the inequality symbol is now reversed.
c. $-6(x + 1) > 12$ $-6x - 6 > 12$ $-6x > 18$ $x < -3$	1. Expand the brackets according to the distributive law. 2. Add 6 to both sides. 3. Divide both sides by -6 and reverse the inequality symbol.

Exercise 3.9

Solve the following inequalities.

a. $3x + 6 < 21$

b. $4(x + 4) > 24$

c. $2x - 4 \leq 8x + 8$

d. $2(x - 1) \leq 3(x + 2)$

3.10 Applying linear inequalities

As with linear and simultaneous equations, linear inequalities can also be applied to real-life situations. When interpreting and solving practical problems involving linear inequalities, you should follow these steps.

- Define each unknown quantity by assigning a pronumeral to it.
- Translate the problem into an inequality using the definitions of each pronumeral.
- Solve the problem.
- Clearly state the solution to the problem.

Example

At Universal World, Jane went on various rides. The cost of each ride was \$14.50. She bought her lunch for \$12.50. If she had \$99 to spend, determine the maximum number of rides she could take.

✓ ***Solution***

Working	Explanation
Let $r =$ the number of rides taken by Jane.	**1.** Define the variable.
$14.5r + 12.5 \leq 99$ $14.5r \leq 86.5$ $r \leq 5.97$	**2.** Set up an inequality and solve it.
The maximum number of rides taken by Jane is 5.	**3.** Answer the question. As the number of rides has to be an integer, the maximum number of rides must be 5, which is still less than or equal to 5.97.

Example

A group of Year 10 students are selling handmade cards to raise money for a charity. They earn \$0.40 for each card they sell. Their goal is to earn more than \$327. Determine the minimum number of cards they need to sell to achieve their aim.

✓ ***Solution***

Working	Explanation
Let $c =$ the number of cards sold by the students.	**1.** Define a variable.
$0.4c \geq 327$ $c \geq 817.5$	**2.** Set up an inequality and solve it.
The students must sell at least 818 cards to achieve their target of \$327.	**3.** Answer the question. As the number of cards sold has to be an integer, the minimum number of cards the students need to sell must be 818, which is still greater than or equal to 817.5.

Exercise 3.10

a. When 3 is subtracted from a certain number, the result is less than or equal to 5. Determine the possible values of the number.

b. It costs \$1 to send a letter weighing less than 20 g. A sheet of paper weighs 3 g. Determine the number of pages that can be sent for \$1.

c. A student receives marks of 66 and 72 on two assessments. What is the lowest mark he can obtain on the third assessment to have an average score for all three assessments greater than or equal to 75?

3.11 Half-planes

When a linear equation is graphed on the Cartesian plane, the line splits the plane into two halves. Each half is called a **half-plane**.

A linear inequality with two variables can also be graphed. Instead of just graphing the line, we need to include all the ordered pairs that are solutions to the inequality. This is done by shading the half-plane that includes the solutions, as shown in the diagram on the right.

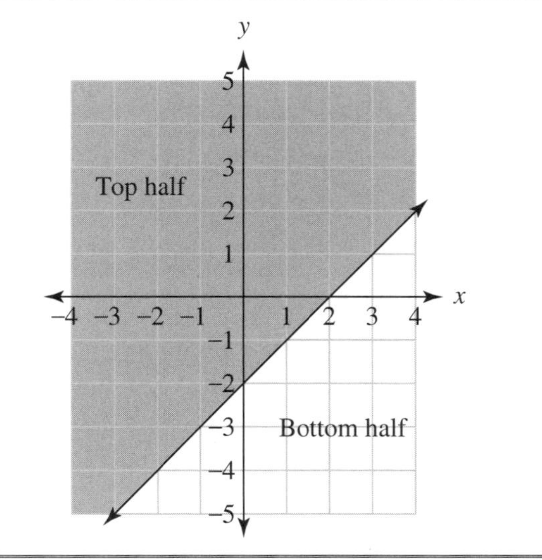

To graph an inequality, follow these steps.

1. Sketch the inequality as if it were a linear equation (i.e. with the inequality sign replaced with an equals sign).
   - If the inequality sign includes an equals (i.e. it is $\leq$ or $\geq$) draw a solid line. This indicates that points on the line are included in the solution.
   - If the inequality sign does not include an equals (i.e. it is $<$ or $>$) draw a dashed line. This indicates that points on the line are excluded from the solution.
2. Determine the half-plane that includes the solutions. To do this, substitute the coordinates of any point – such as $(0, 0)$ – into the inequality.
   - If the substitution satisfies the inequality, we shade the half-plane that includes the point.
   - If the substitution does not satisfy the inequality, we shade the other half-plane.

Example

Sketch the inequality $y > 2x - 3$, shading the half-plane to show all solutions.

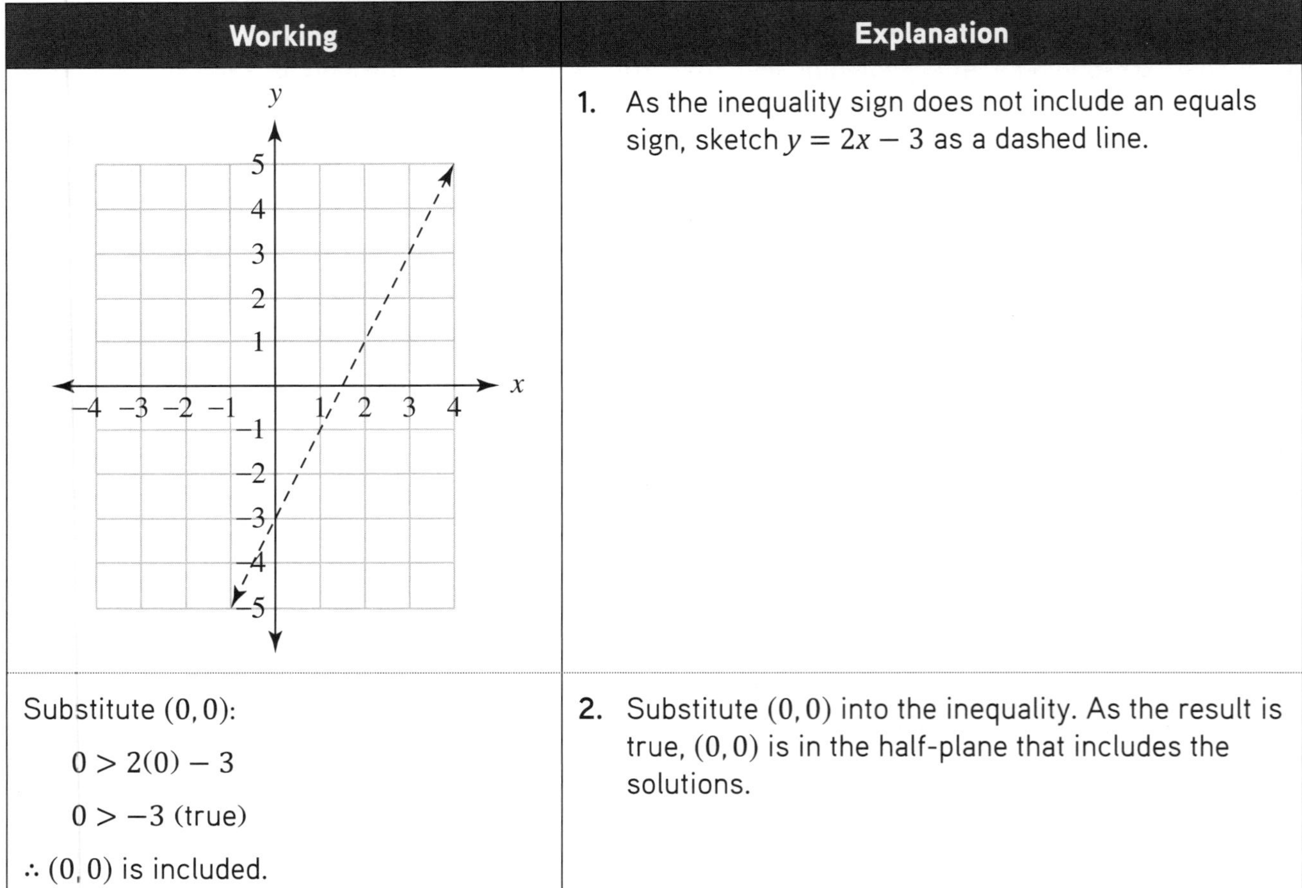

✓ *Solution*

Working	Explanation
	1. As the inequality sign does not include an equals sign, sketch $y = 2x - 3$ as a dashed line.
Substitute $(0, 0)$: $0 > 2(0) - 3$ $0 > -3$ (true) $\therefore (0, 0)$ is included.	2. Substitute $(0, 0)$ into the inequality. As the result is true, $(0, 0)$ is in the half-plane that includes the solutions.

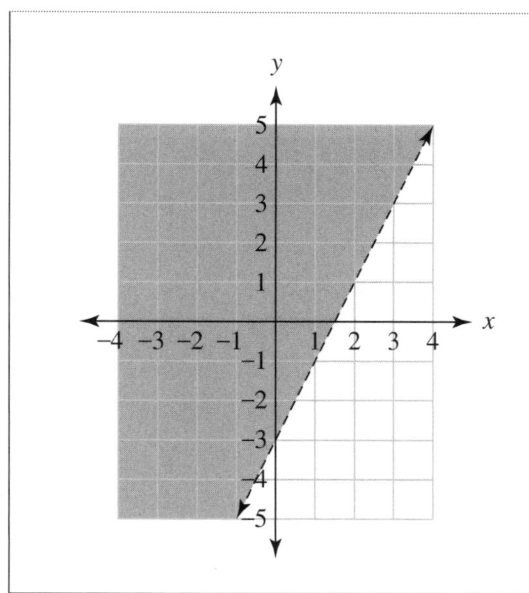	3. Shade the half-plane that includes $(0,0)$.

Example

Sketch the inequality $y + 3x \geq 6$, shading the half-plane to show all solutions.

✓ *Solution*

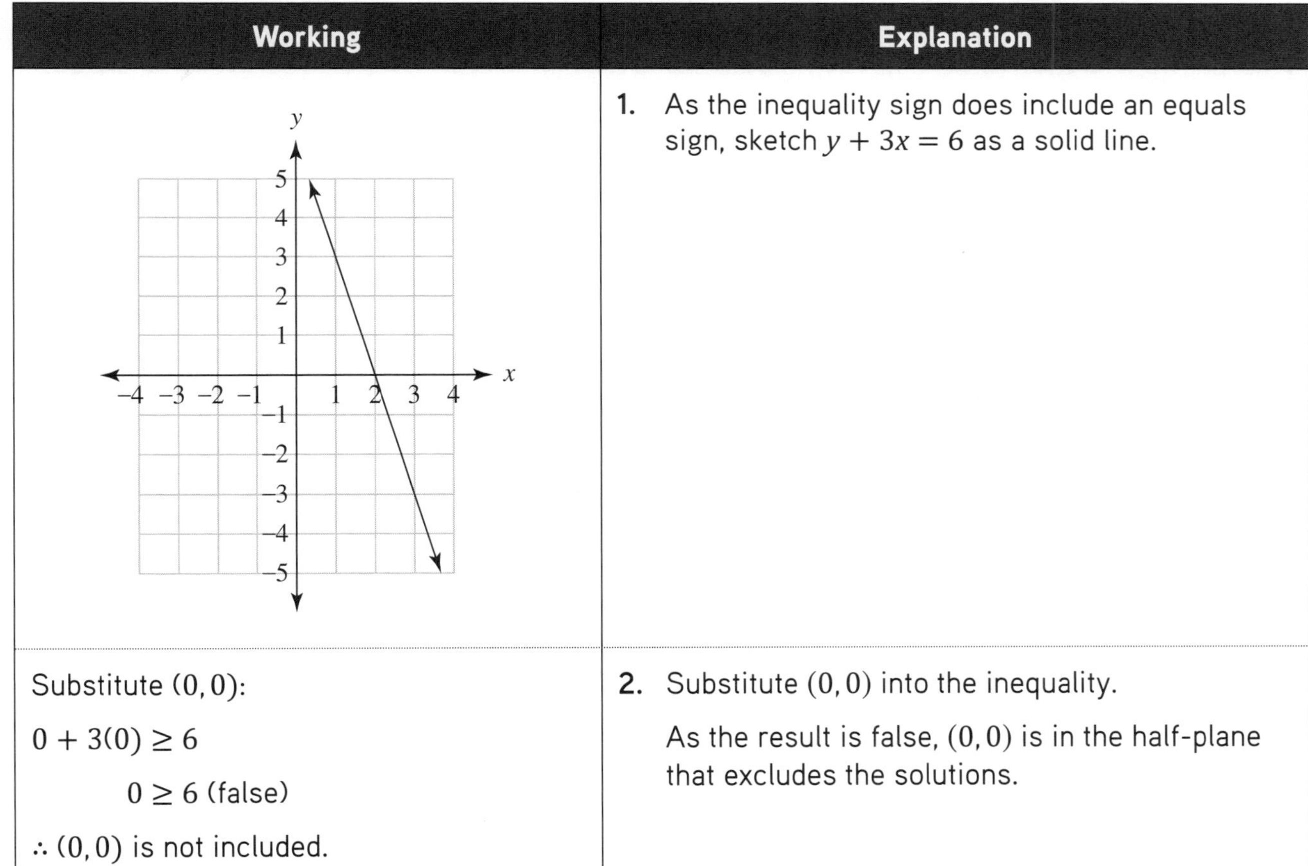

Working	Explanation
(graph)	1. As the inequality sign does include an equals sign, sketch $y + 3x = 6$ as a solid line.
Substitute $(0,0)$: $0 + 3(0) \geq 6$ $0 \geq 6$ (false) $\therefore (0,0)$ is not included.	2. Substitute $(0,0)$ into the inequality. As the result is false, $(0,0)$ is in the half-plane that excludes the solutions.

➡

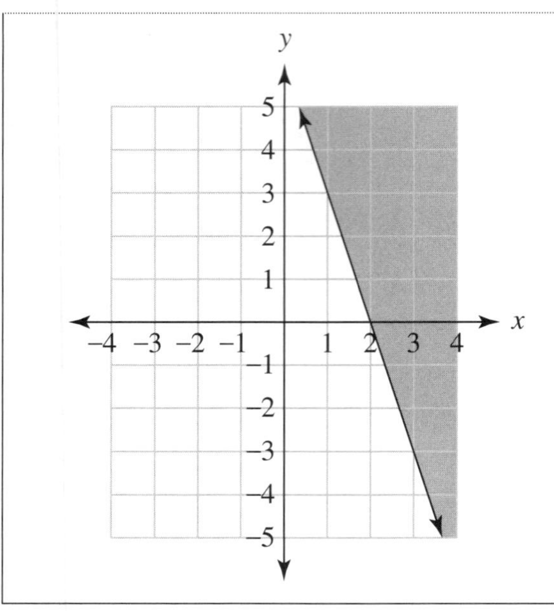	**3.** Shade the half-plane that excludes $(0, 0)$.

Example

Sketch the inequality $x > 4$, shading the half-plane to show all solutions.

✓ ***Solution***

Working	Explanation
	1. As the inequality sign does not include an equals sign, sketch $x = 4$ as a dashed line.
Substitute $(0, 0)$: $0 \geq 4$ (false) $\therefore (0, 0)$ is not included.	**2.** Substitute $(0, 0)$ into the inequality. As the result is false, $(0, 0)$ is in the half-plane that excludes the solutions.

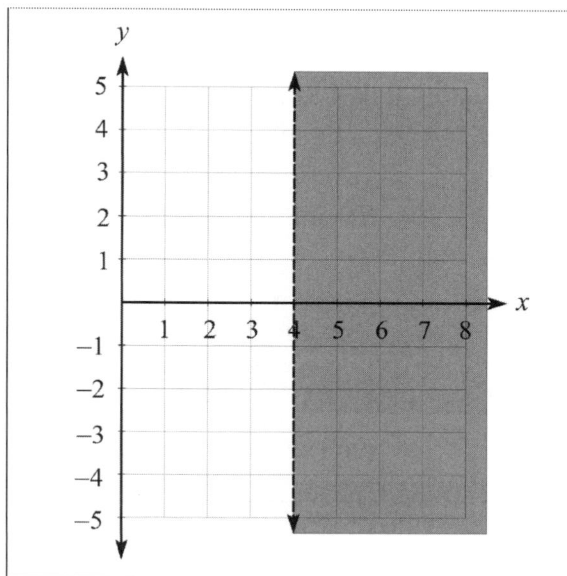	**3.** Shade the half-plane that excludes $(0, 0)$.

Example

One kilogram of a coffee blend is made by mixing type A and type B coffee beans. Type A coffee beans cost \$9.00 per kg and type B coffee beans cost \$7.00 per kg. Find all possible mixtures of the two coffee beans for which the blended cost is \$8.50 or less.

✓ Solution

Working	Explanation
Let x = weight of type A coffee beans. Let y = weight of type B coffee beans.	**1.** Define the variables.
$9x + 7y \leq 8.50$	**2.** Formulate the inequality.
When $x = 0, y = 1.21$ (y-intercept) When $y = 0$, $x = 0.944$ (x-intercept)	**3.** Sketch $9x + 7y = 8.50$ by finding the intercepts. As the equals sign is included, in the inequality sign, sketch a solid line.
Substitute $(0, 0)$ into the inequality: $9(0) + 7(0) \leq 8.50$ $0 \leq 8.50$ (true) $\therefore (0, 0)$ is included.	**4.** Test whether $(0, 0)$ is in the half-plane that includes the solutions.

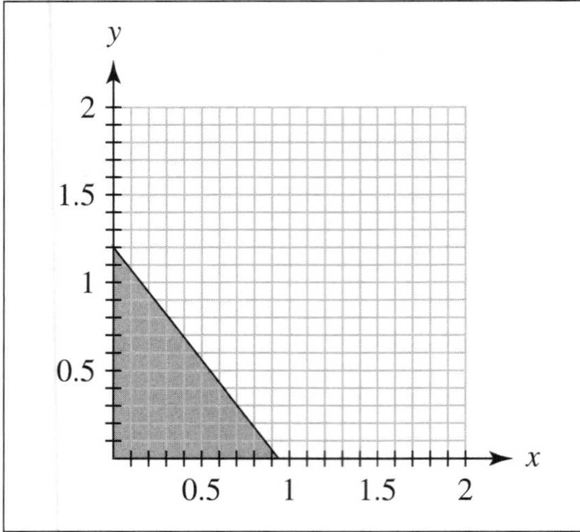	**5.** Shade the region that includes $(0, 0)$. **Note:** only the first quadrant of the coordinate plane is graphed because coffee beans cannot have a negative weight.

Exercise 3.11.1

Sketch the following inequalities, shading the half-plane to show all the solutions.

a. $3x - 4y \geq 12$

b. $2x + 5y > -10$

Exercise 3.11.2

a. Lily has \$30 to spend on food for a class barbecue. A hot dog costs \$0.75 and a burger costs \$1.25. Sketch a graph that shows all the combinations of hot dogs and burgers she could buy for the barbecue while spending less than \$30.00.

b. At the local grocery store, oranges cost \$3.00 per kilogram and apples cost \$4.50 per kilogram. If I have \$20 to spend on oranges and apples, sketch a graph to show what combinations of each I can buy and spend at most \$20.

Chapter 4 – Quadratic equations

4.1 Introduction

A quadratic equation is a polynomial equation in which the highest power of x is 2. There are three main forms.

- **General form**: $y = ax^2 + bx + c$, where a, b and c are constants and $a \neq 0$.
- **Turning-point form**: $y = a(x - h)^2 + k$, where a, h and k are constants and $a \neq 0$. This form presents a quadratic equation in terms of its turning point, (h, k), the point where the parabola defined by the equation reaches its maximum or minimum value. We can obtain the turning-point form from the general form using the technique of completing the square. (The turning-point form is also known as the **vertex form** or **completing-the-square form**.)
- **Factorised form**: $y = a(x - m)(x - n)$, where a, m and n are constants and $a \neq 0$. This form allows us to easily identify the roots of the quadratic equation, if there are any. Note that not all quadratic expressions can be factorised. We can obtain the factorised form by factorising the general form using the techniques learnt in Section 1.2.

4.2 Factorising by completing the square

To obtain the turning-point form of a quadratic equation from its general form, we use the process of completing the square. We will start by considering **monic quadratic equations**. These are quadratic equations where $a = 1$, that is, of the form $y = x^2 + bx + c$.

Completing the square for monic quadratic equations

Step 1

Add $\left(\frac{b}{2}\right)^2$ to the equation and then balance it by subtracting $\left(\frac{b}{2}\right)^2$. This ensures that part of the equation becomes a perfect square trinomial.

$$y = \underbrace{x^2 + bx + \left(\frac{b}{2}\right)^2}_{\text{Perfect square trinomial}} - \left(\frac{b}{2}\right)^2 + c$$

Step 2

Factorise the perfect square trinomial and simplify.

$$y = \left(x + \frac{b}{2}\right)^2 - \left(\frac{b}{2}\right)^2 + c$$

Step 3

If possible, factorise using the difference of perfect squares according to the template $(a^2 - b^2) = (a - b)(a + b)$.

Example

Factorise $y = x^2 + 4x - 6$ by completing the square.

✓ ***Solution***

Working	Explanation
$y = x^2 + 4x - 6$ $= x^2 + 4x + \left(\frac{4}{2}\right)^2 - \left(\frac{4}{2}\right)^2 - 6$	Complete the square by adding $\left(\frac{4}{2}\right)^2$ and balance the equation by subtracting $\left(\frac{4}{2}\right)^2$.
$= \left(x + \frac{4}{2}\right)^2 - \left(\frac{4}{2}\right)^2 - 6$ $= (x + 2)^2 - 4 - 6$ $= (x + 2)^2 - 10$	Factorise the perfect square trinomial and simplify.
$= (x + 2)^2 - (\sqrt{10})^2$ $= (x + 2 - \sqrt{10})(x + 2 + \sqrt{10})$	Express 10 as $(\sqrt{10})^2$, as this creates a difference of perfect squares and thus enables the equation to be further factorised.
Note: $y = x^2 + 4x - 6$ is the general form. $y = (x + 2)^2 - 10$ is the turning-point form. $y = (x + 2 - \sqrt{10})(x + 2 + \sqrt{10})$ is the factorised form.	

Example

Factorise $y = x^2 - 2x + 8$ by completing the square.

✓ ***Solution***

Working	Explanation
$y = x^2 - 2x + 8$ $= x^2 - 2x + \left(\frac{2}{2}\right)^2 - \left(\frac{2}{2}\right)^2 + 8$	Complete the square by adding $\left(\frac{2}{2}\right)^2$ and balance the equation by subtracting $\left(\frac{2}{2}\right)^2$.
$= \left(x - \frac{2}{2}\right)^2 - \left(\frac{2}{2}\right)^2 + 8$ $= (x - 1)^2 - 1 + 8$ $= (x - 1)^2 + 7$	Factorise the perfect square trinomial and simplify. **Note:** this is not in the form of a difference of perfect squares; hence we cannot further factorise it. We must leave the equation in turning-point form.

Exercise 4.2.1

Factorise the following equations by completing the square.

a. $y = x^2 + 2x - 6$ **b.** $y = x^2 - 12x + 2$ **c.** $y = x^2 - 4x + 1$

d. $y = x^2 + 4x - 3$ **e.** $y = x^2 - 30x + 150$ **f.** $y = x^2 + 3x + 7$

Completing the square for non-monic quadratic equations

Non-monic quadratic equations are quadratic equations of the form $y = ax^2 + bx + c$, where $a > 1$. We can factorise a non-monic quadratic equation by first factorising out the common factor that leaves a monic quadratic equation as one of the factors.

Example

Factorise $y = 2x^2 + 8x - 12$ by completing the square.

✓ *Solution*

Working	Explanation
$y = 2x^2 + 8x - 12 = 2(x^2 + 4x - 6)$	Factorise out the common factor: 2. We now have two factors, one of which is a monic quadratic equation.
$y = 2(x^2 + 4x - 6)$ $= 2(x + 2 - \sqrt{10})(x + 2 + \sqrt{10})$	Ignore the common factor for the moment and factorise the monic factor by completing the square. (We factorised this particular monic quadratic equation in an example in the previous section.) Then add back the common factor you took out at the start.

Exercise 4.2.2

Factorise the following equations by completing the square.

a. $y = 2x^2 + 12x + 4$ **b.** $y = 3x^2 + 18x + 3$ **c.** $y = 4x^2 + 8x - 16$

4.3 Solving quadratic equations by factorisation

Solving quadratic equations in factorised form requires the application of the **null factor law**. The null factor law states that if the product of two numbers equals zero, then either or both numbers are zero.

Consider the equation $m \times n = 0$.

We can conclude that $m = 0$, $n = 0$ or $m = n = 0$.

Therefore if $(x + 1)(x - 5) = 0$, we can say that $(x + 1) = 0$ or $(x - 5) = 0$.

Solving both linear equations gives $x = -1$ or 5.

To solve quadratic equations using factorisation the process is:

1. If necessary, rearrange the equation so that zero is on its own on one side of the equation.
2. Factorise the equation using techniques learnt in Chapter 1.
3. Apply the null factor law.
4. Solve for the values of x.

Example

Solve $x^2 - 8x + 12 = 0$ by factorisation.

✓ ***Solution***

Working	Explanation
$x^2 - 8x + 12 = 0$ $(x - 6)(x - 2) = 0$ $x - 6 = 0, \quad x - 2 = 0$ $x = 6, \qquad x = 2$	1. Check to see if the equation needs to be rearranged. In this example it doesn't. 2. Factorise the equation. 3. Apply the null factor law. 4. Solve for the values of x.

Example

Solve $2x^2 = 5x - 3$ by factorisation.

✓ ***Solution***

Working	Explanation
$2x^2 = 5x - 3$ $2x^2 - 5x + 3 = 0$ $(x - 1)(2x - 3) = 0$ $x - 1 = 0, \quad 2x - 3 = 0$ $x = 1, \qquad x = \frac{3}{2}$	1. Rearrange the equation. 2. Factorise the equation. 3. Apply the null factor law. 4. Solve for the values of x.

Exercise 4.3

Solve the following using factorisation.

a. $x^2 - 2x = 0$

b. $x^2 - 9 = 0$

c. $x^2 + 6x + 9 = 0$

d. $x^2 + 2x - 15 = 0$

e. $x^2 - 2x - 8 = 0$

f. $2x^2 - x - 6 = 0$

g. $x^2 = 13x - 30$

h. $10 - x = 3x^2$

i. $4x^2 + 3 = 8x$

4.4 Solving quadratic equations by completing the square

In Section 4.2 we learnt how to fully factorise quadratic expressions by completing the square. In this section we will solve quadratic equations by the following steps:

1. If necessary, rearrange the equation so that zero is on its own on one side of the equation.
2. If there is a common factor in all terms, factorise out the common factor.
3. Factorise the equation by completing the square.
4. Apply the null factor law.
5. Solve for the values of x.

Example

Solve $x^2 + 3x + 1 = 0$ by completing the square. Give your answers in exact form.

✓ *Solution*

Working	Explanation
$x^2 + 3x + 1 = 0$ $x^2 + 3x + \left(\frac{3}{2}\right)^2 - \left(\frac{3}{2}\right)^2 + 1 = 0$ $\left(x + \frac{3}{2}\right)^2 - \frac{9}{4} + 1 = 0$ $\left(x + \frac{3}{2}\right)^2 - \frac{5}{4} = 0$	There is no need here to rearrange the equation, nor are there any common factors to consider. Apply the technique of completing the square.
$\left(x + \frac{3}{2}\right)^2 - \left(\frac{\sqrt{5}}{2}\right)^2 = 0$ $\left(x + \frac{3}{2} - \frac{\sqrt{5}}{2}\right)\left(x + \frac{3}{2} + \frac{\sqrt{5}}{2}\right) = 0$	Factorise using the difference of perfect squares.
$x + \frac{3}{2} - \frac{\sqrt{5}}{2} = 0,\ x + \frac{3}{2} + \frac{\sqrt{5}}{2} = 0$ $x = -\frac{3}{2} + \frac{\sqrt{5}}{2},\quad x = -\frac{3}{2} - \frac{\sqrt{5}}{2}$	Apply the null factor law to solve for the values of x.
$x = \frac{-3 + \sqrt{5}}{2},\ x = \frac{-3 - \sqrt{5}}{2}$	Combine the results into single fractions.
$x = \frac{-3 \pm \sqrt{5}}{2}$	Combine the results using the $\pm$ symbol.

Example

Solve $2x^2 = 8x - 2$ by completing the square. Give your answers in exact form.

✓ *Solution*

Working	Explanation
$2x^2 = 8x - 2$ $2x^2 - 8x + 2 = 0$	Rearrange the equation so that zero is on its own.
$2(x^2 - 4x + 1) = 0$ $x^2 - 4x + 1 = 0$	Factorise out the common factor, 2, and then divide both sides by 2.

$x^2 - 4x + \left(\frac{4}{2}\right)^2 - \left(\frac{4}{2}\right)^2 + 1 = 0$ $(x-2)^2 - 4 + 1 = 0$ $(x-2)^2 - 3 = 0$	Apply the technique of completing the squares.
$(x-2)^2 - (\sqrt{3})^2 = 0$ $(x - 2 - \sqrt{3})(x - 2 + \sqrt{3}) = 0$	Factorise using the difference of perfect squares.
$x - 2 - \sqrt{3} = 0,\ x - 2 + \sqrt{3} = 0$ $x = 2 + \sqrt{3},\ x = 2 - \sqrt{3}$	Apply the null factor law to solve for the values of x.
$x = 2 \pm \sqrt{3}$	Combine the results using the $\pm$ symbol.

Exercise 4.4

Solve the following by completing the square.

a. $x^2 + 2x - 5 = 0$
b. $x^2 + 4x - 3 = 0$
c. $x^2 - 12x + 2 = 0$
d. $x^2 + 150 = 30x$
e. $4x^2 = 8x + 16$
f. $3x^2 - 6x = 3$
g. $x^2 + x - 4 = 0$
h. $x^2 - 5x + 1 = 0$
i. $x^2 = 7x - 2$

4.5 Solving quadratic equations using the quadratic formula

Quadratic equations of the general form (that is, $ax^2 + bx + c = 0$, where a, b and c are constants and $a \neq 0$) can be solved using the quadratic formula.

$$x = \frac{-b \pm \sqrt{b^2 - 4ac}}{2a}$$

The expression under the square root sign, $b^2 - 4ac$, is known as the discriminant (Δ). It helps us to determine the number of solutions to a quadratic equation.

Discriminant, $\Delta = b^2 - 4ac$	Number of solutions
$b^2 - 4ac < 0$	The quadratic has 0 real solutions.
$b^2 - 4ac = 0$	The quadratic has 1 real solution: $x = \frac{-b \pm \sqrt{0}}{2a} = -\frac{b}{2a}$
$b^2 - 4ac > 0$	The quadratic has 2 real solutions: $x = \frac{-b \pm \sqrt{b^2 - 4ac}}{2a}$

Example

Determine the number of solutions to the quadratic equation $2x^2 + 4x - 3 = 0$ and find the exact solution(s) where applicable.

✓ Solution

Working	Explanation
$2x^2 + 4x - 3 = 0$ $a = 2, b = 4, c = -3$	Determine the values of a, b and c.
$\Delta = b^2 - 4ac$ $= (4)^2 - 4(2)(-3)$ $= 40$	Substitute the values into the discriminant formula.
Since $\Delta > 0$, there are 2 solutions.	Determine the number of solutions to the equation based on the result.
$x = \frac{-b \pm \sqrt{b^2 - 4ac}}{2a}$ $= \frac{-4 \pm \sqrt{40}}{2(2)}$ $= \frac{-4 \pm 2\sqrt{10}}{4}$ $= \frac{-2 \pm \sqrt{10}}{2}$	Substitute a, b and c into the quadratic formula and simplify.

Example

Determine the number of solutions to the quadratic equation $x^2 + 8x + 16 = 0$ and find the exact solution(s) where applicable.

✓ Solution

Working	Explanation
$x^2 + 8x + 16 = 0$ $a = 1, b = 8, \ c = 16$	Determine the values of a, b and c.
$\Delta = b^2 - 4ac$ $= (8)^2 - 4(1)(16)$ $= 0$	Substitute the values into the discriminant formula.
Since $\Delta = 0$ there is only one solution.	Determine the number of solutions to the equation based on the result.
$x = \frac{-b \pm \sqrt{b^2 - 4ac}}{2a}$ $= \frac{-8 \pm \sqrt{0}}{2(1)}$ $= -4$	Substitute a, b and c into the quadratic formula and simplify.

Example

Determine the number of solutions to $2x^2 - 3x + 4 = 0$ and find the exact solution(s) where applicable.

✓ Solution

Working	Explanation
$2x^2 - 3x + 4 = 0$ $a = 2, b = -3, c = 4$	Determine the values of a, b and c.
$\Delta = b^2 - 4ac$ $= (-3)^2 - 4(2)(4)$ $= -23$	Substitute the values into the discriminant formula.
Since $\Delta < 0$ there are no solutions.	Determine the number of solutions to the equation based on the result.

Exercise 4.5

Determine the number of solutions to the following quadratic equations. For those with one or more solutions, find the exact solution(s).

a. $x^2 - 3x + 2 = 0$
b. $x^2 + 2x + 1 = 0$
c. $3x^2 - 9x + 5 = 0$
d. $2x^2 - 10x + 15 = 0$
e. $x^2 + 3x + 4 = 0$
f. $x^2 + 12x - 36 = 0$
g. $4x^2 + 5x + 3 = 0$
h. $x^2 - 5x + 1 = 0$
i. $-5x^2 + 8x + 3 = 0$

4.6 Solving linear and quadratic equations simultaneously

In Section 3.7, when we examined how to solve two linear equations simultaneously, we found the point of intersection between the corresponding linear graphs.

We can also solve a linear equation and a quadratic equation simultaneously by noting if or how the straight line corresponding to the linear equation intersects with the parabola corresponding to the quadratic equation.

2 points of intersection $\Delta = b^2 - 4ac > 0$	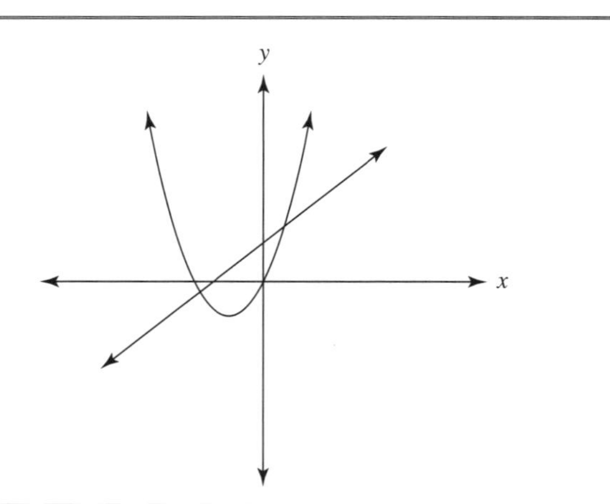

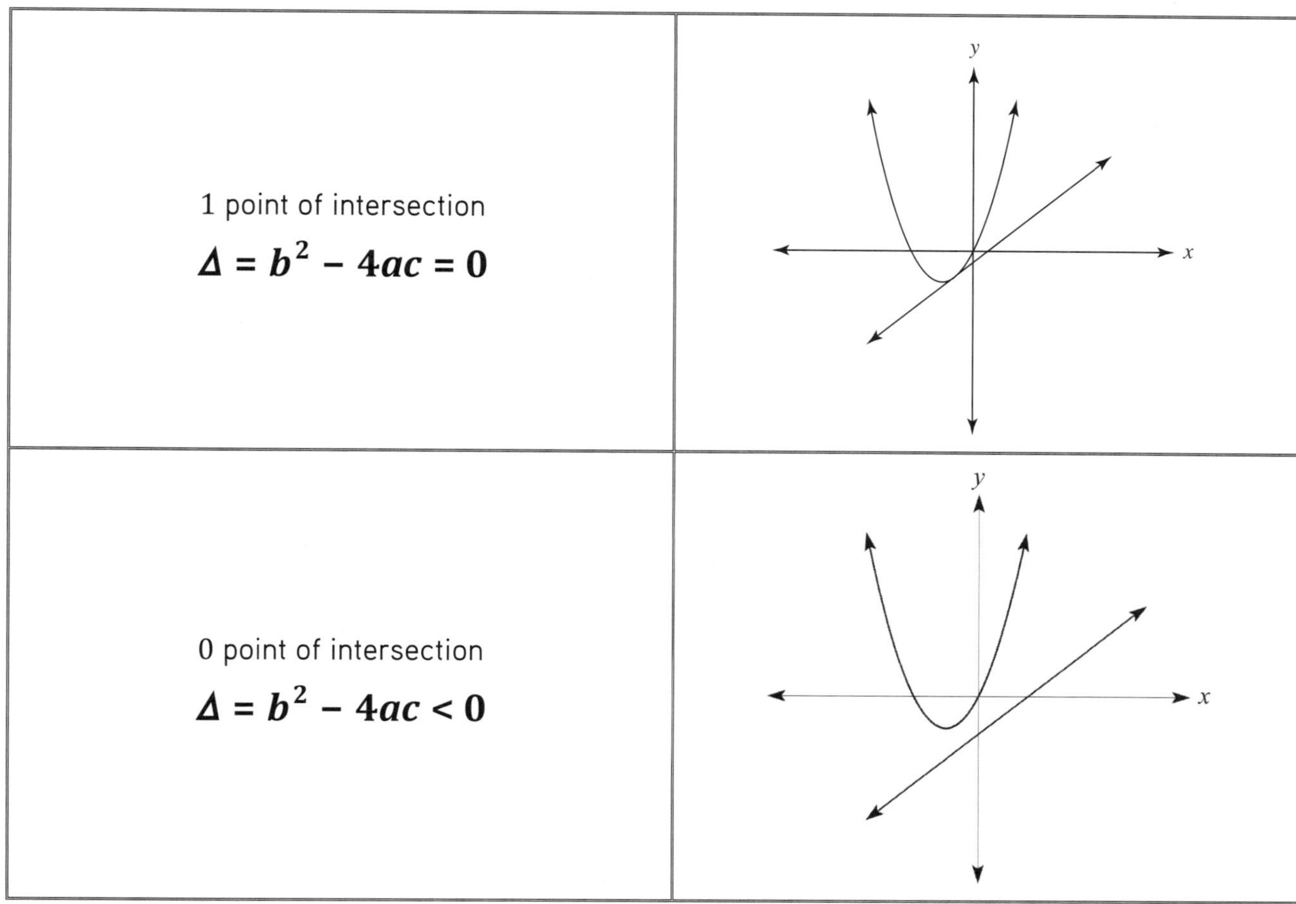

We can use the following steps to determine the number of intersection points between a parabola of the form $y = ax^2 + bx + c_1$ and a line of the form $y = mx + c_2$, then find them if they exist.

1. Substitute one equation into the other.

$$ax^2 + bx + c_1 = mx + c_2$$

2. Rearrange the new equation so that zero is on its own on one side.

$$ax^2 + (b - m)x + (c_1 - c_2) = 0$$

3. Calculate the discriminant to determine the number of intersection points.
4. If intersection points exist, solve the equation for x.
5. Substitute the x-value(s) into the equation of the line to find the y-values.

Example

Determine the number of points of intersection between the quadratic equation $y = x^2 + 2x - 1$ and the linear equation $y = x + 1$. If there are points of intersection, find their coordinates.

✓ Solution

Working	Explanation
$x^2 + 2x - 1 = x + 1$	Substitute one equation into the other.
$x^2 + 2x - x - 1 - 1 = 0$ $x^2 + x - 2 = 0$	Rearrange the new equation so that 0 is on its own on one side.
$\Delta = b^2 - 4ac$ $= 1^2 - 4(1)(-2)$ $= 1 + 8$ $= 9$ Since $\Delta > 0$, there are 2 points of intersection.	Calculate the discriminant to determine the number of intersection points.
$x^2 + x - 2 = 0$ $(x + 2)(x - 1) = 0$ $x = -2,\ x = 1$	Use any technique to solve for x.
Substitute $x = -2$ into $y = x + 1$: $y = -1$ Substitute $x = 1$ into $y = x + 1$: $y = 2$	Substitute the x-values into the linear equation.
The points of intersection are $(-2, -1)$ and $(1, 2)$.	Answer the question.

Example

Determine the number of points of intersection between the quadratic equation $y = x^2 - 6x + 8$ and the linear equation $y = -2x + 4$. If there are points of intersection, find their coordinates.

✓ Solution

Working	Explanation
$x^2 - 6x + 8 = -2x + 4$	Substitute one equation into the other.
$x^2 - 6x + 2x + 8 - 4 = 0$ $x^2 - 4x + 4 = 0$	Rearrange the new equation so that 0 is on its own on one side.
$\Delta = b^2 - 4ac$ $= (-4)^2 - 4(1)(4)$ $= 16 - 16$ $= 0$ Since $\Delta = 0$, there is 1 point of intersection.	Calculate the discriminant to determine the number of intersection points.

$x^2 - 4x + 4 = 0$ $(x-2)^2 = 0$ $x = 2$	Use any technique to solve for x.
$y = -2(2) + 4 = 0$	Substitute the x-value into the linear equation.
The point of intersection is (2, 0).	Answer the question.

Example

Determine the number of points of intersection between the quadratic equation $y = x^2 + x - 1$ and the linear equation $y = x - 2$. If there are points of intersection, find their coordinates.

✓ *Solution*

Working	Explanation
$x^2 + x - 1 = x - 2$	Substitute one equation into the other.
$x^2 + x - x - 1 + 2 = 0$ $x^2 + 1 = 0$	Rearrange the new equation so that 0 is on its own on one side.
$\Delta = b^2 - 4ac$ $= (0)^2 - 4(1)(1)$ $= -4$	Calculate the discriminant to determine the number of intersection points.
Since $\Delta < 0$, there are no points of intersection.	Answer the question.

Exercise 4.6

Determine the number of points of intersection between the following pairs of equations. If there are points of intersection, find their coordinates.

a. $y = x^2 + 2x - 8$ and $y = -x + 2$

b. $y = x^2 - 2x + 6$ and $y = 4x - 3$

c. $y = 2x^2 + 11x + 10$ and $y = 3x + 2$

d. $y = 6 - x - x^2$ and $y = -2(x + 1)$

e. $y = 3x^2 - x + 6$ and $y = 4 - 2x$

f. $y = x^2$ and $4y + 5x = 21$

4.7 Determining quadratic rules

We looked at the different forms a quadratic equation can take at the beginning of this chapter. The appropriate form to use depends on the information we are given.

Given information	Form to use
the coordinates of at least three points on the parabola (either from the graph or from a table of values)	general: $y = ax^2 + bx + c$
the coordinates of the turning point and one other point	turning point: $y = a(x - h)^2 + k$
two x-intercepts and the coordinates of one other point	factorised: $y = a(x - m)(x - n)$

Example

A parabola has x-intercepts of -5 and 2 and passes through the point $(-1, 24)$. Determine the corresponding quadratic equation.

✓ *Solution*

Working	Explanation
$y = a(x - m)(x - n)$	Since we are given the x-intercepts and one other point, we use the factorised form to determine the rule.
Substitute $m = -5$, $n = 2$: $y = a(x - (-5))(x - 2)$ $y = a(x + 5)(x - 2)$	Substitute the values of the x-intercepts into the equation: $m = -5$ and $n = 2$.
Substitute $x = -1, y = 24$: $24 = a(-1 + 5)(-1 - 2)$ $24 = a(4)(-3)$ $a = -2$	Substitute the coordinates of the known point to determine a.
$y = -2(x + 5)(x - 2)$	Write the equation.

Example

A parabola has a turning point at $(3, -7)$ and passes through the point $(4, -4)$. Determine the corresponding quadratic equation.

✓ *Solution*

Working	Explanation
$y = a(x - h)^2 + k$	Since we are given the turning point and one other point, we use the turning-point form to determine the rule.
Substitute $h = 3$, $k = -7$: $y = a(x - 3)^2 - 7$	Substitute the values of the turning point into the equation: $h = 3$ and $k = -7$.
Substitute $x = 4, y = -4$: $-4 = a(4 - 3)^2 - 7$ $a = 3$	Substitute the coordinates of the known point to determine a.
$y = 3(x - 3)^2 - 7$	Write the equation.

Example

A parabola passes through the points $(1, 3)$, $(3, 17)$ and $(0, 2)$. Determine the corresponding quadratic equation.

✓ ***Solution***

Working	Explanation
$y = ax^2 + bx + c$	Since we are given three coordinates, we use the general form to determine the rule.
Substitute $x = 1, y = 3$: $3 = a + b + c \quad (1)$ Substitute $x = 3, y = 17$: $17 = 9a + 3b + c \quad (2)$ Substitute $x = 0, y = 2$: $2 = c \quad (3)$	Substitute the values of three coordinates into the general form to create three equations.
Substitute (3) into (1) and (2): $3 = a + b + 2 \quad (4)$ $17 = 9a + 3b + 2 \quad (5)$ $(4) \times 3 \quad 9 = 3a + 3b + 6 \quad (6)$ $(5) - (6) \quad 8 = 6a - 4$ $12 = 6a$ $a = 2$ Subst. $a = 2$ into (4): $3 = 2 + b + 2$ $b = -1$	Solve the simultaneous linear equations to determine the three unknowns.
$y = 2x^2 - x + 2$	Write the equation.

In Chapter 3, we noted that a given table of values represents a linear function if consecutive values have a constant first-order difference. If the first-order differences between consecutive terms are not constant, we can conclude that the relationship between the variables is not linear.

If we find that the second-order differences – that is, the differences between consecutive terms of the first-order differences – are constant, then the relationship between the variables is quadratic.

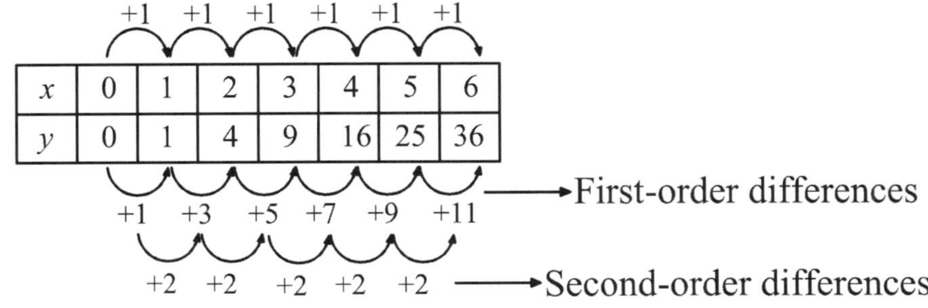

Example

Determine if the values in the following table represent a quadratic equation. If they do, determine its rule.

x	-1	0	1	2	3	4
y	28	13	4	1	4	13

✓ *Solution*

Working	Explanation
x: −1, 0, 1, 2, 3, 4; y: 28, 13, 4, 1, 4, 13 First differences: −15, −9, −3, +3, +9 Second differences: +6, +6, +6, +6	Determine the first-order differences. Note that they are not constant. Determine the second-order differences. Note that they are constant. Hence the values in the table represent a quadratic equation.
$y = ax^2 + bx + c$ Substitute $x = -1, y = 28$: $28 = a - b + c$ (1) Substitute $x = 0, y = 13$: $13 = c$ (2) Substitute $x = 1, y = 4$: $4 = a + b + c$ (3)	Since at least three coordinates are known (there are six in the table of values), we can use the general form of the quadratic equation to determine the rule. Substitute the values of three coordinates into the general form to create three linear equations with three unknowns. **Note**: where possible, choose coordinates where $x = 0$ or $x = 1$.
Substitute (2) into (1) and (3): $28 = a - b + 13$ (4) $4 = a + b + 13$ (5) (4) + (5): $32 = 2a + 26$ $6 = 2a$ $a = 3$ Substitute $a = 3$ into (5): $4 = 3 + b + 13$ $b = -12$	Solve the simultaneous linear equations to determine the three unknowns.
$y = 3x^2 - 12x + 13$	Write the equation.

Example

Determine if the values in the following table represent a quadratic equation. If so, determine its rule.

x	0	1	2	3	4
y	1	0.5	0.25	0.125	0.0625

✓ ***Solution***

<table>
<tr><th>Working</th><th>Explanation</th></tr>
<tr><td>

x	0	1	2	3	4
y	1	0.5	0.25	0.125	0.0625

The values in the table do not represent a quadratic equation.</td><td>Determine the first-order differences. Note that they are not constant.

Determine the second-order differences. Note that they too are not constant. Hence the values in the table do not represent a quadratic equation.

(This table of values represents an exponential function, since as x increases by 1, y decreases multiplicatively by a constant factor of $\frac{1}{2}$.)</td></tr>
</table>

Exercise 4.7.1

a. Determine the rule of the quadratic equation whose graph has a turning point at $(2, 8)$ and passes through the point $(4, 0)$.

b. Determine the rule of the quadratic equation whose graph has intercepts at $(2, 0)$ and $(-8, 0)$ and passes through the point $(0, 48)$.

c. Determine the rule of the quadratic equation whose graph has a turning point at $(-2, 4)$ and passes through the point $(3, -46)$.

d. Determine the rule of the quadratic equation whose graph has intercepts at $(-2, 0)$ and $(6, 0)$ and passes through the point $(1, -30)$.

e. Determine the rule of the quadratic equation whose graph passes through the points $(0, 4)$, $(2, 2)$ and $(4, 4)$.

Exercise 4.7.2

Determine if the values in the following tables represent a quadratic equation. If they do, determine its rule.

a.

x	0	1	2	3	4
y	0	1	8	27	64

b.

x	0	1	2	3	4
y	-3	-1	0	0	-1

4.8 Practical applications of quadratics

Quadratic equations can be used to solve problems in many practical situations, such as calculating an area, the path of a projectile or the shape of the arch of a bridge.

Keep the following steps in mind when interpreting and solving practical problems involving quadratic equations.

1. Assign variables to the unknown quantities.
2. Translate the problem into a quadratic equation using the assigned variables.
3. Solve the problem by using any of the techniques you have learnt.
4. Clearly state the solution to the problem.

Example

The product of two consecutive positive odd numbers is 195. Determine the numbers.

✓ ***Solution***

Working	Explanation
Let x be a positive odd number. It follows that $x + 2$ is the next odd number.	Assign a variable to the unknown value.
$x(x + 2) = 195$ $x^2 + 2x - 195 = 0$ $(x + 15)(x - 13) = 0$ $x = -15, \ x = 13$ Since we are told that x is a positive number, we can reject $x = -15$.	Formulate the equation and solve it.
The two consecutive numbers are 13 and 15.	State the solution.

Example

The perimeter and area of a rectangle are 22 cm and 30 cm^2 respectively. Determine the length and width of the rectangle if the length is the longer side.

✓ *Solution*

Working	Explanation
Let x = length of the rectangle. Let y = width of the rectangle.	Assign a variable to each unknown value.
$2x + 2y = 22$ (1) $xy = 30$ (2)	Formulate the equations. For the perimeter you add the sides of the rectangle: equation (1). For the area you multiply the sides of the rectangle: equation (2).
From (1), $y = 11 - x$ (3) Substitute (3) into (2): $x(11 - x) = 30$ $11x - x^2 = 30$ $x^2 - 11x + 30 = 0$ $(x - 5)(x - 6) = 0$ $x = 5,\ x = 6$ Since length is the longer side, the length must be 6 cm. Substitute $x = 6$ into (2) to get $y = 5$.	Solve the simultaneous equations.
The length and width of the rectangle are 6 cm and 5 cm respectively.	State the solution.

Exercise 4.8

a. The product of two consecutive positive odd numbers is 255. Determine the two numbers.

b. The sides of a right-angled triangle are x cm, $(x + 1)$ cm and $(x + 3)$ cm. Show that $x^2 - 4x - 8 = 0$ and solve this equation to find the lengths of the sides of the triangle. Give your answers to two decimal places.

c. A wire of length 60 cm is cut into two parts and each part is bent to form a square. If the sum of the areas of the two squares is 125 cm^2, determine the lengths of the sides of the two squares.

d. Joe kicks a soccer ball vertically upwards. The height, h metres, of the ball after t seconds is given by $h = 27t - 6t^2$. Determine the time required for the ball to return to the ground.

Chapter 5 – Parabolas

5.1 Sketching parabolas

As we learnt in the previous chapter, the general form of a quadratic equation is $y = ax^2 + bx + c$, where a, b and c are constants and $a \neq 0$.

The graph of a quadratic equation is called a **parabola**. We can observe the shape of a parabola in many real-life features, such as the arch of a bridge or the trajectory of a ball.

We are not always required to plot a graph, as that can be time consuming. Instead, we can sketch a graph.

There are numerous ways to sketch a parabola, such as:

- by plotting the values in a table of values based on the parabola's equation
- by plotting the key features that can be determined from the equation (e.g. intercepts and turning points)
- by transforming points from another parabola.

Creating a table of values to sketch

Given a quadratic equation, we can sketch the graph of the corresponding parabola by first creating a table of values. The table will give the coordinates of points that can be plotted.

Example

Complete a table of values from $x = -2$ to 4 for the quadratic equation $y = -x^2 + 2x + 3$, then sketch the graph.

✓ *Solution*

<table>
<tr><th>Working</th><th>Explanation</th></tr>
<tr><td>

x	-2	-1	0	1	2	3	4
y	-5	0	3	4	3	0	-5

</td><td>Create a table of values by substituting each x-value into the quadratic equation to determine the corresponding y-value.</td></tr>
</table>

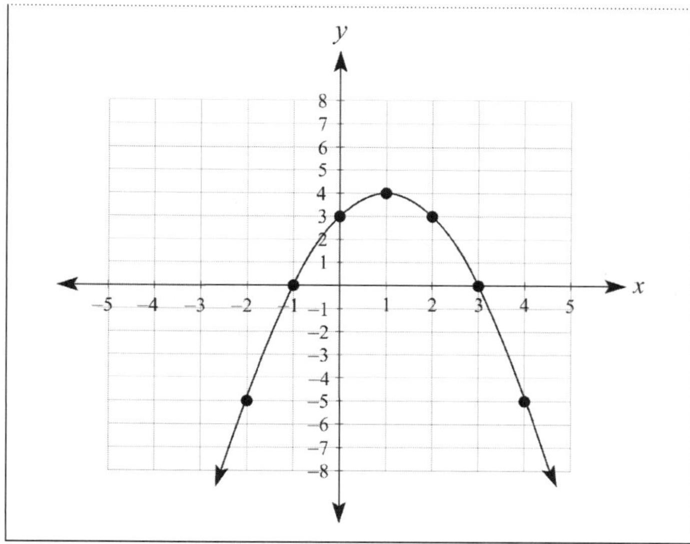	Plot the corresponding pairs of values as coordinates on the Cartesian plane and join them with a smooth line.

Exercise 5.1

a. Complete a table of values from $x = -5$ to $x = 3$ for the quadratic equation $y = x^2 + 2x - 8$, then sketch the graph.

b. Complete a table of values from $x = -3$ to $x = 3$ for the quadratic equation $y = x^2 - 4$, then sketch the graph.

c. Complete a table of values from $x = -2$ to $x = 4$ for the quadratic equation $y = -x^2 + 2x$, then sketch the graph.

Determining key features of a parabola from its equation

We can sketch a parabola by determining its key features from the parabola's equation. These features include the:

- behaviour of the graph (that is, whether it is concave up or concave down)
- line of symmetry
- turning point (and whether it occurs at a maximum or a minimum)
- y-intercept
- x-intercept(s) (or roots).

In the previous chapter, we considered the three forms of a quadratic equation. Each of these forms can provide information about some of the key features of the graph of a quadratic equation.

General form: $y = ax^2 + bx + c$

- if $a > 0$: the graph is concave up; if $a < 0$: the graph is concave down
- y-intercept: $(0, c)$
- line of symmetry: $x = -\frac{b}{2a}$
- turning point: this lies on the line of symmetry, so calculate the y-value corresponding to the x-value of the line of symmetry
- number of roots: calculate the discriminant $(b^2 - 4ac)$
- actual roots (if any): solve $ax^2 + bx + c = 0$ for x

Example

For the quadratic equation $y = x^2 - 2x + 2$, determine the key features of the corresponding parabola and sketch it.

✓ *Solution*

Working	Explanation
y-intercept: $(0, 2)$	Substitute $x = 0$ to determine the y-intercept.
Line of symmetry: $x = -\frac{-2}{2(1)} = 1$	Line of symmetry: $x = -\frac{b}{2a}$
Substitute $x = 1$ into $y = (1)^2 - 2(1) + 2 = 1$ Turning point: $(1, 1)$	The turning point must lie on the line of symmetry, hence the x-coordinate of the turning point is the line of symmetry. We can substitute that coordinate into the equation to solve for the y-coordinate.
The graph is concave up and the turning point is a minimum.	The nature of the turning point can be determined from $a > 0$. Since $a = 1$, the graph is concave up. Hence the turning point is a minimum.
$\Delta = b^2 - 4ac$ $\Delta = (-2)^2 - 4(1)(2)$ $= -4 < 0$ There are no roots.	To determine if there are any roots, calculate the discriminant. Since $\Delta < 0$, there are 0 roots.
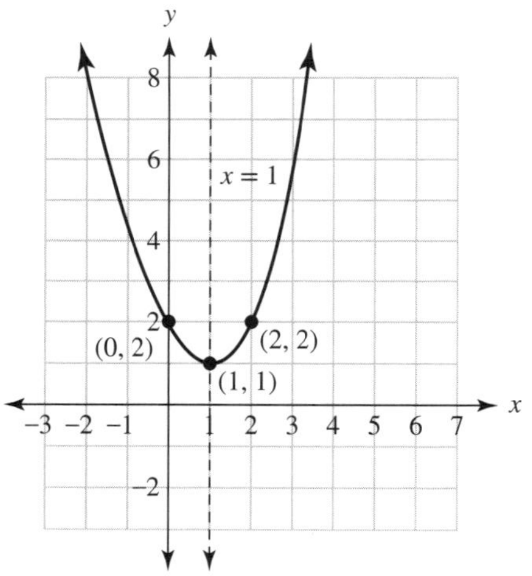	Plot the key points found on a set of axes. Plot the point symmetrical to (0, 2). This will help you to sketch the graph. Sketch the parabola by drawing a smooth line through the plotted points, ensuring that the graph is symmetrical about the line of symmetry.

Turning-point form: $y = a(x - h)^2 + k$

- if $a > 0$: the graph is concave up; if $a < 0$: the graph is concave down
- y-intercept: substitute $x = 0$: $y = a(0 - h)^2 + k = a(h)^2 + k$
- line of symmetry: $x = h$
- turning point: (h, k)
- roots (if any): solve $a(x - h)^2 + k = 0$ for x

Example

For the quadratic equation $y = 2(x - 2)^2 - 5$, determine the key features of the corresponding parabola and sketch it.

✓ *Solution*

Working	Explanation
Line of symmetry: $x = 2$	Line of symmetry: $x = h$
Turning point: $(2, -5)$	Turning point: (h, k)
The graph is concave up and the turning point is a minimum.	The nature of the turning point can be determined from $a > 0$. Since $a = 2$, the graph is concave up. Hence the turning point is a minimum.
y-intercept: $(0, 3)$	Substitute $x = 0$ to determine the y-intercept.
$y = 2(x - 2)^2 - 5$ $0 = 2(x - 2)^2 - 5$ $(x - 2)^2 = \frac{5}{2}$ $x - 2 = \pm\sqrt{\frac{5}{2}}$ $x = 2 \pm \frac{\sqrt{10}}{2}$ x-intercepts: $\left(2 - \frac{\sqrt{10}}{2}, 0\right)$, $\left(2 + \frac{\sqrt{10}}{2}, 0\right)$	Substitute $y = 0$ to determine the x-intercepts.

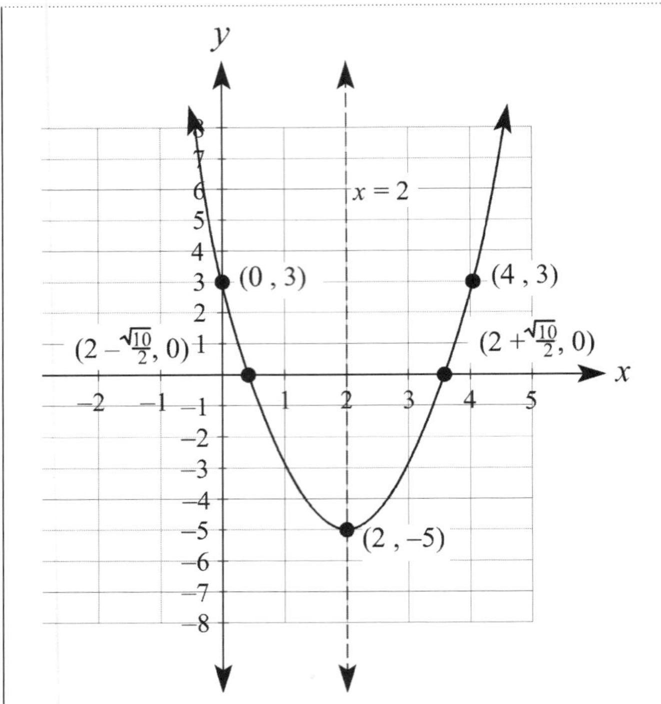

Plot the key points found on the axes.

Plot the point symmetrical to (0, 3). This will help you to sketch the graph.

Sketch the parabola by drawing a smooth line through the plotted points, ensuring that the graph is symmetrical about the line of symmetry.

Factorised form: $y = a(x - m)(x - n)$

- if $a > 0$: the graph is concave up; if $a < 0$: the graph is concave down
- y-intercept: $a(-m)(-n)$
- line of symmetry: $x = \dfrac{m+n}{2}$
- turning point: substitute the line of symmetry into $y = a(x - m)(x - n)$
- roots: $x = m$, $x = n$

Example

For the quadratic equation $y = (x + 1)(x - 5)$, determine the key features of the corresponding parabola and sketch it.

✓ *Solution*

Working	Explanation
y-intercept: $(0, -5)$	Substitute $x = 0$ to determine the y-intercept.
$(x + 1)(x - 5) = 0$ $x = -1, x = 5$ x-intercepts: $(-1, 0), (5, 0)$	Substitute $y = 0$ to determine the x-intercepts.
Line of symmetry: $x = \dfrac{-1+5}{2} = 2$	The line of symmetry will cut the x-axis at the mid-way point between the roots. $\therefore x = \dfrac{m+n}{2}$

Turning point: substitute $x = 2$: $y = (2 + 1)(2 - 5) = -9$	The turning point must lie on the line of symmetry, hence the x-coordinate of the turning point is the line of symmetry. We can substitute the x-coordinate into the equation to determine the y-coordinate of the turning point.
The turning point is a minimum.	Since $a = 2 > 0$, the graph is concave up and the turning point is a minimum.
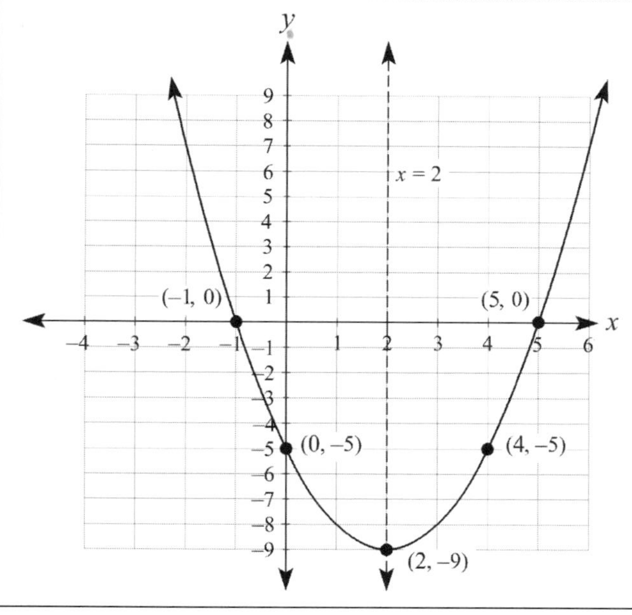	Plot the key points found on the axes. Plot the point symmetrical to (0, −5). This will help you to sketch the graph. Sketch the parabola by drawing a smooth line through the key points, ensuring that the graph is symmetrical about the line of symmetry.

Exercise 5.1.2

a. For the quadratic equation $y = x^2 + 2x - 8$, determine the key features of the corresponding parabola and sketch it.

b. For the quadratic equation $y = -2x^2 + 4x + 1$, determine the key features of the corresponding parabola and sketch it.

c. For the quadratic equation $y = (x - 5)(x + 2)$, determine the key features of the corresponding parabola and sketch it.

d. For the quadratic equation $y = (x + 2)(x + 4)$, determine the key features of the corresponding parabola and sketch it.

e. For the quadratic equation $y = (x + 1)^2 - 4$, determine the key features of the corresponding parabola and sketch it.

f. For the quadratic equation $y = -2(x + 1)^2 - 3$, determine the key features of the corresponding parabola and sketch it.

Transforming the quadratic equation $y = x^2$

We can also sketch a quadratic equation by transforming it from another quadratic. (A transformation is any change that can be made to a graph by **dilation**, **reflection** or **translation**.)

First, consider the basic quadratic equation: $y = x^2$. The graph of $y = x^2$ is shown to the right. It has the following key features.

- Since $a > 0$, the graph is concave up.
- It is symmetrical about the y-axis, so the line of symmetry is $x = 0$.
- The x-intercept is the same as the y-intercept: $(0, 0)$.
- It has a turning point (also known as the vertex) at the origin $(0, 0)$ and, since the graph is concave up, it is a minimum.

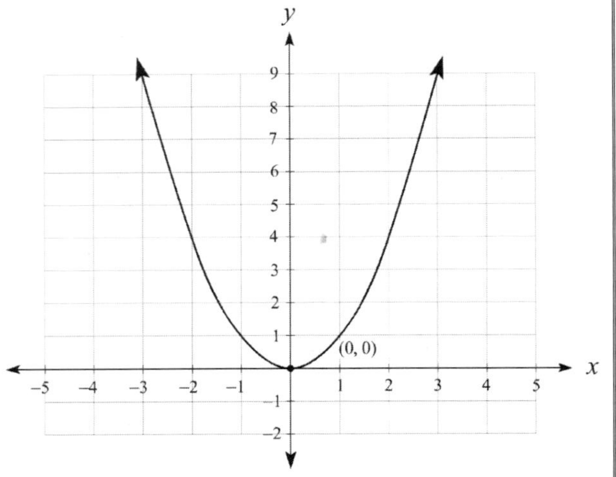

Dilation and reflection of $y = x^2$

Consider graphs of the form $y = ax^2$.

The coefficient a dilates the graph of $y = x^2$ by a scale factor of a parallel to the y-axis. Additionally:

- when $a > 1$, the graph is narrower than $y = x^2$
- when $0 < a < 1$, the graph is wider than $y = x^2$
- when $a < 0$, the graph is reflected about the x-axis.

The graphs of $y = x^2$, $y = 2x^2$, $y = -2x^2$ and $y = \frac{1}{2}x^2$ are shown below.

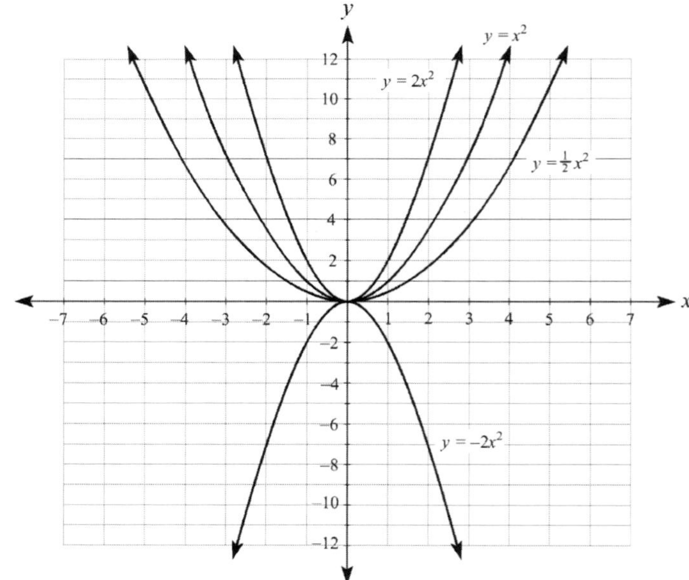

- For the graph of $y = 2x^2$, $a = 2$, so the graph of $y = x^2$ is dilated by a scale factor of 2 parallel to the y-axis. The graph is narrower than $y = x^2$.
- For the graph of $y = -2x^2$, $a = -2$, so the graph is the same as $y = 2x^2$ but reflected about the x-axis.
- For the graph of $y = \frac{1}{2}x^2$, $a = \frac{1}{2}$, so the graph of $y = x^2$ is dilated by a scale factor of $\frac{1}{2}$ parallel to the y-axis. The graph is wider than $y = x^2$.

Vertical translation of $y = x^2$

Consider graphs of the form $y = x^2 + k$.

The k value translates the graph of $y = x^2$ vertically up or down by k units. Additionally:

- When $k > 0$, the graph of $y = x^2$ is translated up (and hence the turning point is translated up).
- When $k < 0$, the graph of $y = x^2$ is translated down (and hence the turning point is translated down).

The graphs of $y = x^2$, $y = x^2 + 2$ and $y = x^2 - 3$ are shown below.

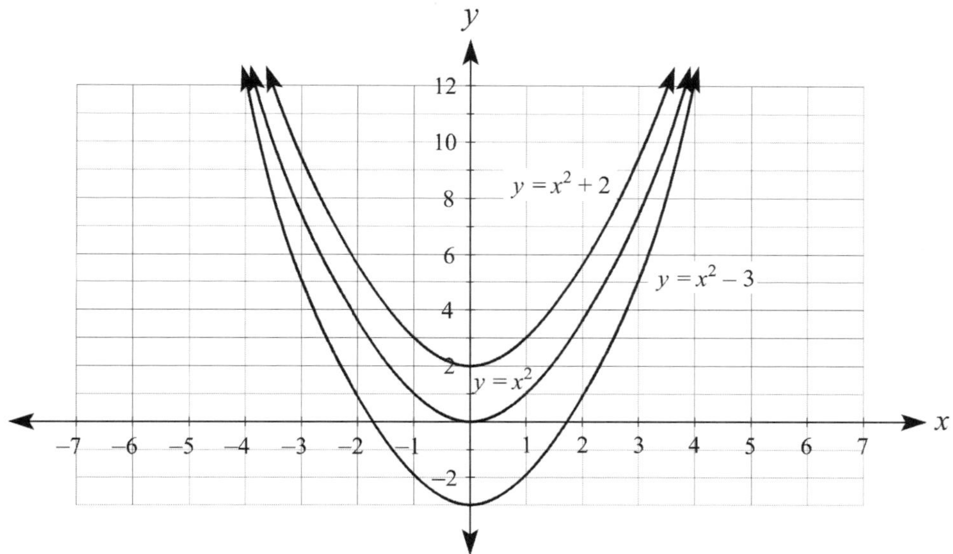

- For the graph of $y = x^2 + 2$, $k = 2$, so the graph of $y = x^2$ is translated vertically up by 2 units. The turning point is now $(0, 2)$.
- For the graph of $y = x^2 - 3$, $k = -3$, so the graph of $y = x^2$ is translated vertically down by 3 units. The turning point is now $(0, -3)$.

Horizontal translation of $y = x^2$

Consider graphs of the form $y = (x - h)^2$.

The h value translates the graph horizontally left and right by h units. Additionally:

- When $h > 0$, the graph of $y = x^2$ is translated right (and the turning point is translated right).
- When $h < 0$, the graph of $y = x^2$ is translated left (and the turning point is translated left).

The graphs of $y = x^2$, $y = (x - 2)^2$ and $y = (x + 2)^2$ are shown below.

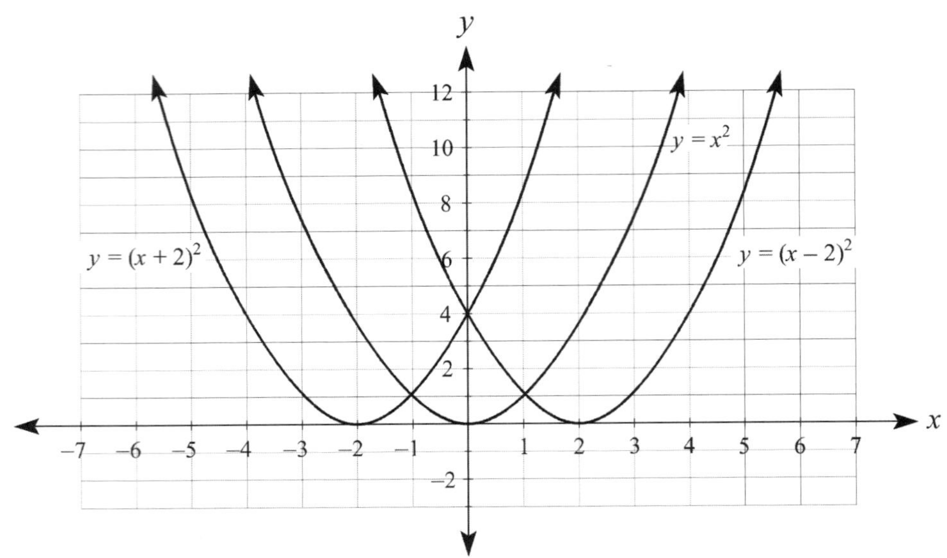

- For the graph of $y = (x - 2)^2$, $h = 2$, so the graph of $y = x^2$ is translated right by 2 units. The turning point is now $(2, 0)$.
- For the graph of $y = (x + 2)^2$, $h = -2$, so the graph of $y = x^2$ is translated left by 2 units. The turning point is now $(-2, 0)$.

Combinations of transformations

We can sketch the graph of any quadratic equation expressed in turning-point form using translations. For example, for $y = a(x - h)^2 + k$:

- a dilates the graph parallel to the y-axis by a scale factor of a. If $a < 0$, the graph is reflected about the x-axis
- h translates the graph horizontally
- k translates the graph vertically
- The turning point is (h, k)
- The line of symmetry is $x = h$.

Example

Sketch the graphs of the following quadratic equations, labelling the turning point and the y-intercept of each.

a. $y = -3x^2$

b. $y = x^2 - 1$

c. $y = (x - 1)^2$

d. $y = -(x + 1)^2 + 1$

✓ *Solution*

Working	Explanation
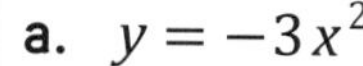 **a.** $y = -3x^2$ 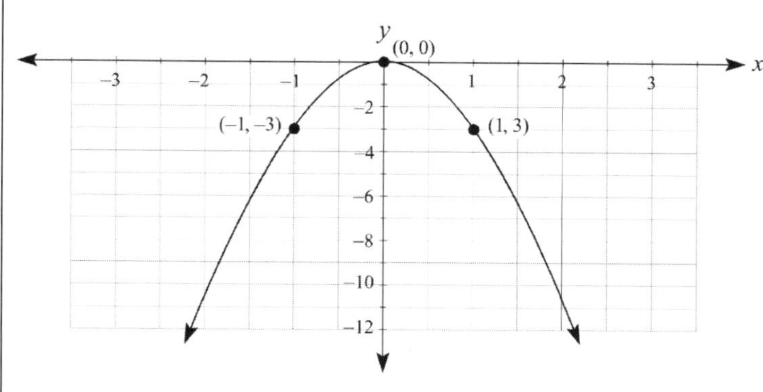	To transform $y = x^2$ to $y = -3x^2$, the graph of $y = x^2$ is dilated by a scale factor of 3. Hence the graph is narrower. As a is negative, the graph is also reflected about the x-axis. Hence the graph is concave down. The turning point remains the same at $(0, 0)$. We can substitute $x = 1$ and $x = -1$ to obtain two other coordinates to help sketch the graph.
b. $y = x^2 - 1$ 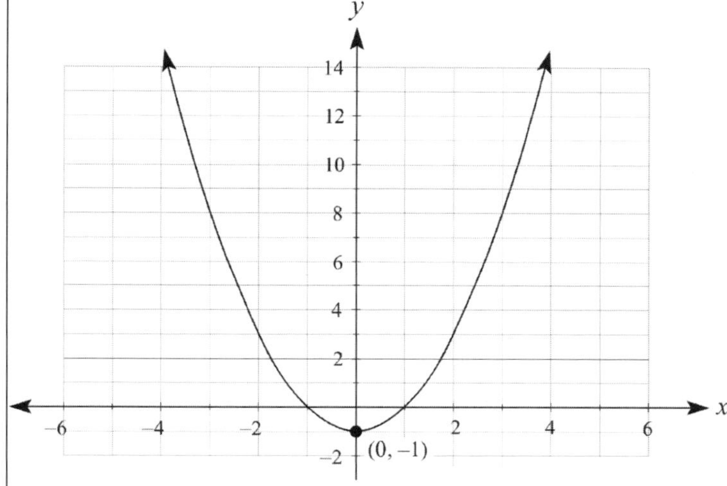	To transform $y = x^2$ to $y = x^2 - 1$, the graph of $y = x^2$ is translated down by 1 unit. The new turning point is $(0, -1)$. The y-intercept is $(0, -1)$.
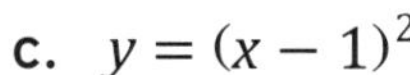 **c.** $y = (x - 1)^2$ 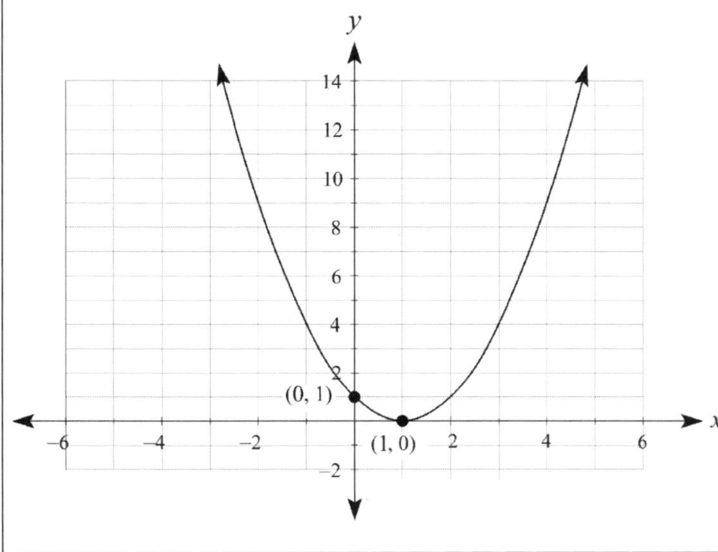	To transform $y = x^2$ to $y = (x - 1)^2$, the graph of $y = x^2$ is translated right by 1 unit. The new turning point is $(1, 0)$. The y-intercept is $(0, 1)$.

d. $y = -(x+1)^2 + 1$	To transform $y = x^2$ to $y = -(x+1)^2 + 1$, the graph of $y = x^2$ is reflected about the x-axis (since a is negative).
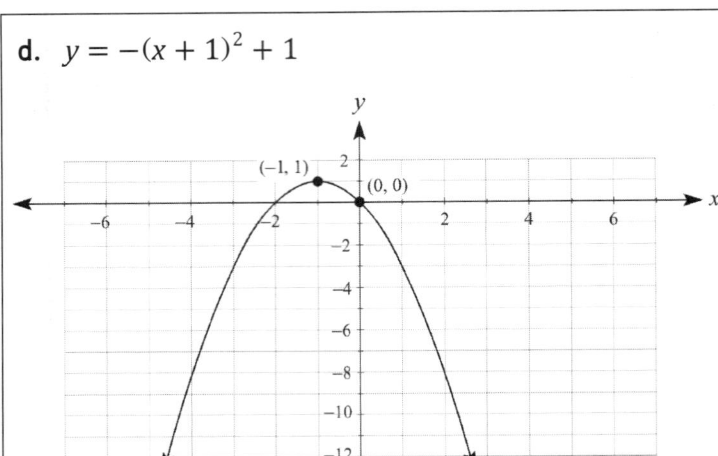	Since $h = -1$, $k = 1$, the turning point is $(-1, 1)$. The graph is translated left by 1 unit and up by 1 unit. The y-intercept is $(0, 0)$.

Exercise 5.1.3

Sketch the graph of each of the following quadratic equations, labelling the turning point and the y-intercept.

a. $y = 2x^2$

b. $y = -\frac{1}{3}x^2$

c. $y = -x^2 + 2$

d. $y = (x+3)^2$

e. $y = (x-4)^2 - 3$

f. $y = -(x+3)^2 + 4$

5.2 Parabolas in practice

Parabolas can be used to solve many practical problems. When applying your knowledge of parabolas to solving practical problems, follow these steps.

- Assign variables to the unknown quantities.
- Formulate the problem as a quadratic equation using the assigned variables.
- Solve the equation.
- Sketch the graph, showing key features.
- Find the turning point.
- Clearly state the solution to the problem.

Example

James wants to enclose a rectangular area in his backyard to keep his dog locked in. He wishes to use existing fencing along one side of the rectangle and has 20 m of wire to fence the other three sides. Let x be the width of the rectangle.

a. Write an equation for the length of the rectangle in terms of x.

b. Write an equation for the area of the rectangle in terms of x.

c. Determine a suitable range of values for x.

d. Sketch the graph.

e. Determine the maximum area that James can surround with wire.

f. Determine the dimensions of the rectangle that will give the maximum area.

✓ ***Solution***

Working	Explanation
a. Fencing = Length + $2x$ $20 =$ Length + $2x$ Length $= 20 - 2x$	A sketch of the situation is 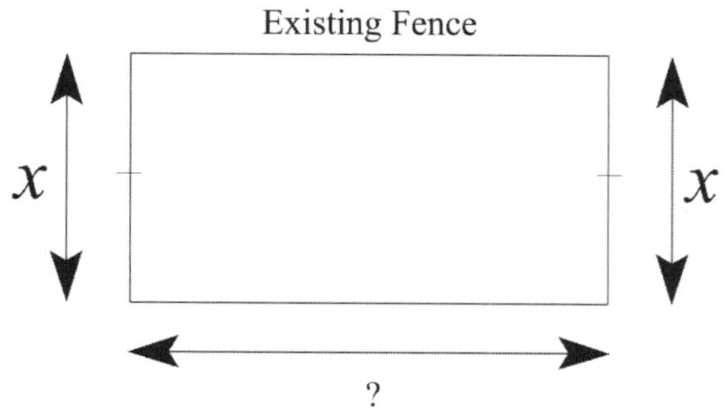 The new fencing is made with 20 metres of wire and the width of the rectangle is x. We can use this information to formulate an equation for the length of the rectangle.
b. Area $= x(20 - 2x)$	We can use the same information to formulate an equation for the area of the rectangle. **Note:** this a quadratic equation in factorised form.
c. As the width and length must both be positive, it follows that $x > 0$ and $20 - 2x > 0$ $20 > 2x$ $x < 10$ $0 < x < 10$	Knowing that both the length and width of the rectangle must be positive, we can work out the domain of x.
d. 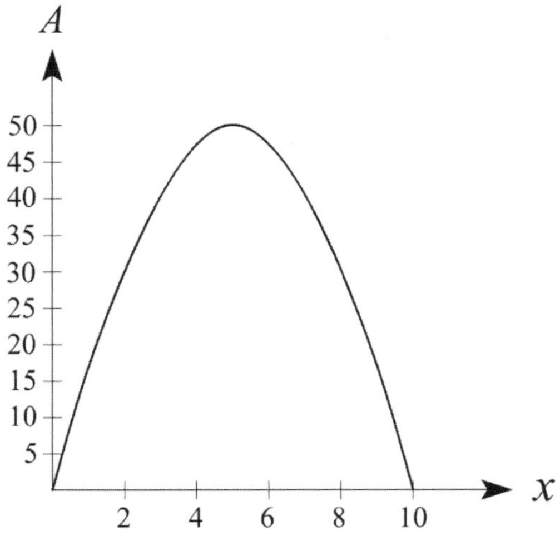	From the quadratic equation for area $(20x - 2x^2)$ determine the x-intercepts: 0 and 10. The turning point must have an x-value halfway between the x-intercepts, that is, at $x = 5$. Substitute $x = 5$ into the area equation to find the corresponding y-value: 50. Thus the coordinates of the turning point are (5, 50). We now have enough information to be able to sketch the graph. **Note:** the x-axis does not extend past 10 and neither axis extends past 0 as the area cannot be negative and the length cannot be less than or equal to 0.
e. The maximum area is 50 m^2.	The maximum area is the y-coordinate of the turning point.

f. The width needed to achieve the maximum area is $x = 5$ m. The corresponding length is $20 - 2(5) = 10$ m.	The maximum area occurs when $x = 5$. Substitute this value into the length equation. We now have the dimensions of the rectangle that give the maximum area.

Exercise 5.2.1

A gardener has 10 m of fencing and wishes to fence off a rectangular area to plant some vegetables. Let x be the width of the rectangle.

a. Use the formula for the perimeter of a rectangle to write an equation for the length of the rectangle in terms of x.

b. Write an equation for the area of the rectangle in terms of x.

c. Sketch the graph of A for a suitable range of values of x.

d. Use the graph to determine the maximum area the fence can enclose and the dimensions of the rectangle that give the maximum area.

Exercise 5.2.2

A piece of wire 80 cm long is bent into the shape of a rectangle.

a. If x is the length of the rectangle and A is the area enclosed by the rectangle, write an equation for A in terms of x.

b. Sketch the graph of A for a suitable range of values of x.

c. Use the graph to determine the maximum area enclosed by the wire.

Exercise 5.2.3

A ball is thrown into the air and follows a path given by the relationship $h = -t^2 + 10t$, where h is the height of the ball in metres after t seconds of flight.

a. Sketch the graph of the relationship.

b. Use the graph to determine the maximum height the ball reaches.

Chapter 6 – Circles

6.1 Introduction

A circle is a shape on which all points are the same distance from a reference point. The reference point is called the centre of the circle and the distance from the reference point to any point on the circle is called the radius, r.

The equation of a circle has two main forms: the **centre–radius form** (also known as the standard form) and the **general form**.

The centre–radius form is

$$(x - a)^2 + (y - b)^2 = r^2$$

where the centre of the circle is point (a, b) and the radius is r.

The general form – which can be obtained by expanding the centre–radius form – is

$$x^2 + y^2 - 2ax - 2by + c = 0$$

where a, b and c are constants.

The centre–radius form can be obtained from the general form by completing the square.

We can determine the coordinates of the centre of a circle and its radius from its equation. We can also determine a circle's equation if we know its radius and the coordinates of its centre.

Example

Determine the centre and radius of the circle with equation $(x + 2)^2 + (y - 4)^2 = 4$.

✓ Solution

Working	Explanation
$(x + 2)^2 + (y - 4)^2 = 4$ $(x + 2)^2 + (y - 4)^2 = 2^2$ centre: $(-2, 4)$, radius: 2	The equation is expressed in centre–radius form $(x - a)^2 + (y - b)^2 = r^2$ where the centre is (a, b) and the radius is r.

Example

Determine the centre and radius of the circle with equation $2x^2 + 2y^2 = 50$.

✓ Solution

Working	Explanation
$2x^2 + 2y^2 = 50$ $x^2 + y^2 = 25$ $x^2 + y^2 = 5^2$ centre: $(0, 0)$, radius: 5	Express the equation in centre–radius form by dividing both sides by 2.

Example

State the equation of the circle with centre $(-3, 5)$ and radius 2.

✓ Solution

Working	Explanation
$(x-a)^2+(y-b)^2=r^2$ $(x-(-3))^2+(y-5)^2=2^2$ $(x+3)^2+(y-5)^2=4$	Since the centre and radius of the circle are given: $(a, b)=(-3, 5)$ and $r=2$, we substitute them into the centre–radius form of the circle equation.

Example

Determine the coordinates of the centre and the radius of the circle with equation $x^2+y^2-2x+6y-6=0$.

✓ Solution

Working	Explanation
$x^2+y^2-2x+6y-6=0$ $x^2-2x+y^2+6y=6$ $(x-1)^2-(1)^2+(y+3)^2-(3)^2=6$ $(x-1)^2+(y+3)^2-1-9=6$ $(x-1)^2+(y+3)^2=16$ $(x-1)^2+(y+3)^2=4^2$ centre: $(1, -3)$, radius: 4	Express the equation in centre–radius form by completing the square. **1.** Rearrange the equation to group the x-terms and y-terms together and move the constant to the right of the equals sign. **2.** Complete the square of the x-terms and the y-terms. **3.** Rearrange the terms to match the centre–radius form. State the centre and radius.

Exercise 6.1

a. Determine the centre and radius of the circles with the following equations.

i. $4x^2+4y^2=9$ ii. $(x-1)^2+(y+2)^2=9$

b. State the equations of the circles with the following properties, in centre–radius form.

i. centre $(-2, 3)$ and radius 5 ii. centre $(3, -4)$ and diameter 6

c. Determine the coordinates of the centre and the radius of the circles with the following equations.

i. $x^2+y^2+6x-14y=6$ ii. $x^2+y^2-4x+16y-32=0$

6.2 Sketching circles

Consider the **unit circle**, whose equation is $x^2 + y^2 = 1^2$.

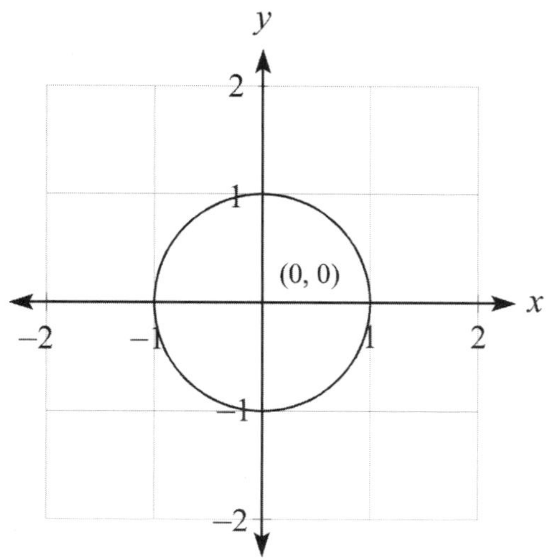

Note the following features of the unit circle:

- centre: $(a, b) = (0, 0)$
- radius: $r = 1$
- x-intercepts: $(1, 0)$ and $(-1, 0)$
- y-intercepts: $(0, 1)$ and $(0, -1)$.

All circles can be sketched as transformations of the unit circle. To see this, consider the centre–radius form of the circle equation, $(x - a)^2 + (y - b)^2 = r^2$. This equation is the equation for the unit circle:

- translated horizontally by a units
- translated vertically by b units.

Note that:

- if $a > 0$, the unit circle is translated right by a units
- if $a < 0$, the unit circle is translated left by a units
- if $b > 0$, the unit circle is translated up by b units
- if $b < 0$, the unit circle is translated down by b units.

Example

Sketch the graph of $x^2 + y^2 = 9$.

✓ *Solution*

Working	Explanation
$x^2 + y^2 = 9$ centre: (0, 0) radius: 3	1. Note that the equation is the centre–radius form of the circle equation. Thus, we can determine the centre and radius of the circle just by examining the equation.
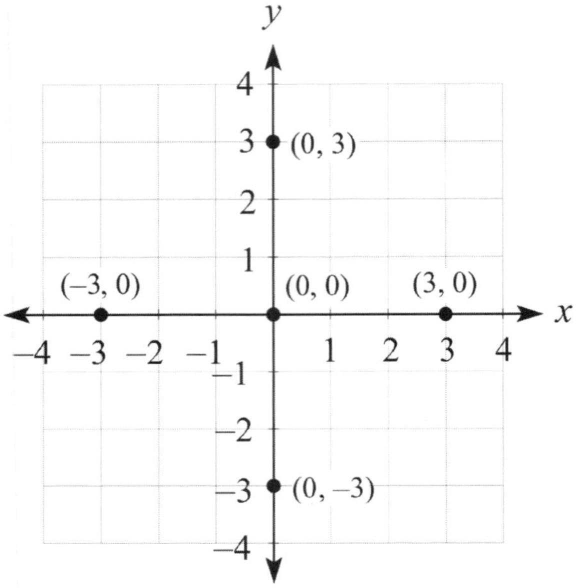	2. Plot the centre: (0, 0). 3. Plot 4 points that are 3 units away from the centre in the up, down, right and left directions. Since the centre is (0, 0): • up $(0, 0 + 3) = (0, 3)$ • down $(0, 0 - 3) = (0, -3)$ • right $(0 + 3, 0) = (3, 0)$ • left $(0 - 3, 0) = (-3, 0)$.
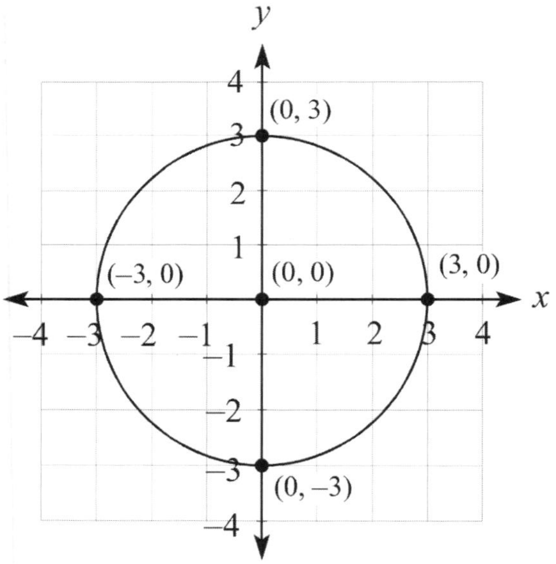	4. Sketch the circle.

Example

Sketch the graph of $(x + 2)^2 + (y - 4)^2 = 9$.

✓ *Solution*

Working	Explanation
Note that $(x+2)^2+(y-4)^2=9$ is a transformation of $x^2+y^2=9$, the graph sketched in the previous exercise. There are two methods for sketching this new graph.	
Method 1: Sketch by transformation The new graph is translated 2 units left and 4 units up.	**Method 1** 1. Identify the translations of the graph $(x+2)^2+(y-4)^2=9$ from the graph of $x^2+y^2=9$.
The 4 translated points are: $(0-2, 3+4)=(-2, 7)$ $(0-2, -3+4)=(-2, 1)$ $(3-2, 0+4)=(1, 4)$ $(-3-2, 0+4)=(-5, 4)$	2. Determine 4 new points by translating the 4 points found in the previous example by 2 units left and 4 units up. 3. Plot the new points and sketch the graph (see below).
Method 2: Sketch by determining the centre and radius $(x+2)^2+(y-4)^2=9$ centre: $(-2, 4)$ radius: 3	**Method 2** 1. Determine the centre and radius.
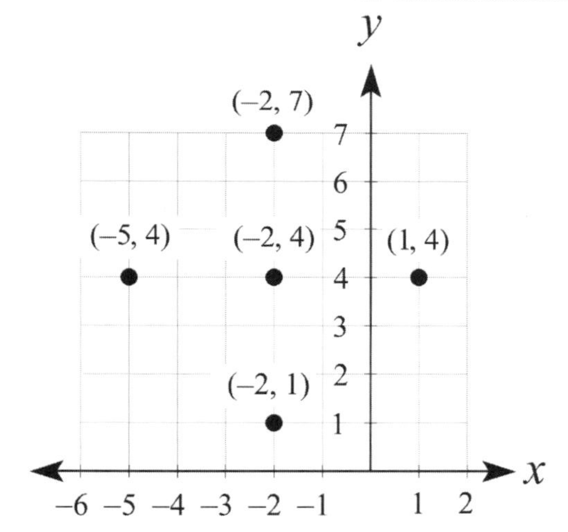	2. Plot 4 points that are 3 units away from the centre in the up, down, right and left directions. Since centre is $(-2, 4)$: Up: $(-2, 4+3)=(-2, 7)$ Down: $(-2, 4-3)=(-2, 1)$ Right: $(-2+3, 4)=(1, 4)$ Left: $(-2-3, 4)=(-5, 4)$
Sketch the circle 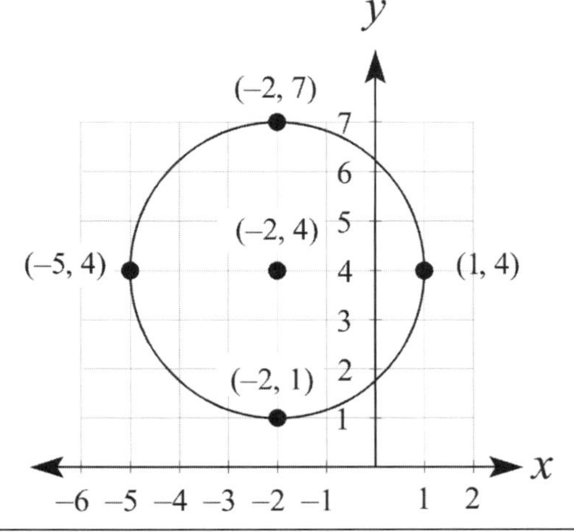	

Example

Sketch the graph of $x^2 + y^2 - 2x - 4y - 4 = 0$.

✓ Solution

Working	Explanation
$x^2 + y^2 - 2x - 4y - 4 = 0$ $x^2 - 2x + y^2 - 4y = 4$ $(x-1)^2 - (1)^2 + (y-2)^2 - (2)^2 = 4$ $(x-1)^2 + (y-2)^2 = 9$	1. Note that the equation is in the general form of the circle equation. Use the techniques discussed in Section 6.1 to transform the equation into the centre–radius form.
centre: (1, 2), radius: 3	2. Identify the centre point and radius.
(1, 5), (1, −1), (4, 2), and (−2, 2)	3. Use either of the methods outlined in the previous example to determine 4 points to plot.
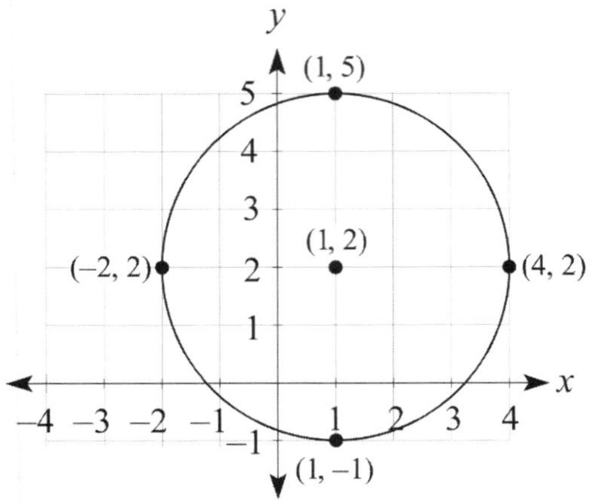	4. Sketch the graph.

Exercise 6.2.1

Sketch the following graphs.

a. $x^2 + y^2 = 16$

b. $2x^2 + 2y^2 = 50$

Exercise 6.2.2

Sketch the following graphs.

a. $(x+1)^2 + (y-2)^2 = 16$

b. $(x-2)^2 + (y-3)^2 = 25$

Exercise 6.2.3

Sketch the following graphs.

a. $x^2 + y^2 - 6x - 2y = 6$

b. $x^2 + y^2 + 2x + 4y - 20 = 0$

6.3 Solving linear and circle equations simultaneously

We can solve linear and circle equations simultaneously by looking to see if their graphs have points of intersection. There may be 2, 1 or 0 points of intersection.

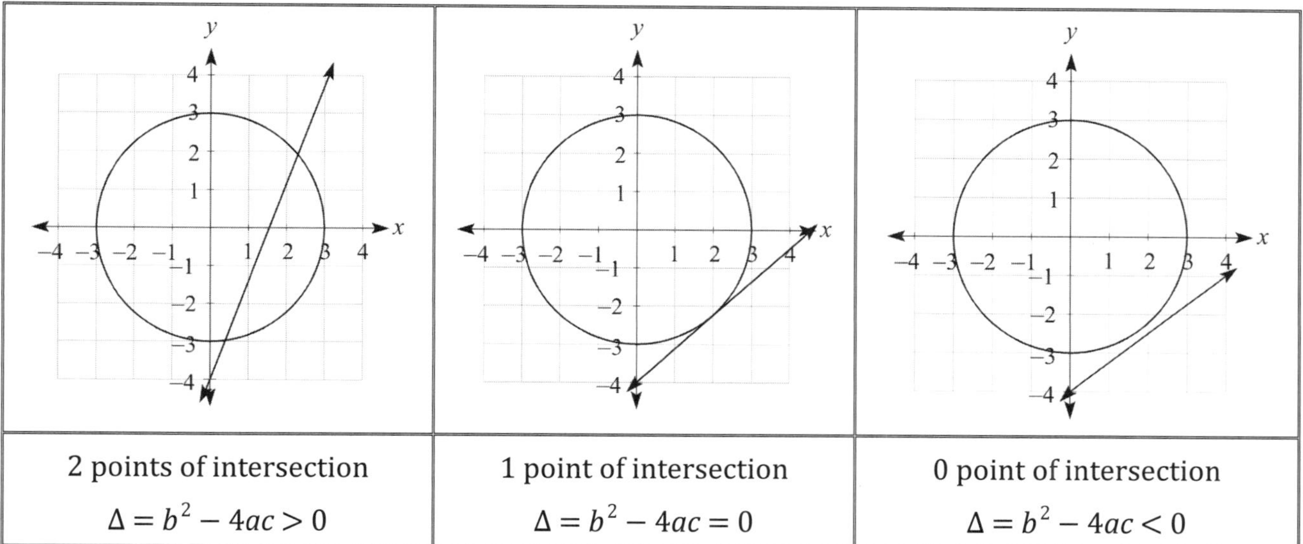

2 points of intersection	1 point of intersection	0 point of intersection
$\Delta = b^2 - 4ac > 0$	$\Delta = b^2 - 4ac = 0$	$\Delta = b^2 - 4ac < 0$

To determine the number of points of intersection between a circle of the form $(x - a)^2 + (y - b)^2 = r^2$ and a line of the form $y = mx + c$, as well as the locations of the intersection points:

1. Substitute $mx + c$ for y in the equation for the circle:

$$(x - a)^2 + (mx + c - b)^2 = r^2$$

2. Expand and rearrange the equation so that all the terms are on one side of the equation and zero is on the other side.
3. Group the x^2, x and constant terms together to form a quadratic equation.
4. Calculate the discriminant. This tells us the number of intersection points (see the table above).
5. If there are intersection points, solve the equation for x.
6. Substitute the x-value(s) into the equation of the line to find the corresponding y-values.

Example

Determine the number of points of intersection between $x^2 + y^2 = 2$ and $y = 7x + 10$. Then locate them, if they exist.

✓ Solution

Working	Explanation
$x^2 + y^2 = 2$ (1) $y = 7x + 10$ (2) $x^2 + (7x + 10)^2 = 2$ $50x^2 + 140x + 98 = 0$	**1.** Substitute equation (2) into equation (1) and rearrange the equation to form a quadratic equation.
$\Delta = b^2 - 4ac$ $= 140^2 - 4(50)(98)$ $= 0$	**2.** Calculate the discriminant to determine the number of solutions.
There is one point of intersection.	**3.** Answer the first part of the question.
$50x^2 + 140x + 98 = 0$ $x = \frac{-140}{2(50)} = -\frac{7}{5}$	**4.** Use any technique to solve for x.
Substitute $x = -\frac{7}{5}$ into (2) and solve. $y = \frac{1}{5}$	**5.** Substitute the x-value into equation (2) and solve for y.
The point of intersection is $\left(-\frac{7}{5}, \frac{1}{5}\right)$.	**6.** Answer the final part of the question.

Example

Determine the number of points of intersection between $x^2 + y^2 - 2x + 6y - 27 = 0$ and $y = x + 1$. Then locate these points of intersection, if they exist.

✓ Solution

Working	Explanation
$x^2 + y^2 - 2x + 6y - 27 = 0$ (1) $y = x + 1$ (2) $x^2 + (x + 1)^2 - 2x + 6(x + 1) - 27 = 0$ $2x^2 + 6x - 20 = 0$	**1.** Substitute equation (2) into equation (1) and rearrange it to form a quadratic equation.
$\Delta = 6^2 - 4(2)(-20)$ $= 36 + 160$ $= 196 > 0$	**2.** Calculate the discriminant to determine the number of solutions.
There are two points of intersection.	**3.** Answer the first part of the question.

$2x^2 + 6x - 20 = 0$ $(x + 5)(x - 2) = 0$ $x = -5, x = 2$	**4.** Use any technique to solve for x.
Substitute $x = -5$ into (2) and solve. Substitute $x = 2$ into (2) and solve. $y = -4$ and 3	**5.** Substitute the x-values into equation (2) and solve for y.
The points of intersection are $(-5, -4)$ and $(2, 3)$.	**6.** Answer the final part of the question.

Example

Determine the number of points of intersection between $(x - 1)^2 + (y + 2)^2 = 9$ and $y = 2x + 5$. If there are points of intersection, find the points.

✓ ***Solution***

Working	Explanation
$(x - 1)^2 + (y + 2)^2 = 9$ (1) $y = 2x + 5$ (2) $(x - 1)^2 + (2x + 5 + 2)^2 = 9$ $5x^2 + 26x + 41 = 0$	**1.** Substitute equation (2) into equation (1) and rearrange it to form a quadratic equation.
$\Delta = 26^2 - 4(5)(41)$ $= -144 < 0$	**2.** Calculate the discriminant to determine the number of solutions.
There are no points of intersection.	**3.** Answer the first part of the question.

Exercise 6.3

Determine the number of points of intersection for the following pairs of equations. Then locate them, if they exist.

a. $(x + 4)^2 + (y - 2)^2 = 4^2$ and $y = x - 1$

b. $x^2 + y^2 + 6x - 2y - 7 = 0$ and $y = -4x + 6$

c. $(x - 1)^2 + (y + 1)^2 = 16$ and $y = 2x + 1$

Chapter 7 – Trigonometry

7.1 Pythagoras' theorem in three dimensions

Pythagoras' theorem states that for any right-angled triangle, the square of the length of the hypotenuse is the sum of the square of the lengths of the other two sides of the triangle. (The hypotenuse is the longest side and is always opposite the right angle.)

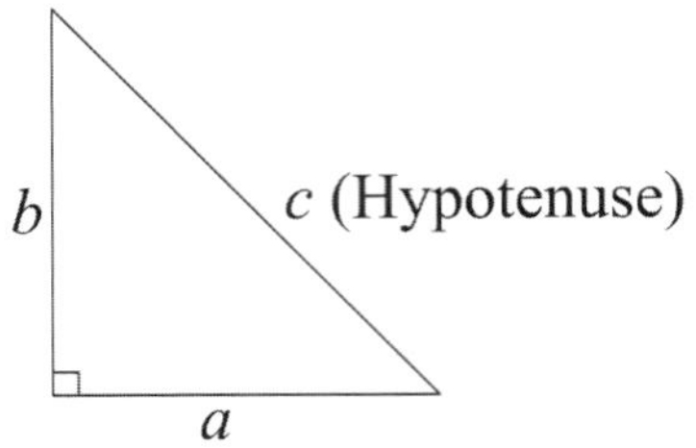

> Pythagoras' theorem
>
> $a^2 + b^2 = c^2$

Pythagoras' theorem can also be used to calculate distances in three dimensions. In some cases, we need to apply the theorem twice: once to find a surface diagonal and again to find the three-dimensional object's diagonal.

For example, suppose we want to find the distance from the bottom left front corner to the top right back corner of the rectangular prism shown to the right.

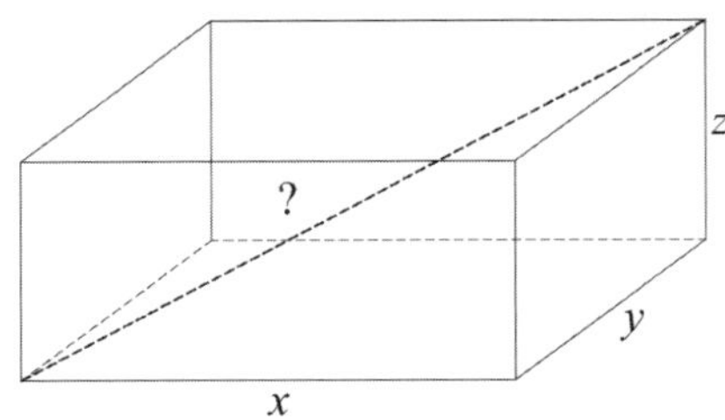

First, we determine the diagonal of the base which, by Pythagoras' theorem, is $\sqrt{x^2 + y^2}$.

Now we can make another triangle, with the base as $\sqrt{x^2 + y^2}$ and height as z. We then apply Pythagoras' theorem again to calculate the diagonal.

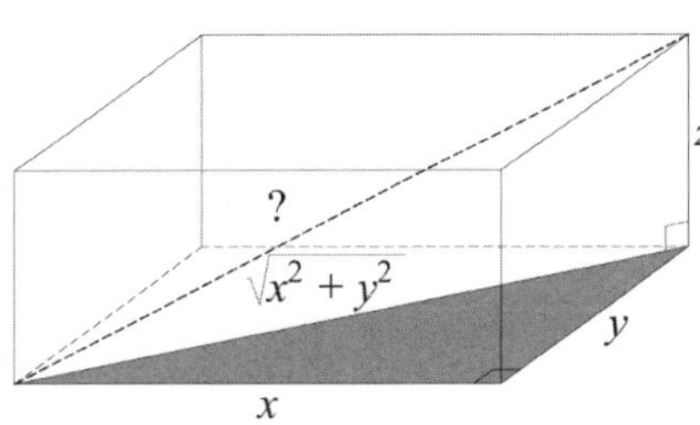

Example

a. Find the slant height, s, of the following cone, correct to two decimal places.

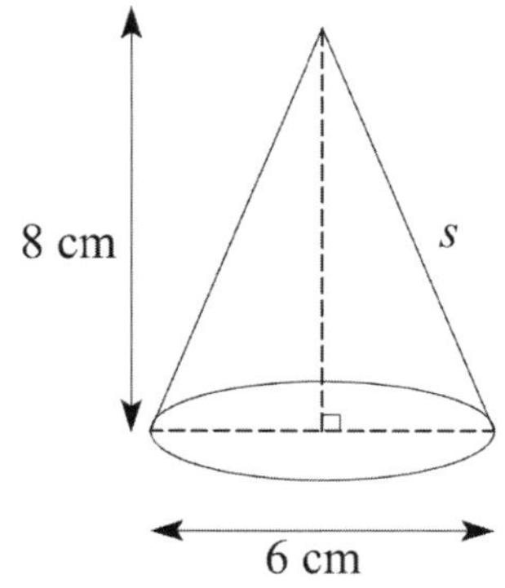

b. Find the perpendicular height, x, of the following pyramid, correct to two decimal places.

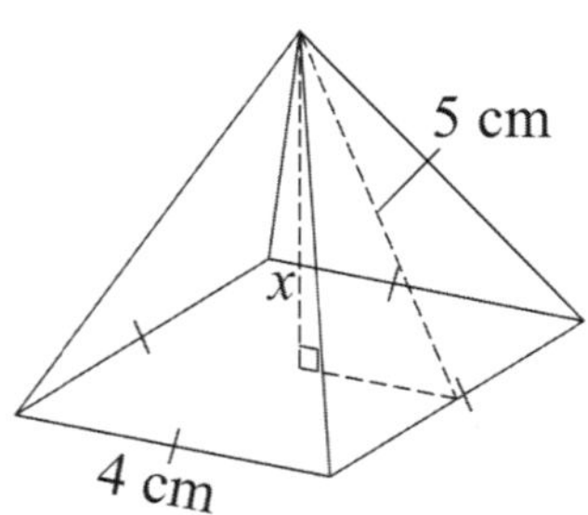

c. Find the distance, y, from one corner of the following rectangular prism to the opposite corner, correct to two decimal places.

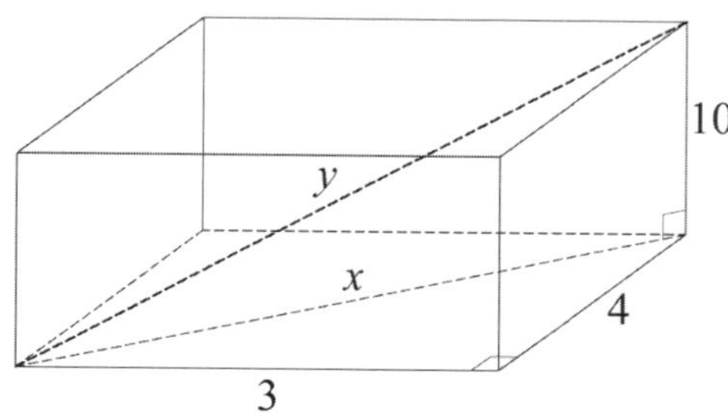

✓ ***Solution***

Working	Explanation
a. $c^2 = a^2 + b^2$ $s^2 = 3^2 + 8^2$ $s = \sqrt{73}$ $s = 8.54$ cm	Draw the right-angled triangle with the two known sides. Substitute $a = 3$, $b = 8$ and $c = s$ into Pythagoras' theorem. Solve for s.
b. $c^2 = a^2 + b^2$ $5^2 = x^2 + 2^2$ $x^2 = 25 - 4$ $x^2 = 21$ $x = \sqrt{21}$ $x = 4.58$ cm	Draw the right-angled triangle with the two known sides. Substitute $a = x$, $b = 2$ and $c = 5$ into Pythagoras' theorem. Solve for x.
c. $c^2 = a^2 + b^2$ $x^2 = 3^2 + 4^2$ $x = \sqrt{25}$ $x = 5$ cm	Draw the right-angled triangle required to calculate x. Substitute $a = 3$, $b = 4$ and $c = x$ into Pythagoras' theorem. Solve for x.
$c^2 = a^2 + b^2$ $y^2 = 5^2 + 10^2$ $y = \sqrt{125}$ $y = 11.18$ cm	Draw the right-angled triangle required to calculate y. Substitute $a = 5$, $b = 10$ and $c = y$ into Pythagoras' theorem. Solve for y.

Exercise 7.1

a. Find the perpendicular height of the following cone given that the slant height is 10 cm. Give your answer correct to two decimal places.

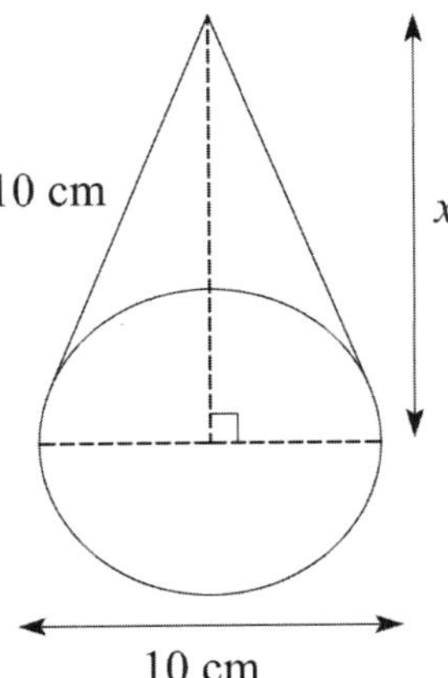

b. Find the slant height of the pyramid below given that the perpendicular height is 2 m. Give your answer correct to two decimal places.

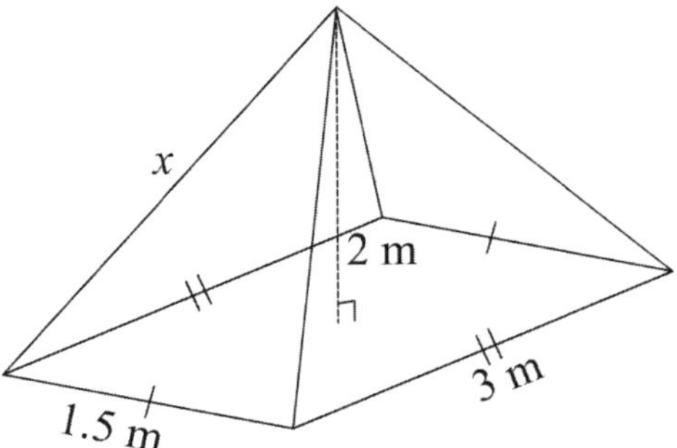

c. Find the width of the rectangular prism shown below, given that the diagonal from the bottom left to the top right corner of the prism is 10 cm. Give your answer correct to two decimal places.

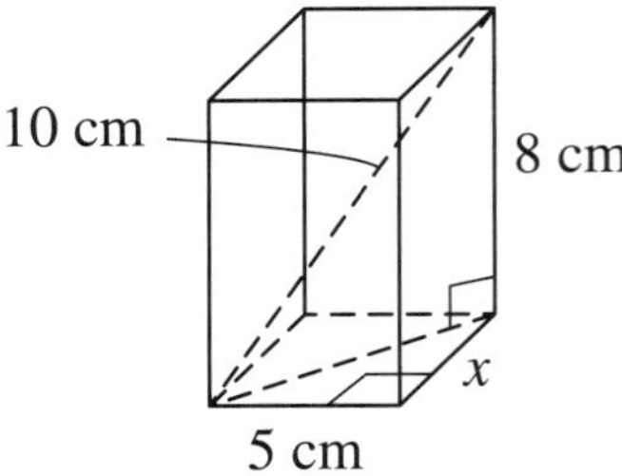

d. Joe has a rectangular box that is 8 cm long by 10 cm wide by 15 cm deep. Determine the longest object (to the nearest cm) he can keep in the box.

7.2 Trigonometric ratios

Trigonometry is the study of the relationships between the sides and the acute angles of a right-angled triangle. These relationships are used determine an unknown angle or side of a right-angled triangle.

If we assign one of the acute angles in a right-angled triangle as the reference angle, θ, we can give the sides of the triangle a standard name that is relative to θ.

As shown in the diagram to the right, the side next to θ is named 'adjacent' and the side opposite θ is named 'opposite'. The longest side is always named 'hypotenuse'.

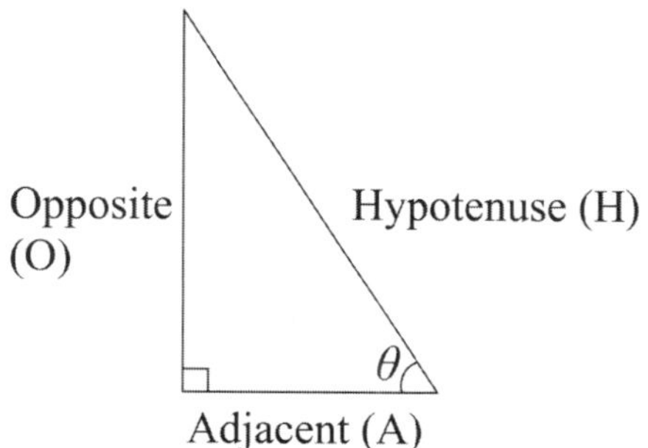

The three trigonometric ratios relating the reference angle to the sides are given below. The acronym **SOHCAHTOA** can help you remember these ratios.

$\text{sine } \theta = \dfrac{\text{opposite}}{\text{hypotenuse}}$	$\text{cosine } \theta = \dfrac{\text{adjacent}}{\text{hypotenuse}}$	$\text{tangent } \theta = \dfrac{\text{opposite}}{\text{adjacent}}$
$\sin(\theta) = \frac{\text{O}}{\text{H}}$	$\cos(\theta) = \frac{\text{A}}{\text{H}}$	$\tan(\theta) = \frac{\text{O}}{\text{A}}$
SOH	CAH	TOA

Consider the right-angled triangle below.

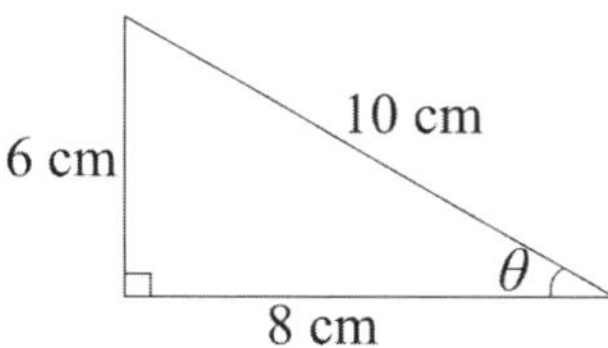

The trigonometric ratios for the angle θ are

$$\sin\theta = \frac{6}{10} = \frac{3}{5} \qquad \cos\theta = \frac{8}{10} = \frac{4}{5} \qquad \tan\theta = \frac{6}{8} = \frac{3}{4}$$

The ratios can be simplified fractions or decimals. There are no units for trigonometric ratios.

Finding unknown sides

If you know an angle and the length of a side of a right-angled triangle, you can use trigonometry to determine the lengths of the other sides.

- Use $\sin\theta = \frac{\text{O}}{\text{H}}$ if you know the opposite (or the hypotenuse) and want to know the hypotenuse (or the opposite).
- Use $\cos\theta = \frac{\text{A}}{\text{H}}$ if you know the adjacent (or the hypotenuse) and want to know the hypotenuse (or the adjacent).
- Use $\tan\theta = \frac{\text{O}}{\text{A}}$ if you know the opposite (or the adjacent) and want to know the adjacent (or the opposite).

Example

Determine the lengths of the unknown sides of the following right-angled triangles, correct to two decimal places.

a.

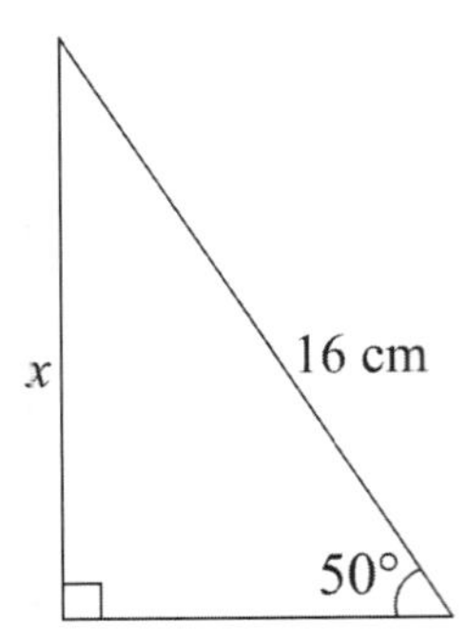

b.

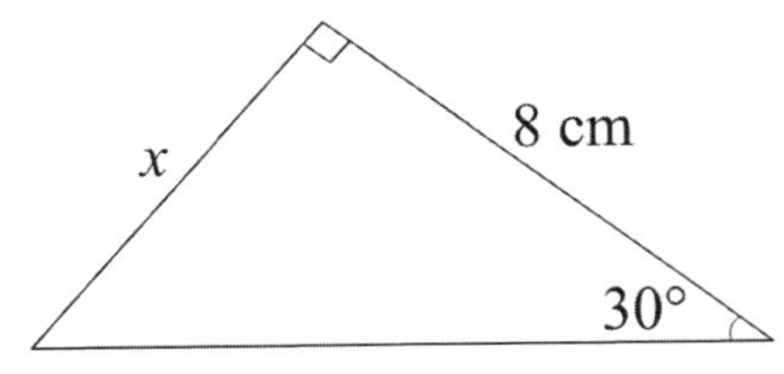

c.

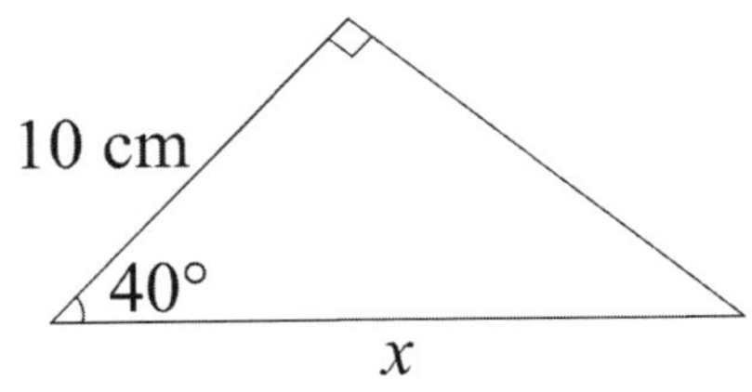

✓ Solution

Working	Explanation
a. (O) x 16 cm (H) 50° $\sin(\theta) = \frac{\text{O}}{\text{H}}$ $\sin(50) = \frac{x}{16}$ $x = 16\sin(50)$ $x = 12.26$ cm	1. Identify the adjacent, opposite and hypotenuse of the triangle in reference to the known angle. 2. Determine the trigonometric ratio to use. Since we know H and want to find O, we should use $\sin\theta = \frac{\text{O}}{\text{H}}$. 3. Substitute $\theta = 50$, $\text{O} = x$ and $\text{H} = 16$ into the ratio. 4. Solve for x.
b. (O) x 8 cm (A) 30° $\tan(\theta) = \frac{\text{O}}{\text{A}}$ $\tan(30) = \frac{x}{8}$ $x = 8\tan(30)$ $x = 4.62$ cm	1. Identify the adjacent, opposite and hypotenuse of the triangle in reference to the known angle. 2. Determine the trigonometric ratio to use. Since we know A and want to find O, we should use $\tan\theta = \frac{\text{O}}{\text{A}}$. 3. Substitute $\theta = 30$, $\text{O} = x$, and $\text{A} = 8$ into the ratio. 4. Solve for x.

c. 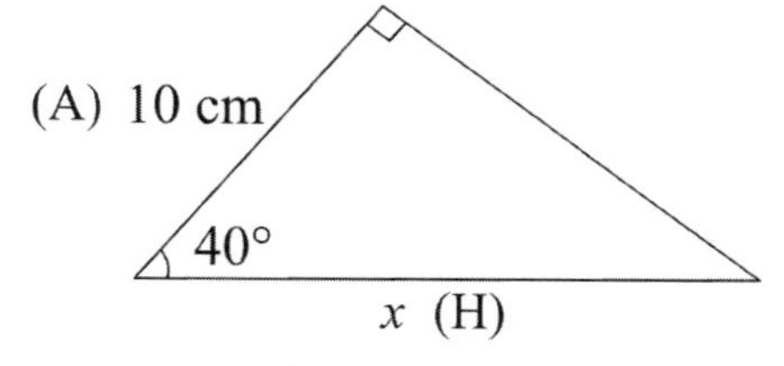 $\cos(\theta) = \frac{A}{H}$ $\cos(40) = \frac{10}{x}$ $x = \frac{10}{\cos(40)}$ $x = 13.05$ cm	1. Identify the adjacent, opposite and hypotenuse of the triangle in reference to the known angle. 2. Determine the trigonometric ratio to use. Since we know A and want to find H, we should use $\cos\theta = \frac{A}{H}$. 3. Substitute $\theta = 40$, $A = 10$ and $H = x$ into the ratio. 4. Solve for x

Exercise 7.2.1

Determine the lengths of the unknown sides (labelled x and y) in the following right-angled triangles.

a.

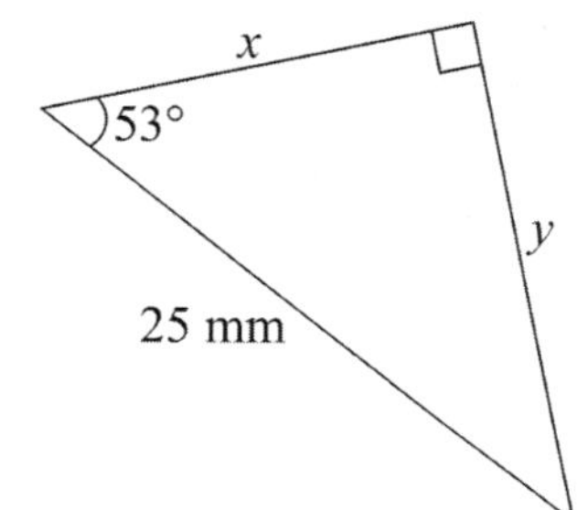

b.

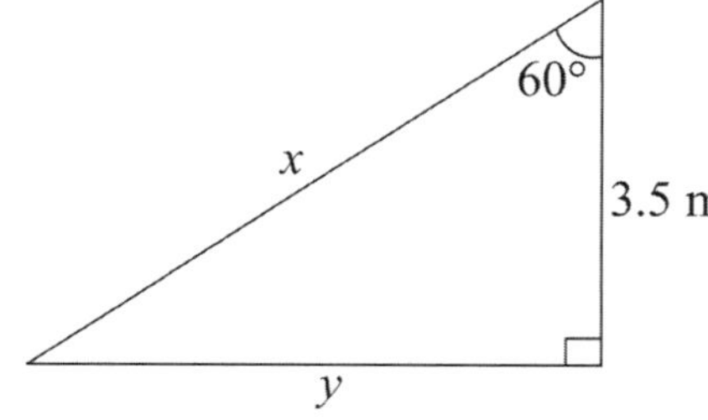

c.

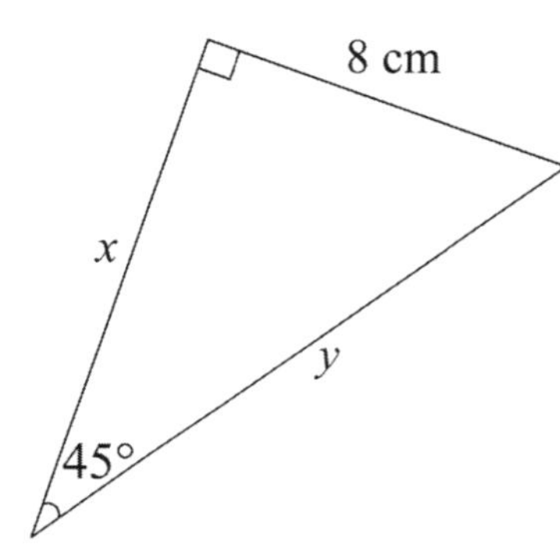

Finding unknown angles

If you know two sides of a right-angled triangle, you can use trigonometry to determine an unknown angle.

To find an angle from the given trigonometric ratios or decimals, you need to use an inverse function (which is easiest to work out using a calculator).

If we know that $\sin\theta = 0.56$, θ is found by calculating inverse sin 0.56, written as $\sin^{-1} 0.56$. In this case θ is $34.06°$.

If we know that $\cos\theta = 0.28$, θ is found by calculating inverse cos 0.28, written as $\cos^{-1} 0.28$. In this case θ is $73.74°$.

If we know that $\tan\theta = \frac{28}{32}$, θ is found by calculating inverse tan $\frac{28}{32}$, written as $\tan^{-1}\frac{28}{32}$. In this case θ is $41.19°$.

Example

Determine the angle labelled θ in each of the following right-angled triangles.

a.

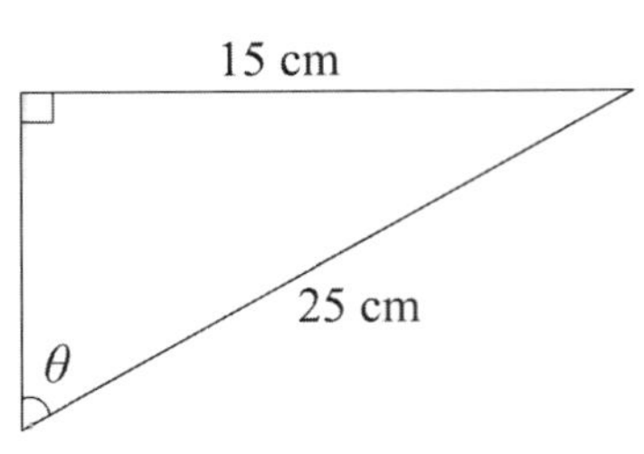

b.

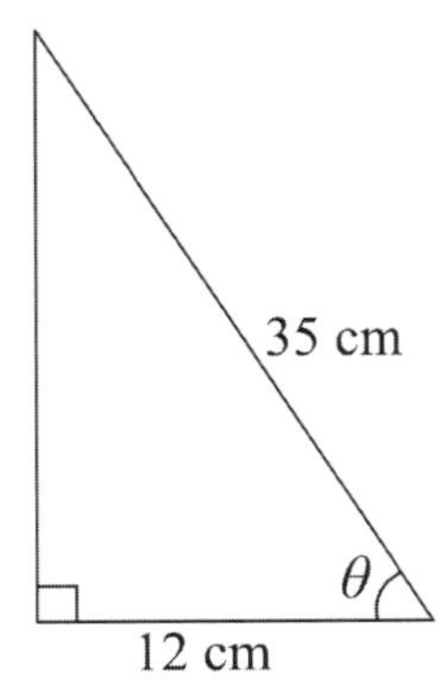

c.

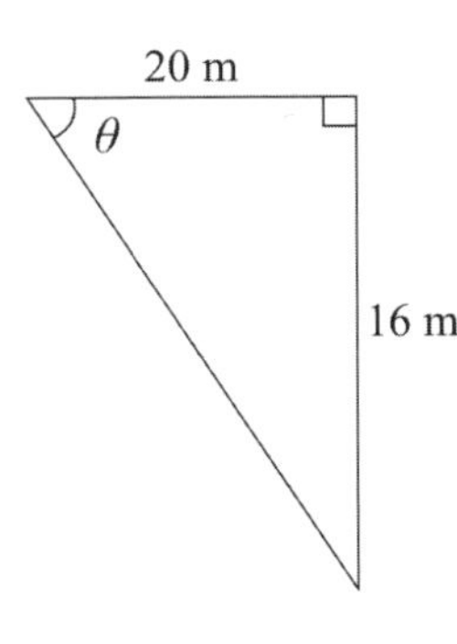

✓ *Solution*

Working	Explanation
a. 15 cm (O) 25 cm (H) θ $\sin(\theta) = \frac{\text{O}}{\text{H}}$ $\sin(\theta) = \frac{15}{25}$ $\theta = \sin^{-1}\frac{15}{25}$ $\theta = 36.87°$	1. Identify the adjacent, opposite and hypotenuse of the triangle in reference to the unknown angle. 2. Determine the trigonometric ratio to use. Given that we know O and H, we should use $\sin\theta = \frac{\text{O}}{\text{H}}$. 3. Substitute $\text{O} = 15$ and $\text{H} = 25$ into the ratio. 4. Solve for θ using the inverse of sine.
b. 35 cm (H) θ 12 cm (A) $\cos(\theta) = \frac{\text{A}}{\text{H}}$ $\cos(\theta) = \frac{12}{35}$ $\theta = \cos^{-1}\frac{12}{35}$ $\theta = 69.95°$	1. Identify the adjacent, opposite and hypotenuse of the triangle in reference to the unknown angle. 2. Determine the trigonometric ratio to use. Given that we know A and H, we should use CAH ratio. 3. Substitute $\text{A} = 12$, and $\text{H} = 35$ into the ratio. 4. Solve for θ using the inverse of cosine.

c. 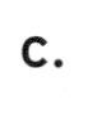 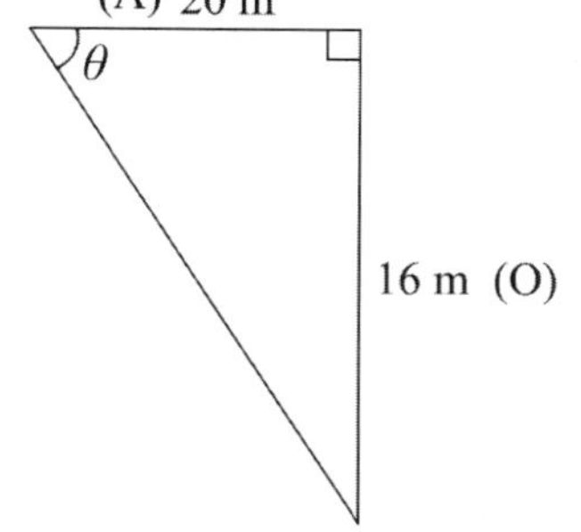 $\tan(\theta) = \frac{O}{A}$ $\tan(\theta) = \frac{16}{20}$ $\theta = \tan^{-1}\frac{16}{20}$ $\theta = 38.66°$	1. Identify the adjacent, opposite and hypotenuse of the triangle in reference to the unknown angle. 2. Determine the trigonometric ratio to use. Given that we know O and A, we should use the TOA ratio. 3. Substitute $O = 16$ and $A = 20$ into the ratio. 4. Solve for θ using the inverse of tangent.

Exercise 7.2.2

Determine θ in each of the following right-angled triangles.

a.

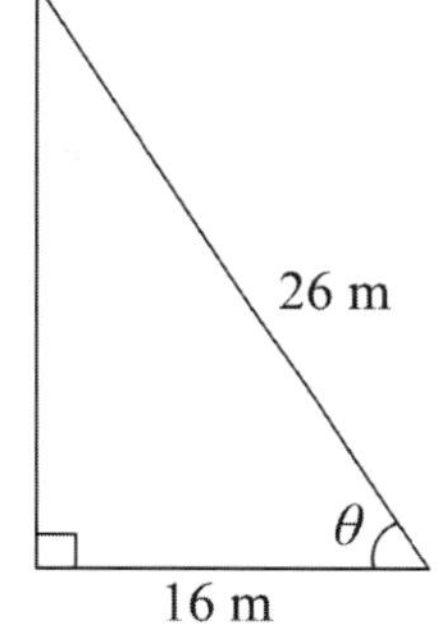

b.

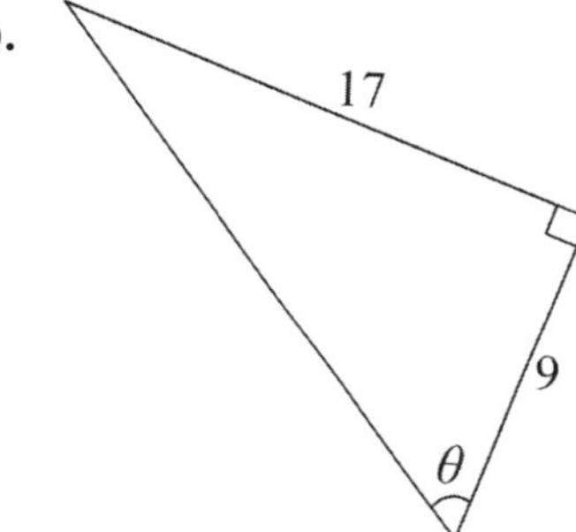

c.

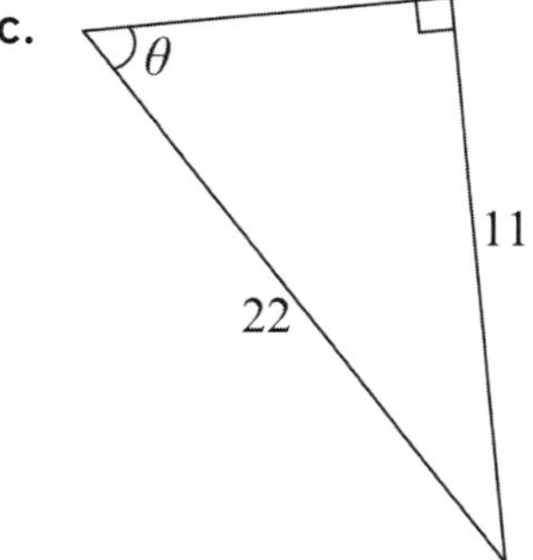

7.3 Angles of elevation and depression

Both the **angle of elevation** and the **angle of depression** are angles between a horizontal line and the line of sight.

If the line of sight is upwards from the horizontal line, the angle made with the horizontal line is the angle of elevation.

If the angle is downwards from the horizontal line, the angle made with the horizontal line is the angle of depression.

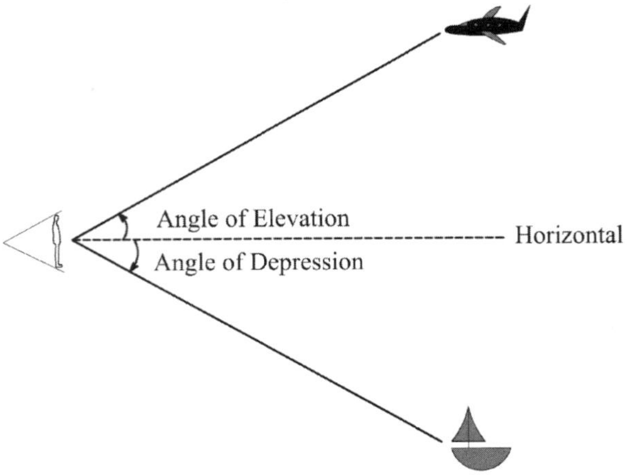

Example

Jerry is 1.6 m tall and is standing 20 m away from a building. He is looking at the top of the building and the angle of elevation from the top of his head is 58°. Determine the height of the building, to the nearest metre.

✓ *Solution*

Working	Explanation
a. 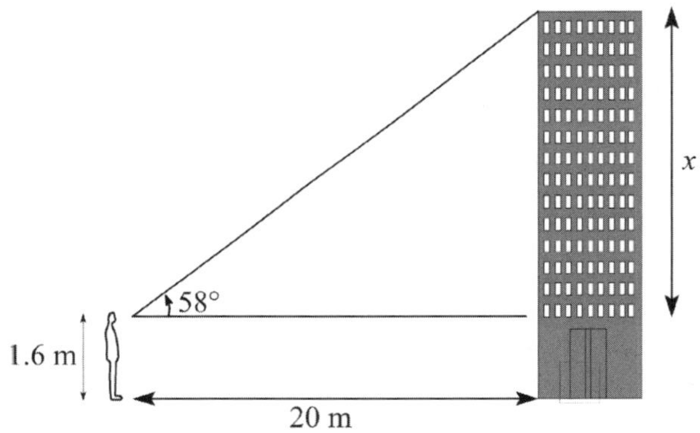	1. Represent the situation by sketching a right-angled triangle. Include the known measurements.
$\tan 58° = \frac{x}{20}$ $x = 20\tan 58°$ $x = 32.01$ $32.01 + 1.6 = 33.61$ m The height of the building is 34 m to the nearest metre.	2. Use trigonometry to determine the value of x. 3. The height of the building must include Jerry's height as the angle of elevation is measured from his head. 4. State the height of the building to the nearest metre.

Example

From the top of a cliff 110 m above sea level, the angle of depression to a boat sailing below is 35°. Determine how far the ship is from the base of the cliff, to the nearest metre.

✓ ***Solution***

Working	Explanation
b. 110 m, 35°, θ, x	1. Represent the situation by sketching a right-angled triangle. Include the known measurements.
$\theta = 90° - 35° = 55°$	2. Determine the angle θ.
$\tan 55° = \frac{x}{110}$ $x = 110 \tan 55°$ $x = 157.10$ m	3. Use trigonometry to determine the distance of the boat from the base of the cliff.
The boat is 157 m from the base of the cliff.	4. State the distance, to the nearest metre.

Exercise 7.3

a. A radar station detects a plane at an angle of elevation of 15° and an altitude of 2.3 kilometres. What is the horizontal distance of the plane from the radar station, correct to two decimal places?

b. When the angle of elevation of the sun is 40°, a tree casts a shadow of length 18 m. What is the height of the tree, correct to the nearest metre?

c. From the top of a 200 m tower, the angle of depression to a fire is 21°. How far away is the fire, correct to the nearest metre?

d. A person measures the angle of elevation to the top of a building as 20° and the angle of depression to the bottom of the building as 38°. The building is 35 m away from the person. Determine the height of the building, correct to two decimal places.

e. A person measures the angle of elevation to the top of a building as 28°. Given that the building is 36 m away and the height of the building is 45 m, what is the angle of depression to the bottom of the building?

f. An observer 35 m out from the foot of a vertical rock wall measures the angle of elevation to a rock climber as 33°. If the climber ascends a further 15 m, what is the angle of elevation to the rock climber?

7.4 Bearings

Bearings are a way of expressing direction. They are commonly used in navigation, surveying and engineering. Bearings are usually measured in degrees clockwise from north.

True bearing (°T) is the angle measured clockwise from the north direction to the object or point of interest. It is written using three digits.

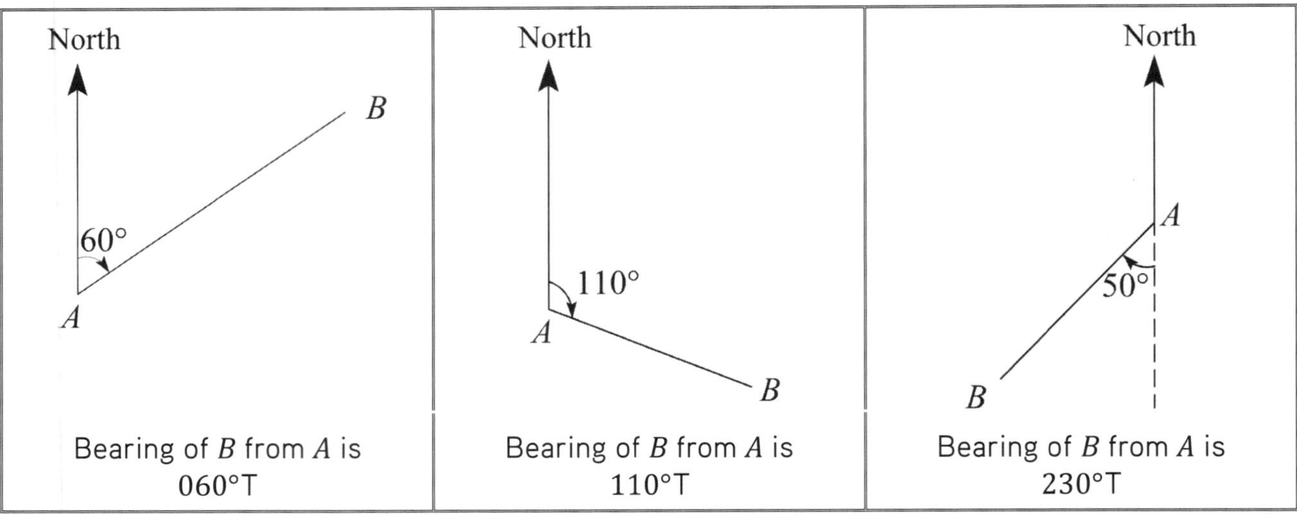

Bearing of B from A is 060°T

Bearing of B from A is 110°T

Bearing of B from A is 230°T

Example

Sarah leaves her campsite and walks on a bearing of 120°T for 10 km. How far east of the camp is she?

✓ *Solution*

Working	Explanation
	Draw a compass with the camp at the centre. Draw a line from the camp to the hiker 10 km away and 120° clockwise from the north. Draw a right-angled triangle and label the appropriate angle $(120 - 90 = 30°)$ and length (10 km). Label the distance that needs to be calculated (x).
$\cos 30 = \frac{x}{10}$ $x = 10\cos 30$ $x = 8.66$ km Sarah is 8.66 km east of the camp.	Use the appropriate trigonometric ratio to solve for x.

Example

Ivan walks from his campsite directly to a lookout 5 km west and 6 km south of his starting point. In what direction, to the nearest degree, has he walked to reach the lookout?

✓ *Solution*

Working	Explanation
N, 5 km, Camp, θ, 6 km	Draw a compass with the camp at the centre. Mark 5 km west and then 6 km south. Draw a line from Ivan to the campsite.
$\tan\theta = \frac{6}{5}$ $\theta = \tan^{-1}\left(\frac{6}{5}\right)$ $\theta = 50°$ (to the nearest degree)	Use the appropriate trigonometric ratio to solve for θ.
True bearing $= 270 - 50 = 220°$T	As direction is measured from north to the object, we have to subtract the angle from 270 to get the true bearing.

✎ Exercise 7.4

a. Determine the true bearing of B from A in each of the following diagrams.

i.

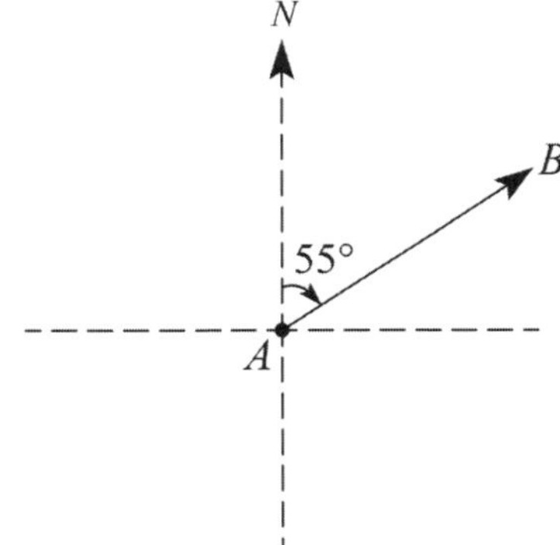

ii.

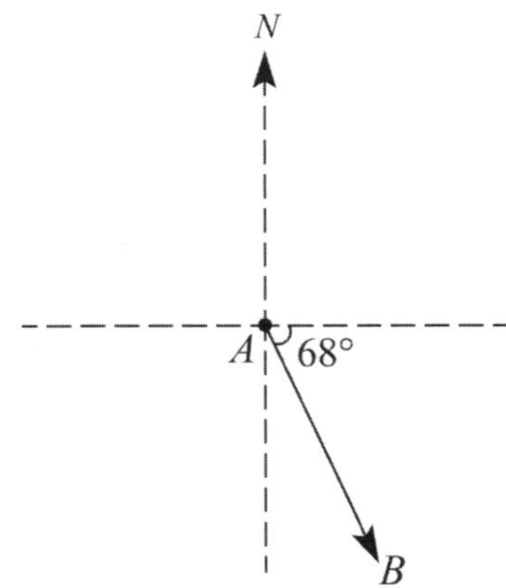

iii.

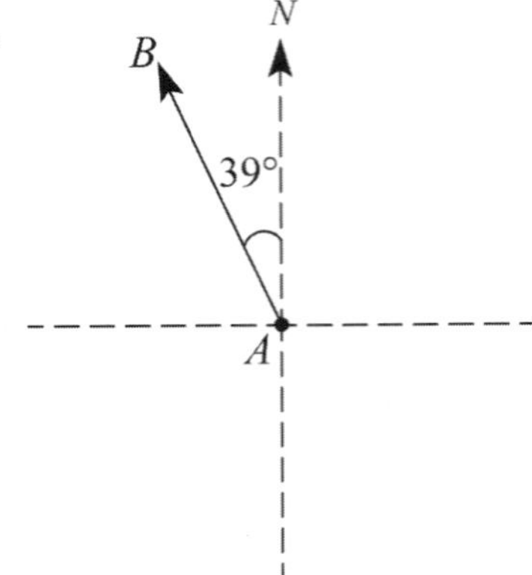

b. A motorbike travels 14 km east and then 9 km north. Determine the true bearing of its finishing point from its starting point.

c. Starting from A, a car travels 20 km north to B and then 26 km west to C. Determine the true bearing of C from A.

d. A driver travels on a bearing of 145° for 28.5 km. How far east of the starting point is the driver?

e. A hiker walks in the direction of 215° and stops when he is 2 km south of his starting point. How far did he walk?

f. A helicopter travels on a bearing of 295° until it is 200 km west of its starting point. How far did it travel on this bearing, correct to the nearest km?

7.5 Applications of trigonometry in three dimensions

Just as we can use Pythagoras' theorem in three dimensions, we can use trigonometry in three dimensions if we have right-angled triangles and enough information.

Example

Calculate the length of the diagonal labelled x in the following diagram, correct to 2 decimal places.

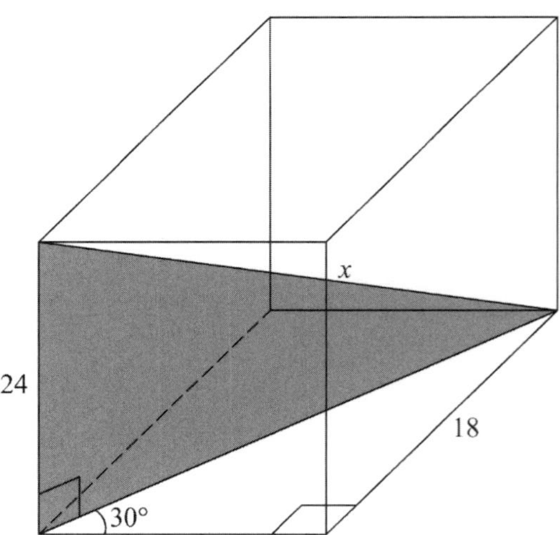

✓ *Solution*

Working	Explanation
$\sin 30 = \dfrac{18}{y}$ $y = \dfrac{18}{\sin 30}$ $y = 36$	Draw a right-angled triangle with the known side and angle. Let y be the length of the diagonal on the base. Use trigonometry to solve for the unknown.
$x^2 = 24^2 + 36^2$ $x = \sqrt{1872}$ $x = 43.27$	Draw a second right-angled triangle using the information just calculated. Use Pythagoras' theorem to determine x.

Example

A vertical pole is supported by two cables extending from two points, A and B, as illustrated below. The cable from point A is 26 metres long and is at an angle of 42° to the horizontal. Point B is 18 metres from the base of the pole. Determine the angle to the horizontal of the cable extending from point B, to two decimal places.

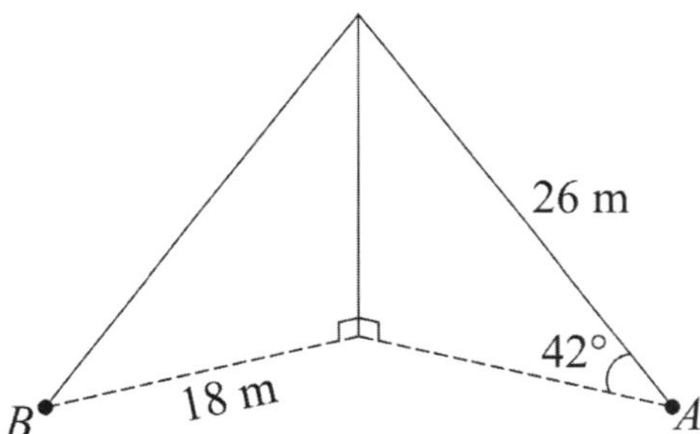

✓ *Solution*

Working	Explanation
$\sin 42 = \dfrac{x}{26}$ $x = 26\sin 42$ $x = 17.40$	Draw a right-angled triangle to represent the cable from point A. Use trigonometry to calculate the height of the pole.

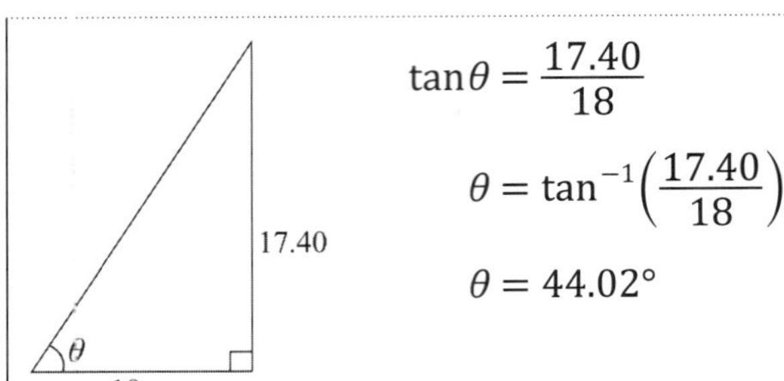 $\tan\theta = \frac{17.40}{18}$ $\theta = \tan^{-1}\left(\frac{17.40}{18}\right)$ $\theta = 44.02°$	Draw a right-angled triangle to represent the cable from point B. Use Pythagoras' theorem with the information just calculated to determine the unknown angle.

Exercise 7.5

a. A drinking straw extends 4 cm above the top of a glass with diameter 6 cm and height 11 cm. What angle does the straw make with the base of the glass? How long is the straw?

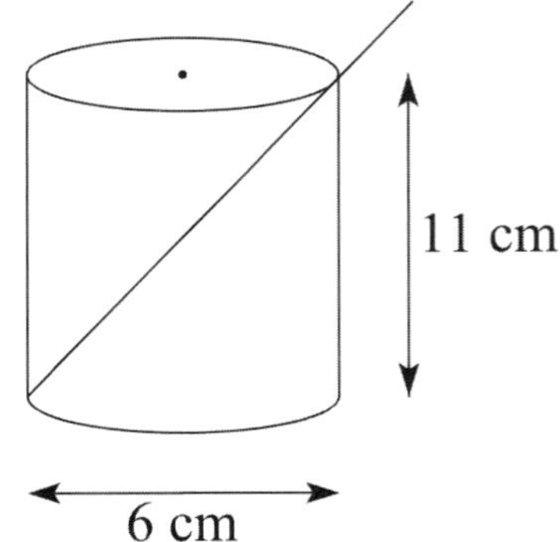

b. A ramp of length 1.2 m and width 0.5 m is raised 10 cm, as shown below. Determine $\angle CBE$.

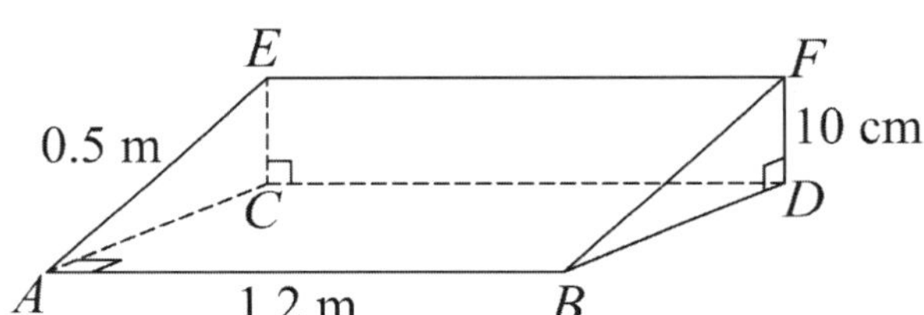

c. A vertical mast is supported at the top by two cables extending from two points: A and B. The cable from point B is 33 metres long and at an angle of 51° to the horizontal. Point A is 27 metres from the base of the mast. Determine the angle to the horizontal of the cable from point A, to two decimal places.

d. In a right square-based pyramid, the length of a side of the base is 5.7 cm. If the angle between the triangular face and the base is 68°, determine the perpendicular height and the slant height, s, of the pyramid.

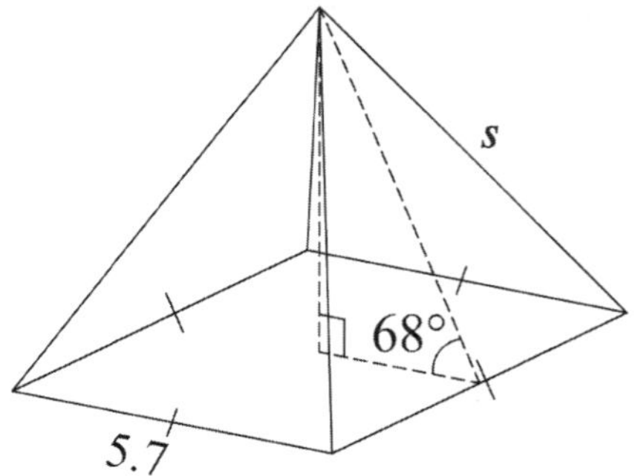

Chapter 8 – Measurement

8.1 Length and area

Basic shapes

The formulas for the perimeter and area of basic two-dimensional shapes are listed below. We will apply these formulas in the next section.

Shape	Diagram	Formula	
		Perimeter	Area
Square	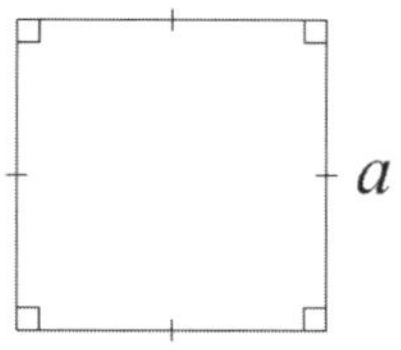 a	$4a$	a^2
Rectangle	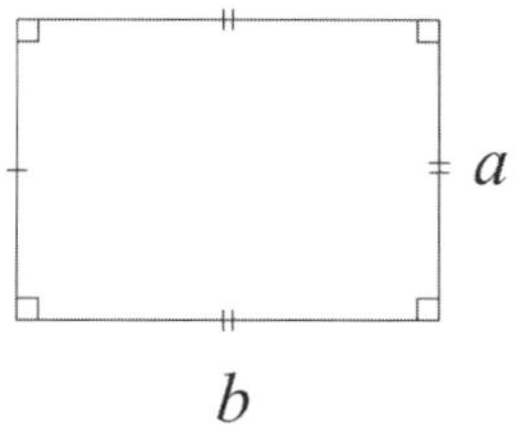 a, b	$2(a + b)$	ab
Triangle	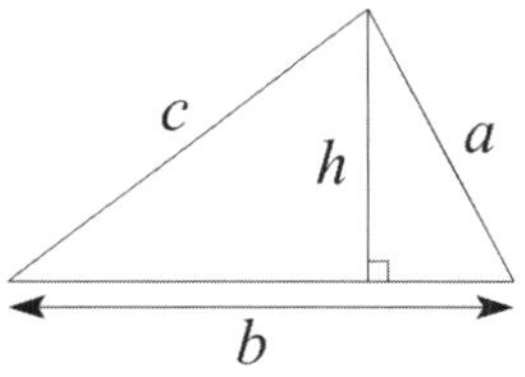 c, h, a, b	$a + b + c$	$\frac{1}{2}bh$
Parallelogram	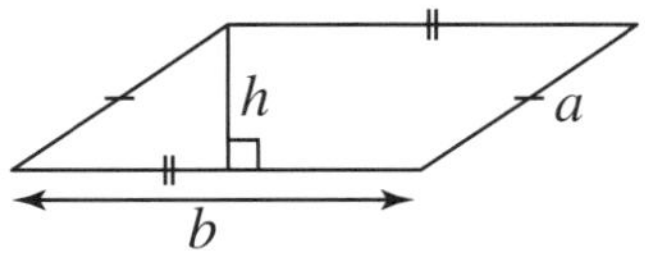 h, a, b	$2(a + b)$	bh
Trapezium	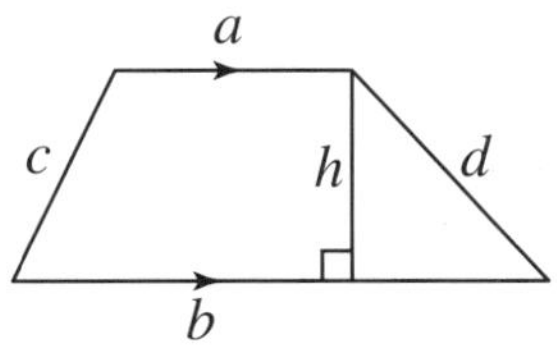 a, c, h, d, b	$a + b + c + d$	$\frac{1}{2}(a + b)h$
Rhombus	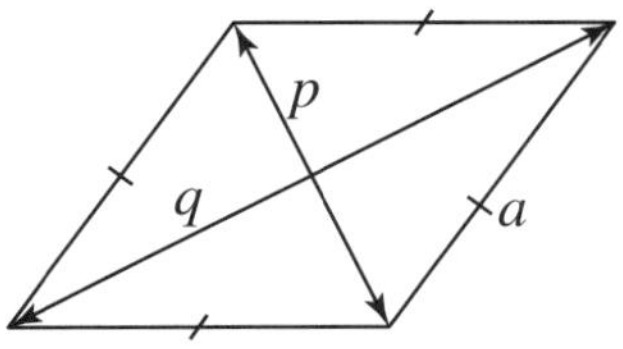 p, q, a	$4a$	$\frac{1}{2}pq$

Kite		$2(a+b)$	$\frac{1}{2}pq$
Circle		$2\pi r$ **Note:** the term 'circumference' is used for a circle instead of perimeter.	πr^2

Another shape that you may encounter is a sector of a circle, illustrated below.

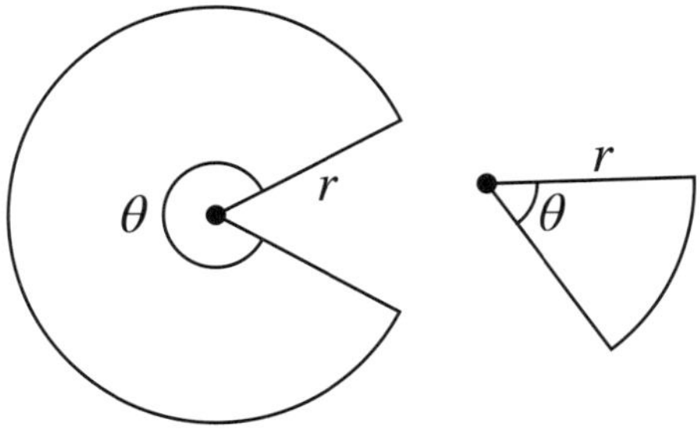

The area of a sector is $$\frac{\theta}{360}\pi r^2$$	The perimeter of a sector is $$\frac{\theta}{360}2\pi r + 2r = \frac{\theta}{180}\pi r + 2r$$

Composite shapes

A composite shape is one composed of two or more basic shapes. The area of a composite shape is obtained by adding or subtracting the areas of the component basic shapes.

Example

Calculate the perimeter and the area of the following composite shape.

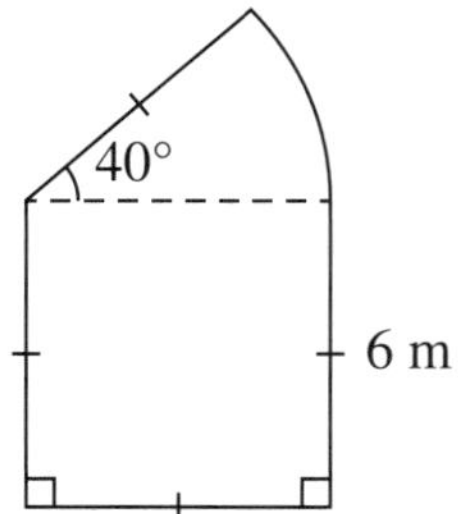

✓ ***Solution***

Working	Explanation
Arc length $= \frac{\theta}{360} \times 2 \times \pi \times r$ $= \frac{40}{360} \times 2 \times \pi \times 6$ $= \frac{4}{3}\pi$	This is a composite shape made up of a sector and a square. One component of the perimeter is the arc of the sector. We can calculate the length of an arc from the formula for the perimeter of a sector given opposite: just remove $2r$ from the formula. **1.** Calculate the arc length of the sector. **Note:** when calculating the area or circumference of a circle (or part of a circle) an answer with π is the exact value. When you give an answer as a decimal, always give it to two decimal places.
Perimeter $= \frac{4}{3}\pi + 4 \times 6$ $= 28.19$ m	**2.** Calculate the perimeter. This is found by adding up the length of all the straight sides plus the arc length.
Area of sector $= \frac{\theta}{360} \times \pi r^2$ $= \frac{40}{360} \times \pi 6^2$ $= 4\pi$	**3.** Calculate the area of the sector.
Area of square $= 6^2$ $= 36$	**4.** Calculate the area of the square.
Area of shape $= 36 + 4\pi$ $= 48.57$ m^2	**5.** Add both areas together.

Example

Calculate the perimeter and the area of the following composite shape.

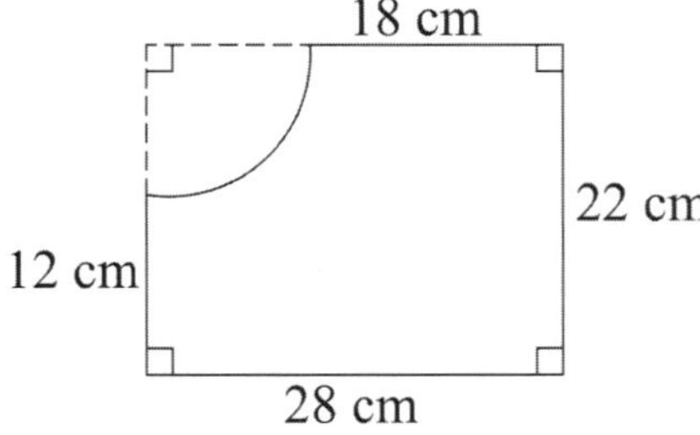

✓ Solution

Working	Explanation
Radius $= 28 - 18$ $= 10$ cm	This is a composite shape made up of a rectangle missing a quarter of a circle. 1. Determine the radius of the circle.
Arc length $= \frac{1}{4} \times 2 \times \pi \times r$ $= \frac{1}{4} \times 2 \times \pi \times 10$ $= 5\pi$	2. Determine the arc length of the curved edge.
Perimeter $= 5\pi + 18 + 22 + 28 + 12$ $= 95.71$ cm	3. Calculate the perimeter.
Area of quarter circle $= \frac{1}{4} \times \pi r^2$ $= \frac{1}{4} \times \pi 10^2$ $= 25\pi$	4. Calculate the area of the quarter circle.
Area of rectangle $= 28 \times 22$ $= 616$	5. Calculate the area of the rectangle.
Area of shape $= 616 - 25\pi$ $= 537.46$ cm^2	6. Calculate the area of the composite shape by subtracting the area of the quarter circle from the area of the rectangle.

Exercise 8.1

a. Calculate the perimeter and the area of the following composite shapes. Give your answers correct to two decimal places.

i.

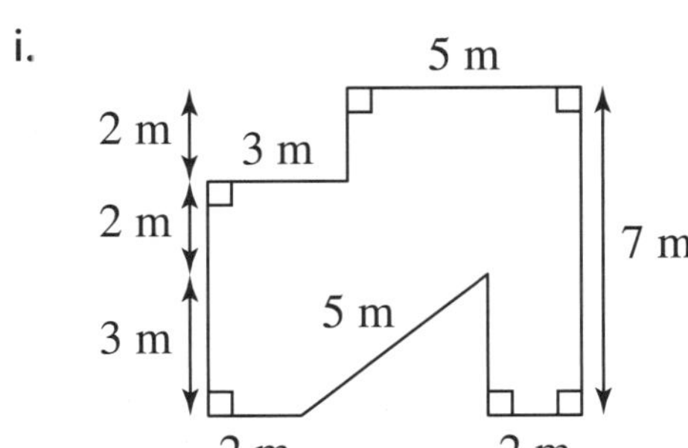

ii.

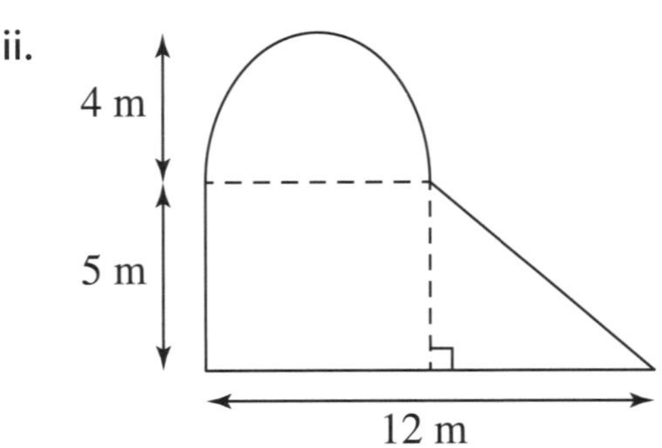

b. Calculate the area of the shaded regions of the following composite shapes. Give your answer correct to the nearest whole number.

i.

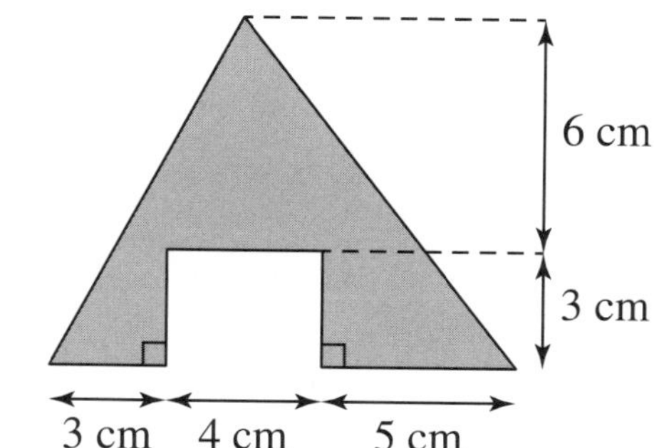

ii.

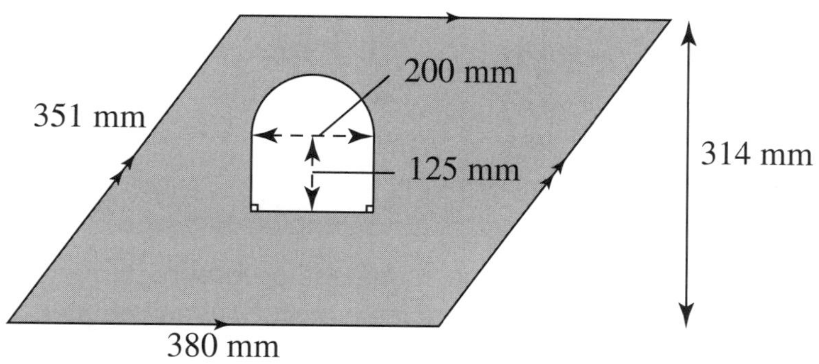

8.2 Surface area and volume of prisms and cylinders

For a three-dimensional object, the total surface area (TSA) is the sum of the areas of each of the shapes that make up the surface of the object. Draw a net of a three-dimensional solid to determine the shapes of the component surfaces. You can then use the area formulas to calculate the TSA.

Note: three-dimensional objects are sometimes referred to as **solids**.

The following table shows the nets of some common three-dimensional objects.

Three-dimensional object	Net of the object	Two-dimensional shapes
Rectangular prism		The surface of a rectangular prism is made up of 6 rectangles.

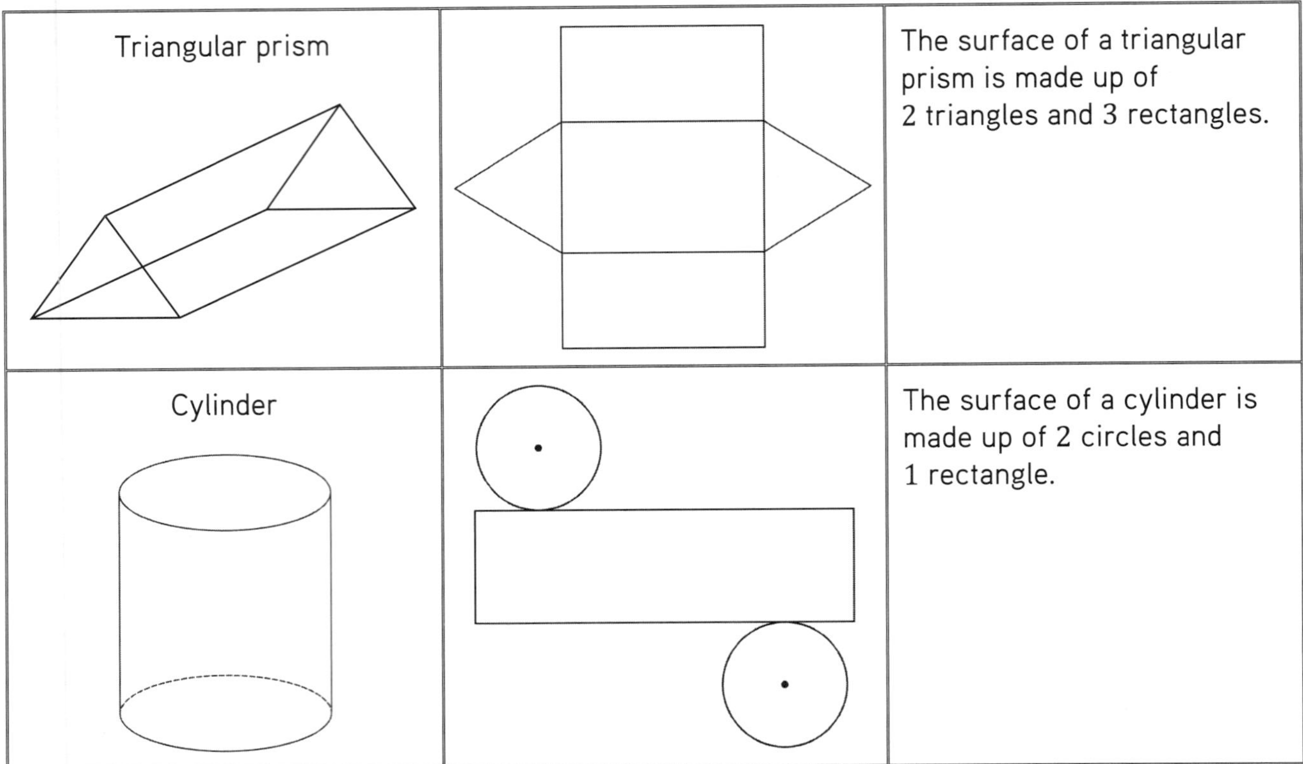

Triangular prism		The surface of a triangular prism is made up of 2 triangles and 3 rectangles.
Cylinder		The surface of a cylinder is made up of 2 circles and 1 rectangle.

A right prism is a prism with two parallel bases of the same shape and several rectangular faces joining the parallel faces. The bases and the rectangular faces meet at 90°. Two examples of a right prism are the rectangular prism and the triangular prism, shown above.

The volume of a right prism is given by the following formula:

volume = area of base × height

Example

Determine the TSA and volume of a cuboid with 5 cm sides.

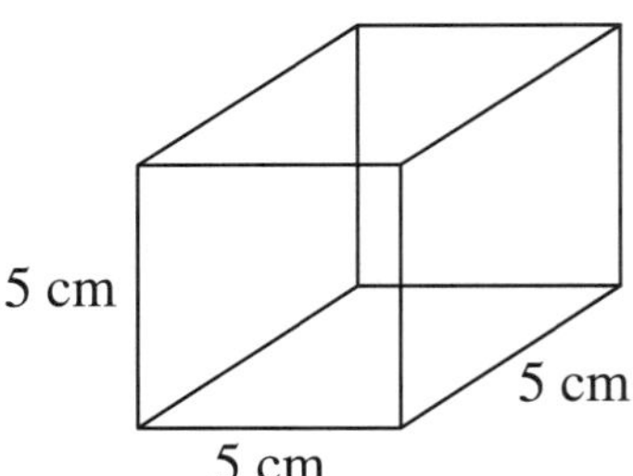

✓ *Solution*

Working	Explanation
5 cm 5 cm Area of one face $= 5^2 = 25$ $\text{TSA} = 25 \times 6 = 150 \text{ cm}^2$ $\text{Volume} = 25 \times 5 = 125 \text{ cm}^3$	A cuboid is made up of 6 square faces. Determine the area of one face and multiply it by the number of surfaces to find the TSA. The volume is found by multiplying the height of the object by the area of one of its faces.

Example

Determine the TSA and volume of the following trapezoidal prism.

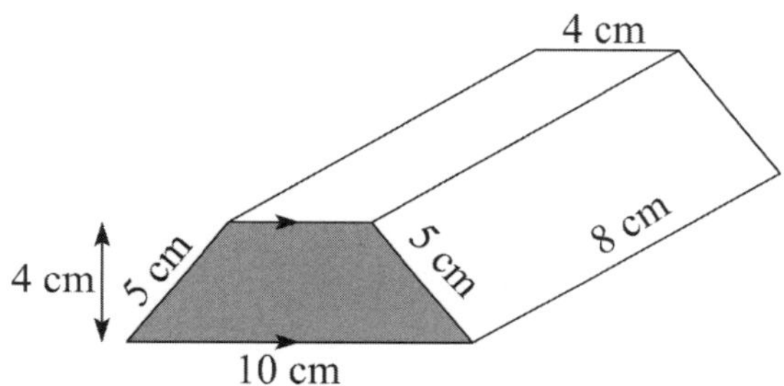

✓ *Solution*

Working	Explanation
4 cm 4 cm 5 cm 4 cm *A* 5 cm 10 cm *D* *B* *C* *B* 8 cm *A* Area $A = \frac{1}{2}(4 + 10) \times 4 = 28$ Area $B = 5 \times 8 = 40$ Area $C = 10 \times 8 = 80$ Area $D = 4 \times 8 = 32$ $\text{TSA} = 2 \times 28 + 2 \times 40 + 80 + 32 = 248 \text{ cm}^2$ $\text{Volume} = 28 \times 8 = 224 \text{ cm}^3$	1. Draw the net of the trapezoidal prism and include the measurements. 2. Label similar shapes of the same dimensions. 3. Calculate the area of each shape. 4. Sum the areas to determine the TSA of the prism. 5. Calculate the volume of prism by multiplying the area of the base (Area A) by the depth (8 cm).

Example

Determine the TSA and volume of the following cylinder.

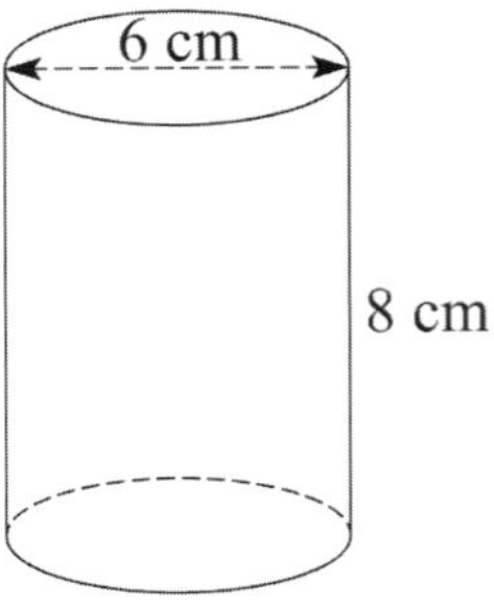

✓ ***Solution***

Working	Explanation
3 cm, A, x, B, 8 cm, A	**1.** Draw the net of the cylinder and include the measurements.
Area of the circle $= \pi 3^2 = 9\pi$	**2.** Determine the area of the base (which is a circle). **Note:** the original diagram provides the diameter of the circle, so you have to halve it to get the radius.
$x = 2\pi(3) = 6\pi$ (the circumference of the circle)	**3.** Determine the length of the rectangle, x. **Note:** the length of the rectangle is the circumference of the cylinder's base.
Area of body $= 6\pi \times 8 = 48\pi$	**4.** Calculate the area of the cylinder's body.
TSA $= 2 \times 9\pi + 48\pi = 207.35$ cm^2 Volume $= 9\pi \times 8 = 226.19$ cm^3	**5.** Sum the areas to determine the TSA of the cylinder. **6.** Calculate the volume using the volume formula (that is, area of base × height).

Exercise 8.2

Determine the volume and the total surface area of the following objects.

a. a triangular prism

b. a hexagonal prism

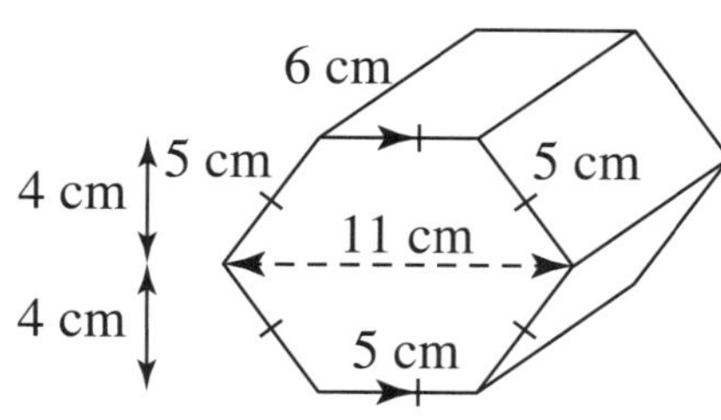

c. a cylinder

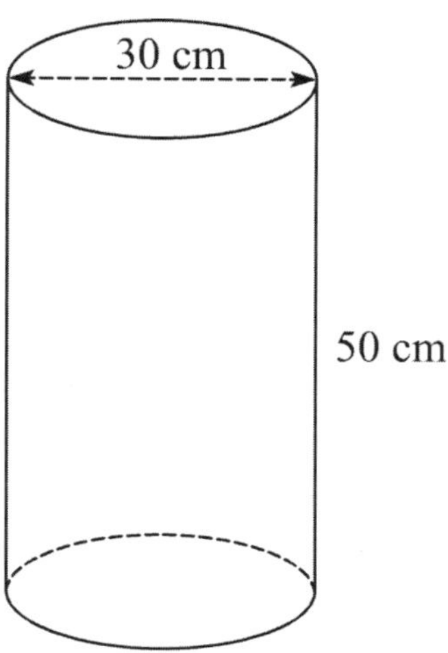

8.3 Surface area and volume of pyramids and cones

The following table shows the net of pyramids and cones.

Three-dimensional object	Net of the object	Two-dimensional shapes
Pyramid 4		A pyramid has a polygon base and its remaining faces are triangles that meet at the apex.

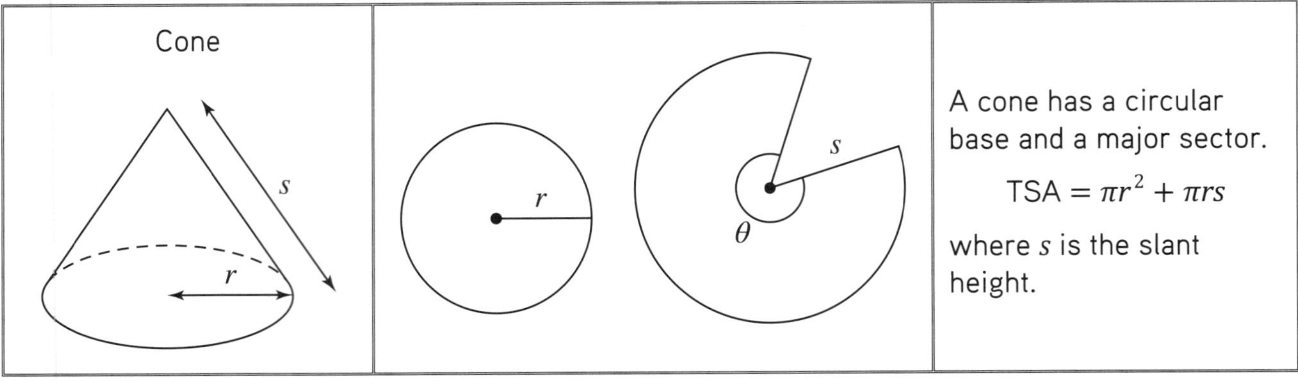

The formula for the volume of pyramids and cones is

$$\textbf{volume} = \frac{1}{3} \times \textbf{area of base} \times \textbf{perpendicular height}$$

Example

Determine the volume and surface area of the following square pyramid, where the apex is vertically above the centre of the base.

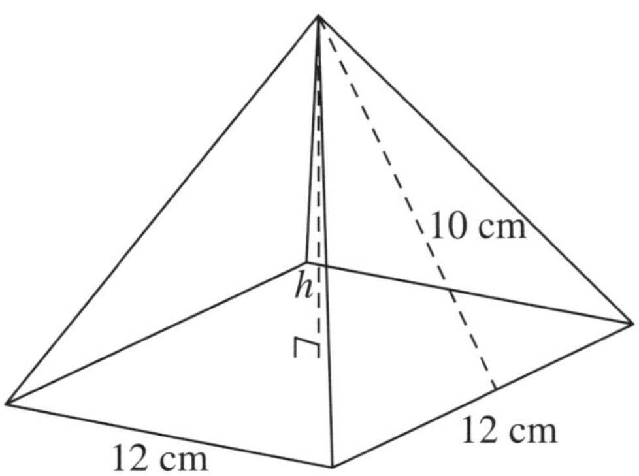

✓ ***Solution***

Working	Explanation
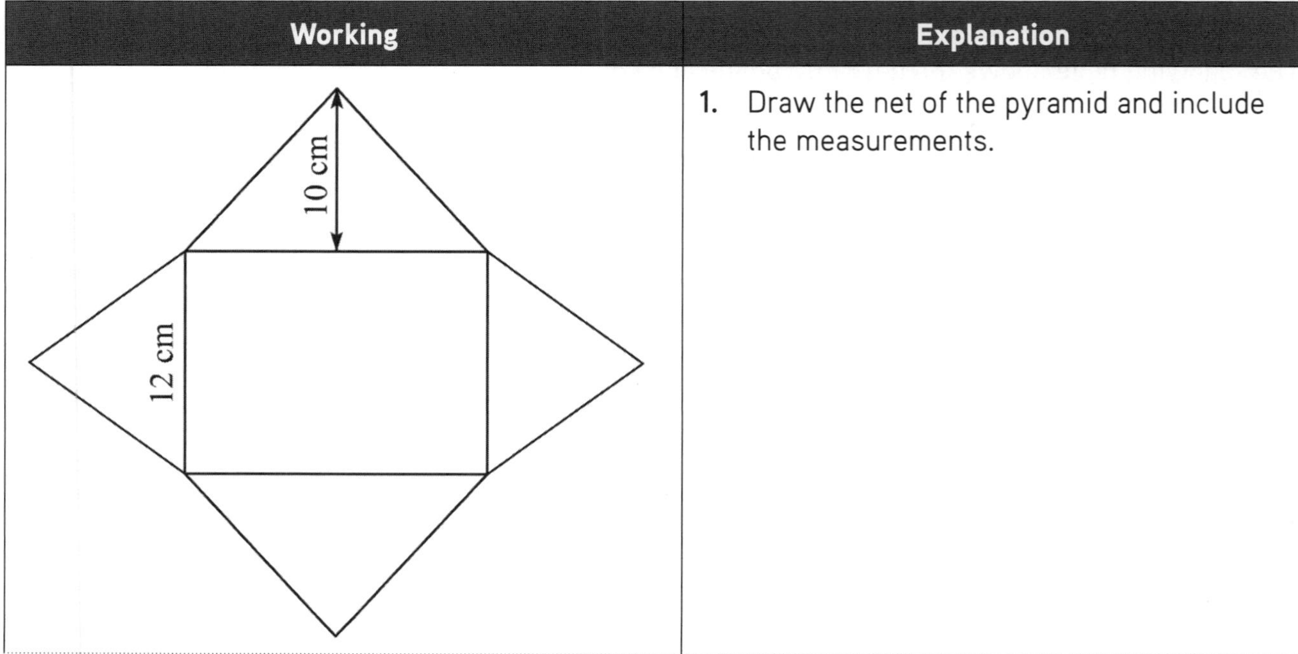	1. Draw the net of the pyramid and include the measurements.

Area of square $= 12^2$ $= 144$	**2.** Determine the area of the base (which is a square).
Area of triangle $= \frac{1}{2} \times 12 \times 10$ $= 60$	**3.** Determine the area of one triangular face.
TSA $= 4 \times 60 + 144$ $= 384 \text{ cm}^2$	**4.** Sum the areas to determine the TSA of the pyramid.
$h = \sqrt{10^2 - 6^2} = 8$	**5.** We need to determine the perpendicular height, h, before we can calculate the volume. This can be found using Pythagoras' theorem.
Volume $= \frac{1}{3} \times 144 \times 8$ $= 384 \text{ cm}^3$	**6.** Use the volume formula to determine the volume of the pyramid.

Example

Determine the volume and surface area of the following cone.

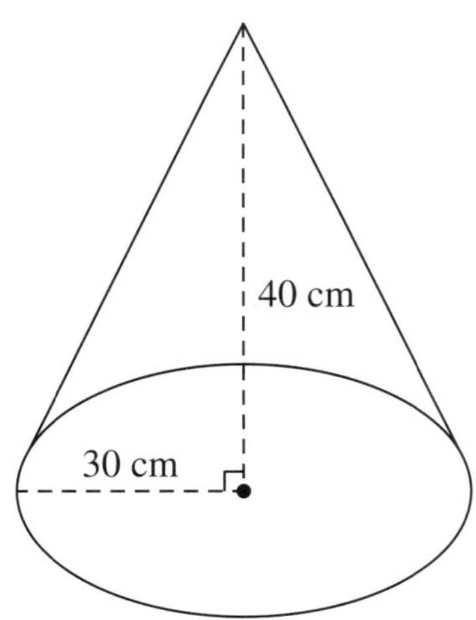

✓ ***Solution***

Working	Explanation
$s = \sqrt{40^2 + 30^2} = 50$	**1.** Calculate the slant height of the cone using Pythagoras' theorem.
$\text{TSA} = \pi r^2 + \pi rs$ $= \pi 30^2 + \pi(30)(50)$ $= 7539.82\ \text{cm}^2$	**2.** Calculate the TSA using the TSA formula for a cone.
$\text{Volume of cone} = \frac{1}{3} \times \pi \times 30^2 \times 40$ $= 37\,699.11\ \text{cm}^3$	**3.** Calculate the volume using the volume formula for a cone.

Exercise 8.3

Determine the surface area and volume of the following solids.

a. a rectangular pyramid with the apex vertically above the centre of the base

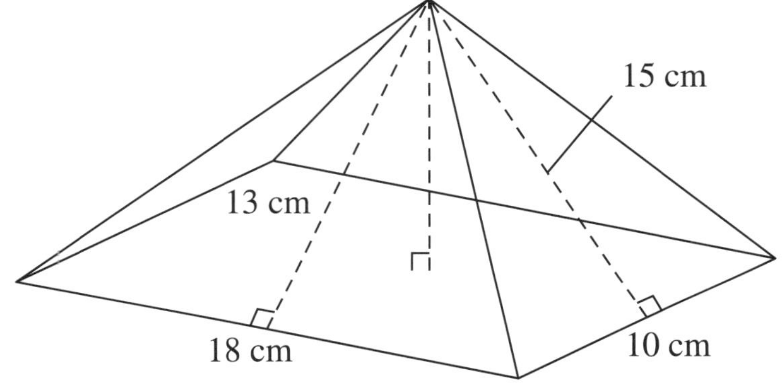

b. a cone with a diameter of 20 cm and a perpendicular height of 17 cm

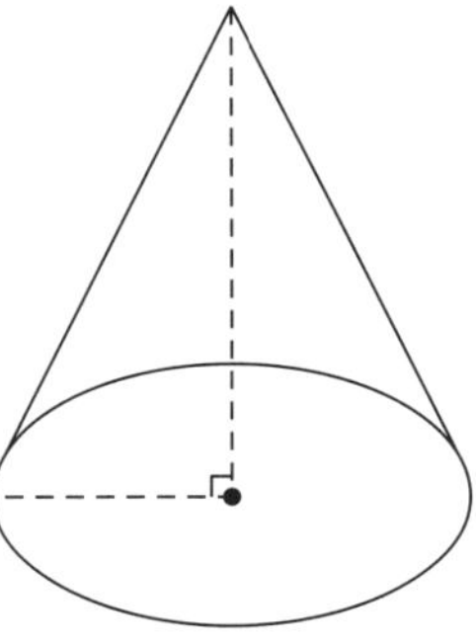

8.4 Surface area and volume of spheres

The surface area and volume of a sphere can be calculated using the following formulas, where *r* is the radius of the sphere.

$$\textbf{surface area} = 4\pi r^2 \qquad \textbf{volume} = \frac{4}{3}\pi r^3$$

Example

a. Determine the surface area and volume of a sphere with a diameter of 10 cm, correct to two decimal places.

b. Determine the radius of a sphere with a volume of 6 m^3, correct to two decimal places.

✓ *Solution*

Working	Explanation
a. Radius $= \frac{10}{2} = 5$ cm	**1.** Determine the radius of the sphere.
TSA $= 4\pi \times 5^2$ $= 314.16$ cm^2	**2.** Apply the TSA formula.
Volume $= \frac{4}{3} \times \pi \times 5^3$ $= 523.60$ cm^3	**3.** Apply the volume formula.
b. Volume $= \frac{4}{3}\pi r^3$	**1.** Substitute what we know into the volume formula for a sphere.
$6 = \frac{4}{3} \times \pi \times r^3$ $r^3 = \frac{18}{4\pi}$ $r = \sqrt[3]{\frac{18}{4\pi}}$ $r = 1.13$ m	**2.** Rearrange the formula to make r^3 the subject. **3.** Find the cube root to solve for r.

Exercise 8.4

a. Determine the surface area and volume of a sphere with a diameter of 18 cm, correct to two decimal places.

b. Determine the radius of a sphere with a volume of 15 cm^3.

c. Determine the diameter of a sphere with a surface area of 20 m^2.

8.5 Surface area and volume of composite solids

A composite solid is a solid made by combining two or more solids (or subtracting one solid from another). To calculate the surface area of a composite solid, we calculate only the visible area of the surfaces.

To calculate the total volume of a composite solid, we first separate the solid into its component solids, calculate the volume of each component and then add or subtract the individual volumes accordingly.

Example

A solid cone of radius 9 cm and height 12 cm is placed symmetrically on top of a solid hemisphere of radius 11 cm to form the composite solid shown at the right. Calculate the volume and surface area of the composite solid.

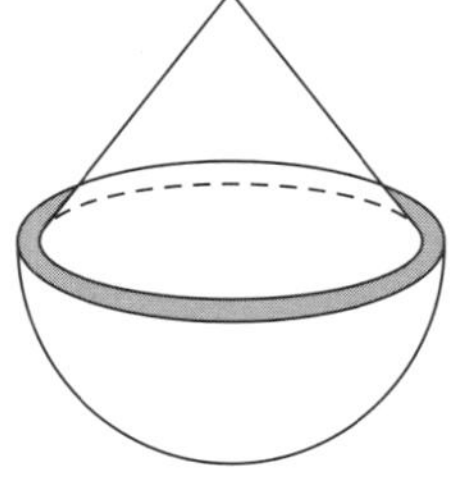

Working	Explanation
Volume of cone $= \frac{1}{3} \times \pi \times 9^2 \times 12$ $= 324\pi$	1. Determine the volume of the cone.
Volume of hemisphere $= \frac{1}{2} \times \frac{4}{3}\pi \times 11^3$ $= \frac{2662}{3}\pi$	2. Determine the volume of the hemisphere (which is half a sphere).
Total volume $= 324\pi + \frac{2662}{3}\pi$ $= 3805.52$ cm^3	3. Sum the two volumes.
$s = \sqrt{12^2 + 9^2} = 15$ cm	4. Determine the slant height of the cone.
Surface area of curved surface of cone $= \pi \times 9 \times 15$ $= 135\pi$	5. Determine the area of the curved face of the cone.
Surface area of curved hemisphere $= \frac{1}{2} \times 4 \times \pi \times 11^2$ $= 242\pi$	6. Determine the surface area of the hemisphere.
Area of shaded region $= \pi 11^2 - \pi 9^2$ $= 40\pi$	7. Determine the area of the shaded region.
Surface area $= 135\pi + 242\pi + 40\pi$ $= 1310.04$ cm^2	8. Sum the individual surface areas.

Example

Tennis balls are stored in a cylindrical container with a diameter of 4 cm, as shown in the diagram on the right. The tennis balls fill the entire vertical space of the container. Determine the amount of unused space inside the container.

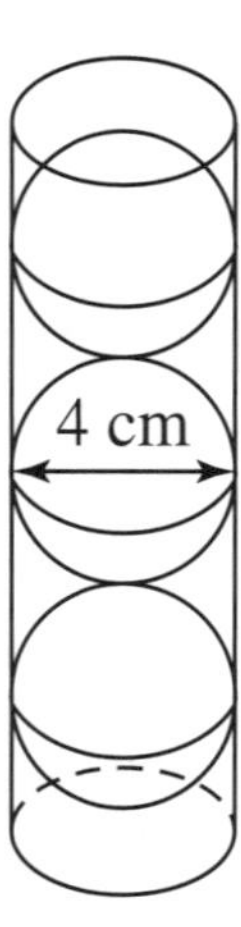

✓ ***Solution***

Working	Explanation
Volume of 1 tennis ball $= \frac{4}{3}\pi \times 2^3$ $= \frac{32}{3}\pi$	1. Determine the volume of one tennis ball.
Volume of 3 tennis balls $= \frac{32}{3}\pi \times 3$ $= 100.53\ \text{cm}^3$	2. Determine the volume of three tennis balls.
Volume of container $= \pi 2^2 \times 3 \times 4$ $= 150.80\ \text{cm}^3$	3. Determine the volume of the container.
Unused space $= 150.80 - 100.53$ $= 50.27\ \text{cm}^3$	4. Subtract the volume of the tennis balls from the volume of the cylinder to find the volume of the unused space.

Exercise 8.5

a. The diagram below shows the cross-section of a metal pipe of length 50 cm. The inner diameter of the pipe is 20 cm and the outer diameter is 30 cm. Calculate the volume of metal needed to make the pipe and its total surface area, including the inside surface.

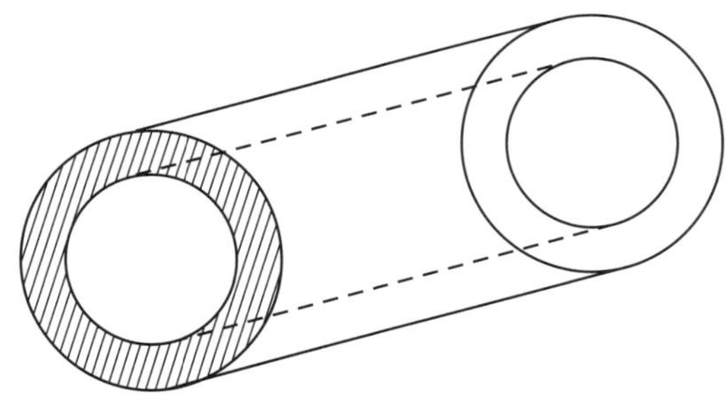

b. A cylindrical rainwater tank measuring 2.1 metres high and with a diameter of 180 cm collects rainwater at a rate of 900 ml per hour. Assuming that the tank was empty to begin with and that no water evaporates, determine the number of days it has to rain for the tank to fill completely.

c. A rectangular prism measuring 30 cm by 40 cm by 8 cm has a circular hole bored through its centre, as shown below.

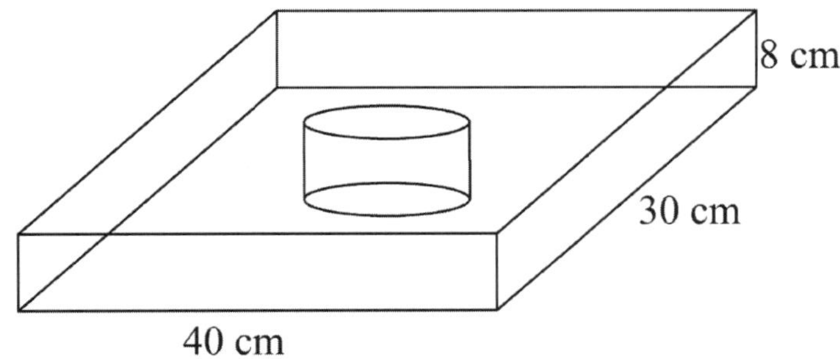

i. What was the volume of the rectangular prism before the circular hole was bored?

ii. After the circular hole was bored, the volume of the remaining prism was half the original volume. Show that the radius of the circular hole must be 13.82 cm.

iii. Determine the total surface area of the solid that remains after the circular hole is bored, correct to the nearest cm^2.

d. Joe is looking for a cylindrical container to hold 5 tennis balls. Each tennis ball has a volume of $180\ cm^3$.

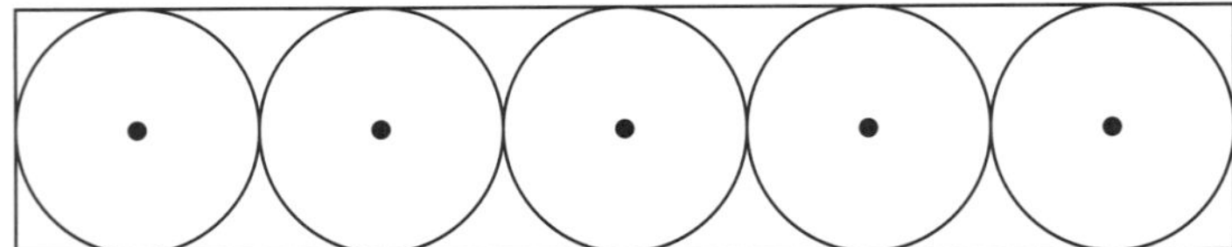

i. Determine the diameter and length of the cylinder that can fit 5 tennis balls.

ii. Determine the volume of empty space in the cylinder after the balls are placed in it.

8.6 Effect of rounding errors

Rounding a measurement can affect the accuracy of results, leading to serious errors or biased findings. Understanding the consequences of rounding is crucial for obtaining reliable data and drawing valid conclusions.

Example

A cylindrical tank has a radius of 3.6 metres and a height of 8.2 metres. If the measurements are rounded to the nearest metre before calculating the volume of the tank, what is the rounded volume of the tank? Determine the difference between the rounded volume and the exact volume.

✓ *Solution*

Working	Explanation
Radius ≈ 4 m Height ≈ 8 m	1. Round the given values.
Approximate volume of cylinder $= \pi \times 4^2 \times 8$ $\approx 402\ m^3$	2. Determine the volume of the cylinder based on the rounded values.
Volume of cylinder $= \pi \times 3.6^2 \times 8.2$ $= 333.86\ m^3$	3. Determine the actual volume of the cylinder.
Difference in volume $= 402 - 333.86$ $= 68.14\ m^3$	4. Calculate the difference.

Example

A household budget allocates $\$414$ for groceries, $\$253$ for utilities and $\$158$ for entertainment each month. If the budgeted amounts are rounded to the nearest ten dollars before totalling, what is the difference between the rounded total budget and the actual total budget? Comment on the difference.

✓ Solution

Working	Explanation
Groceries $\approx \$410$ Utilities $\approx \$250$ Entertainment $\approx \$160$	**1.** Round the given values.
Rounded budget $= 410 + 250 + 160 = \$820$	**2.** Calculate the budget based on the rounded figures.
Unrounded budget$= 414 + 253 + 158 = \$825$	**3.** Calculate the budget based on the actual figures.
Difference $= 825 - 820 = \$5$	**4.** Determine the difference.
If the household had budgeted based on the rounded budget, it would be $5 short each month.	**5.** Comment on the difference.

Exercise 8.6

a. A rectangular prism has dimensions 3.4 cm by 5.9 cm by 7.2 cm. If each dimension is rounded to the nearest centimetre before calculating the surface area, what is the difference between the rounded and actual surface area of the prism?

b. Amy and John want to purchase some fencing for their rectangular garden. Amy measured the dimensions of the garden as 7.94 metres long and 5.49 metres wide. As fences are bought by the metre, John says that they can just round the measurements to the nearest metre to determine the number of metres of fence they need to purchase. Calculate the perimeter using the rounded measurements and the actual measurements, and comment on John's claim.

c. You invest $\$5000$ in a savings account with an annual interest rate of 4.8%. However, due to a rounding error, the bank advertises the rate as 5%. If the interest is compounded annually for 5 years, what is the difference in the final amount you receive compared to the amount you would have received with the advertised interest rate?

Chapter 9 – Geometry

9.1 Similarity

Two figures are said to be similar if the following conditions are met.

- Condition 1: all pairs of corresponding sides are in the same ratio.
- Condition 2: all pairs of corresponding angles are equal.

Consider the following rectangles: X, Y and Z.

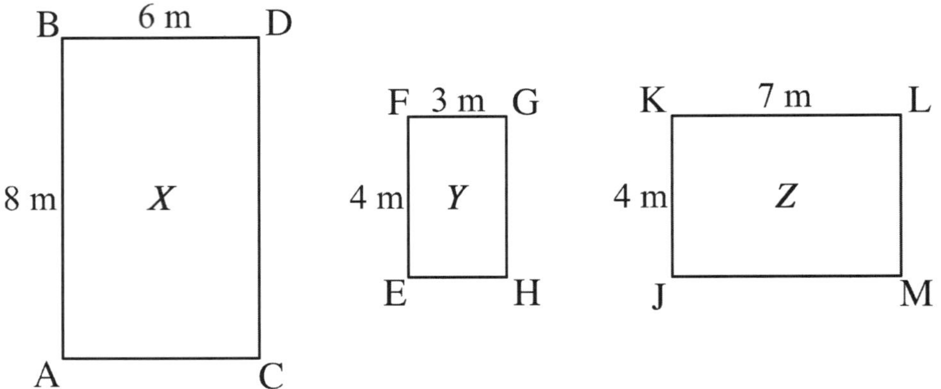

Although all of these are rectangles, only two are similar.

Condition 2 is met for all rectangles, as the corresponding angles are equal (90°).

For condition 1 to be met, all corresponding sides must have the same ratio.

Consider rectangles X ($ABDC$) and Y ($EFGH$). The corresponding pairs of sides are AB and EF, BD and FG, DC and GH, and CA and HE. The ratios of these sides are

$$\frac{AB}{EF} = \frac{BD}{FG} = \frac{DC}{GH} = \frac{CA}{HE} = 2$$

So condition 1 is also met for rectangles X and Y: all pairs of sides have the same ratio. Hence X and Y are similar rectangles.

Now consider rectangles Y ($EFGH$) and Z ($JKLM$). Note that

$$\frac{EF}{JK} = \frac{GH}{LM} = 1$$

so some ratios are equal. However

$$\frac{FG}{KL} = \frac{HE}{MJ} = \frac{3}{7} \neq 1$$

so, as the ratios of all corresponding sides are not equal, condition 1 is not met. Therefore, rectangles Y and Z are not similar.

Applying a scale factor to area and volume

If objects are similar and one is an enlargement of the other, some useful ratios can be applied. Consider the following similar objects.

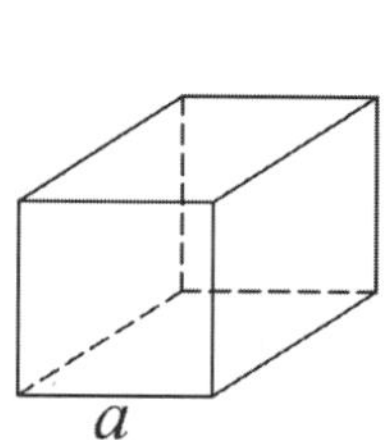

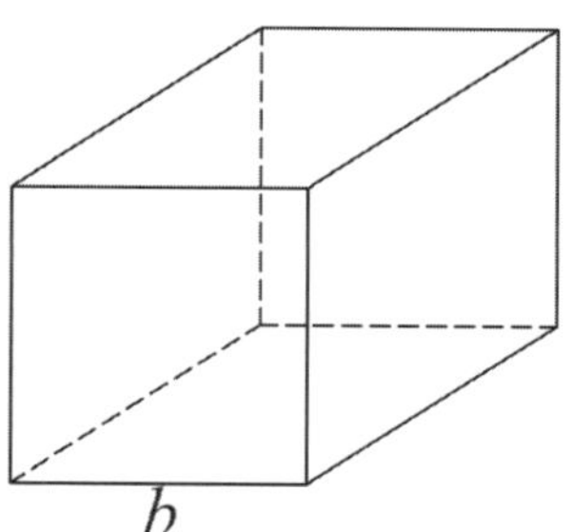

Length ratio $= a{:}b$ Scale factor $= \frac{b}{a}$

Area ratio $= a^2{:}b^2$ Scale factor $= \frac{b^2}{a^2}$

Volume ratio $= a^3{:}b^3$ Scale factor $= \frac{b^3}{a^3}$

Example

The two prisms shown below are similar. The surface area of the small prism is $288\ \text{cm}^2$ and its volume is $240\ \text{cm}^3$. Find the surface area and volume of the larger prism.

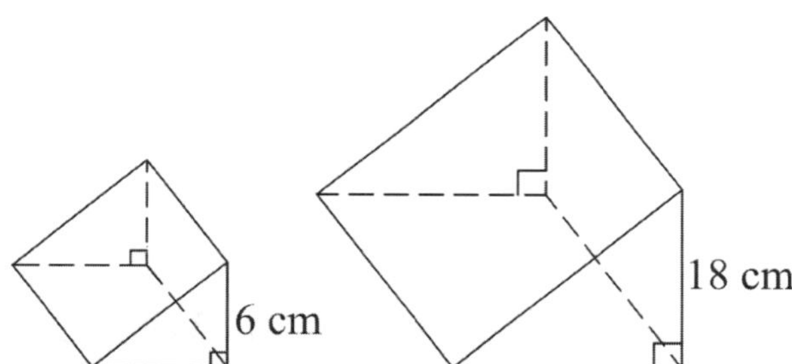

✓ *Solution*

Working	Explanation
Surface area Length ratio $= 6{:}18 = 1{:}3$	1. Write the length ratio and simplify it.
Area ratio $= 1^2{:}3^2 = 1{:}9$	2. Determine the area ratio by squaring the length ratio.
Area scale factor $= \frac{\text{TSA of large prism}}{\text{TSA of small prism}}$ $\frac{\text{TSA of large prism}}{\text{TSA of small prism}} = \frac{9}{1} = 9$	3. Rewrite the ratio as a scale factor.

$\frac{\text{TSA of large prism}}{288} = 9$	**4.** Substitute the surface area of the small prism.
$\text{TSA of large prism} = 9 \times 288 = 2592\ \text{cm}^2$	**5.** Rearrange the equation to find the surface area of the large prism.
Volume $\text{Volume ratio} = 1^3:3^3 = 1:27$	**1.** Determine the volume ratio by cubing the length ratio.
$\text{Vol. scale factor} = \frac{\text{Vol. of large prism}}{\text{Vol. of small prism}}$ $\frac{\text{Vol. of large prism}}{\text{Vol. of small prism}} = \frac{27}{1} = 27$	**2.** Rewrite the ratio as a scale factor.
$\frac{\text{Vol. of large prism}}{240} = 27$	**3.** Substitute the volume of the small prism.
$\text{Vol. of large prism} = 27 \times 240 = 6480\ \text{cm}^3$	**4.** Rearrange the equation to find the volume of the large prism.

Example

The two prisms shown below are similar. The surface area of the large prism is $94\,\text{cm}^2$ and its volume is $60\ \text{cm}^3$. Find the surface area and volume of the smaller prism.

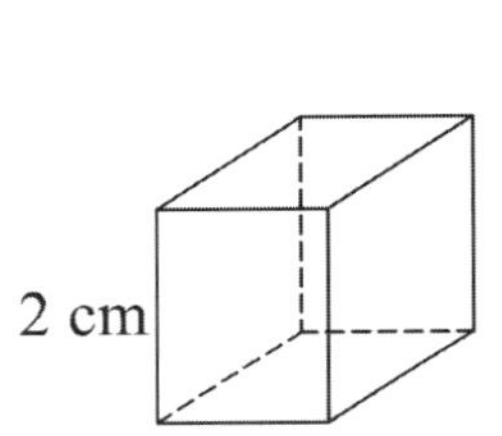

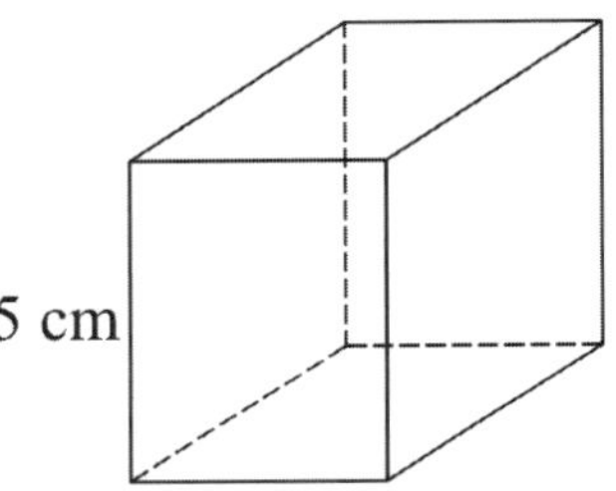

Working	Explanation
Surface area $\text{Length ratio} = 2:5$	**1.** Write the length ratio.
$\text{Area ratio} = 2^2:5^2 = 4:25$	**2.** Determine the area ratio by squaring the length ratio.
$\text{Area scale factor} = \frac{\text{TSA of large prism}}{\text{TSA of small prism}}$ $\frac{\text{TSA of large prism}}{\text{TSA of small prism}} = \frac{25}{4}$	**3.** Rewrite the ratio as a scale factor.
$\frac{94}{\text{TSA of small prism}} = \frac{25}{4}$	**4.** Substitute the surface area of the large prism.
$\text{TSA of small prism} = \frac{4}{25} \times 94 = 15.04\ \text{cm}^2$	**5.** Rearrange the equation to find the surface area of the small prism.

Volume Volume ratio $= 2^3:5^3 = 8:125$	1. Determine the volume ratio by cubing the length ratio.
$\text{Vol. scale factor} = \dfrac{\text{Vol. of large prism}}{\text{Vol. of small prism}}$ $\dfrac{\text{Vol. of large prism}}{\text{Vol. of small prism}} = \dfrac{125}{8}$	2. Rewrite the ratio as a scale factor.
$\dfrac{60}{\text{Vol. of small prism}} = \dfrac{125}{8}$	3. Substitute the volume of the large prism.
$\text{Vol. of small prism} = \dfrac{8}{125} \times 60 = 3.84 \text{ cm}^3$	4. Rearrange the equation to find volume of the small prism.

Example

The surface area ratio of cone A to cone B is 1:25. If cone A has a volume of 9 cm^3, determine the volume of cone B.

✓ *Solution*

Working	Explanation
Area ratio = cone A:cone B = 1:25 Length ratio = 1:5	1. Determine the length ratio by taking the square root of the area ratio.
Volume ratio $= 1^3:5^3 = 1:125$	2. Determine the volume ratio by cubing the length ratio.
$\text{Vol. scale factor} = \dfrac{\text{Vol. of cone B}}{\text{Vol. of cone A}}$ $\dfrac{\text{Vol. of cone B}}{\text{Vol. of cone A}} = \dfrac{125}{1} = 125$	3. Rewrite the ratio as a scale factor.
$\dfrac{\text{Vol. of cone B}}{9} = 125$	4. Substitute the volume of cone A.
$\text{Vol. of cone B} = 125 \times 9 = 1125 \text{ cm}^3$	5. Rearrange the equation to find the volume of cone B.

Exercise 9.1

a. The two prisms shown below are known to be similar. From the information provided, find the surface area and volume of the larger prism.

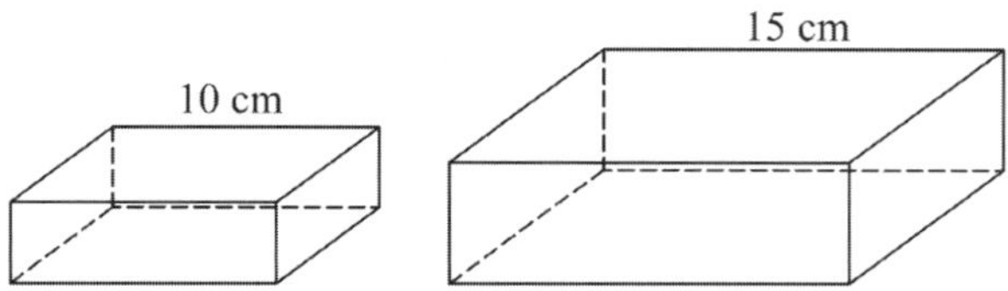

Volume of smaller prism: 60 cm^3

Surface area of smaller prism: 112 cm^2

b. The two prisms shown below are known to be similar. From the information provided, find the surface area and volume of the smaller prism.

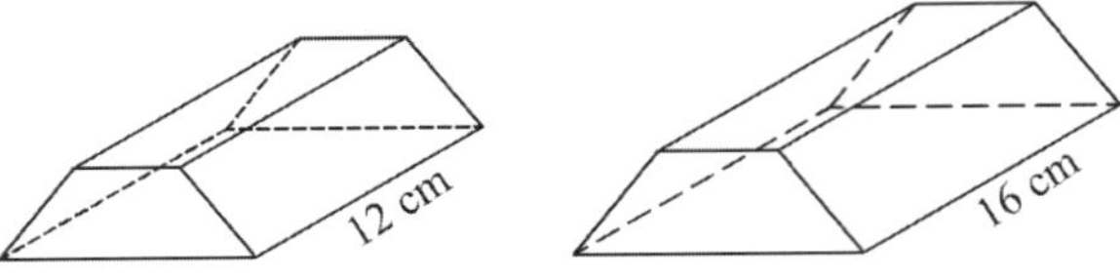

Volume of larger prism: $28\,\text{cm}^3$

Surface area of larger prism: $40\,\text{cm}^2$

c. The ratio of the surface area of sphere A to that of sphere B is 1:16. If sphere A has a volume of $50\,\text{cm}^3$, what is the volume of sphere B?

d. Rowan builds a scale model of a bookcase with a height of 3 cm, shown below. He would like the actual bookcase to have a volume of $4\,\text{m}^3$. Find the length scale ratio between Rowan's drawing and the actual bookcase, and determine the volume of the scale model bookcase in cubic centimetres. (**Note:** $1\,\text{m} = 100\,\text{cm}$ and $1\,\text{m}^3 = 1\,000\,000\,\text{cm}^3$.)

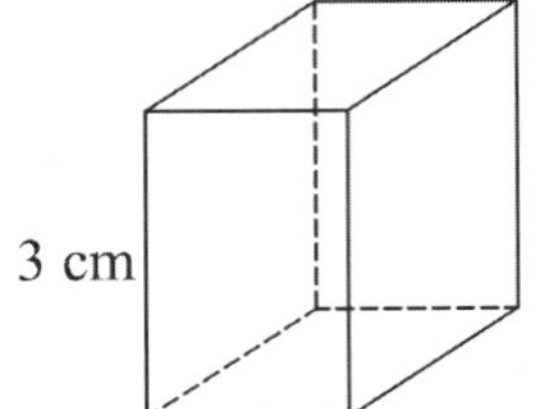

Actual bookcase

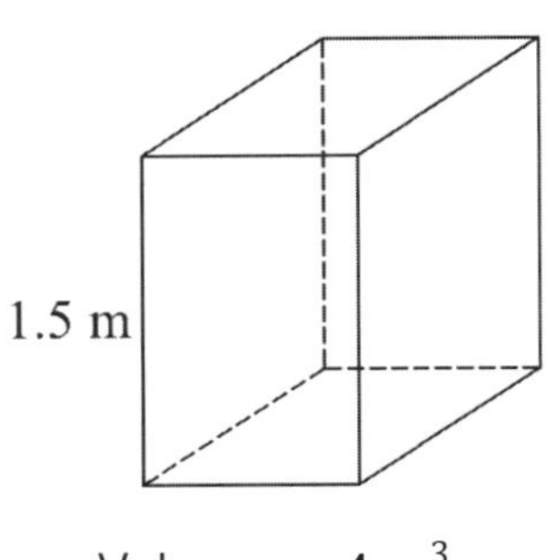

Volume = $4\,\text{m}^3$

9.2 Applications of similarity

We can use similarity in practical applications such as mapping and architectural design.

Example

A triangular flag needs its dimensions enlarged by a factor of 5. If the flag has a base of 30 cm and a perpendicular height of 45 cm, determine the difference in the area of material needed to make each flag.

✓ *Solution*

Working	Explanation
Length ratio = 1:5	**1.** Write the length ratio.
Area ratio = $1^2:5^2 = 1:25$	**2.** Determine the area ratio by squaring the length ratio.
Area scale factor $= \dfrac{\text{Area of enlarged flag}}{\text{Area of original flag}}$ $\dfrac{\text{Area of enlarged flag}}{\text{Area of original flag}} = \dfrac{25}{1} = 25$	**3.** Rewrite the ratio as a scale factor.

Area of current flag $= \frac{1}{2} \times 30 \times 45$ $= 675\ \text{cm}^2$ $\frac{\text{Area of enlarged flag}}{675} = 25$	4. Calculate the area of the current flag and substitute it into the ratio.
Area of enlarged flag $= 25 \times 675 = 16\,875\ \text{cm}^2$	5. Rearrange the equation to find the area of the enlarged flag.
Difference $= 16\,875 - 675 = 16\,200\ \text{cm}^2$	6. Determine the difference.

Example

A map has a scale of 1:50 000, which means that 1 cm on the map is equivalent to 50 000 cm (or 500 m) in real life. An area of parkland occupies $4.5\ \text{cm}^2$ on the map. What is the area of this parkland in real life, in square kilometres?

Note: $1\ \text{km}^2 = 10\ 000\ 000\ 000\ \text{cm}^2$.

✓ Solution

Working	Explanation
Length ratio = 1:50 000	1. Write the length ratio.
Area ratio $= 1^2{:}50\ 000^2$ Area scale factor of enlargement $= 50\,000^2$	2. Determine the area ratio by squaring the length ratio.
Area of actual parkland $= 50\,000^2 \times 4.5$	3. Determine actual area by multiplying the map area by the scale factor.
Area of parkland $= (50\,000^2 \times 4.5) \div 10\ 000\ 000\ 000$ $= 1.125\ \text{km}^2$	4. Convert the result to km^2.

Exercise 9.2

a. A solid sphere of radius 1 m is made of a particular metal. The metal in the sphere is worth \$70 000. How much is a solid sphere made of the same metal but with a radius 2 m worth?

b. A model of a sailing boat is made to a scale of 1:50 (that is, a length of 1 cm on the model is equivalent to 50 cm on the real yacht). If one of the sails on the real yacht has an area of $50\ 000\ \text{cm}^2$, what is the area of the same sail on the model?

c. A map has a scale of 1:10 000. What area on the map is equivalent to an actual area of $8000\ \text{m}^2$? **Note:** $1\ \text{m}^2 = 10\ 000\ \text{cm}^2$.

d. A map has a scale of 1:50 000.

   i. On the map, a straight line between two locations is 1.54 cm long. How far are these locations actually apart?

   ii. On the map, the grounds of a shopping centre are $1\ \text{cm}^2$. What area does the shopping centre actually occupy?

9.3 Similar triangles

Two triangles are said to be similar if they are the same shape but are different in size. Corresponding angles will be same (i.e. congruent) and corresponding sides will be in the same ratio. (This ratio is the scale factor.)

There are four tests for determining whether two triangles are similar. They are summarised in the table below.

Similarity test	Explanation	
Angle, Angle, Angle (AAA)	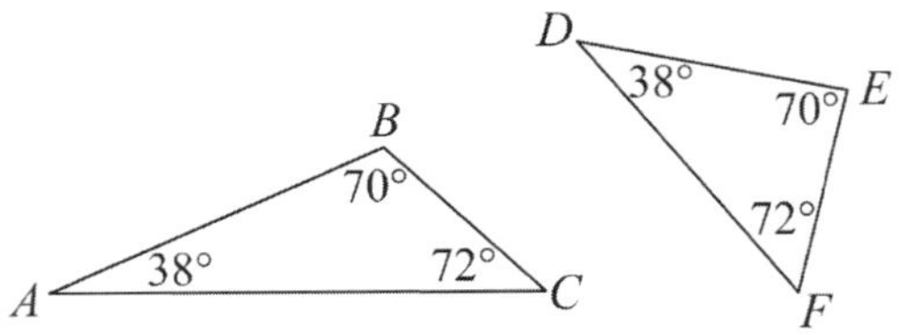 A, B, C, 38°, 70°, 72°; D, E, F, 38°, 70°, 72°	$\angle ABC = \angle DEF = 70°$ $\angle BCA = \angle EFD = 72°$ $\angle CAB = \angle FDE = 38°$ All angles are the same, therefore ΔABC is similar to ΔDEF (AAA).
Side, Side, Side (SSS)	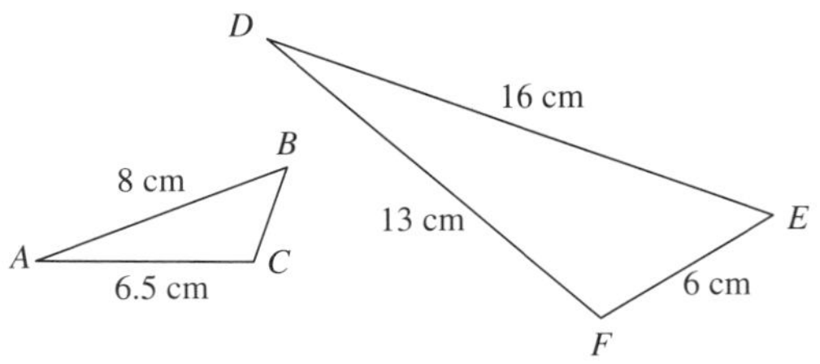 A, B, C, 8 cm, 6.5 cm; D, E, F, 16 cm, 13 cm, 6 cm	$\frac{AB}{DE} = \frac{BC}{EF} = \frac{CA}{FD} = \frac{1}{2}$ All corresponding sides have the same ratio, therefore ΔABC is similar to ΔDEF (SSS).
Side, Angle, Side (SAS)	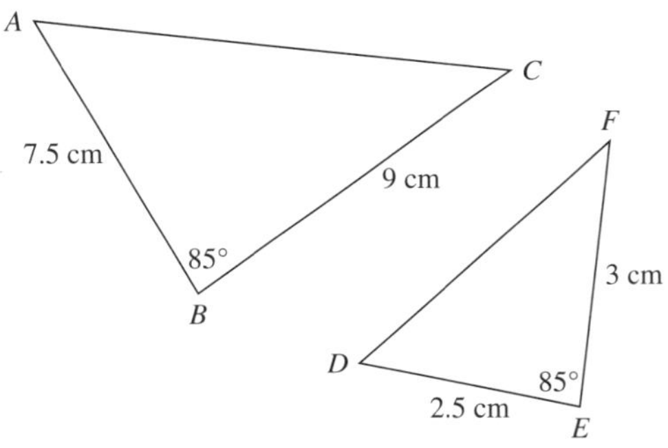 A, B, C, 7.5 cm, 9 cm, 85°; D, E, F, 2.5 cm, 3 cm, 85°	$\angle ABC = \angle DEF = 85°$ $\frac{AB}{DE} = \frac{BC}{EF} = 3$ An angle is the same and two pairs of corresponding sides have the same ratio, therefore ΔABC is similar to ΔDEF (SAS). **Note:** for the SAS test to apply, the angle must be between the two sides that are in the same proportion (1:3 in this example).
Right angle, Hypotenuse, Side (RHS)	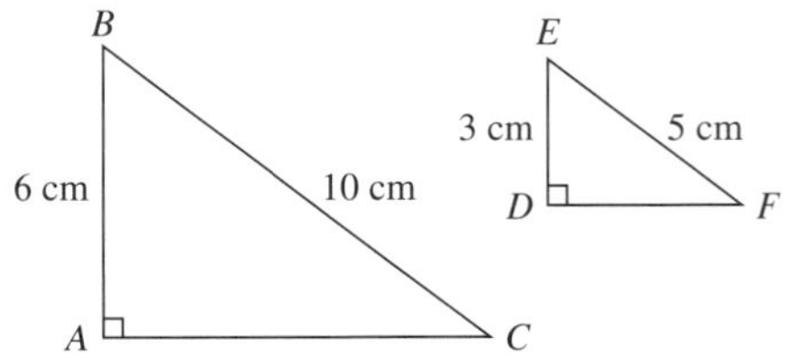 A, B, C, 6 cm, 10 cm; D, E, F, 3 cm, 5 cm	$\angle CAB = \angle FDE = 90°$ $\frac{AB}{DE} = \frac{BC}{EF} = 2$ There is a shared right angle, and the ratios of the hypotenuses and the other corresponding sides are the same, therefore ΔABC is similar to ΔDEF (RHS).

The notation used to indicate that triangles are similar is

$$\Delta ABC \sim \Delta DEF \text{ or } \Delta ABC \;|||\; \Delta DEF$$

You need to be able to write proofs and provide reasons as to why two triangles are similar. For example, suppose you had to prove that the following triangles are similar.

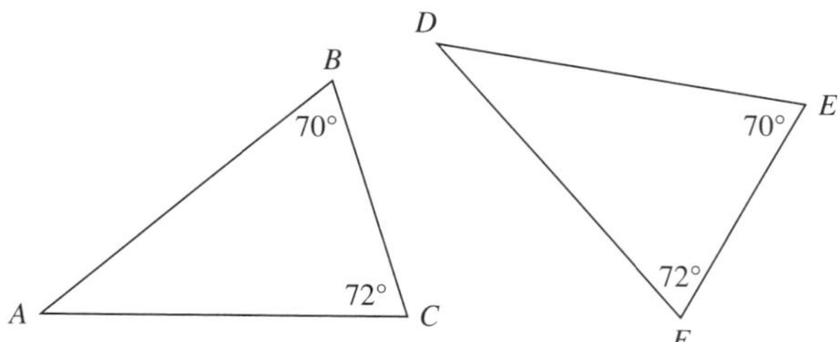

The table below shows the structure you should follow in providing your proof.

Structure	What is required
Introduction: what needs to be proven?	Required to prove (RTP) that $\Delta ABC \sim \Delta DEF$
Statements and reason	In ΔABC and ΔDEF: • $\angle ABC = \angle DEF = 70°$ (given) • $\angle BCA = \angle EFD = 72°$ (given) • $\angle CAB = \angle FDE = 38°$ (as the sum of the internal angles in a triangle is 180°) The corresponding angles in both triangles are the same.
Conclusion and the test that was used	$\therefore \Delta ABC \sim \Delta DEF$ (AAA)

Example

Prove that the following triangles are similar.

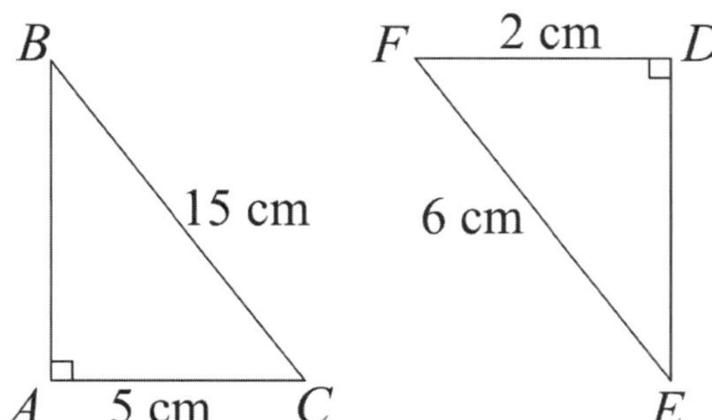

✓ Solution

Working	Explanation
RTP $\Delta ABC \sim \Delta DEF$	1. Write what is required to be proven. Always ensure that the vertices of the triangles are listed in corresponding order.
In ΔABC and ΔDEF: • $\angle BAC = \angle EDF = 90°$ (given) • $\frac{BC}{EF} = \frac{15}{6} = \frac{5}{2}$ (ratio of the hypotenuses) • $\frac{AC}{DF} = \frac{5}{2} = \frac{5}{2}$ (ratio of the given sides)	2. For each triangle, the information given is one angle and two sides, one of which is the hypotenuse. Since the angle is a right angle, the test to use is RHS. 3. Write out the statements and reasons.
$\therefore \Delta ABC \sim \Delta DEF$ (RHS)	4. Conclude that the two triangles are similar and state the test.

Example

Prove that the following triangles are similar.

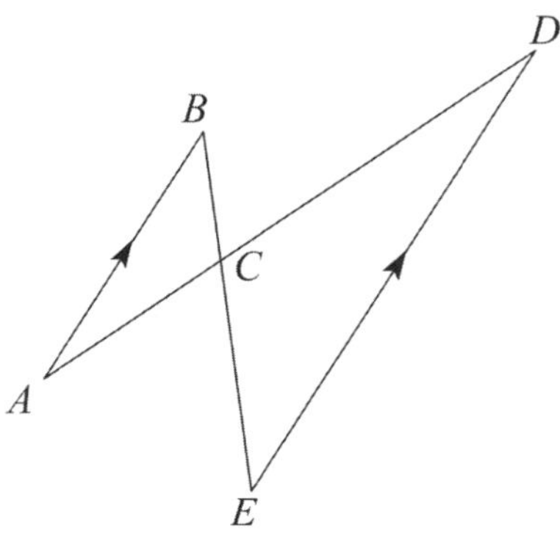

✓ Solution

Working	Explanation
RTP $\Delta ABC \sim \Delta EDC$	1. Write what is required to be proven. Always ensure that the vertices of the triangles are listed in corresponding order. There are no measurements or angles given but, because of the parallel lines, and the fact that the two lines, AD and BE, intersect at C, we can use our knowledge of geometry to provide a proof.
In ΔABC and ΔEDC: • $\angle ACB = \angle DCE$ (vertically opposite angles) • $\angle ABC = \angle DEC$ (alternate angles, $AB \parallel DE$) • $\angle BAC = \angle EDC$ (alternate angles, $AB \parallel DE$)	2. Write out the statements and reasons. **Note:** $AB \parallel DE$ means AB is parallel to DE.
$\therefore \Delta ABC \sim \Delta EDC$ (AAA)	3. Conclude that the two triangles are similar and state the test.

Exercise 9.3

Prove that the following pairs of triangles are similar.

a.

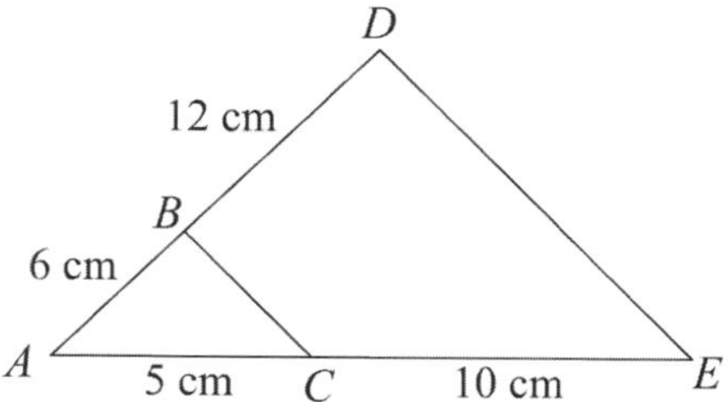

b.

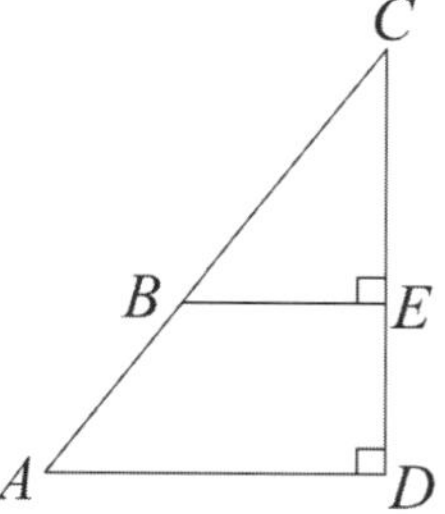

c.

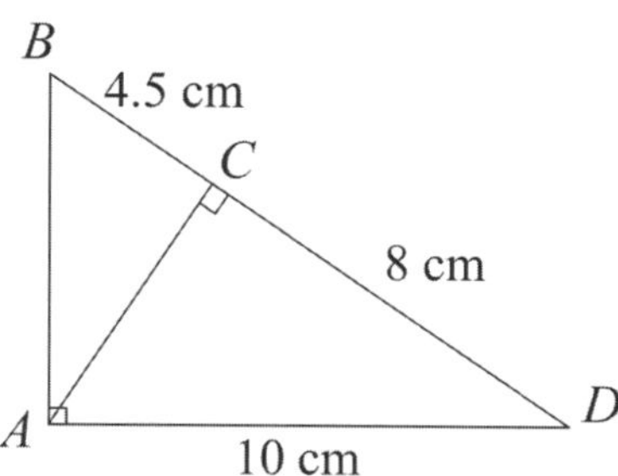

9.4 Applications of similar triangles

The similarity of triangles can be put to many uses. For example, once you have established that two triangles are similar, you can determine certain dimensions and angles of one triangle from the dimensions and angles of the other triangle.

Example

In the diagram below, $DE = 3\,\text{cm}$, $EF = 6\,\text{cm}$ and $EH = 2\,\text{cm}$. Prove that $\Delta DHE \sim \Delta DGF$ and hence determine the length of FG.

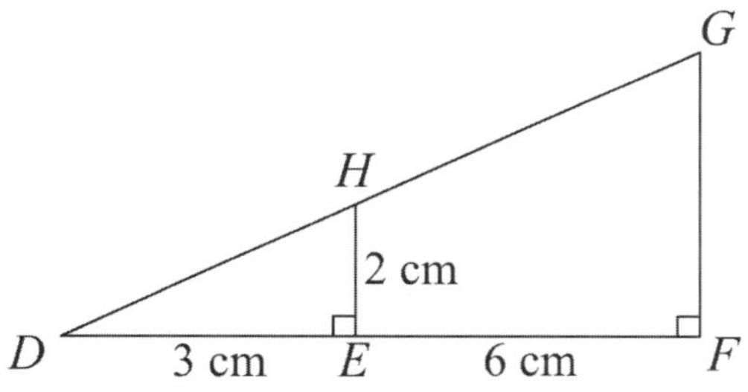

✓ *Solution*

Working	Explanation
RTP $\Delta DEH \sim \Delta DFG$	**1.** Write what is required to be proven. Always ensure that the vertices of the triangles are listed in corresponding order. Some measurements and one angle are given. Further, there is a common angle, since both triangles share vertex D. Hence the test to apply is AAA.
In ΔDEH and ΔDFG: • $\angle HED = \angle GFD = 90°$ (given) • $\angle HDE = \angle GDF$ (common angle) • $\angle DHE = \angle DGF$ (sum of the internal angles in a triangle $= 180°$)	**2.** Write out the statements and reasons.

$\Delta DEH \sim \Delta DFG$ (AAA)	**3.** Conclude that the two triangles are similar and state the test.
Since $\Delta DEH \sim \Delta DFG$: $\frac{DF}{DE} = \frac{9}{3} = 3$ $\frac{FG}{EH} = 3$ $\frac{FG}{2} = 3$ $FG = 6$ cm	**4.** Use the scale factor (ratio) to determine the length of FG.

Example

Gillian is 1.3 m tall and stands 7 m away from a tree, as shown in the diagram below. Her shadow is 1.8 m long. The top of the shadow cast by the tree is at the same point as the top of the head of Gillian's shadow.

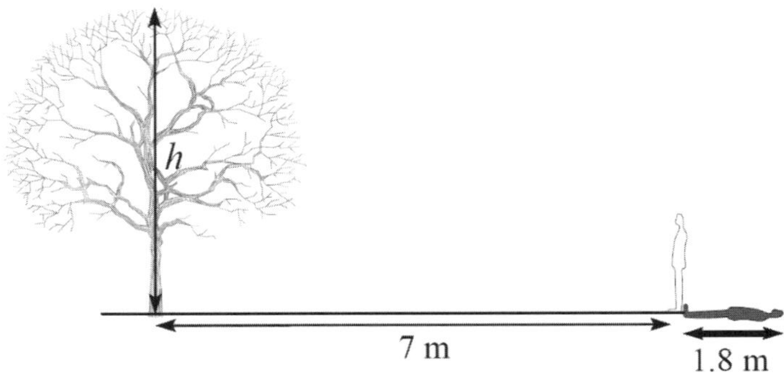

a. Draw a pair of triangles to represent this situation and prove that the triangles are similar.

b. Determine the height of the tree, h, to the nearest metre.

✓ *Solution*

Working	Explanation
a. D, h, B, 1.3 m, E, A, 7 m, C, 1.8 m	**1.** Draw the triangles. The height, h, is indicated on the diagram, and we know that it is one of the sides of a right-angled triangle. Gillian is standing 7 m away and casts a shadow of 1.8 m. We can therefore construct two triangles. **Note:** you can assume that the tree and Gillian are standing at 90° to the ground.
RTP $\Delta ABC \sim \Delta ADE$	**2.** Write what is required to be proven. Some measurements and one angle are given. Further, there is a common angle, since both triangles share vertex A. Hence, the test to apply is AAA.

In ΔABC and ΔADE: • $\angle CAB = \angle EAD$ (common) • $\angle BCA = \angle DEA = 90°$ (given) • $\angle ABC = \angle ADE$ (sum of the internal angles in a triangle $= 180°$)	**3.** Write out the statements and reasons.
$\therefore \Delta ABC \sim \Delta ADE$ (AAA)	**4.** Conclude that the two triangles are similar and state the test.
b. Since $\Delta ABC \sim \Delta ADE$: $\frac{AE}{AC} = \frac{7 + 1.8}{1.8} = \frac{8.8}{1.8} = 4.8\dot{8}$ Therefore $h = 4.8\dot{8} \times 1.3 = 6.3\dot{5}$ The height of the tree is 6 m.	Use the scale factor to determine the height of the tree to the nearest metre.

Exercise 9.4

a. An 8 m ladder is placed with its foot on horizontal ground and its top just reaching the top of a vertical wall of height 7 m. With the ladder remaining in contact with both the wall and the ground, the base of the ladder is pulled a further 1 m from the wall. How far does the top of the ladder move down the wall?

b. Liam and Lucy want to calculate the height of a large tree in their backyard. One mid-afternoon they measure the tree's shadow to be 7.6 m. At the same time, they place a 1.5 m stick vertically in the ground that gives an 84 cm shadow (as shown below). Calculate the height of the tree in metres, correct to two decimal places.

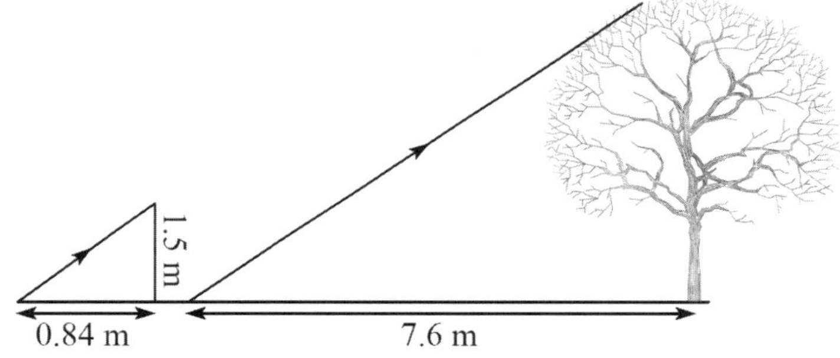

c. Luke wanted to know the height of his house walls so that he could order some paint. He placed a 4 m ladder on an angle so that it touched the top of the wall, as shown in the diagram below. The ladder has rungs every 50 cm (that is, the first rung is at 50 cm, the second at 1 m and so on). If Luke, who is 170 cm tall, stood directly under the ladder and his head came into contact with the fifth rung, determine:

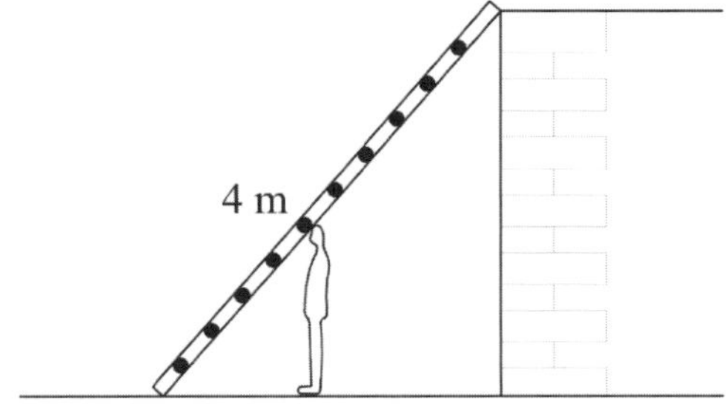

i. the length of the ladder where it touched Luke's head

ii. the height of Luke's walls, correct to two decimal places.

9.5 Congruency

Two objects are said to be congruent if they are identical: that is, they have the same shape and size. The following conditions must be met.

- Condition 1: corresponding sides are equal.
- Condition 2: corresponding angles are equal.

The symbol '≡' or '≅' denotes congruence.

Consider the following quadrilaterals. If we rotate and flip quadrilateral $ABCD$ and place it over quadrilateral $PQRS$, we will find that they match exactly.

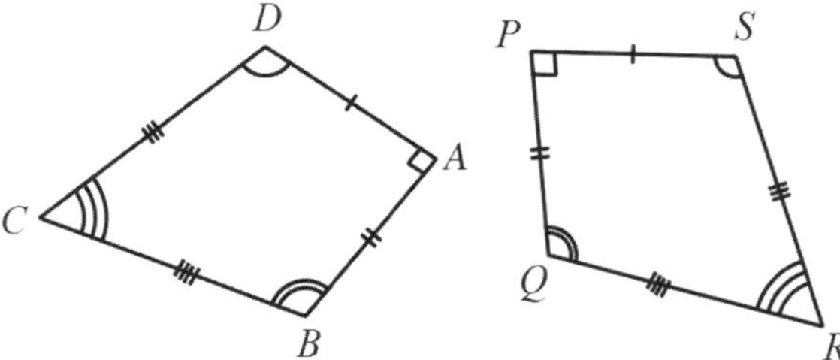

Corresponding sides are equal: $AB = PQ$, $AD = PS$, $CD = RS$, $BC = QR$. Therefore, condition 1 is met.

Corresponding angles are equal: $\angle ADC = \angle PSR$, $\angle DCB = \angle SRQ$, $\angle ABC = \angle PQR$ and $\angle DAB = \angle SPQ$. Therefore, condition 2 is met. Hence, $ABCD \equiv PQRS$.

Note: when comparing shapes, it is important that vertices are labelled in corresponding order.

Congruent triangles

There are four tests to determine if two triangles are congruent. They are explained in the following table.

Congruence test	Explanation	
Side, Side, Side (SSS)		In ΔABC and ΔPQR: • $AB = PQ = 4$ cm (given) • $AC = PR = 2$ cm (given) • $BC = QR = 7$ cm (given) $\therefore \Delta ABC \equiv \Delta PQR$ (SSS)
Side, Angle, Side (SAS)		In ΔABC and ΔDEF: • $\angle ABC = \angle DEF = 81°$ • $AB = DE = 4.8$ cm (given) • $BC = EF = 3$ cm (given) $\therefore \Delta ABC \equiv \Delta DEF$ (SAS)
	Note: for SAS, the angles that are equal must be between corresponding pairs of sides.	

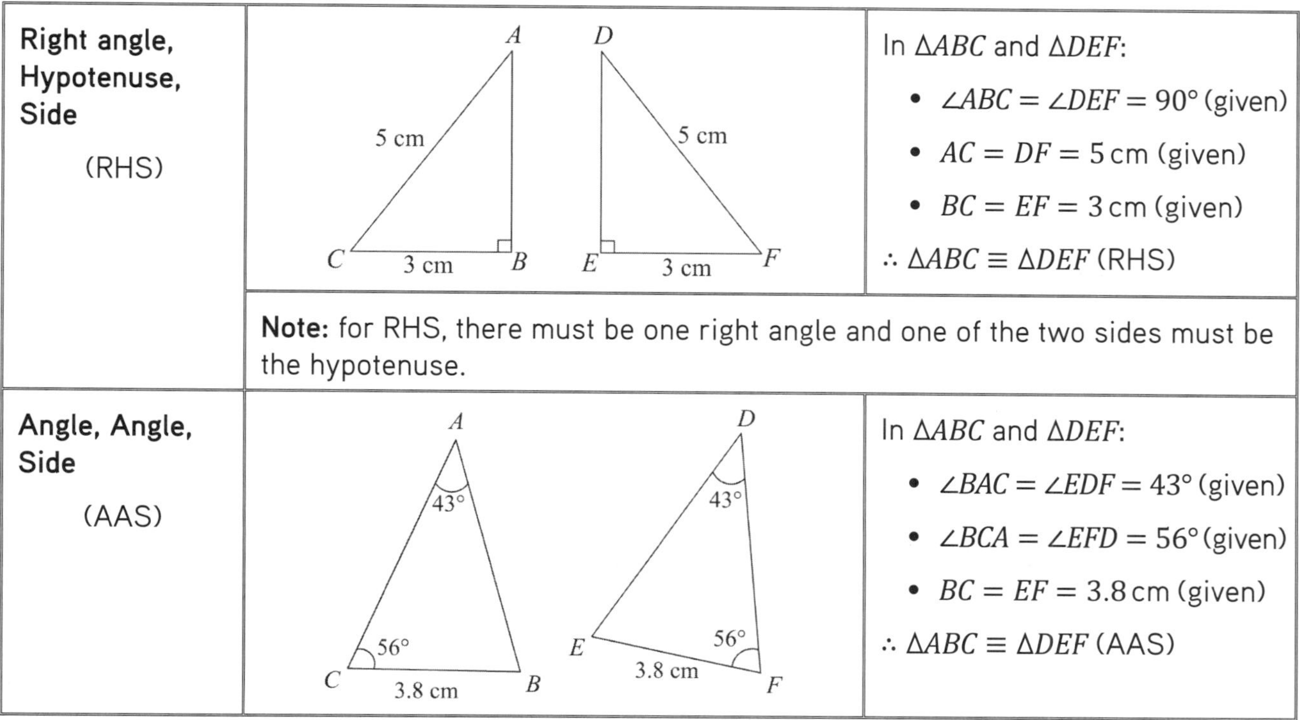

Right angle, Hypotenuse, Side (RHS)		In ΔABC and ΔDEF: • $\angle ABC = \angle DEF = 90°$ (given) • $AC = DF = 5$ cm (given) • $BC = EF = 3$ cm (given) $\therefore \Delta ABC \equiv \Delta DEF$ (RHS)
	Note: for RHS, there must be one right angle and one of the two sides must be the hypotenuse.	
Angle, Angle, Side (AAS)		In ΔABC and ΔDEF: • $\angle BAC = \angle EDF = 43°$ (given) • $\angle BCA = \angle EFD = 56°$ (given) • $BC = EF = 3.8$ cm (given) $\therefore \Delta ABC \equiv \Delta DEF$ (AAS)

You need to be able to write proofs and provide reasons why two triangles are congruent. Suppose you were asked to prove that the following triangles are similar.

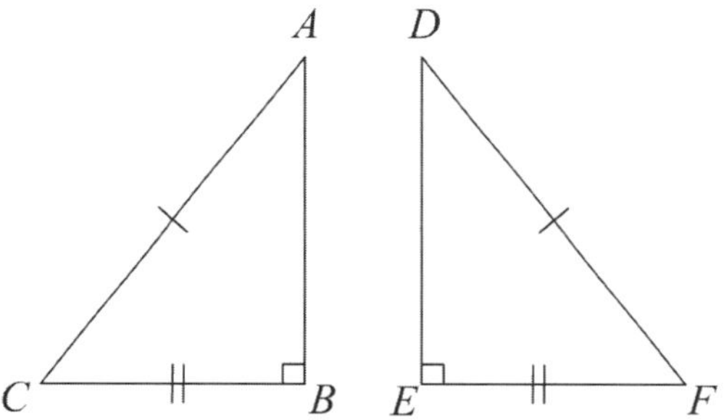

The table below gives the structure you should follow. Note that it is identical to the structure to be followed in proving that two triangles are similar.

Structure	What is required
Introduction: what needs to be proven?	Required to prove (RTP) $\Delta ABC \equiv \Delta DEF$
Statements and reasons	In ΔABC and ΔDEF: • $\angle ABC = \angle DEF = 90°$ (given) • $AC = DF$ (given) • $BC = EF$ (given)
Conclusion (and the test that was used)	$\therefore \Delta ABC \equiv \Delta DEF$ (RHS)

Example

Prove that the following triangles are congruent.

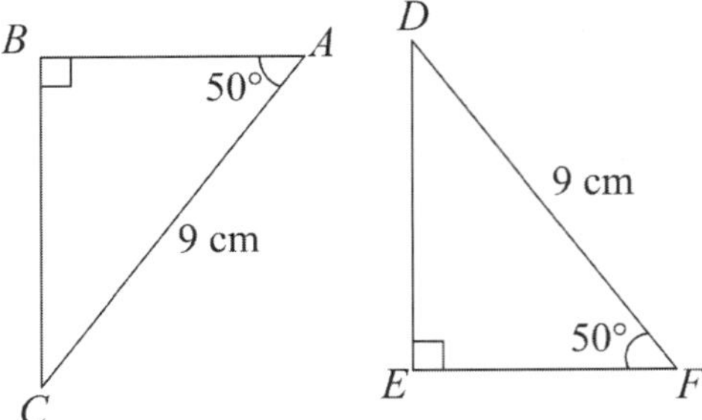

✓ ***Solution***

Working	Explanation
RTP $\Delta ABC \equiv \Delta FED$ In ΔABC and ΔFED: • $\angle ABC = \angle FED = 90°$ (given) • $\angle BAC = \angle EFD = 50°$ (given) • $AC = FD = 9$ cm (given) $\therefore \Delta ABC \equiv \Delta FED$ (AAS)	1. Write what is required to be proven. Always ensure that the vertices of the triangles are listed in corresponding order. 2. For each triangle, the information given is two angles and one side. The appropriate test is AAS. 3. Write out the statements and reasons. 4. Conclude that the two triangles are congruent and state the test.

Example

Prove that the following triangles are congruent.

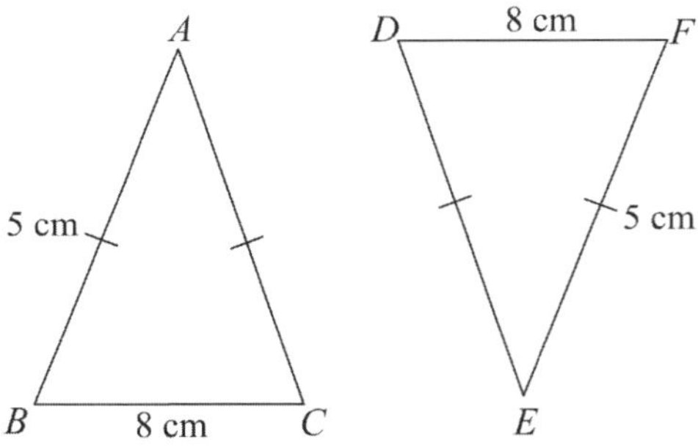

✓ ***Solution***

Working	Explanation
RTP $\Delta ABC \equiv \Delta EDF$ In ΔABC, $AB = AC = 5$ cm In ΔEDF, $EF = ED = 5$ cm In ΔABC and ΔEDF: • $AB = ED = 5$ cm (given) • $AC = EF = 5$ cm (given) • $BC = DF = 8$ cm (given) $\Delta ABC \equiv \Delta EDF$ (SSS)	1. Write what is required to be proven. 2. As per the equality notations, we know the length of AC given the length of AB, and the length of ED given the length of EF. 3. For each triangle, the information given is 3 sides. The appropriate test is SSS. 4. Write out the statements and reasons. 5. Conclude that the two triangles are congruent and state the test.

Example

Prove that the following triangles are congruent.

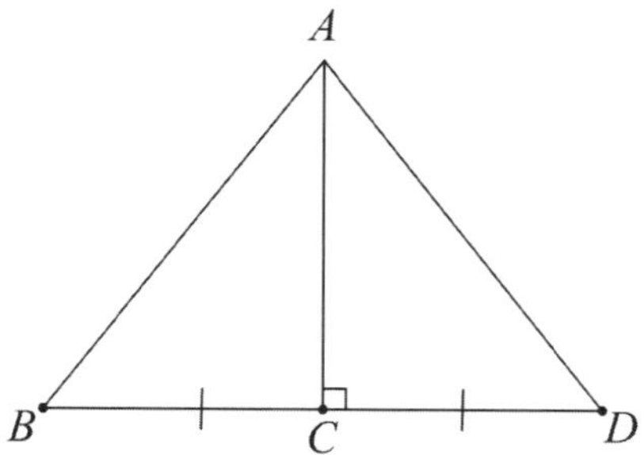

✓ ***Solution***

Working	Explanation
RTP $\Delta ABC \equiv \Delta ADC$ In ΔABC and ΔADC: • $AC = AC$ (common side of both triangles) • $\angle ACB = \angle ACD = 90°$ (supplementary angles) • $BC = DC$ (given) $\Delta ABC \equiv \Delta ADC$ (SAS)	**1.** Write what is required to be proven. **2.** For each triangle, the information provided is 2 sides and an angle. The appropriate test is SAS. **3.** Write out the statements and reasons. **4.** Conclude that the two triangles are congruent and state the test.

Exercise 9.5.1

a. Identify the pairs of congruent triangles from the triangles below.

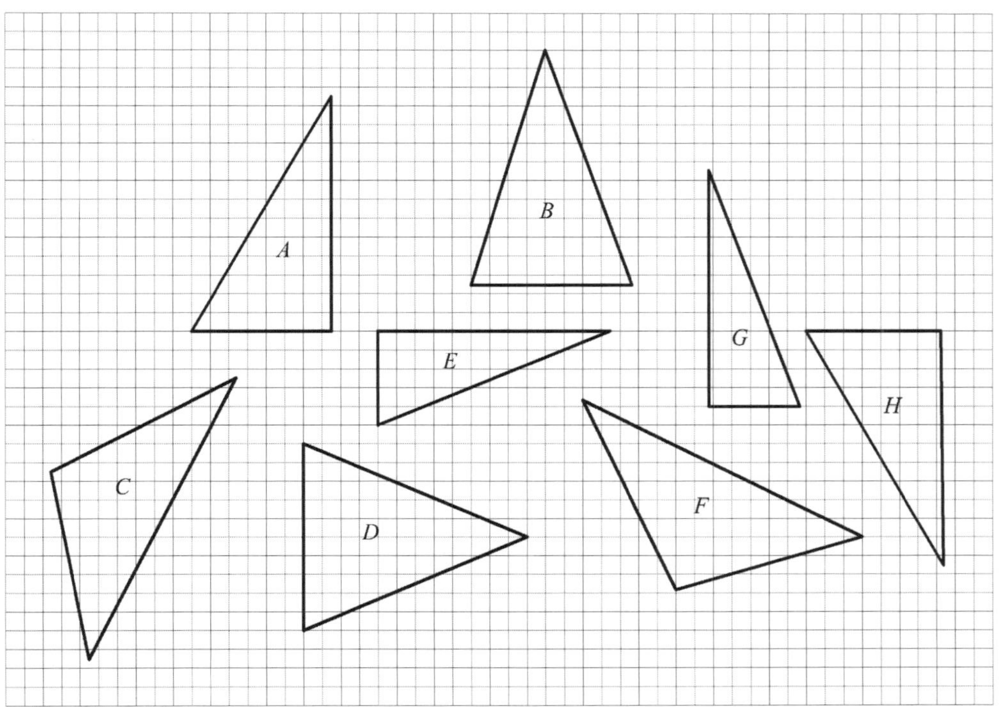

b. Prove that the following pairs of triangles are congruent.

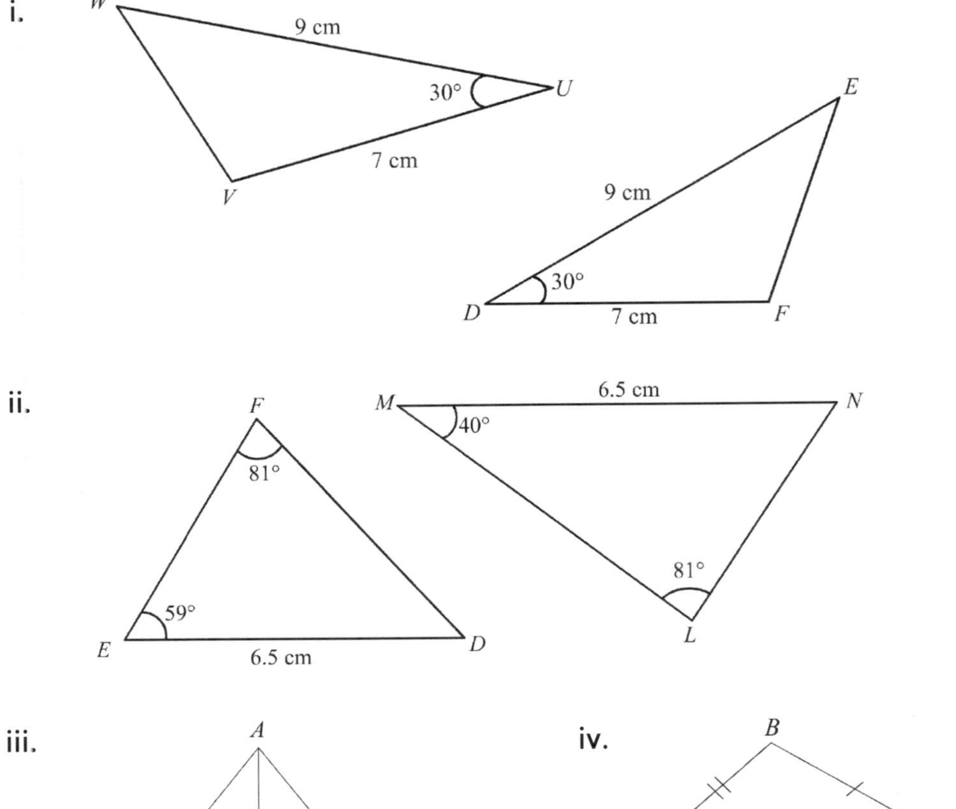

Applications of congruency

Congruent triangles are widely used in construction, engineering and manufacturing to ensure the accurate assembly of structures and components. Once you have established that two triangles are congruent, you can determine certain dimensions and angles of one triangle from the dimensions and angles of the other triangle.

Example

Prove that $\Delta ABC \equiv \Delta ADC$ and hence determine the value of x.

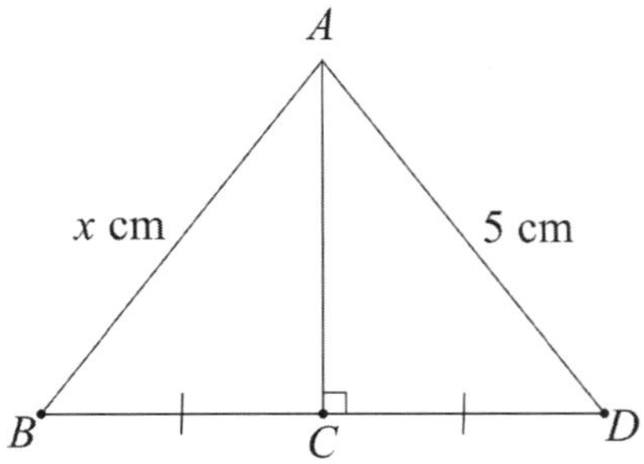

✓ *Solution*

Working	Explanation
RTP $\Delta ABC \equiv \Delta ADC$ In ΔABC and ΔADC: • $AC = AC$ (common side of both triangles) • $\angle ACB = \angle ACD = 90°$ (supplementary angles) • $BC = DC$ (given) $\therefore \Delta ABC \equiv \Delta ADC$ (SAS) $AB = AD$ (corresponding sides in congruent triangles) $\therefore x = 5$ cm	1. Write what is required to be proven. 2. For each triangle, the information given is two sides and an angle. The appropriate test is SAS. 3. Write out the statements and reasons. 4. Conclude that the two triangles are congruent and state the test. 5. Since corresponding sides in congruent triangles are equal, determine x.

Example

Prove that $\Delta ABC \equiv \Delta EDC$ and hence prove that AB is parallel to DE.

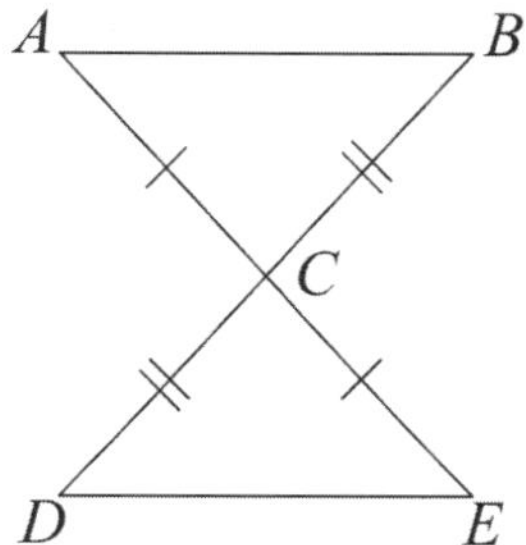

✓ *Solution*

Working	Explanation
RTP $\Delta ABC \equiv \Delta EDC$ In ΔABC and ΔEDC: • $AC = EC$ (given) • $\angle ACB = \angle ECD$ (vertically opposite angles) • $BC = DC$ (given) $\therefore \Delta ABC \equiv \Delta EDC$ (SAS) $\angle BAC = \angle DEC$ (corresponding angles in congruent triangles) $\therefore AB \parallel DE$ (alternate angles in parallel lines are equal)	1. Write what is required to be proven. 2. For each triangle, the information given is two sides and there is one pair of equal corresponding angles. The appropriate test is SAS. 3. Write out the statements and reasons. 4. Conclude that the two triangles are congruent and state the test. 5. Note that corresponding angles in congruent triangles are equal. 6. Since alternate angles are equal then AB and DE must be parallel.

Exercise 9.5.2

a. In each diagram below, prove that the two triangles are congruent and hence determine the value of x.

i.

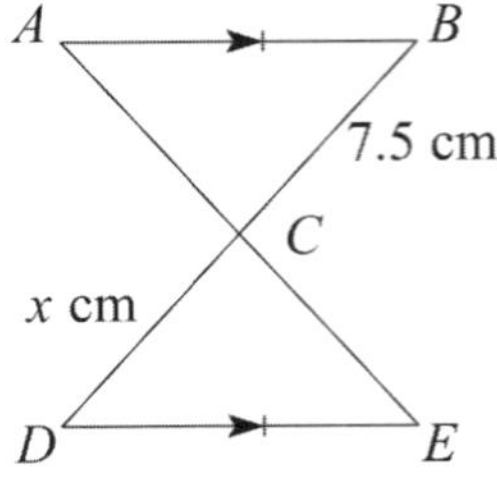

ii.

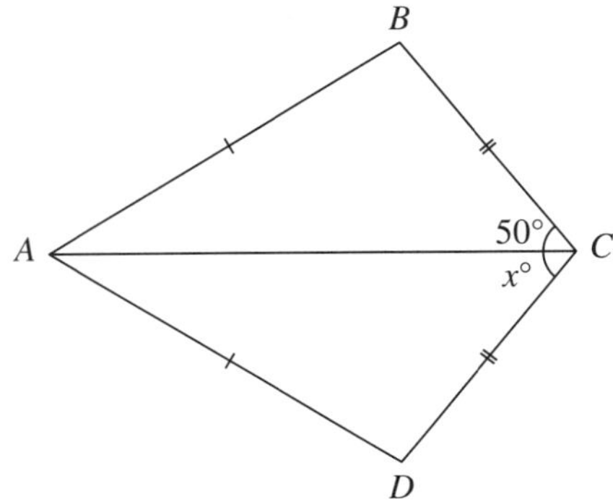

b. Prove that $\Delta ABD \equiv \Delta CDB$ and hence prove that AD is parallel to BC.

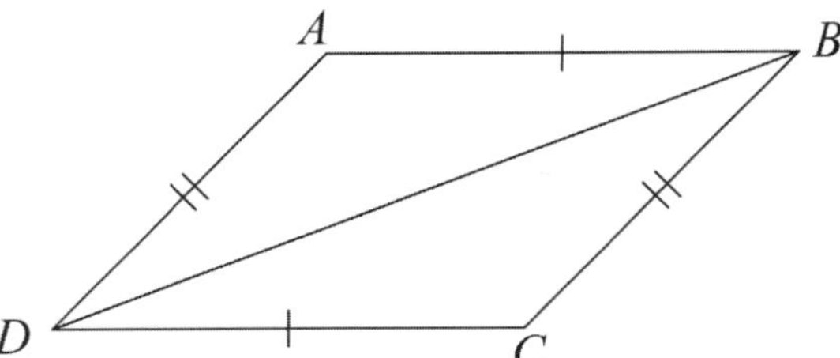

c. Prove that $\Delta ABC \equiv \Delta ADC$ and hence prove that AC bisects $\angle BAD$. (**Note:** 'bisect' means to divide into two equal parts.)

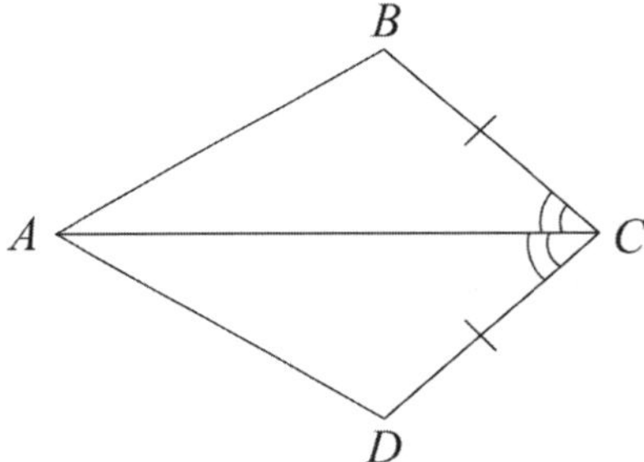

d. Prove that $\Delta ABC \equiv \Delta ADC$ and hence prove that ΔABD is an isosceles triangle.

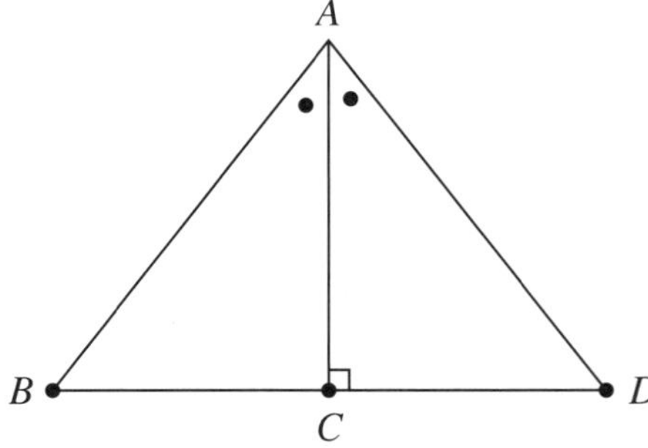

Chapter 10 – Probability

10.1 Review of probability

Probability is the branch of mathematics that deals with the occurrence of random events. The probability of a random event is between 0 and 1 (inclusive). A probability of 0 means that the event is impossible, while a probability of 1 means that the event is certain to happen.

For example, if we have a regular six-sided die, we can never roll a 7 with it. Hence the probability of rolling a 7 on a regular die is 0. Tossing a coin will give us an even chance (that is, a probability of 0.5) of getting a head (or a tail). We know for certain that the sun will set every day and so the probability of the sun setting today is 1.

Key terms

probability	the likelihood of a particular event occurring, e.g. the probability of rolling a 6 with a regular six-sided die is $\frac{1}{6}$
experiment (or **trial**)	a situation involving chance or probability that leads to one or more outcomes, e.g. rolling a die
outcome	the result of a single trial of an experiment, e.g. the occurrence of a 6 appearing on a die
event	one or more outcomes of an experiment
sample space	the set of all possible outcomes of an experiment, e.g. the sample space when rolling a six-sided die is $\{1, 2, 3, 4, 5, 6\}$

The probability of an event occurring is defined as

$$\textbf{\textit{Pr(event)}} = \frac{\textbf{\textit{number of possible outcomes}}}{\textbf{\textit{total number of outcomes}}}$$

$$0 \le \textbf{\textit{Pr(event)}} \le 1$$

Venn diagram and set notation

The **sample space** is the total number of outcomes. It is also called the **universal set**, U. In the context of rolling a regular six-sided die, the sample space can be written in set notation as

$$U = \{1, 2, 3, 4, 5, 6\}$$

This can be represented in a diagram, as shown on the right.

We know that there are 6 possible outcomes, and we can use the following notation to indicate this.

$$n(U) = 6$$

U 5 4
1 2 6
3

Consider the trial of rolling a regular six-sided die. Let:

- A be the event of rolling an even number
- B be the event of rolling a prime number.

The various outcomes can be represented by a Venn diagram and in set notation, as the following table shows.

Situation	Venn diagram	Set notation
A only	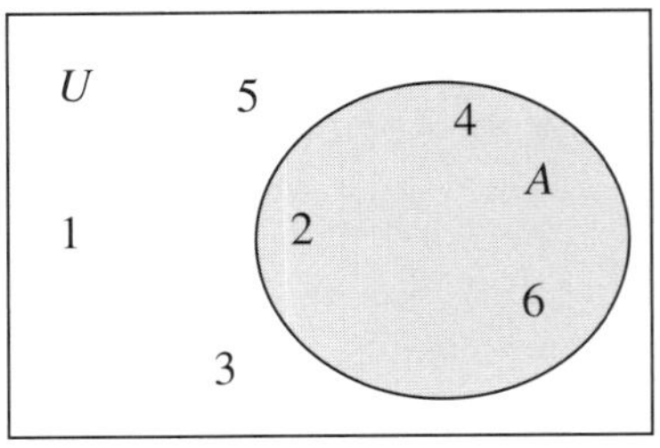	$A = \{2, 4, 6\}$
B only	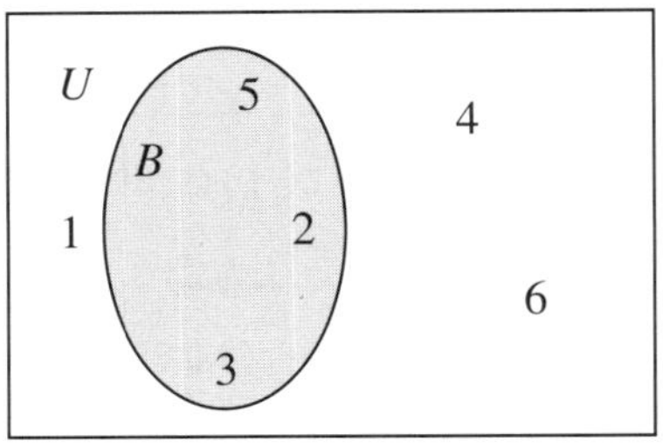	$B = \{2, 3, 5\}$
A AND B (intersection)	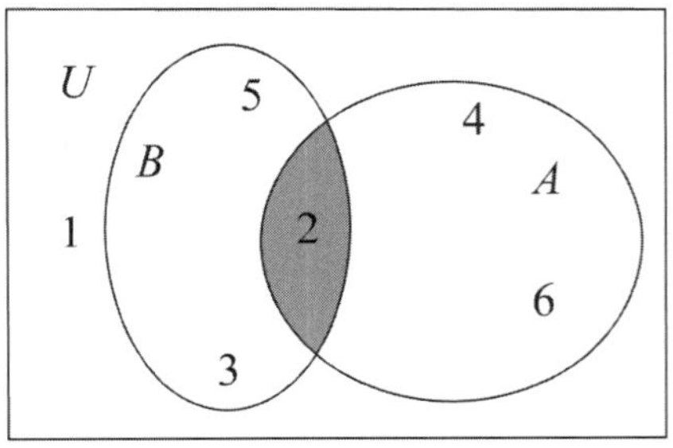	$A \cap B = \{2\}$
A OR B (union)	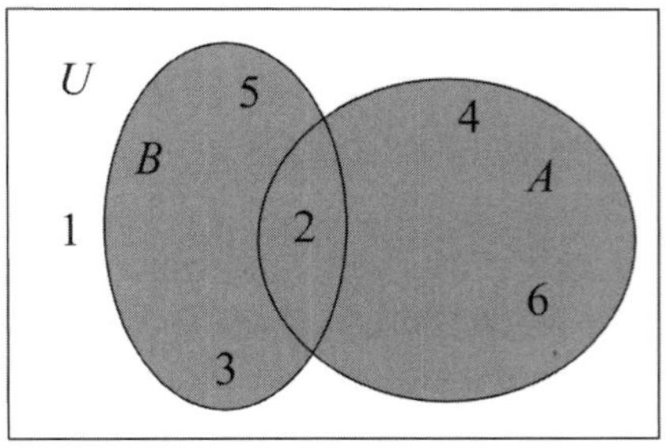	$A \cup B = \{2, 3, 4, 5, 6\}$
NOT A (complement)	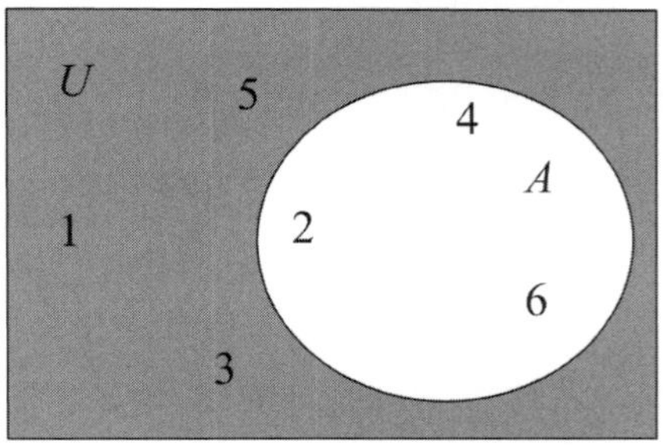	$A' = \bar{A} = A^{c} = \{1, 3, 5\}$

Let C be the event that an odd number occurs, that is, $C = \{1, 3, 5\}$. The Venn diagram showing both A and C is shown to the right.

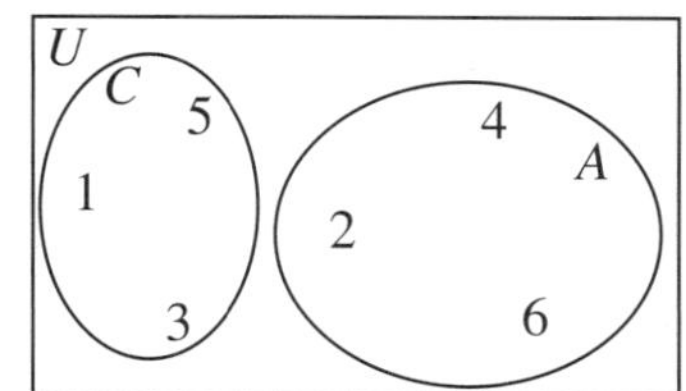

Note that these two events have nothing in common. We can write their intersection as

$$A \cap C = \{\,\} \text{ or } A \cap C = \emptyset$$

The signs $\{\,\}$ and $\emptyset$ are signs for the **null set**.

Events that have no common elements are called **mutually exclusive** events.

You shade various areas (or regions) of a Venn diagram to indicate the relationship between the sets being compared. Some examples of shading are shown below.

$A \cap B$	$A \cup B$
Shading = the area that is common to both A and B, i.e. their intersection.	Shading = A and B, including their intersection.
A	A'
Shading = all of A, including the intersection of A and B.	Shading = the area that is the complement of A, i.e. not A.
$A \cap B'$	$A \cup B'$
Shading = all of A except the intersection of A and B.	Shading = everything that is not just B, including the intersection of A and B.

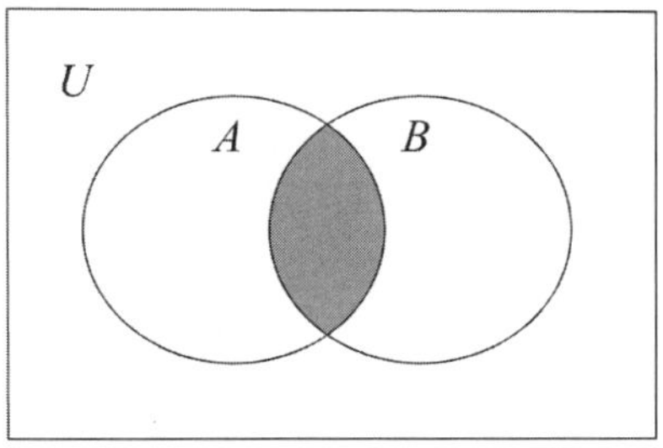

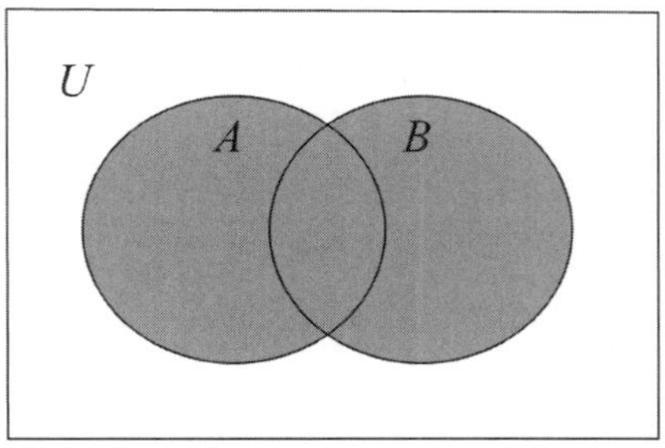

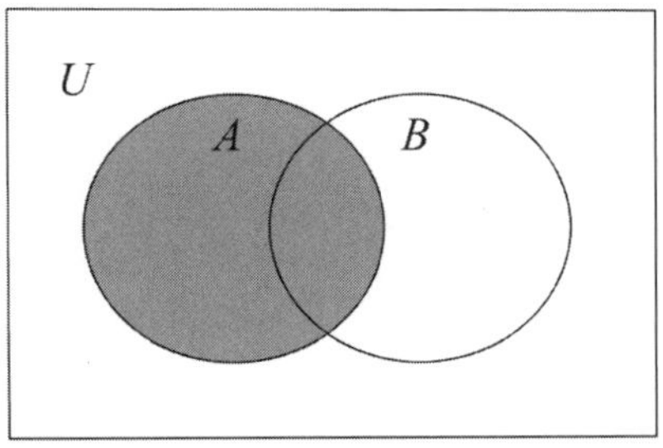

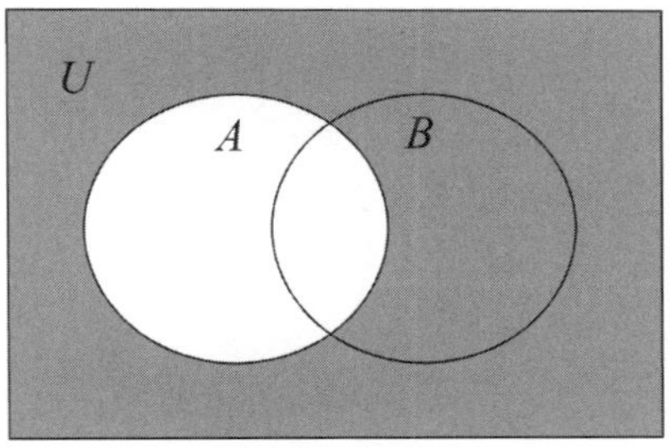

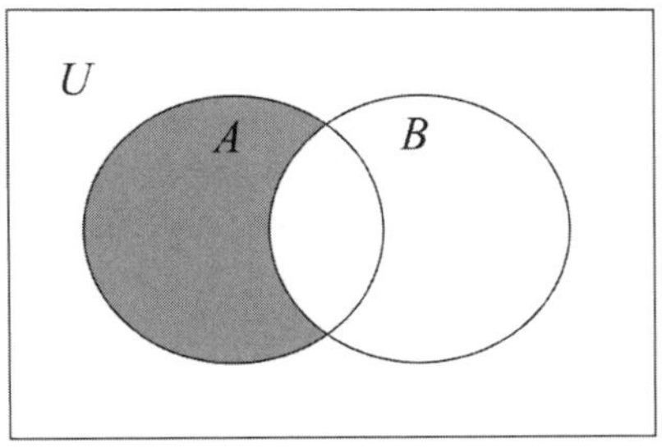

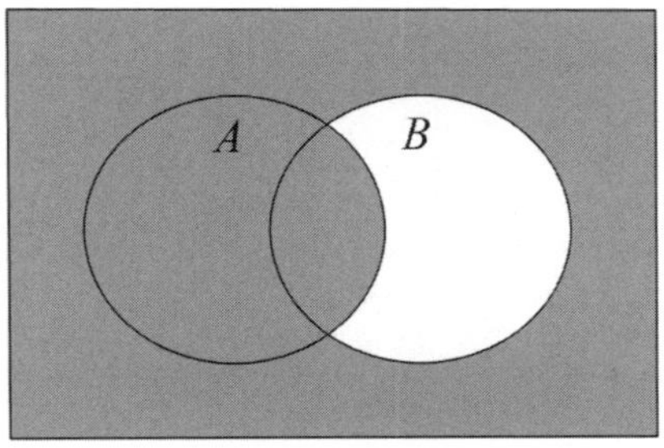

$(A \cap B)'$ or $A' \cup B'$	$(A \cup B)'$ or $A' \cap B'$
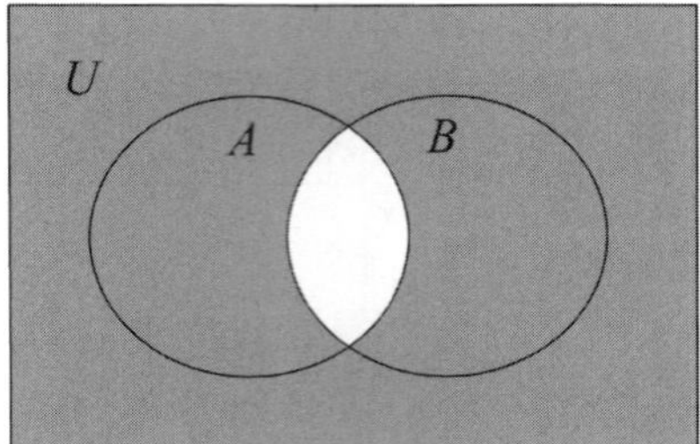	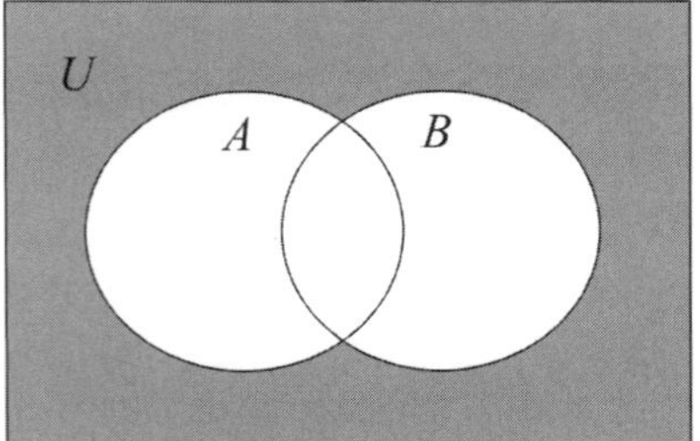
Shading = the complement of $A \cap B$, i.e. everything that is not A and everything that is not B.	Shading = the complement of $A \cup B$, i.e. everything that is not A and not B.

Example

Suppose that A is the set of factors of 12 and B is the set of prime numbers less than 10. If a number is chosen at random from the integers from 1 to 20, draw a Venn diagram and use it to determine the following probabilities.

a. $\Pr(A)$ **b.** $\Pr(B)$ **c.** $\Pr(A \cap B)$ **d.** $\Pr(A \cup B)$

✓ *Solution*

Working	Explanation
U=20 A: 1, 4, 6, 12 $A \cap B$: 2, 3 B: 5, 7 8, 9, 10, 11, 12, 13, 14, 15, 16, 17, 18, 19, 20	List the items in A and B: $A = \{1, 2, 3, 4, 6, 12\}$ $B = \{2, 3, 5, 7\}$
a. $\Pr(A) = \frac{6}{20} = \frac{3}{10}$ **b.** $\Pr(B) = \frac{4}{20} = \frac{1}{5}$ **c.** $\Pr(A \cap B) = \frac{2}{20} = \frac{1}{10}$ **d.** $\frac{\Pr(A \cup B)}{20} = \frac{8}{20} = \frac{2}{5}$	Count the items belonging to each set and express the number as a fraction of 20. Simplify your answer.

Example

In a survey of 100 university students, a market research company found that 70 students owned a smartphone, 45 owned a car and 35 owned both a smartphone and a car.

a. Draw a Venn diagram to represent the results of the survey.

b. If a student from the group surveyed is chosen at random, determine the probability that the student owns:

i. neither a car nor a smartphone

ii. either a car or a smartphone, but not both.

✓ Solution

Working	Explanation
a. U=100; A smartphones; B cars; 70; x; 35; y; 45; z $n(A \text{ only}) = x = 70 - 35 = 35$ $n(B \text{ only}) = y = 45 - 35 = 10$ $n(\text{neither } A \text{ or } B) = z$ $= 100 - 35 - 35 - 10$ $= 20$	1. Define the two events. • Let A be the set of students who owned smart phones. • Let B be the set of students who owned cars. 2. Represent the given information in a Venn diagram. 3. Assign a pronumeral to represent each unknown, then calculate its value.
b. i. $\Pr(\text{neither } A \text{ nor } B) = \frac{20}{100} = \frac{1}{5}$ ii. $\Pr(\text{either } A \text{ or } B \text{ but not both}) = \frac{35 + 10}{100}$ $= \frac{45}{100} = \frac{9}{20}$	• As $n(A) = 70$, $n(A \text{ only}) = 35$ • As $n(B) = 45$, $n(B \text{ only}) = 10$ The number of students who own neither a smartphone nor a car is found by subtracting those who own a smartphone, a car or both from the number of students surveyed. Use the values in the Venn diagram to calculate these probabilities.

Exercise 10.1.1

a. Suppose that a number is randomly drawn from the set of the first 10 positive integers. Suppose further that $A = \{1, 2, 3, 4\}$ and $B = \{2, 4, 6\}$. Draw a Venn diagram and use it to determine the probability of the following events.

i. $\Pr(\text{neither } A \text{ nor } B)$ ii. $\Pr(A \cap B)$ iii. $\Pr(B')$

b. Suppose that a number is randomly drawn from the set of the first 12 positive integers. Suppose further that A is the set of even numbers and B is the set of multiples of three. Draw a Venn diagram and use it to determine the probability of the following events.

i. Pr(neither A nor B) **ii.** $\Pr(A)$ **iii.** $\Pr(B)$ **iv.** $\Pr(A \cap B)$

c. A group of eighty students commenced a university course together. Of these students, 42 studied physics in their last year at school and 46 studied chemistry. If 25 students studied both subjects, determine the probability that a student randomly selected from the group studied neither subject.

Two-way tables

The information in a Venn diagram can also be represented in a **two-way table**. The general form of a two-way table is shown below.

	A	A'	**Total**
B	$n(A \cap B)$	$n(B \text{ only}) = n(A' \cap B)$	$n(B)$
B'	$n(A \text{ only}) = n(A \cap B')$	$n(\text{neither } A \text{ nor } B) = n(A' \cap B')$	$n(B')$
Total	$n(A)$	$n(A')$	$n(U)$

To illustrate how a two-way table can represent sets, consider the following situation. Ms Chong, the mathematics teacher, surveyed her class of 30 students. She found that 16 students had a cat (C) as their pet and 19 students had a dog (D). She also found that 11 students had both a dog and a cat.

We can represent this information in a Venn diagram.

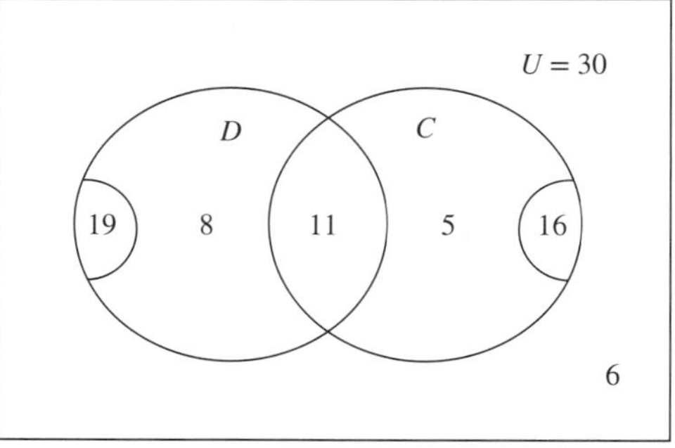

We can also represent the information in a two-way table.

	D	D'	**Total**
C	11	5	16
C'	8	6	14
Total	19	11	30

If we put the Venn diagram and the two-way table side by side, we can easily see how they are related:

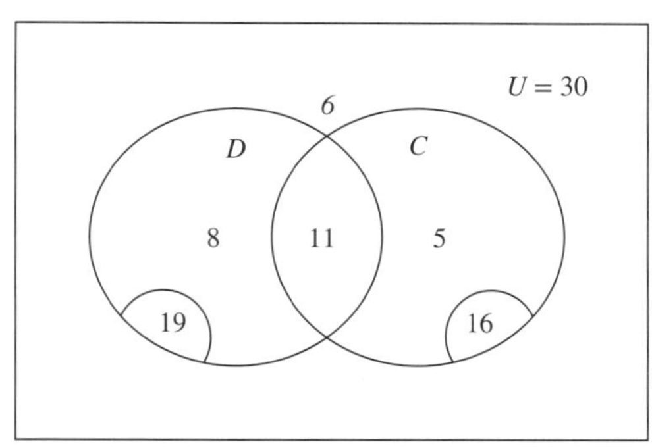

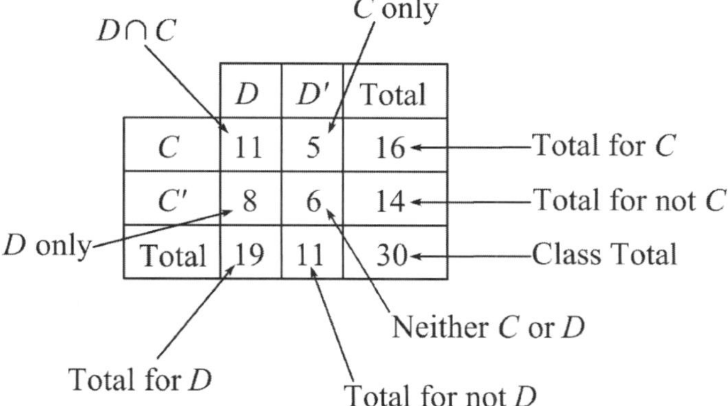

Example

A supermarket offers free apples and bananas to children. On a particular day, 180 children went to the supermarket. Of the 180 children, 102 took an apple (A), 89 took a banana (B) and 30 took both.

a. Display this information in a two-way table.

b. Determine the number of children who did not take any fruit.

c. What is the probability that a child selected at random took a banana but not an apple?

✓ Solution

Working	Explanation
a.	Construct a two-way table, filling in the cells with the information provided.
b. The number of children who took neither is 19.	The number of children who took neither an apple nor a banana can be determined from the table. This situation is represented by $A' \cap B'$.
c. Pr(banana only) $= \frac{59}{180}$	The number of children who took only a banana is 59. This is represented by $A' \cap B$. Therefore the probability of randomly selecting a child who took only a banana is 59 out of the total number of children.

Table for part a:

	A	A'	**Total**
B	30	59	89
B'	72	19	91
Total	102	78	180

Example

The Venn diagram below shows the distribution of elements in two sets, A and B.

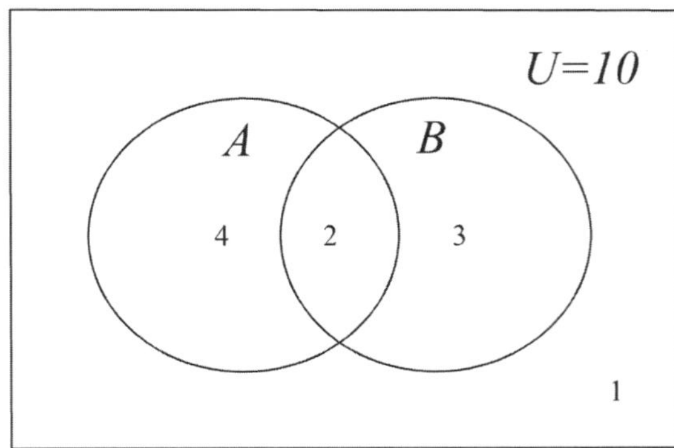

a. Create a two-way table representing the Venn diagram above.

b. Determine $\Pr(A \cap B)$, $\Pr(A')$ and $\Pr(A \cup B)$.

✓ Solution

<table>
<tr><th>Working</th><th>Explanation</th></tr>
<tr><td>a.
<table><tr><td></td><td>A</td><td>A'</td><td>Total</td></tr><tr><td>B</td><td>2</td><td>3</td><td>5</td></tr><tr><td>B'</td><td>4</td><td>1</td><td>5</td></tr><tr><td>Total</td><td>6</td><td>4</td><td>10</td></tr></table></td><td>Transfer the information from the Venn diagram to the two-way table. If necessary, use the table at the start of this section as a guide.</td></tr>
<tr><td>b. $\Pr(A \cap B) = \frac{2}{10} = \frac{1}{5}$
$\Pr(A') = \frac{4}{10} = \frac{2}{5}$
$\Pr(A \cup B) = \frac{2 + 3 + 4}{10} = \frac{9}{10}$</td><td>When calculating probabilities, divide the number of elements that match the event by the total number of elements in the sample space.</td></tr>
</table>

Exercise 10.1.2

a. Customers can order a burger (B), chips (C) or both from the local café. On one particular day, 88 customers ordered both burgers and chips, 3 ordered chips only, 9 ordered a burger only and 25 customers did not order either a burger or chips.

- **i.** Represent this information in a two-way table.
- **ii.** How many customers did the café have that day?
- **iii.** If a customer is chosen at random, what is the probability that the customer ordered a burger?

b. The Venn diagram below shows the distribution of elements in two sets A and B.

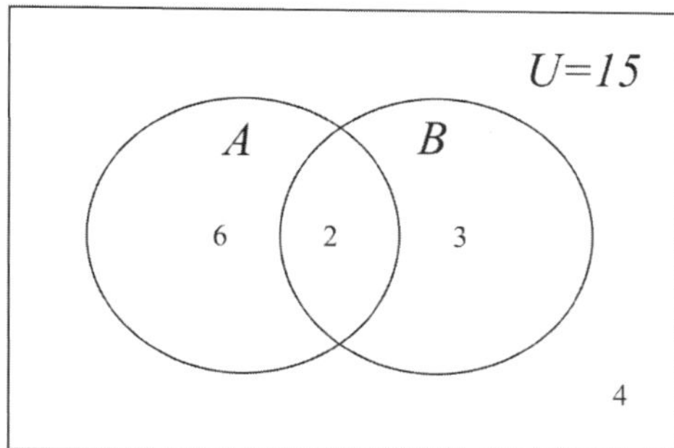

i. Transfer the information in the Venn diagram to a two-way table.

ii. Determine $\Pr(A' \cap B')$, $\Pr(B)$ and $\Pr(A \cup B)$.

c. A group of 16 chefs all enjoy baking cakes and/or pastries. Of the group, 10 chefs enjoy baking cakes and 8 chefs enjoy baking pastries. Construct a two-way table and determine the probability that a chef enjoys baking both cakes and pastries.

10.2 Complement probability and the addition rule

Complement probability

The complement probability of an event is the probability of the event not occurring.

For event A, the complement of A, denoted as A', represents all outcomes that are not in A. The complement probability of A, denoted as $\Pr(A')$, is calculated as

$$\Pr(A') = 1 - \Pr(A)$$

For example, if the probability that it will rain tomorrow is 0.3 (30%), then the complement probability (that is, the probability of it not raining) is 0.7 (70%).

Addition rule

The addition rule in probability allows us to calculate the probability of the union of two events.

If two events, A and B, are not mutually exclusive (that is, they can both occur at the same time), then the probability of either event occurring is the sum of their individual probabilities minus the probability that both events occur simultaneously. (We need to subtract the probability of both events occurring to avoid double counting.)

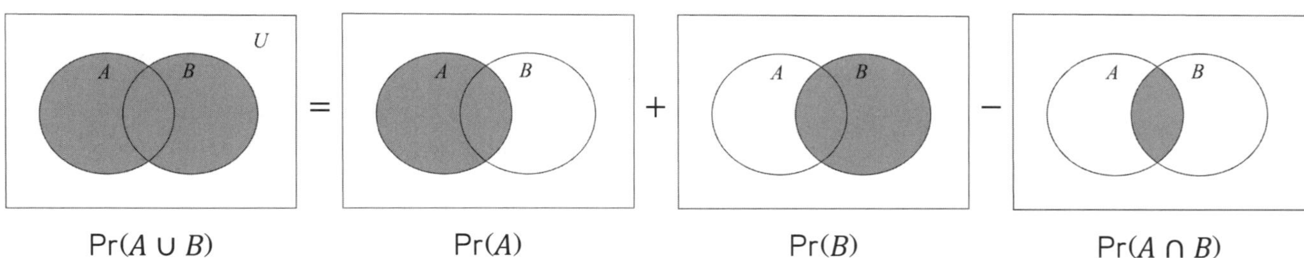

Therefore, the addition rule is

$$\Pr(A \cup B) = \Pr(A) + \Pr(B) - \Pr(A \cap B)$$

The addition rule takes a special form with mutually exclusive events. Two events, A and B, are mutually exclusive (or disjoint) if both events cannot happen at the same time. An example is drawing an even number and an odd number in the one event.

Since both events cannot happen at the same time, $\Pr(A \cap B) = 0$. Therefore, the addition rule for mutually exclusive events is

$$\Pr(A \cup B) = \Pr(A) + \Pr(B)$$

Example

A class of 30 students is surveyed about the type of phone they own. Of the 30 students, 19 own an Android phone, while the others own an iPhone. Determine the probability of randomly selecting a student who owns an Android and hence determine the probability of randomly selecting a student who owns an iPhone.

✓ Solution

Working	Explanation
Let A = the set of students who own an Android phone $\Pr(A) = \frac{19}{30}$ $\Pr(A') = 1 - \frac{19}{30} = \frac{11}{30}$	Define the set of interest. 19 students out of 30 own an Android. The complement of owning an Android is owning an iPhone.

Example

A standard die is rolled. Find the probability of each of the following events.

a. rolling a 2 or a 5

b. rolling an odd number or a number greater than 3

✓ Solution

Working	Explanation
a. Let A = rolling a 2 Let B = rolling a 5 $\Pr(A) = \frac{1}{6}$ $\Pr(B) = \frac{1}{6}$ $\Pr(A \cup B) = \Pr(A) + \Pr(B)$ $= \frac{1}{6} + \frac{1}{6}$ $= \frac{2}{6} = \frac{1}{3}$	**1.** Define the events. **2.** Determine the probability of each event. The events are mutually exclusive, therefore $\Pr(A \cap B) = 0$. **3.** Use the addition rule for mutually exclusive events to determine the probability of either event occurring.

b. Let A = rolling an odd number $= \{1, 3, 5\}$ Let B = rolling a number greater than 3 $= \{4, 5, 6\}$	**1.** Define the events.
$\Pr(A) = \frac{1}{2}$ $\Pr(B) = \frac{1}{2}$	**2.** Determine the probability of each event.
$A \cap B = \{5\}$ $\Pr(A \cap B) = \frac{1}{6}$	**3.** Determine the probability of the intersection of the events.
$\Pr(A \cup B) = \Pr(A) + \Pr(B) - \Pr(A \cap B)$ $= \frac{1}{2} + \frac{1}{2} - \frac{1}{6}$ $= \frac{5}{6}$	**4.** Use the addition rule to determine the probability.

Example

If $\Pr(A) = \frac{1}{6}$, $\Pr(B) = \frac{1}{3}$ and $\Pr(A \cup B) = \frac{5}{18}$, determine $\Pr(A \cap B)$.

✓ ***Solution***

Working	Explanation
$\Pr(A \cup B) = \Pr(A) + \Pr(B) - \Pr(A \cap B)$ $\frac{5}{18} = \frac{1}{6} + \frac{1}{3} - \Pr(A \cap B)$ $\frac{5}{18} = \frac{1}{2} - \Pr(A \cap B)$ $\Pr(A \cap B) = \frac{1}{2} - \frac{5}{18}$ $= \frac{4}{18}$ $= \frac{2}{9}$	**1.** Substitute $\Pr(A)$, $\Pr(B)$ and $\Pr(A \cup B)$ into the addition rule. **2.** Simplify and solve for $\Pr(A \cap B)$.

Exercise 10.2

a. In a survey of 500 people, 60% said they preferred tea over coffee. What is the probability that a randomly chosen person does not prefer tea?

b. In a class of 30 students, 20 study mathematics and 15 study physics. If 8 students study both mathematics and physics, what is the probability that a randomly selected student studies either mathematics or physics?

c. In a bag there are 10 balls numbered 1 to 10. A ball is drawn at random.

  i. What is the probability that the number drawn is either a prime number or an even number?

  ii. What is the probability that the number drawn is either an odd number or divisible by 4?

d. Suppose that $\Pr(A) = \frac{3}{8}$ and $\Pr(B) = \frac{1}{2}$.

  i. Determine $\Pr(A \cup B)$ if $\Pr(A \cap B) = \frac{1}{4}$.

  ii. Determine $\Pr(A \cap B)$ if $\Pr(A \cup B) = \frac{3}{4}$.

  iii. Determine $\Pr(A' \cap B')$ if $\Pr(A \cap B) = \frac{1}{8}$.

10.3 Conditional probability

Conditional probability is the probability of an event occurring given that another event has already occurred. It applies in situations where a prior condition reduces the number of possibilities for an event to occur.

The conditional probability of event A given event B is denoted as $\Pr(A|B)$. The formula is

$$Pr(A|B) = \frac{Pr(A \cap B)}{Pr(B)}$$

Similarly, the conditional probability of event B given event A is denoted as $\Pr(B|A)$. The formula is

$$Pr(B|A) = \frac{Pr(A \cap B)}{Pr(A)}$$

Example

A group of 200 university students was surveyed. It was found that 42 only studied physics, 25 only studied chemistry and 8 study both. Draw a Venn diagram to illustrate this information and hence determine the probability that a student studies physics given that they also study chemistry.

✓ *Solution*

Working	Explanation
$U=200$; P: 42; $P \cap C$: 8; C: 25; outside: 125 Pr(study physics given study chemistry) $= \frac{8}{25+8}$ $= \frac{8}{33}$	Represent the given information in a Venn diagram. Given that the prior condition is that the student studies chemistry, we are only interested in the shaded region $(25 + 8 = 33)$. Of the 33 chemistry students, 8 also study physics.

Example

A bag contains black and blue balls. Some of the balls have A marked on them while others have B marked on them. The number of each type is given in the table below.

	Black	Blue	**Total**
Marked A	50	27	77
Marked B	22	13	35
Total	72	40	112

A ball is randomly taken out of the bag. Determine the probability that

a. it is marked A given that it is a blue ball

b. it is a blue ball given that it is marked B.

✓ ***Solution***

Working	Explanation
a. $\Pr(A\vert\text{Blue}) = \dfrac{n(A \cap \text{Blue})}{n(\text{Blue})} = \dfrac{27}{40}$	$n(\text{Blue}) = 40$ and $n(A \cap \text{Blue}) = 27$ Substitute these values into the conditional probability formula.
b. $\Pr(\text{Blue}\vert B) = \dfrac{n(B \cap \text{Blue})}{n(B)} = \dfrac{13}{35}$	$n(B) = 35$ and $n(\text{Blue} \cap B) = 13$ Substitute these values into the conditional probability formula.

Exercise 10.3

a. In a survey of 200 students, 120 liked pizza, 80 liked burgers and 50 liked both pizza and burgers. If a student is selected at random from the survey group, determine the probability that the student likes pizza given that they like burgers. (Use a Venn diagram as a guide.)

b. In a group of 150 employees, 90 are managers, 60 are engineers and 30 are both managers and engineers. If an employee is chosen at random, what is the probability that the employee is an engineer given that they are a manager? (Use a Venn diagram as a guide.)

c. A survey of students was conducted to determine whether they like maths, science or both. The results are partially summarised in the two-way table below. Complete the table and use it to determine the probability that a randomly selected student does not like maths given that they like science.

	Likes maths	Does not like maths	**Total**
Likes science	50		
Does not like science		10	
Total	70		100

d. A company surveyed its employees to determine their preferences for two types of training programs: online and in-person. The results are partially summarised in the two-way table below. Complete the table and use it to determine the probability that a randomly selected employee is under 30 years of age given that they prefer in-person training.

	Prefers online	Prefers in-person	**Total**
Under 30 years of age		40	
30 years of age or older	30		80
Total			200

10.4 Multi-stage experiments

A multi-stage experiment is one where we repeat the experiment several times, such as tossing a coin multiple times or rolling a die more than once (or rolling two dice). We can use an **array table** or a **tree diagram** to represent these situations.

Multi-stage experiments can be conducted with or without replacement.

With replacement

In an experiment with replacement, each time an item is selected from a set, it is returned to the set before the next selection. This means that the probability of selecting an item doesn't change after each selection, as the size of the set always remains the same.

Without replacement

In an experiment without replacement, once an item is selected from a set, it is not returned to the set before the next selection. This means that the probability of selecting an item changes, as the size of the set decreases after each selection.

Array tables

For two-step experiments, array tables are particularly helpful for listing all possible outcomes. Consider the event of rolling a die twice (or rolling two dice). The array table below shows all the possible outcomes.

		Die 2					
		1	2	3	4	5	6
Die 1	1	(1, 1)	(1, 2)	(1, 3)	(1, 4)	(1, 5)	(1, 6)
	2	(2, 1)	(2, 2)	(2, 3)	(2, 4)	(2, 5)	(2, 6)
	3	(3, 1)	(3, 2)	(3, 3)	(3, 4)	(3, 5)	(3, 6)
	4	(4, 1)	(4, 2)	(4, 3)	(4, 4)	(4, 5)	(4, 6)
	5	(5, 1)	(5, 2)	(5, 3)	(5, 4)	(5, 5)	(5, 6)
	6	(6, 1)	(6, 2)	(6, 3)	(6, 4)	(6, 5)	(6, 6)

We can use this table to obtain the probability of, for example, rolling a 6 on at least one of the dice. We know that there are a total of 36 possible outcomes and 11 outcomes in which at least one 6 appears. The probability is therefore $\frac{11}{36}$.

Example

Two letters are selected one after the other from the word TURN, without replacement.

a. Construct an array table to list the sample space.

b. Determine the probability of selecting

i. two Ts ii. at least one U iii. a U or an R.

✓ *Solution*

<table>
<tr><th>Working</th><th>Explanation</th></tr>
<tr><td>

a.

<table>
<tr><td rowspan="6">1st letter</td><td colspan="5">2nd letter</td></tr>
<tr><td></td><td>T</td><td>U</td><td>R</td><td>N</td></tr>
<tr><td>T</td><td>–</td><td>T, U</td><td>T, R</td><td>T, N</td></tr>
<tr><td>U</td><td>U, T</td><td>–</td><td>U, R</td><td>U, N</td></tr>
<tr><td>R</td><td>R, T</td><td>R, U</td><td>–</td><td>R, N</td></tr>
<tr><td>N</td><td>N, T</td><td>N, U</td><td>N, R</td><td>–</td></tr>
</table>

</td><td>

Letters are selected without replacement, so the same letter cannot be chosen twice.

Total outcomes $= 12$

</td></tr>
<tr><td>

b. i. $\Pr(T, T) = 0$

</td><td>There is no outcome of {T, T}.</td></tr>
<tr><td>

ii. $\Pr(U) = \frac{6}{12} = \frac{1}{2}$

</td><td>6 of the 12 outcomes contain at least one U.</td></tr>
<tr><td>

iii. $\Pr(R) = \frac{6}{12}$

$\Pr(U \cap R) = \frac{2}{12}$

$\Pr(U \cup R) = \Pr(U) + \Pr(R) - \Pr(U \cap R)$

$= \frac{6}{12} + \frac{6}{12} - \frac{2}{12}$

$= \frac{10}{12} = \frac{5}{6}$

</td><td>

Determine the probability of selecting at least one R.

Determine the probability of selecting U and R.

Apply the addition rule to determine the probability of selecting U or R and simplify.

</td></tr>
</table>

Example

Two balls are selected one at a time from a bag with 5 balls, with replacement. The balls are coloured black, white, orange, green and red.

a. Construct an array table to list the sample space.

b. Determine the probability of selecting

i. two balls of the same colour

ii. one red ball and one black ball

iii. a red ball given that a white ball is selected either first or second.

✓ ***Solution***

<table>
<tr><th>Working</th><th>Explanation</th></tr>
<tr><td>a.
<table>
<tr><td rowspan="7">1st</td><td colspan="6">2nd</td></tr>
<tr><td></td><td>B</td><td>W</td><td>O</td><td>G</td><td>R</td></tr>
<tr><td>B</td><td>B, B</td><td>B, W</td><td>B, O</td><td>B, G</td><td>B, R</td></tr>
<tr><td>W</td><td>W, B</td><td>W, W</td><td>W, O</td><td>W, G</td><td>W, R</td></tr>
<tr><td>O</td><td>O, B</td><td>O, W</td><td>O, O</td><td>O, G</td><td>O, R</td></tr>
<tr><td>G</td><td>G, B</td><td>G, W</td><td>G, O</td><td>G, G</td><td>G, R</td></tr>
<tr><td>R</td><td>R, B</td><td>R, W</td><td>R, O</td><td>R, G</td><td>R, R</td></tr>
</table>
</td><td>Total outcomes: $5 \times 5 = 25$</td></tr>
<tr><td>b. i. $\text{Pr(same colour)} = \frac{5}{25} = \frac{1}{5}$</td><td>There are 5 outcomes where balls of the same colour could be drawn.</td></tr>
<tr><td>ii. $\text{Pr(red and black)} = \frac{2}{25}$</td><td>There are 2 outcomes where red and black balls could be drawn: {R, B} and {B, R}.</td></tr>
<tr><td>iii. $n(\text{white}) = 9$
$n(\text{red and white}) = 2$
$\text{Pr(red}|\text{white)} = \frac{2}{9}$</td><td>Determine the number of outcomes where a white ball could be drawn.
Determine the number of outcomes where a red and white ball could be drawn.
Apply the conditional probability formula.</td></tr>
</table>

Exercise 10.4.1

A fair five-sided die is rolled twice.

a. Construct an array table to list the sample space.

b. Determine the probability of

i. rolling a double

ii. rolling a 2 or a 4

iii. rolling a 3 given that a double has been rolled.

Exercise 10.4.2

Two regular dice are rolled.

a. Construct an array table to show the sum of each possible set of rolls.

b. Determine the probability that the sum lies between 4 and 6 inclusive.

Exercise 10.4.3

Two letters are chosen from the word EAT, with replacement.

a. Construct an array table to list the sample space.

b. Determine the probability of

i. selecting at least one T

ii. selecting an A given T was selected

iii. selecting an E and a T

iv. selecting an E or a T.

Exercise 10.4.4

Two letters are chosen from the word TEST without replacement.

a. Construct an array table to list the sample space.

b. Determine the probability of

i. selecting two Ts

ii. selecting an S and a T

iii. selecting two Ts given that at least one T is selected.

Tree diagrams

Tree diagrams can be useful for listing the sample space in experiments involving two or more stages. The example below shows the sample space when tossing a coin three times.

1st toss	2nd toss	3rd toss	Outcomes	Probability
$\frac{1}{2}$ H	$\frac{1}{2}$ H	$\frac{1}{2}$ H	HHH	$\frac{1}{2}\times\frac{1}{2}\times\frac{1}{2}=\frac{1}{8}$
		$\frac{1}{2}$ T	HHT	$\frac{1}{2}\times\frac{1}{2}\times\frac{1}{2}=\frac{1}{8}$
	$\frac{1}{2}$ T	$\frac{1}{2}$ H	HTH	$\frac{1}{2}\times\frac{1}{2}\times\frac{1}{2}=\frac{1}{8}$
		$\frac{1}{2}$ T	HTT	$\frac{1}{2}\times\frac{1}{2}\times\frac{1}{2}=\frac{1}{8}$
$\frac{1}{2}$ T	$\frac{1}{2}$ H	$\frac{1}{2}$ H	THH	$\frac{1}{2}\times\frac{1}{2}\times\frac{1}{2}=\frac{1}{8}$
		$\frac{1}{2}$ T	THT	$\frac{1}{2}\times\frac{1}{2}\times\frac{1}{2}=\frac{1}{8}$
	$\frac{1}{2}$ T	$\frac{1}{2}$ H	TTH	$\frac{1}{2}\times\frac{1}{2}\times\frac{1}{2}=\frac{1}{8}$
		$\frac{1}{2}$ T	TTT	$\frac{1}{2}\times\frac{1}{2}\times\frac{1}{2}=\frac{1}{8}$

In a tree diagram, you should list all possible outcomes in the sample space, label each branch with its probability and give the probability of each outcome. The sum of the probabilities of all outcomes should equal 1.

Multi-stage experiments with and without replacement

Consider the following two situations.

Situation 1: Each of the letters of the word START is written on a card. The cards are placed facedown on a table and jumbled. A card is chosen at random and its letter revealed, then it is returned facedown to the table. The cards are rejumbled and a second card is chosen.

Situation 2: Each of the letters of the word START is written on a card. The cards are placed facedown on a table and jumbled. A card is chosen at random and its letter revealed, then it is put to one side. A second card is chosen from the cards remaining on the table.

We can represent these situations using tree diagrams (see below). Note that in this case we have simplified the tree. There are two Ts in START, and instead of adding a branch for each possible T, we have added just one branch but specified a probability of $\frac{2}{5}$ when it was possible that either of the Ts could be selected.

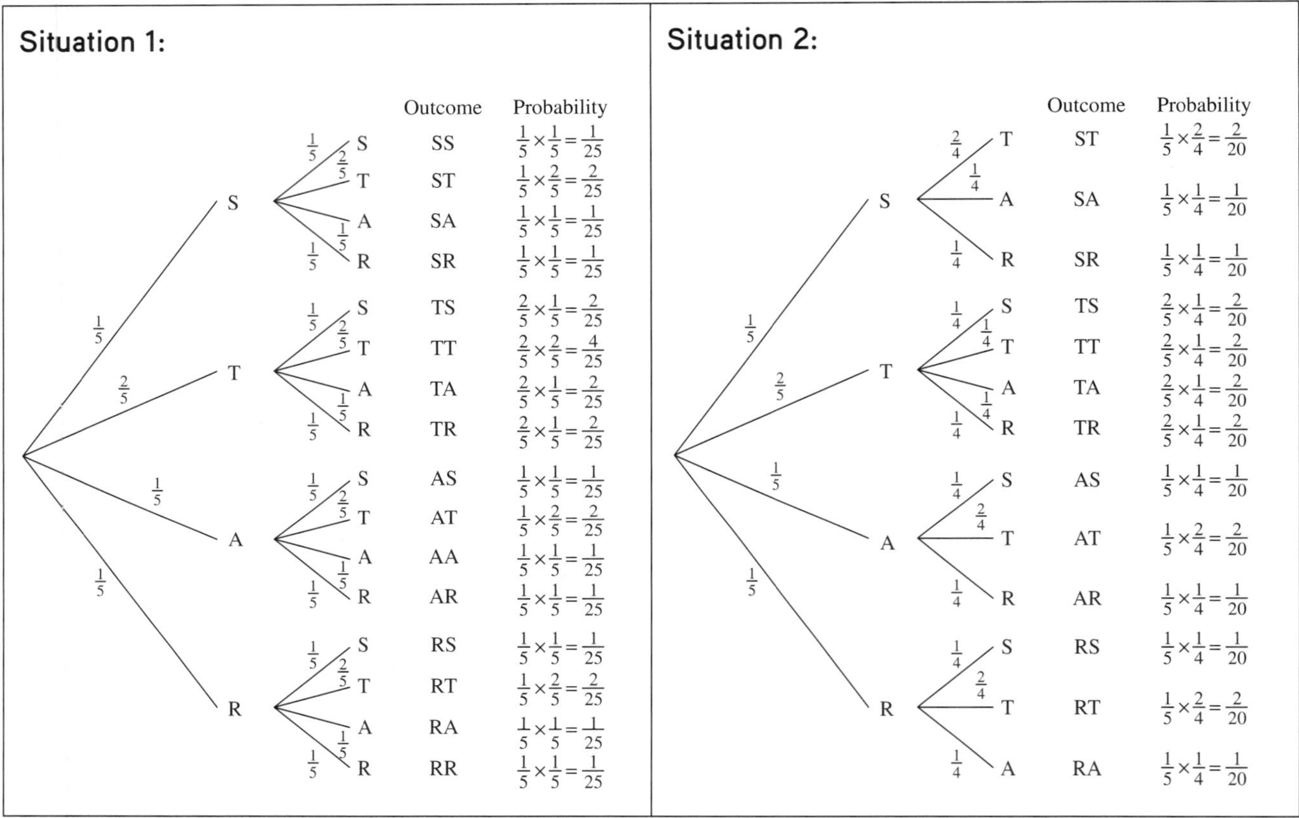

The difference between situation 1 and situation 2 is whether the first card is replaced. In situation 1, the odds of drawing a specific card the second time are not affected by any card having been put to one side. In situation 2, the odds of drawing a specific card the second time are affected by the fact that the first card has not been replaced and there is now one card less to choose from. The probabilities for the second draw in situation 1 have not changed, but the probabilities for the second draw in situation 2 have changed. We can also see from the tree diagram that there are more possible outcomes in situation 1 than in situation 2.

In summary, two events are **independent** if the result of one event has no effect on the probability of the second event. Two events are **dependent** if the result of one event affects the probability of the second event.

Example

A bag contains two green balls and one pink ball. One ball is selected at random and its colour noted. The ball is placed back in the bag. Another ball is selected and its colour noted. Draw a tree diagram to show all possible outcomes and then determine

a. Pr(drawing a pink and a green ball in any order)

b. Pr(drawing two pink balls)

c. Pr(drawing a green followed by a pink ball).

✓ *Solution*

Working	Explanation
a. 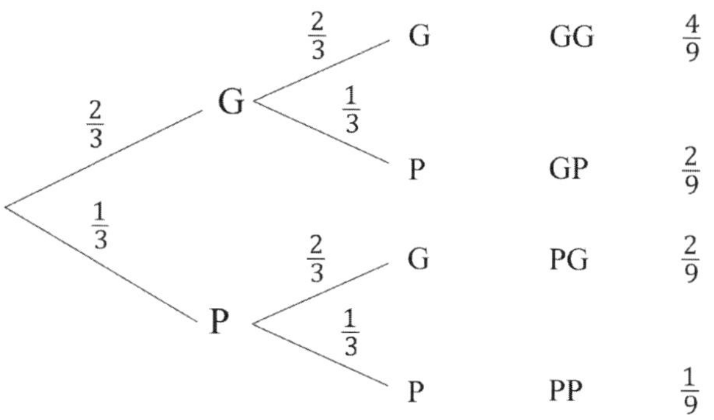 $\frac{2}{3}$ G: $\frac{2}{3}$ G → GG $\frac{4}{9}$; $\frac{1}{3}$ P → GP $\frac{2}{9}$ $\frac{1}{3}$ P: $\frac{2}{3}$ G → PG $\frac{2}{9}$; $\frac{1}{3}$ P → PP $\frac{1}{9}$	Draw a tree diagram starting with two branches, showing G and P. Note that there are 3 balls in total of which 2 are green and 1 is pink. Hence the probability of drawing a green ball is $\frac{2}{3}$ and the probability of drawing a pink ball is $\frac{1}{3}$. Label the branches with their probabilities.
$\Pr(PG \text{ or } GP) = \frac{2}{9} + \frac{2}{9} = \frac{4}{9}$	Since the order does not matter – it can be GP or PG – we add the two probabilities together.
b. $\Pr(PP) = \frac{1}{9}$	These probabilities can be read directly from the tree diagram.
c. $\Pr(GP) = \frac{2}{9}$	

Example

The letters MATH are each written on cards. The cards are placed facedown on a table and jumbled. A card is chosen and its letter revealed, then it is put to one side. Then a second card is chosen from the cards remaining on the table.

a. Draw a tree diagram to show all outcomes.

b. Determine the probability that the two letters chosen are T and A in that order.

c. Determine the probability of choosing a card with M on it.

✓ *Solution*

Working	Explanation
a. 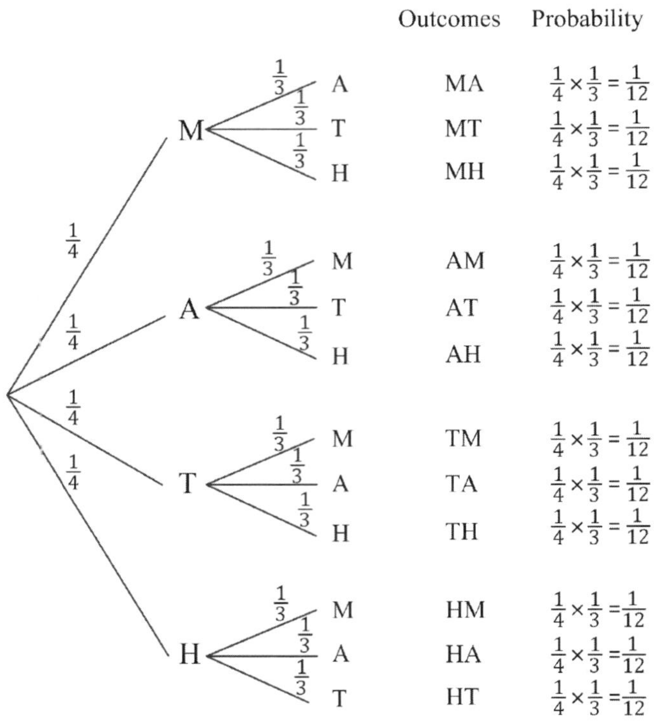 $\frac{1}{4}$ M: $\frac{1}{3}$ A, $\frac{1}{3}$ T, $\frac{1}{3}$ H $\frac{1}{4}$ A: $\frac{1}{3}$ M, $\frac{1}{3}$ T, $\frac{1}{3}$ H $\frac{1}{4}$ T: $\frac{1}{3}$ M, $\frac{1}{3}$ A, $\frac{1}{3}$ H $\frac{1}{4}$ H: $\frac{1}{3}$ M, $\frac{1}{3}$ A, $\frac{1}{3}$ T Outcomes — Probability MA — $\frac{1}{4}\times\frac{1}{3}=\frac{1}{12}$ MT — $\frac{1}{4}\times\frac{1}{3}=\frac{1}{12}$ MH — $\frac{1}{4}\times\frac{1}{3}=\frac{1}{12}$ AM — $\frac{1}{4}\times\frac{1}{3}=\frac{1}{12}$ AT — $\frac{1}{4}\times\frac{1}{3}=\frac{1}{12}$ AH — $\frac{1}{4}\times\frac{1}{3}=\frac{1}{12}$ TM — $\frac{1}{4}\times\frac{1}{3}=\frac{1}{12}$ TA — $\frac{1}{4}\times\frac{1}{3}=\frac{1}{12}$ TH — $\frac{1}{4}\times\frac{1}{3}=\frac{1}{12}$ HM — $\frac{1}{4}\times\frac{1}{3}=\frac{1}{12}$ HA — $\frac{1}{4}\times\frac{1}{3}=\frac{1}{12}$ HT — $\frac{1}{4}\times\frac{1}{3}=\frac{1}{12}$	Draw a tree diagram starting with four branches, one for each letter: M, A, T and H. Label each branch with the corresponding probability ($\frac{1}{4}$). Since the experiment is without replacement, extend each branch of the tree by 3 branches. Label each new branch with the corresponding probability. (As there is one less letter, the probability of drawing each letter increases to $\frac{1}{3}$.) List each outcome and its probability.
b. $\Pr(T, A) = \frac{1}{12}$	There are 12 possible outcomes but only one outcome is T followed by A.
c. $\Pr(\text{outcomes with M}) = \frac{6}{12}$	Six outcomes include an M.

Example

Jenny is participating in a tennis tournament where she has to play three other players. She estimates that she has a 60% chance of winning the first match, an equal chance of winning the second match and a 25% chance of losing the final match.

a. Construct a tree diagram to show the sample space. Clearly label all outcomes and their associated probabilities.

b. Determine the probability that Jenny wins at least two matches.

✓ ***Solution***

Working	Explanation
a. 0.6 W — 0.5 W — 0.75 W — WWW — 0.225 0.6 W — 0.5 W — 0.25 L — WWL — 0.075 0.6 W — 0.5 L — 0.75 W — WLW — 0.225 0.6 W — 0.5 L — 0.25 L — WLL — 0.075 0.4 L — 0.5 W — 0.75 W — LWW — 0.150 0.4 L — 0.5 W — 0.25 L — LWL — 0.050 0.4 L — 0.5 L — 0.75 W — LLW — 0.150 0.4 L — 0.5 L — 0.25 L — LLL — 0.050	Each match is either a win (W) or a loss (L). Begin by calculating the probability of winning or losing each individual match. Match 1 – the probability of W is 0.6 (60%), therefore the probability of L is 0.4 (40%). Match 2 – Jenny has an equal chance of winning and losing, therefore the probability is 0.5 (50%) for each possible outcome. Match 3 – the probability of L is 0.25 (25%), therefore the probability of W is 0.75 (75%). Construct the tree diagram as shown, clearly labelling all branches, and state the outcomes and their associated probabilities.
b. Pr(WWW or WWL or WLW or LWW) $= 0.225 + 0.075 + 0.225 + 0.150 = 0.675$	There are 4 outcomes on the tree diagram that show Jenny winning at least 2 matches (including the outcome that shows her winning all three games). Add up the probability of each of these outcomes occurring to determine the probability of Jenny winning at least 2 games. **Note:** in this case, it is easier to work with decimals rather than percentages.

Exercise 10.4.5

a. James has two containers of sweets. In container A there are three lollipops (L) and one gummy bear (G). In container B there are two lollipops and two gummy bears. James chooses one container at random and then one sweet is chosen from that container, also at random.

  i. Draw a tree diagram to represent all possible outcomes and their probabilities.

  ii. Determine the probability of selecting container A and a gummy bear.

  iii. Determine the probability of selecting a lollipop.

b. Peach and Mario play three games of golf. Peach's chance of winning any single game is $\frac{3}{5}$. Construct a tree diagram to show the sample space. Clearly show all outcomes and their probabilities. Determine the probability that Peach wins at least two games.

c. At a supermarket, cartons of eggs are inspected for broken shells before they are put on sale. The probability that a carton of eggs is rejected is $\frac{1}{10}$. Two cartons of eggs are inspected. Draw a tree diagram to represent this situation and use it to find the probability that

  i. both cartons are rejected **ii.** one carton is rejected.

d. A marble is randomly selected from a bag containing 4 blue marbles and 7 green marbles. It is replaced before a second marble is selected. Draw a tree diagram to represent all possible outcomes and use it to find the probability of

  i. selecting two green marbles **ii.** selecting at least one blue marble.

e. Two cards are drawn, without replacement, from a set of 20 cards that are numbered 1 to 20. Let $P =$ 'a prime number is drawn' and $N =$ 'a prime number is not drawn'. Draw a tree diagram showing all possible outcomes and use it to find the probability of

  i. drawing two prime numbers **ii.** drawing no prime numbers

  iii. drawing at least one prime number.

10.5 Independent and dependent events

Two events are independent if the result of one event has no effect on the probability of the second event occurring. An example is flipping a coin twice. The outcome of the first flip does not affect the outcome of the second flip.

Mathematically, two events A and B are independent if the probability of both events occurring is the product of their individual probabilities.

$$\Pr(A \cap B) = \Pr(A) \times \Pr(B)$$
$$\Pr(A|B) = \Pr(A)$$
$$\Pr(B|A) = \Pr(B)$$

Dependent events are events where the outcome of one event does have an effect on the outcome of the other. An example is drawing cards from a deck without replacement. The probability of drawing a particular card changes depending on what cards have previously been drawn, because the number of cards in the deck changes after each draw.

Example

In a city there are two bus routes, A and B. Suppose that the probability that a bus taking route A will arrive on time is 0.7 and the probability that a bus taking route B arrives on time is 0.6. What is the probability that two buses – one taking route A and the other taking route B – will arrive on time?

✓ *Solution*

Working	Explanation
$\Pr(A \cap B) = \Pr(A) \times \Pr(B)$ $= 0.7 \times 0.6$ $= 0.42$	Since event A and event B clearly occur independently of each other, we can apply the independence rule.

Example

A selection of 10 mobile-phone plans includes 4 that offer unlimited data connection and 5 that offer free international calls. One plan offers both unlimited data and free international calls. Let A be the event 'choosing a mobile-phone plan with unlimited data connection' and B be the event 'choosing a mobile-phone plan with free international calls'.

a. Determine $\Pr(A)$ and $\Pr(A|B)$.

b. State whether or not the events A and B are independent.

✓ *Solution*

Working	Explanation
a. $\Pr(A) = \frac{4}{10} = \frac{2}{5}$	4 out of 10 plans offer unlimited data connection. (One of these also offers free international calls.)
$\Pr(A\|B) = \frac{n(A \cap B)}{n(B)} = \frac{1}{5}$	To determine the conditional probability, apply the rule $\Pr(A\|B) = \frac{n(A \cap B)}{n(B)}$.
b. $\Pr(A\|B) = \frac{1}{5} \neq \Pr(A)$ ∴ events A and B are not independent.	Use the property $\Pr(A\|B) = \Pr(A)$ to determine if events are independent.

Example

For two events A and B, $\Pr(A) = 0.5$, $\Pr(B) = 0.8$ and $\Pr(A \cap B) = 0.4$. Determine whether the events are independent.

✓ *Solution*

Working	Explanation
$\Pr(A) \times \Pr(B) = 0.8 \times 0.5$ $= 0.4$ $= \Pr(A \cap B)$ ∴ events A and B are independent.	Use the property $\Pr(A \cap B) = \Pr(A) \times \Pr(B)$ to determine if the events are independent.

Exercise 10.5

a. A company manufactures two types of products: product A and product B. The probability that product A passes quality control inspection is independent of product B passing quality control inspection. The probability that product A passes quality control inspection is 0.8 and the probability that product B passes inspection is 0.7. What is the probability that both products pass quality control inspection?

b. A selection of 8 offers for vacuum cleaners includes 3 that are cordless and 4 that have a handheld-function. Two have a handheld-function and are cordless. Let A be the event 'choosing a vacuum that is cordless' and B be the event 'choosing a vacuum with a handheld-function'.

i. Determine $\Pr(A)$ and $\Pr(A|B)$.

ii. State whether or not events A and B are independent.

c. The probability of events A and B can be determined from the Venn diagrams below. Determine $\Pr(A)$ and $\Pr(A|B)$, and hence decide whether or not the events are independent.

i.

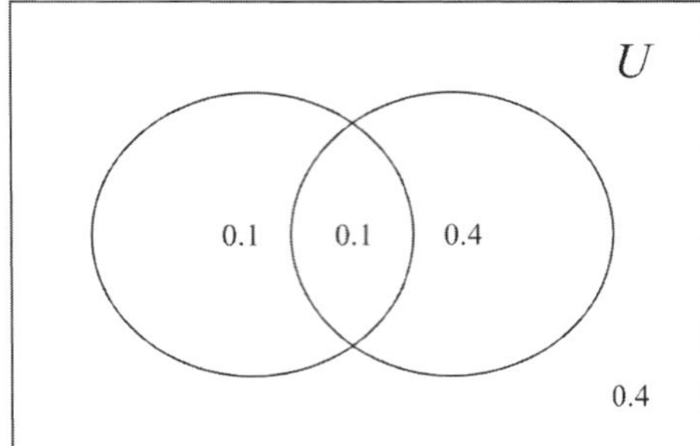

ii.

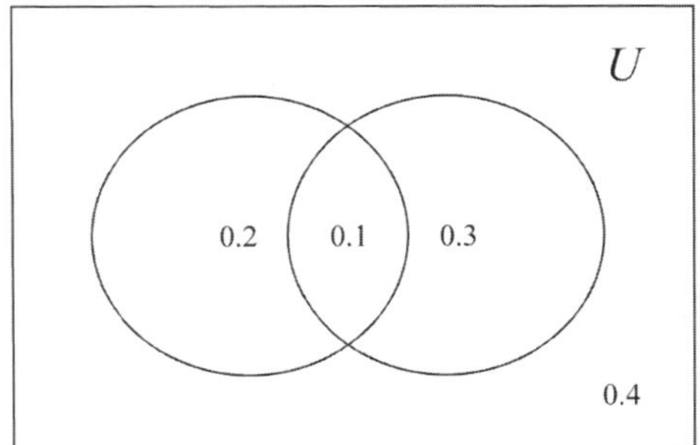

d. For two events, A and B, $\Pr(A) = 0.7$, $\Pr(B) = 0.5$ and $\Pr(A \cup B) = 0.85$. Determine whether the events are independent.

10.6 Relative frequency

Theoretically we know that if we toss a fair coin, the chance of it landing heads or tails is the same. The probability is $\frac{1}{2}$ (or 50% or 0.5). However, in real life, if we toss a coin 1000 times it is possible that we end up with a result that is not exactly 500 heads and 500 tails. We could, for example, get 551 heads and 449 tails. This variation could have a number of causes, such as the way the coin is tossed or a difference in the distribution of mass on the surface of the coin. For this particular coin we can say that

$$\Pr(\text{head}) = \frac{551}{1000} = 55.1\% \text{ and } \Pr(\text{tail}) = \frac{449}{1000} = 44.9\%$$

Based on these probabilities we can predict that the next toss of this coin has a 55.1% probability of landing heads up.

Probability based on an actual number of outcomes is called **experimental probability** or **relative frequency**. We can define experimental probability as

$$\textit{experimental probability} = \frac{\textit{number of times the outcome has occurred}}{\textit{total number of trials in the experiment}}$$

As with standard probability, experimental probability falls between 0 and 1 (inclusive).

Experimental probability can be used as an estimate of theoretical probability if there has been a large number of trials.

Example

Kalum used a simulator to roll a die 3000 times and obtained the following results.

Outcomes	1	2	3	4	5	6
Frequency	578	495	425	534	462	506

Use the table to calculate the probability that the next roll of the die will be

a. a 3 **b.** an odd number **c.** a number less than 3.

✓ Solution

Working	Explanation
a. $P(3) = \frac{425}{3000} = 0.1417$	Use the experimental probability formula to determine the probability of obtaining a 3.
b. $P(\text{odd}) = \frac{578 + 425 + 462}{3000} = 0.4883$	There are three odd numbers (1, 3 and 5), so you need to add up the frequencies of these numbers to obtain the probability.
c. $P(<3) = \frac{578 + 495}{3000} = 0.3577$	There are 2 numbers less than 3 (1 and 2). The frequency of both needs to be added. **Note:** we normally quote the probability to 4 decimal places. This is because we will still have 2 decimal places if the probability is converted to a percentage.

Example

A bowl contains 340 red and 60 black marbles.

a. State the probability of drawing a red marble.

b. What is the expected number of red marbles we will find if we draw 60 marbles from the bowl?

✓ Solution

Working	Explanation
a. $Pr(\text{red}) = \frac{340}{400} = \frac{17}{20}$	The probability is based on the total number of marbles in the bowl ($340 + 60 = 400$).
b. $\frac{17}{20} \times 60 = 51$ The expected number of red marbles in a sample of 60 is 51.	The probability or relative frequency of an outcome can be used to calculate the expected outcomes of future trials. This can be found by: expected number = relative frequency × number of trials Give your answer as a whole number, as you cannot have a fraction of a marble.

Exercise 10.6

a. Estimate the probability of the event specified below occurring from the data given.

i. Pr(tail) if a coin is tossed 100 times and 64 tails are observed.

ii. Pr(three) if a spinner is spun 200 times and lands on the 'three' 20 times.

iii. Pr(two heads) if two coins are tossed 150 times and two heads are observed on 60 occasions.

b. A survey of families yielded the following information about the number of children in each family.

No. of children	No. of families
0	17
1	35
2	58
3	37
4	12
5	4

A family from the survey is chosen at random. Estimate the probability that the family will have

i. no children

ii. two children

iii. no more than two children

iv. at least two children.

c. A biased five-sided die has faces numbered 1 to 5. The probability that the die will land on each of the numbers is given in the table below.

Number	1	2	3	4	5
Relative frequency	$2x$	x	0.2	0.25	0.1

i. What is the relative frequency of rolling a 1 or a 2?

ii. The die is rolled 300 times. What is the expected number of times it will land on an even number?

d. 100 adults were surveyed regarding their political affiliation. The results are shown in the table below.

	Party A	Party B	Party C	Undecided
Male	20	28	2	3
Female	14	16	9	8

A person is chosen at random from this group. Determine the probability that the person is

i. male and a supporter of party B

ii. female or a supporter of party A

iii. a supporter of party A

iv. undecided, given that the person is female.

e. The manufacturer of toothpicks decided to inspect 100 boxes of toothpicks to determine if the label claiming that there are 380 toothpicks in the box is justified. The results of the inspection are shown in the table below.

No. of toothpicks	377	378	379	380	381	382	383	384
No. of boxes	0	2	5	10	44	22	13	4

Determine the probability that the next box off the production line contains

i. 378 toothpicks

ii. 380 or more toothpicks

iii. less than the number stated on the box.

iv. Comment on the manufacturer's concern.

Chapter 11 – Statistics

11.1 Collecting data

We can collect data from the entire population (a **census**) or from part of the population (a **sample**).

An entire population can be very large or difficult to access, making it impractical to conduct a census every time we want to collect data. Hence, we often select a sample of the population and collect the same information from each member of our sample.

Some examples of census data collection are:

- the census carried out by the Australian Bureau of Statistics every five years to collect information about the entire population of Australia
- a survey of all students in a school about their mode of transport in order to plan for a new bicycle parking area.

Some examples of sample data collection are:

- a survey by a market research company asking selected voters what party they intend to vote for in the upcoming state election
- a survey of only a selected number of the students about their mode of transport.

Some of the ways in which data can be collected are:

- surveys
- interviews
- forms (as in the five-yearly census)
- field observation (e.g. counting the number of cars passing through a particular intersection)
- experiments.

Data can be primary or secondary. **Primary data** is the data that you collect. **Secondary data** is the data you use that has been collected by others, such as when we use data collected by the Australian Bureau of Statistics in a school assignment.

Because of the cost and the effort involved, it is sometimes impractical to collect data yourself: therefore, we use data from other sources. One potential disadvantage is that often we do not know how the data was collected or how accurate it is.

There are two sampling methods used when collecting data – **probability sampling** and **non-probability sampling**. The probability sampling method involves random selection. This is a good way of reducing bias and obtaining a representative sample, as each member of the population has an equal chance of participating.

The non-probability sampling method involves non-random selection. An example is restricting a survey to a certain period (such as 8 am to 9 am) or at a particular location (such as outside a railway station). Only people who are present at that time or location are given an opportunity to participate in the survey. This can cause biases, as the population may not be accurately represented.

When collecting sample data, it is also important to ensure that the sample size is large enough to represent the entire population.

11.2 Types of data

Data can be classified as **categorical data** or **numerical data**. Categorical data is data that can be divided into groups or categories. Numerical data is data that can be measured.

Both types of data have two subcategories. These are summarised in the table below.

Data			
Categorical		**Numerical**	
Nominal	**Ordinal**	**Discrete**	**Continuous**
no order is implied by the name of the data	an order is implied by the name of the data	only integers	can be any value, not just an integer
examples: • colours • overseas countries • fruit sold at a market	examples: • pizza sizes (large, medium, small) • movie ratings (1 star to 5 stars)	examples: • number of goals scored in a season • number of students who participated in a race	examples: • the weights of newborn babies at a hospital • the heights of students in Year 10

Example

a. What type of data would the following survey questions generate: categorical–nominal, categorical–ordinal, numerical–discrete or numerical–continuous?

i. How many family members are living in your home?

ii. How do you feel about the movie *Titanic*: don't like it, neutral, like it?

b. A survey is printed in newspapers to determine Australia's favourite TV channel. Would this sample be representative of the views of Australians?

✓ *Solution*

Working	Explanation
a. i. numerical and discrete	The answer to the question is a number and it is a whole number.
ii. categorical and ordinal	The answer is a category and it can be ordered.
b. A survey via newspapers restricts the sample to those people who purchase or have access to a newspaper, omitting those who do not.	The sample may not include some of the younger members of the community who do not purchase newspapers.

Exercise 11.2

a. What type of data would the following survey questions generate?

i. What is your preferred season in the year?

ii. How long does it take you to get to school?

b. Decide whether the following surveys would be representative of the entire Australian population. Justify your answer.

i. making 1000 random phone calls to find out who is likely to win in the coming election

ii. a survey via social media to discover people's favourite radio station

iii. using census data to determine the number of children in each family household

11.3 Displaying data

There are many ways of displaying data. For categorical data, we generally use bar graphs, dot plots or pie charts. These are illustrated in the table below.

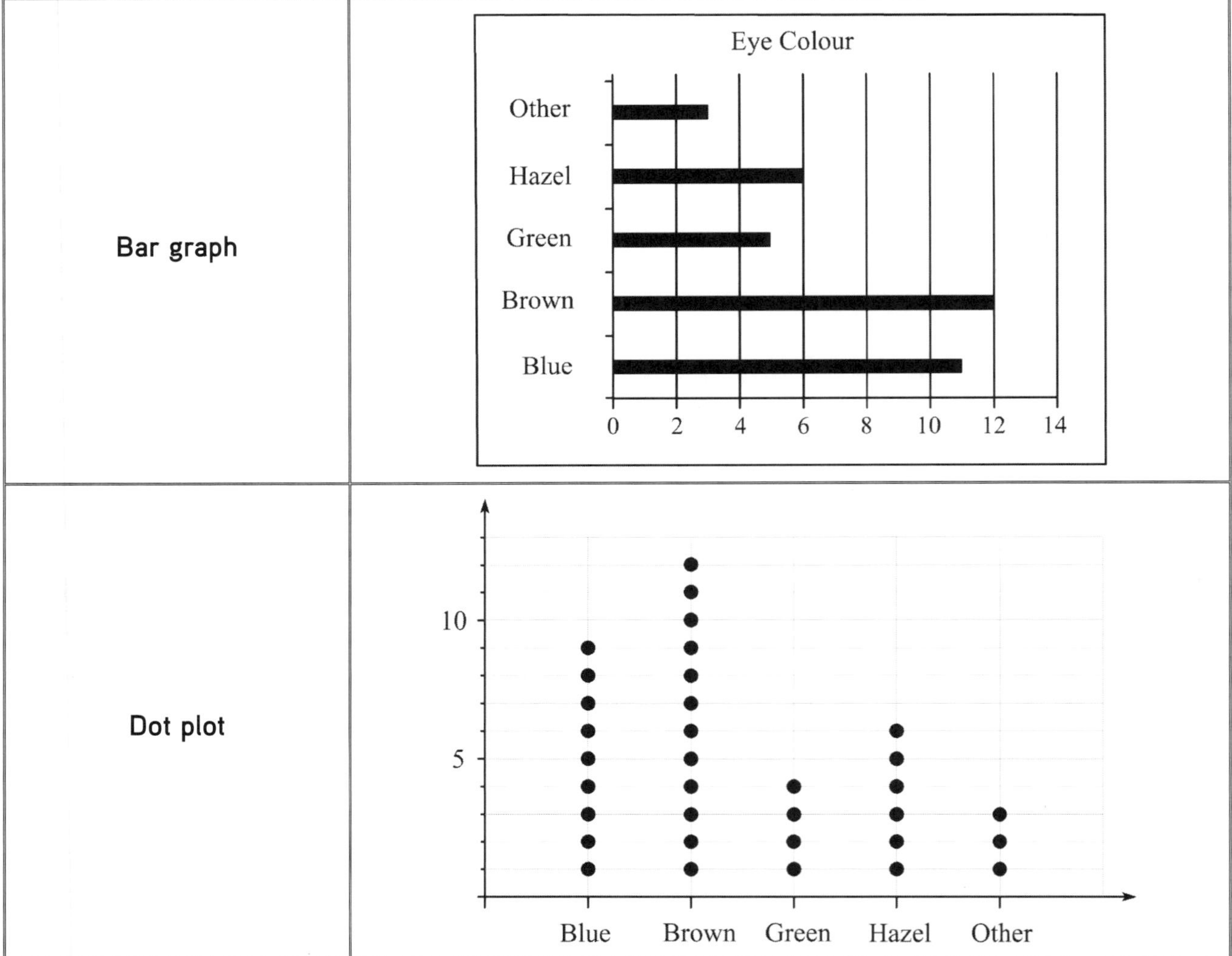

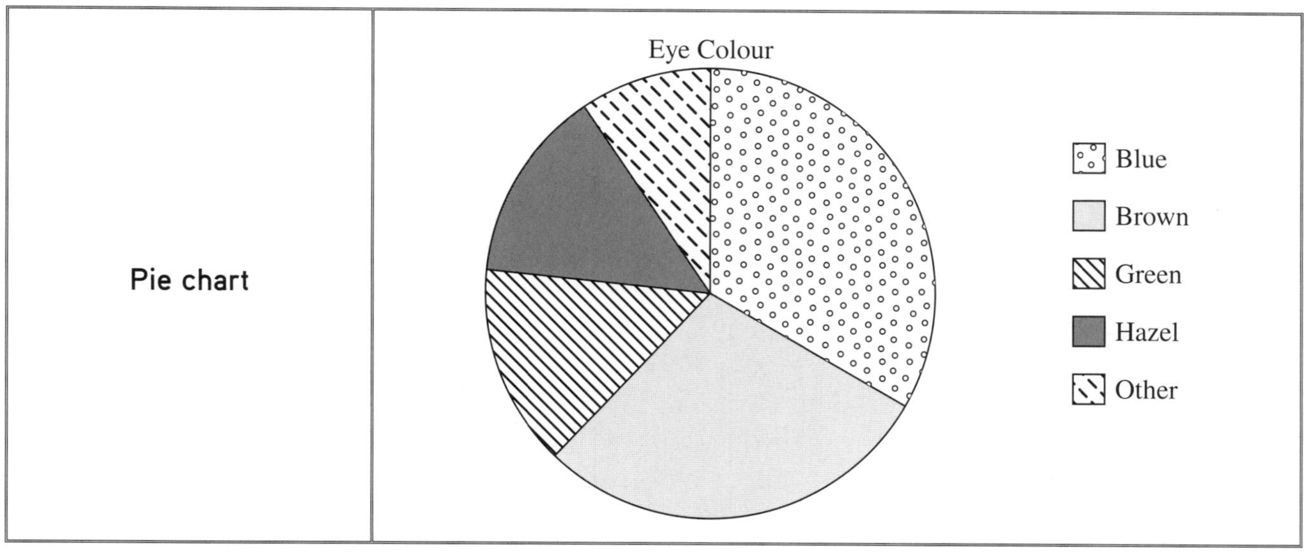

For numerical data, we generally use stem-and-leaf plots, dot plots and histograms. These are illustrated in the table below.

Stem-and-leaf plot

Class A Leaves	Stems	Class B Leaves
8 0	6	0 0
5 0	7	0 1 3 3 5 6 7
6 4	8	4 5 6
6 4 4 2 1 0	9	1 2
0 0	10	

8 | 7 | 5 means 78 marks in class A and 75 marks in class B

Dot plot

Length (cm)	46	47	48	49	50	51	52	53	54	55
Frequency	0	1	3	5	9	14	12	4	2	0

Histogram	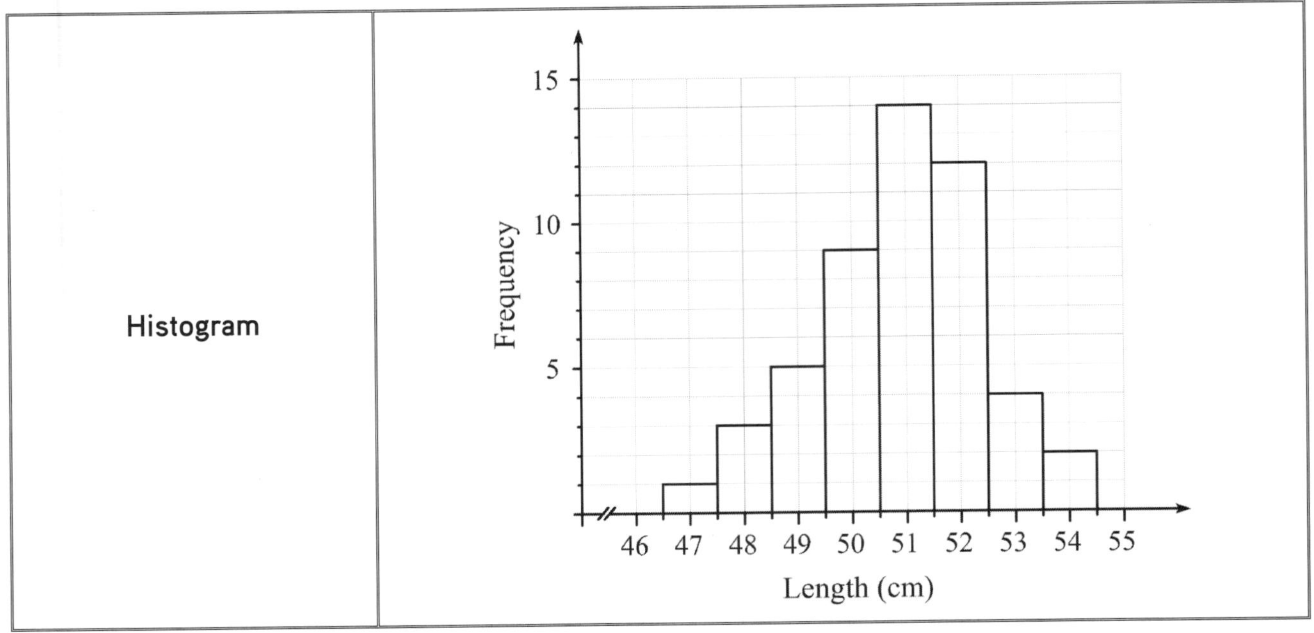

Stem-and-leaf plots

Stem-and-leaf plots (or stem plots) are commonly used to display a single dataset or two related datasets. An example is shown below.

Stem	Leaf
0	6 8
1	4 6 7
2	3 3 3 8
3	5 8 9
4	8 9
5	8

Key: 1|7 means 17

The **Stem** column is the first digit of a two-digit number, or the first two digits of a three-digit number, and so on.

The **Leaf** column is usually the last digit of the value.

The stem-and-leaf plot shown above represents the total rainfall captured in a rain gauge for July 2010. The raw data being represented is as follows.

Total rainfall for July 2010 (cm): 16, 8, 17, 23, 28, 35, 58, 49, 6, 23, 48, 39, 23, 14, 38

The leaves are arranged in order, with the smallest value closest to the stem and the largest furthest away.

You must always provide a key that explains how the stem and leaf combinations are to be interpreted. In the example above, the key indicates that a 1 in the **Stem** column and a 7 in the **Leaf** column should be interpreted as 17.

We can also have a **back-to-back stem-and-leaf plot** in which we can compare two sets of data. For example, if we want to compare the total rainfall for July 2020 to the total rainfall for July 2010, a back-to-back stem-and-leaf plot should be constructed. The raw data for July 2010 is given above and the raw data for July 2020 is as follows.

Total rainfall for July 2020 (cm): 57, 16, 54, 26, 46, 43, 36, 43, 40, 32

The back-to-back stem-and-leaf plot representing both sets of rainfall data is shown below.

July 2020	Stem	July 2010
	0	6 8
6	1	4 6 7
6	2	3 3 3 8
6 2	3	5 8 9
6 3 3 0	4	8 9
7 4	5	8

Key: 6|1|4 means 16 for July 2020 and 14 for July 2010

There are now three columns, with the middle column being the stem. The leaves are again arranged in order, from the smallest (closest to the stem) to the largest (furthest away).

Histograms

It is important to consider the following points when constructing a histogram.

- There should be no gaps between the bars unless the corresponding frequency is 0.
- The y-axis always represents frequency.
- The x-axis always represents numbers grouped into intervals.
- There are usually 6 to 10 equal groups along the x-axis.

A tally table can be handy to work out the frequency of each group.

Let's consider an example. The following data gives the length of a particular type of fish (to the nearest cm) caught at a popular fishing spot in a single day.

11	43	57	25	48	32	48	53	45	22
31	63	45	44	48	54	37	43	51	31
40	24	43	37	30	49	33	37	38	40
38	45	38	36	46	50	32	30	42	58
54	43	34	42	54	45	41	43	33	38
34	38	18	47	48	33	27	47	32	43

To represent this data in a histogram, the data needs to be grouped into equal intervals. By inspecting the dataset, we see that the shortest fish is 11 cm and the longest fish is 63 cm. To have between 6 and 10 equal intervals, we group the data into intervals of 10 cm. These intervals are known as **class intervals**. A tally table can then be used to count the frequency of each class interval.

Length of fish (l)	**Tally**	**Frequency**
$10 \leq l < 20$	||	2
$20 \leq l < 30$	||||	4
$30 \leq l < 40$	𝍸 𝍸 𝍸 𝍸 |	21
$40 \leq l < 50$	𝍸 𝍸 𝍸 𝍸 ||||	24
$50 \leq l < 60$	𝍸 |||	8
$60 \leq l < 70$	|	1

Note: $40 \leq l < 50$ means that any length between 40 cm (including 40 cm) and less than 50 cm is included in the class interval.

The grouped data can now be represented with a histogram.

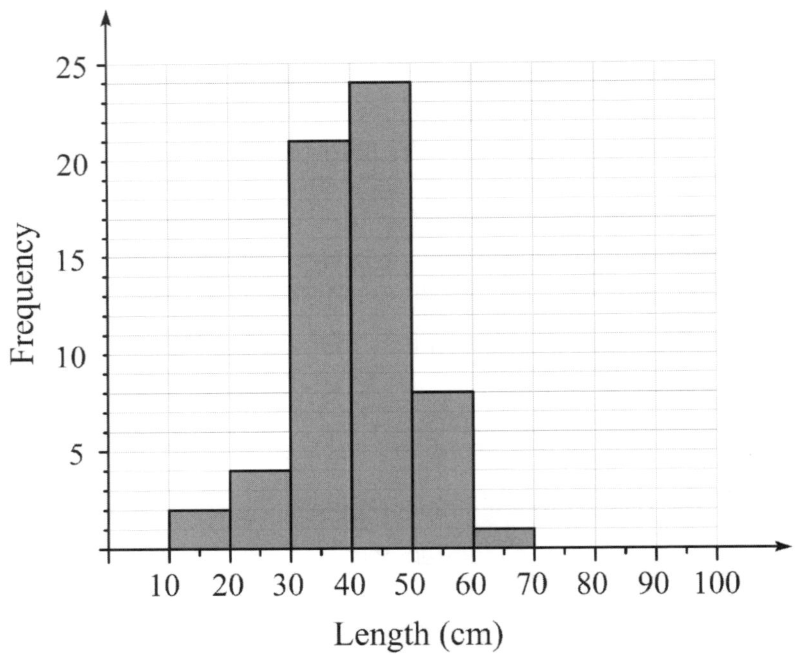

The height of a bar is the frequency of the corresponding class interval. For example, the first bar in the histogram above indicates that 2 of the fish caught were between 10 cm (inclusive) and 20 cm (exclusive).

When you are given a histogram, or a tally table without the original data, the mean of the data can be estimated from the midpoint of each class interval. The table below gives the midpoint of each class interval in the fish example introduced above. The corresponding frequency can be read from the histogram.

Length of fish (l)	Midpoint of class interval	Frequency
$10 \le l < 20$	15	2
$20 \le l < 30$	25	4
$30 \le l < 40$	35	21
$40 \le l < 50$	45	24
$50 \le l < 60$	55	8
$60 \le l < 70$	65	1

The mean can be estimated by multiplying each midpoint by the corresponding frequency, adding all the values and then dividing by the total number of data points.

$$\text{mean} = \frac{(2 \times 15) + (4 \times 25) + (21 \times 35) + (24 \times 45) + (8 \times 55) + (1 \times 65)}{60} = 40.8 \text{ cm}$$

If we use the actual data, we find that the mean is 40.2 cm. Therefore, the mean found using the midpoint of each class interval is just an estimate.

We cannot determine the mode from the grouped data, but we can state the **modal class** (i.e. the class interval with the highest frequency). For the fish data discussed above, the modal class is $40 \le l < 50$ cm. The actual mode derived from the raw data is 43 cm.

Column graphs

A **column graph** may look like a histogram. For both types of displays, the y-axis represents the frequency. The main differences are:

- the x-axis in a histogram represents numerical values while the x-axis in a column graph represents categories
- there should be no gap between the bars of a histogram except when the frequency for the class interval is 0. A gap is permitted in a column graph.

Exercise 11.3

a. The maximum temperature recorded at Perth Airport for each day of December in a particular year is shown in the following data.

Max. temp. (°C)	20–24	25–29	30–34	35–39	40–44
Frequency (no. of days)	3	13	8	6	1

Display this information as a histogram.

b. The speeds of vehicles on a country road with a speed limit of 110 km/h were measured using a speed radar over the course of one hour. The results are listed below.

105	110	99	102	110	108	111	109	112	115
112	98	113	120	100	89	112	110	109	108
110	114	105	109	110	110	148	90	101	106

Display the data as a stem-and-leaf plot.

11.4 Five-number statistics summary

The 5-number statistics summary is a set of five statistics, used for numerical data sets, that give a quick view of the distribution of data. The five statistics are described in the following table.

Minimum	The smallest value in the dataset.
Lower quartile ($Q1$)	The value that 25% of the data falls below.
Median ($Q2$)	The middle value when the data is ordered from least to greatest.
Upper quartile ($Q3$)	The value that 75% of the data falls below.
Maximum	The largest value in the dataset.

From the 5-number summary we can determine the

- range: maximum – minimum
- interquartile range (IQR): $Q3 - Q1$.

Consider the following scores.

$$12,\ 6,\ 10,\ 19,\ 9,\ 12,\ 4,\ 14,\ 8,\ 16,\ 6$$

List the scores in ascending order. This allows us to quickly determine the minimum, $Q1$, median, $Q3$ and maximum.

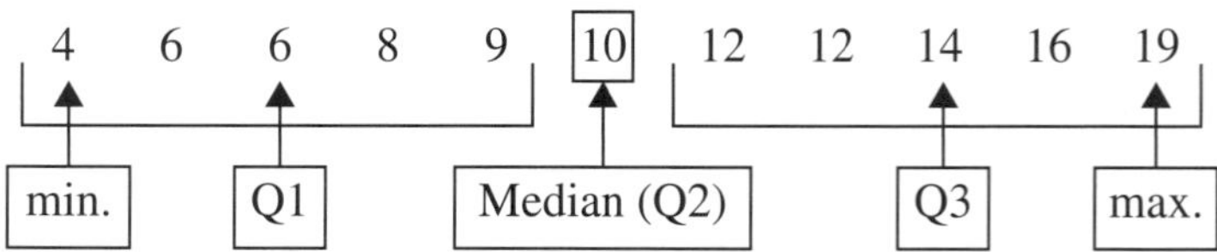

- To locate the median, look for the middle value of the entire dataset.
- $Q1$ is the median of the lower half of the dataset.
- $Q3$ is the median of the upper half of the dataset.

Note: don't include the median when locating $Q1$ and $Q3$.

The dataset of the scores listed above has the following properties.

$$\text{Minimum} = 4$$
$$Q1 = 6$$
$$Q2 = 10$$
$$Q3 = 14$$
$$\text{Maximum} = 19$$
$$\text{Range} = 19 - 4 = 15$$
$$IQR = 14 - 6 = 8$$

Outliers

Outliers are values in a dataset that are far away from the median. The interquartile range – determined from the 5-number statistics summary – is often used to identify potential outliers in the dataset. The process is as follows.

1. Calculate the interquartile range: $Q3 - Q1$.
2. Calculate the lower and upper bounds:
   - Lower bound $= Q1 - 1.5 \times IQR$
   - Upper bound $= Q3 + 1.5 \times IQR$.

Any data point less than the lower bound or greater than the upper bound is considered a potential outlier.

Outliers can affect a dataset in two main ways.

- **By distorting statistical measures.** Outliers can significantly skew the measures of central tendency (mean and median) and dispersion (variance and standard deviation). For instance, a single very high income in a dataset of salaries would inflate the average salary, making it a poor representation of most people's salaries.
- **By masking patterns.** Outliers can obscure underlying trends or relationships within the data. If a large cluster of data points follows a clear pattern, a single outlier can disrupt that pattern and make it harder to identify the overall trend. Imagine a graph showing a steady increase in temperature throughout the year, with one data point much lower due to a recording error. This outlier could cause the overall warming trend to be downplayed.

Example

The following data represents the number of ducks spotted on each day of a 13-day tour of Australia.

$$5,\ 1,\ 2,\ 6,\ 3,\ 3,\ 18,\ 4,\ 4,\ 1,\ 7,\ 2,\ 4$$

a. Determine the range and IQR of the data by first calculating the 5-number summary.

b. Determine what values, if any, are potential outliers.

c. If there are any outliers, provide a possible reason for why they may have occurred.

✓ Solution

Working	Explanation
a. 1 1 2 ↑ 2 3 3 [4] 4 4 5 ↑ 6 7 18 (Q1 between 2 and 2; Median = 4; Q3 between 5 and 6) Minimum = 1 $Q1 = \frac{2+2}{2} = 2$ $Q2 = 4$ $Q3 = \frac{5+6}{2} = 5.5$ Maximum = 18 Range = 18 − 1 = 17 $IQR = 5.5 - 2 = 3.5$	Rearrange the data in ascending order. Locate the median of the full dataset. $Q1$ is the median of the lower half of the dataset. $Q3$ is the median of the upper half of the dataset. Average the two middle values of the lower and upper halves of the dataset to find $Q1$ and $Q3$. Range = Maximum − Minimum $IQR = Q3 - Q1$
b. Lower bound $= 2 - 1.5 \times 3.5 = -3.25$ Upper bound $= 5.5 + 1.5 \times 3.5 = 10.75$ ∴ 18 is an outlier as it is greater than the upper bound.	Calculate the lower and upper bounds. Lower bound $= Q1 - 1.5 \times IQR$ Upper bound $= Q3 + 1.5 \times IQR$ There are no values less than -3.25, but one value is greater than 10.75 : 18.
c. Perhaps the tour visited a location that is home to a flock of ducks.	Give a possible reason for the outlier.

Exercise 11.4

a. Consider the following set of scores.

$$15,\ 23,\ 19,\ 11,\ 17,\ 26,\ 53,\ 14,\ 8,\ 18,\ 22,\ 17,\ 26,\ 16,\ 24$$

- **i.** Determine the range and IQR of the data by first finding the 5-number statistics summary.
- **ii.** Identify any outliers in the set of scores.

b. The reaction times, in milliseconds, for 10 motorists after seeing a brake light are as follows.

$$8.9,\ 6.8,\ 10.7,\ 8.1,\ 6.5,\ 8.6,\ 7.9,\ 11.8,\ 8.7,\ 8.5$$

- **i.** Determine the range and IQR of the data by first finding the 5-number statistics summary.
- **ii.** Identify any outliers in the data and provide a reason why they might have occurred.

11.5 Box plots

Box plots, also known as box-and-whisker plots, are a way of representing the spread and key features of a numerical dataset. They are particularly useful for comparing datasets and identifying outliers. An example is shown below.

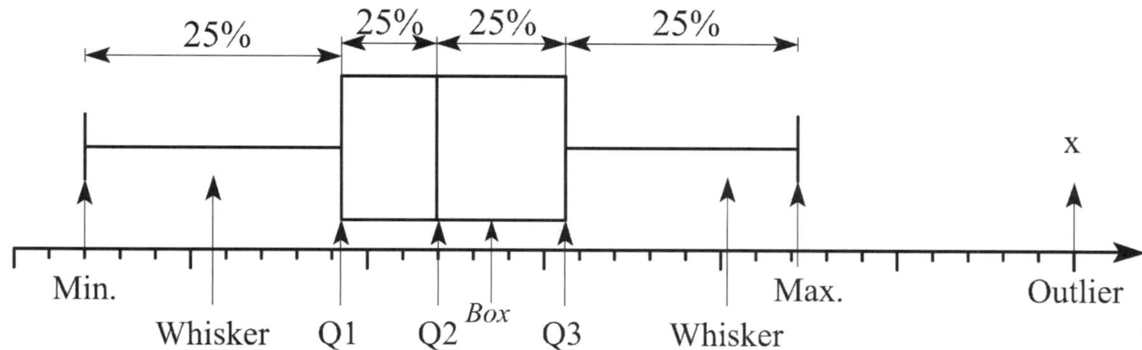

To create a box plot, follow these steps.

1. Arrange the data in ascending order.
2. Calculate the median ($Q2$).
3. Calculate the first quartile ($Q1$) and the third quartile ($Q3$).
4. Determine the size of the box. The box spans from $Q1$ to $Q3$, with a line indicating the median ($Q2$) within the box.
5. Determine the extent of the two whiskers. One whisker extends from the minimum value to $Q1$ and another whisker extends from $Q3$ to the maximum value.
6. Represent outliers as data points beyond the whiskers.

Example

Consider the dataset below. Draw a box plot to summarise the data, marking any outliers, if they exist.

$$12,\ 22,\ 22,\ 23,\ 27,\ 14,\ 27,\ 23,\ 21,\ 30,\ 26,\ 17,\ 23,\ 17$$

✓ *Solution*

Working	Explanation
12 14 17 17 21 22 22 23 23 23 26 27 27 30 Q1 (17), Q2 (between 22 and 23), Q3 (26)	Rearrange the data in ascending order.
$Q2 = 22.5$ $Q1 = 17$ $Q3 = 26$ $IQR = 26 - 17 = 9$ Lower bound $= 17 - 1.5 \times 9 = 3.5$ Upper bound $= 26 + 1.5 \times 9 = 39.5$	Determine the median (which will be $Q2$ on the box plot). Determine $Q1$, which is the middle value of the lower half. Determine $Q3$, which is the middle value of the upper half. Calculate $IQR = Q3 - Q1$. Calculate the lower bound: $Q1 - 1.5 \times IQR$. Calculate the upper bound: $Q3 + 1.5 \times IQR$.
There are no outliers.	There are no data values smaller than 3.5 or larger than 39.5, hence there are no outliers.
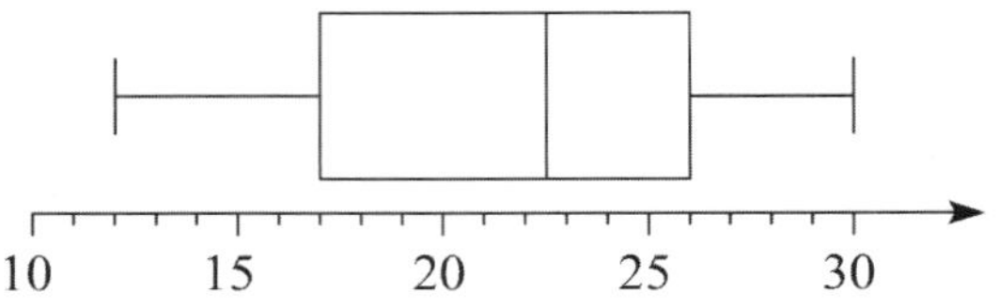 [Box plot on a scale: 10 15 20 25 30]	Draw a line and mark on it a uniform scale extending from 10 to 30. Sketch the box plot using the minimum, $Q1$, $Q2$, $Q3$ and maximum as a guide.

Example

Consider the dataset below. Draw a box plot to summarise the data, marking any outliers, if they exist.

$$11,\ 11,\ 11,\ 8,\ 1,\ 17,\ 10,\ 12,\ 10,\ 14,\ 9,\ 15,\ 9$$

✓ ***Solution***

Working	Explanation
1 8 9 9 10 10 11 11 11 12 14 15 17 Q1 (between 9 and 9), Q2 (11), Q3 (between 12 and 14)	Rearrange the data in ascending order.
$Q2 = 11$ $Q1 = \frac{9+9}{2} = 9$ $Q3 = \frac{12+14}{2} = 13$ $IQR = 13 - 9 = 4$ Lower bound $= 9 - 1.5 \times 4 = 3$ Upper bound $= 13 + 1.5 \times 4 = 19$	Determine the median (which will be $Q2$ on the box plot). Determine $Q1$, which is the middle value of the lower half. Determine $Q3$, which is the middle value of the lower half. Calculate $IQR = Q3 - Q1$. Calculate the lower bound: $Q1 - 1.5 \times IQR$. Calculate the upper bound: $Q3 + 1.5 \times IQR$.
∴ 1 is an outlier.	There are no data values greater than 19, but there is one data value that is less than 3. Hence there is an outlier.
0 5 10 15 20	Draw a line and mark on it a uniform scale extending from 0 to 20. Sketch the box plot using the minimum, $Q1$, $Q2$, $Q3$ and maximum as a guide. Disregard the outlier when marking the minimum value. Place a mark where the outlier is.

Exercise 11.5

Consider the datasets below. Draw a box plot to summarise the data, marking any outliers.

a. 7, 8, 3, 16, 23, 7, 12, 14, 10, 10, 9, 6, 8

b. 21, 18, 28, 30, 23, 17, 30, 27, 28, 19, 29, 20

11.6 Comparing datasets

When you describe data or compare two datasets, you need to consider the location, spread and shape of the data.

- **Location:** a measure of central tendency. The main measures are mean, median and mode.
- **Spread:** range.
- **Shape:** symmetrical or skewed.

For the location, you can choose to give the mean, median or mode of the data. The mean is most often used, but if there are a few very large or very small data points in the dataset, the median is often used. The mode can be used when there is a value that frequently occurs in the dataset.

For the spread, calculate the range (i.e. the largest value minus the smallest value).

For the shape, describe whether the data is scattered, symmetrical, bimodal or multimodal, and if it is positively or negatively skewed. The table below illustrates some of these features.

Box plot

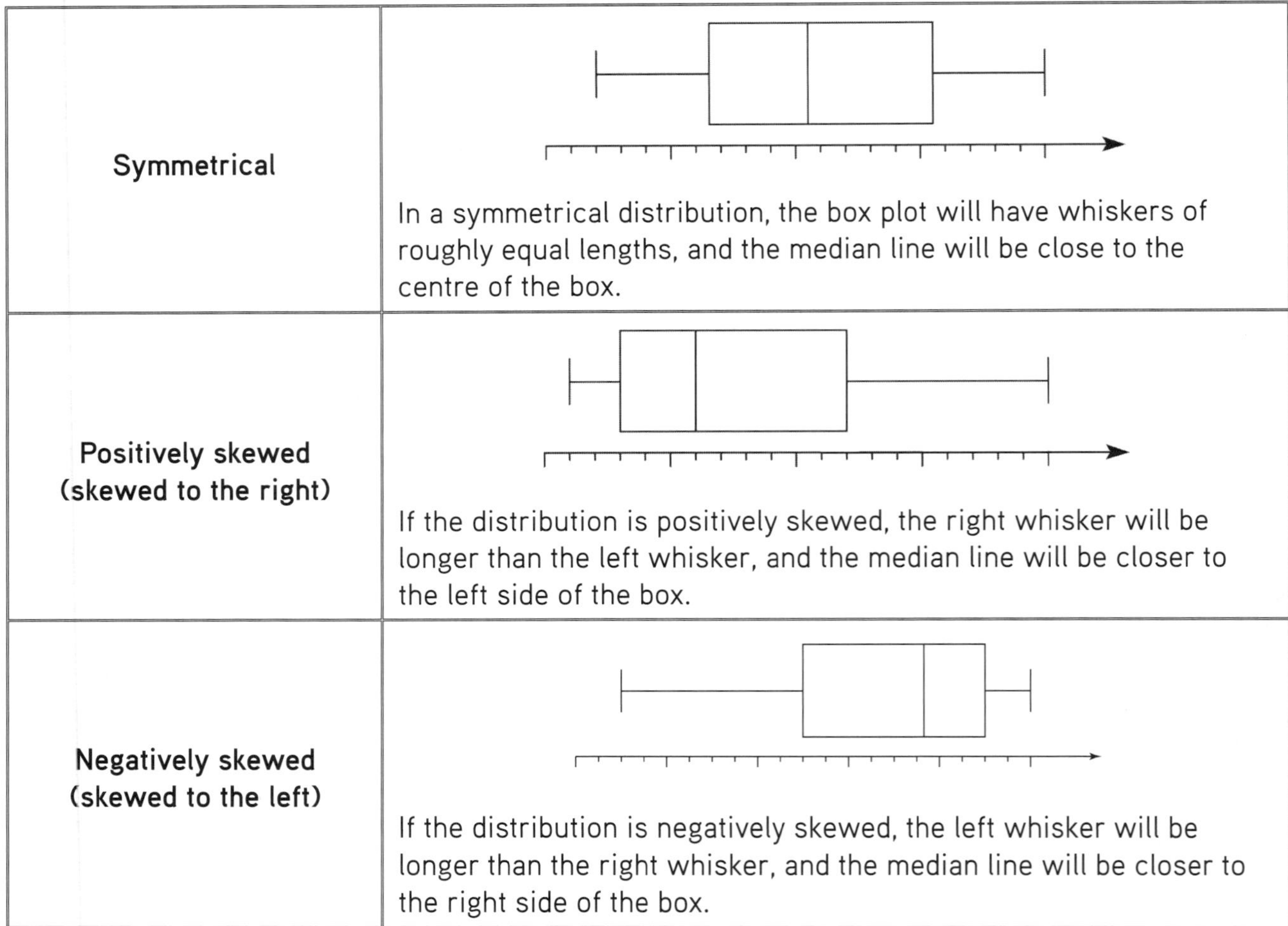

Symmetrical	In a symmetrical distribution, the box plot will have whiskers of roughly equal lengths, and the median line will be close to the centre of the box.
Positively skewed (skewed to the right)	If the distribution is positively skewed, the right whisker will be longer than the left whisker, and the median line will be closer to the left side of the box.
Negatively skewed (skewed to the left)	If the distribution is negatively skewed, the left whisker will be longer than the right whisker, and the median line will be closer to the right side of the box.

Histogram

Symmetrical	**Bimodal**
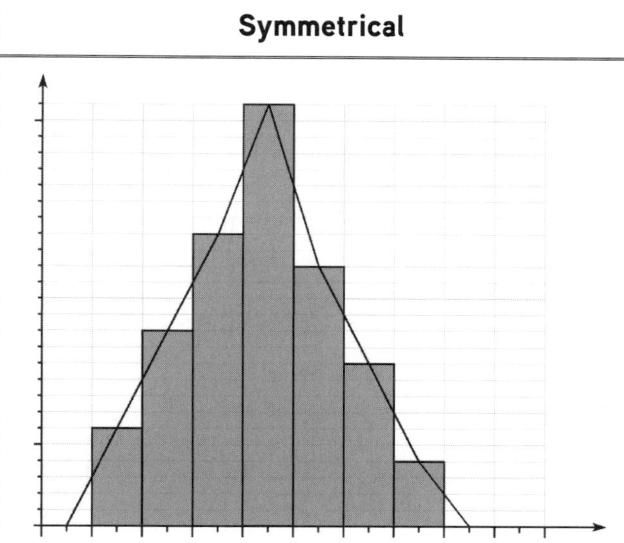 The histogram can be folded in half, with the centre line as the axis of symmetry.	Two bars of approximately the same height are much taller than the other bars.
Positively skewed (skewed to the right)	**Negatively skewed (skewed to the left)**
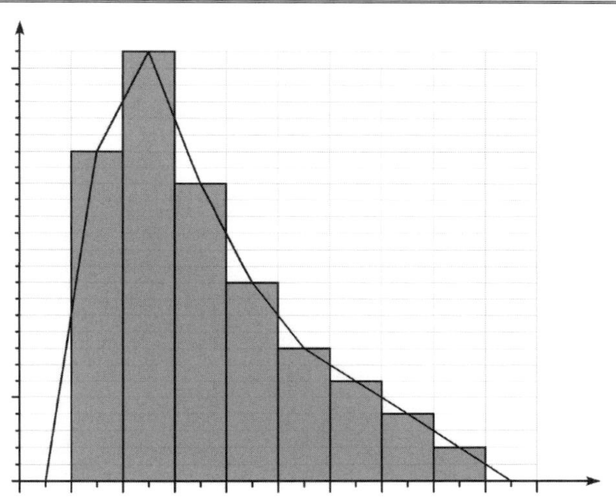 The tail on the right side is longer than the tail on the left side.	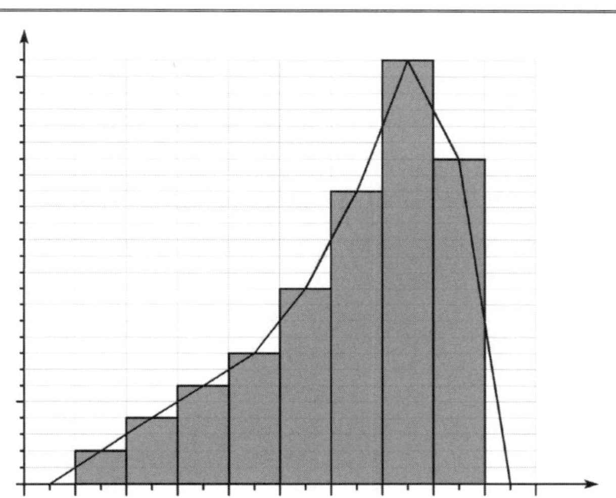 The tail on the left side is longer than the tail on the right side.

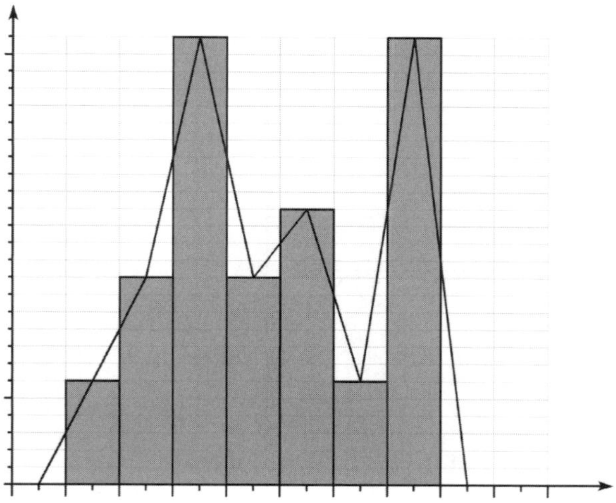

Stem-and leaf plot

Symmetrical	Positively skewed (skewed to the right)	Negatively skewed (skewed to the left)
A curve drawn along the edge of the leaves is evenly distributed around the stem with the most leaves.	The tail of a curve drawn along the edge of the leaves is longer towards the larger data points.	The tail of a curve drawn along the edge of the leaves is longer towards the smaller data points.

Symmetrical

Stem	Leaf
0	5
1	4 6
2	3 3 8
3	2 4 6 8 9
4	2 3 4 4 5 8 9
5	1 3 6 8 8
6	4 5 6
7	6 8
8	9

Positively skewed (skewed to the right)

Stem	Leaf
0	2 2 4 5 7
1	3 4 6 7 8
2	3 3 4 5 6 8 9
3	2 4 4 5 6 6
4	2 3 4 4 5
5	1 3 6
6	3 4
7	2
8	1

Negatively skewed (skewed to the left)

Stem	Leaf
0	5
1	4
2	3 3
3	2 4 6
4	2 3 4 4 5
5	1 3 6 8 8 8 9
6	1 3 4 4 5 6
7	1 3 6 8 8
8	1 2 4 5 7

Box plots compared with histograms

Consider the following histogram and box plot.

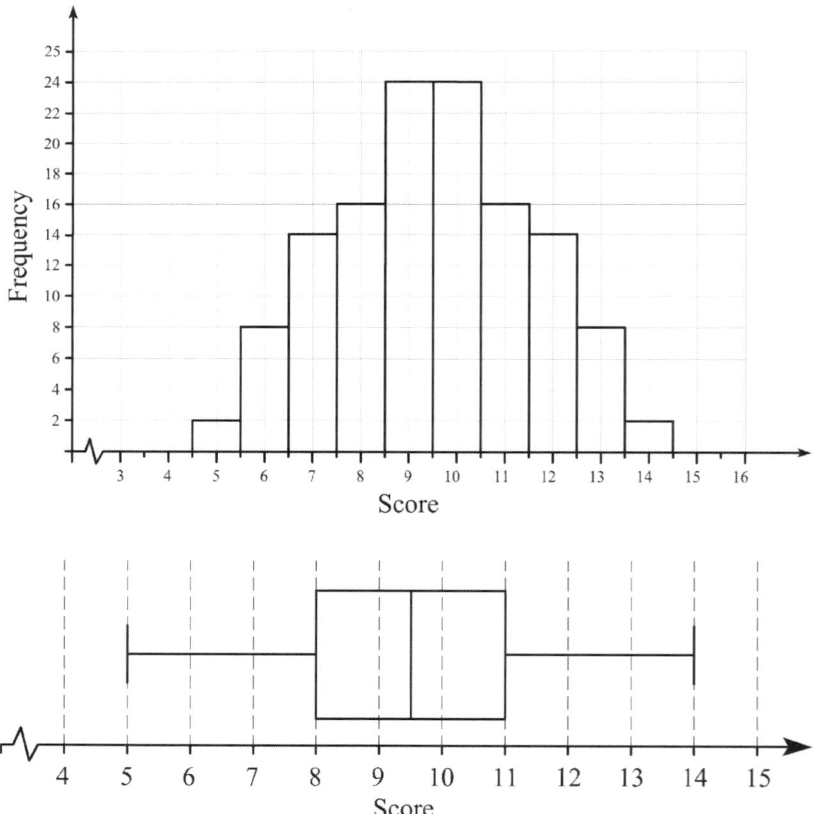

A histogram tells us the number of datapoints in the sample, the mean, median and mode, and the way the data is distributed.

A box plot confirms the information obtained from the histogram regarding the spread, median and distribution. The advantage of a box plot is that we are able to get this information solely by inspection, whereas we need to calculate this information when looking at a histogram. The disadvantage of a box plot is that it only displays the 5-number statistics and gives no information about individual scores (and thus we are unable to calculate the mean and mode).

Box plots are particularly useful when comparing datasets. You can draw parallel box plots – that is, two or more boxplots drawn on the same number line – and visually compare the central tendency and spread.

Example

Comment on the symmetry or asymmetry of the following box plots.

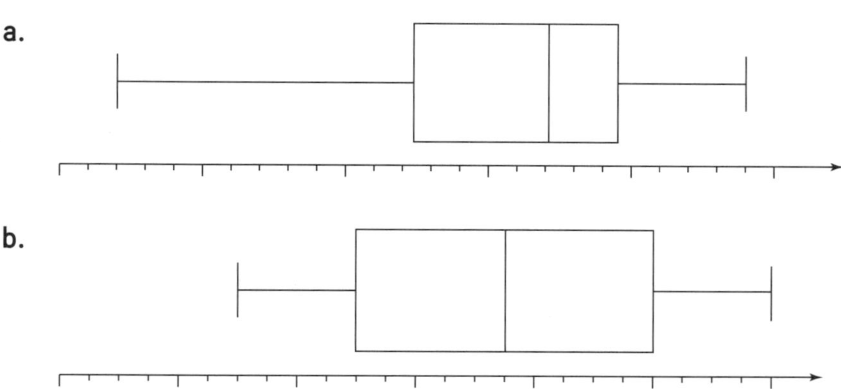

✓ *Solution*

Working	Explanation
a. The box plot is negatively skewed.	The left whisker is longer than the right whisker, and the median line is closer to the right side of the box. Therefore, it is negatively skewed.
b. The box plot is symmetrical about the median.	The whiskers are of roughly equal lengths and the median line is centred within the box. Therefore, it is symmetrical.

Example

The heights (in cm) of the students in two Year 10 classes are recorded below.

10A	148	149	150	150	153	154	154	154	155	155	156	156
	157	157	158	158	158	158	158	160	161	163	165	168
10B	150	151	152	152	152	153	153	154	155	155	155	156
	156	156	157	157	158	160	160	160	161	161	162	163

Draw parallel box plots of the data and compare the median, range and interquartile range of both classes.

✓ ***Solution***

<table>
<tr><th>Working</th><th>Explanation</th></tr>
<tr><td>

	10A	10B
Minimum	148	150
$Q1$	154	153
Median	156.5	156
$Q3$	158	160
Maximum	168	163

</td><td>First determine the 5-number statistics of each class.</td></tr>
<tr><td>145 150 155 160 165 170</td><td>Draw a line with a uniform scale reaching from 145 to 170. As the dataset starts from 145, we can draw a break in the axis to the left of 145.

Sketch the box plots by marking the minimum, $Q1$, $Q2$, $Q3$ and maximum.</td></tr>
<tr><td>Range of 10A $= 168 - 148 = 20$
IQR of 10A $= 158 - 154 = 4$

Range of 10B $= 163 - 150 = 13$
IQR of 10B $= 160 - 153 = 7$</td><td>Determine the range and the IQR.
Range = Maximum – Minimum
$IQR = Q3 - Q1$</td></tr>
<tr><td>The medians for the two classes are almost the same. The range for 10A is much larger than for 10B. However, the IQR for 10A is much smaller than the IQR for 10B.</td><td>Compare the two classes.</td></tr>
</table>

Example

Match each box plot to one of the graphs shown at the right.

i.

A.

ii.

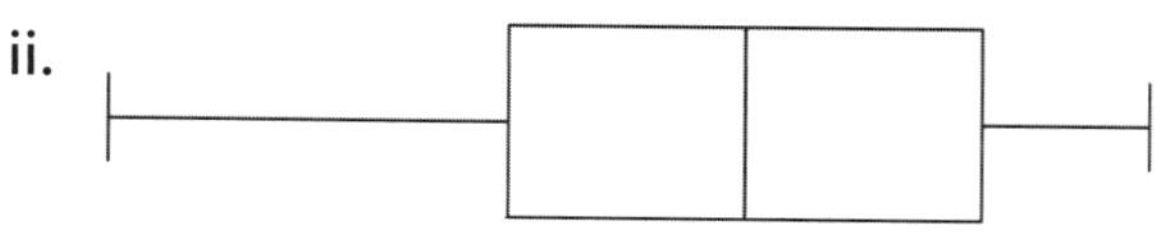

B.

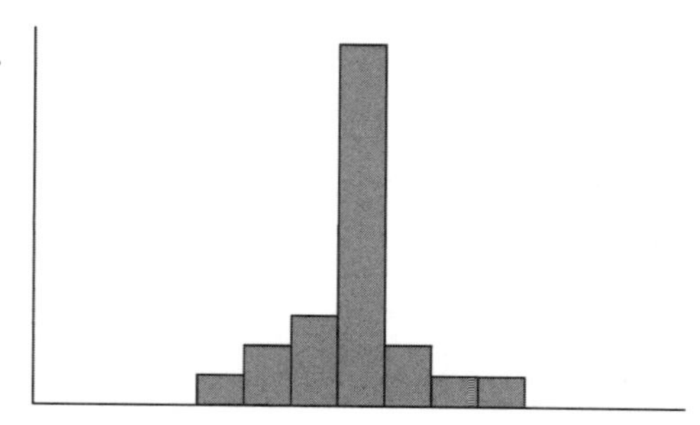

iii.

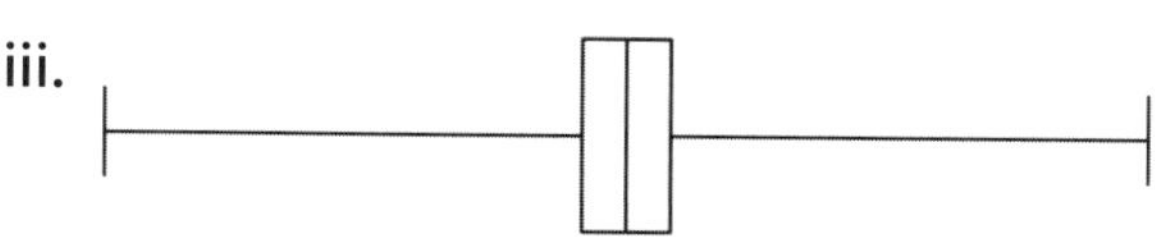

C.

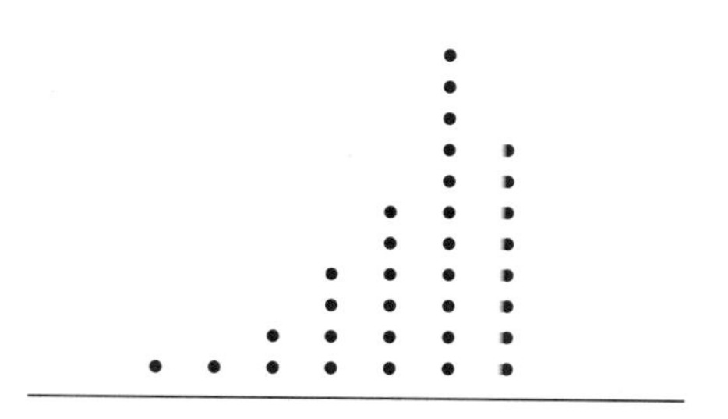

iv.

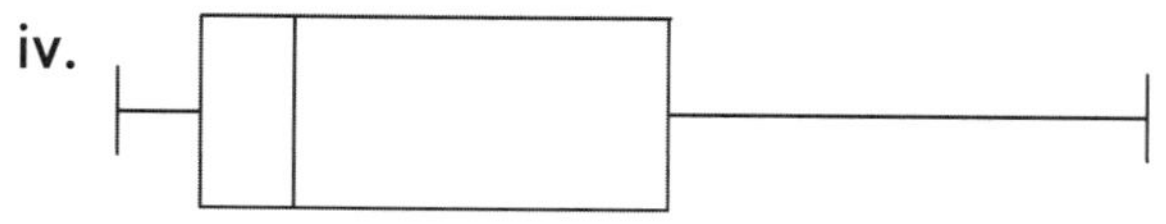

D.

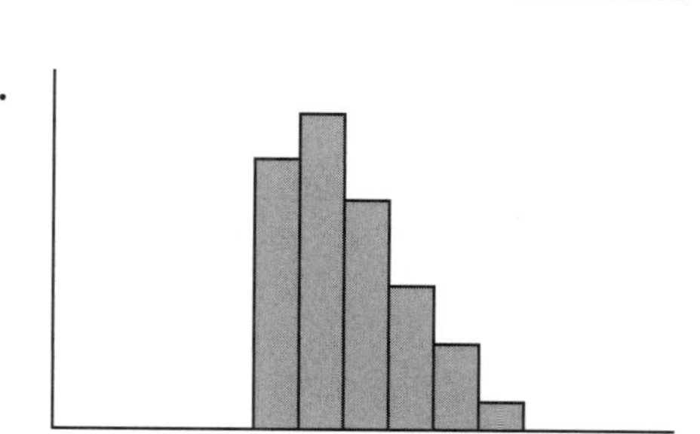

✓ ***Solution***

Working	Explanation
i and C	Both graphs are negatively skewed.
ii and A	Both graphs are symmetrical and the data is distributed evenly.
iii and B	Both graphs are symmetrical with the data centred around the median.
iv and D	Both graphs are positively skewed.

Exercise 11.6

a. Comment on the symmetry or asymmetry of the following box plots:

i.

ii.

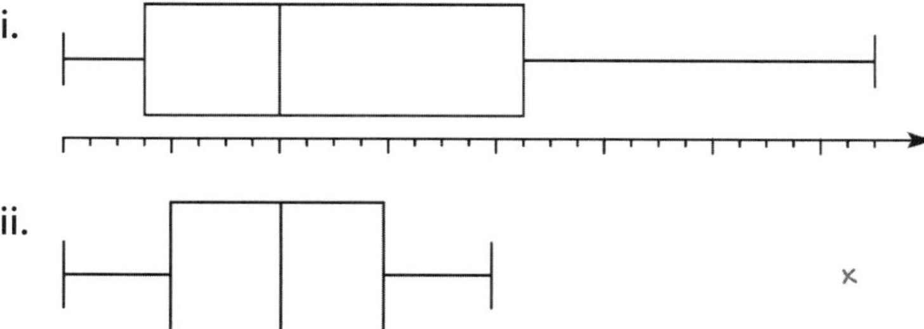

b. Four classes – A, B, C and D – take the same test, with students marked out of 100. The box plots to the right show the results.

i. In which class is the student who scored the highest mark?

ii. In which class is the student who scored the lowest mark?

iii. Which class had the highest median?

iv. Which class had the lowest median?

v. Which class had the smallest interquartile range?

vi. Which class had the greatest range of marks?

vii. Which class had the smallest range of marks?

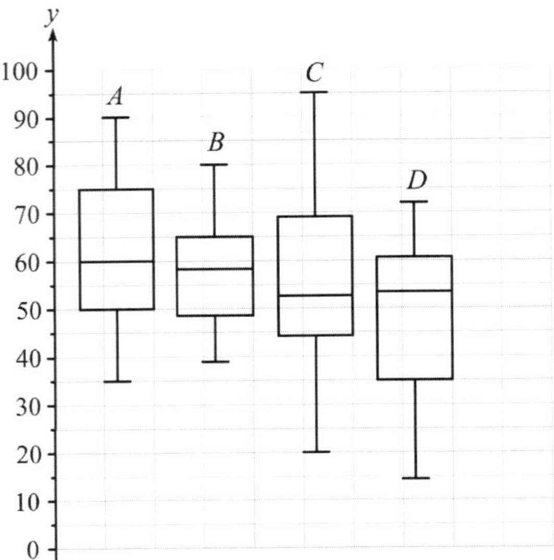

c. For each histogram shown below (labelled I to III), a box plot using the same set of data points has been constructed (labelled A to C). Match each histogram with its corresponding box plot.

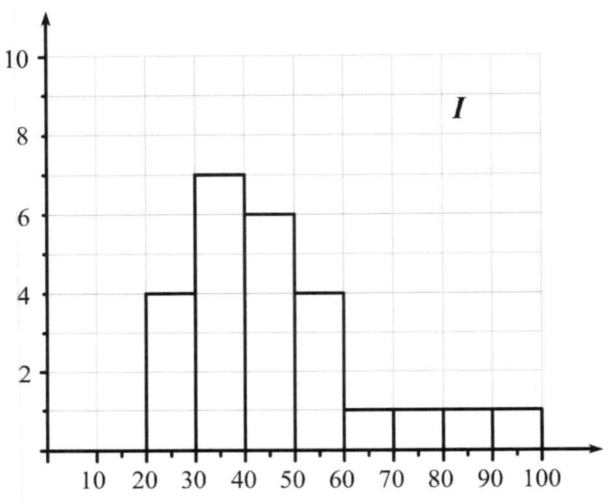

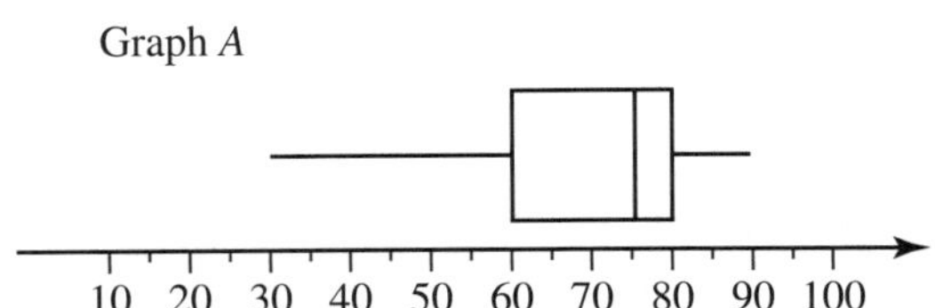

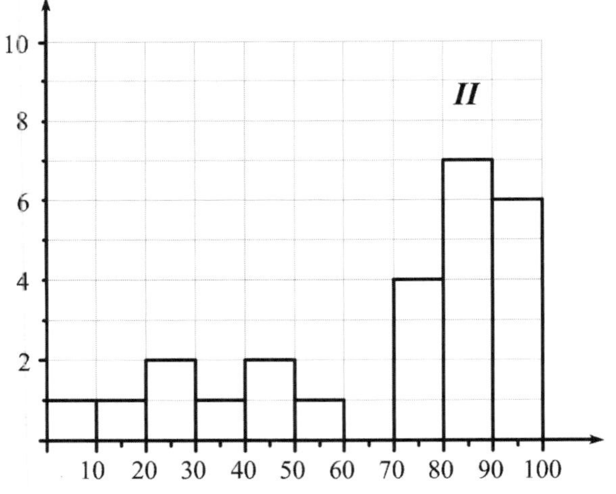

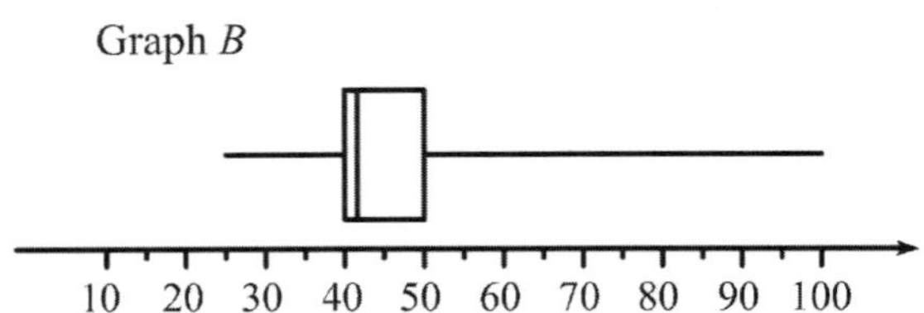

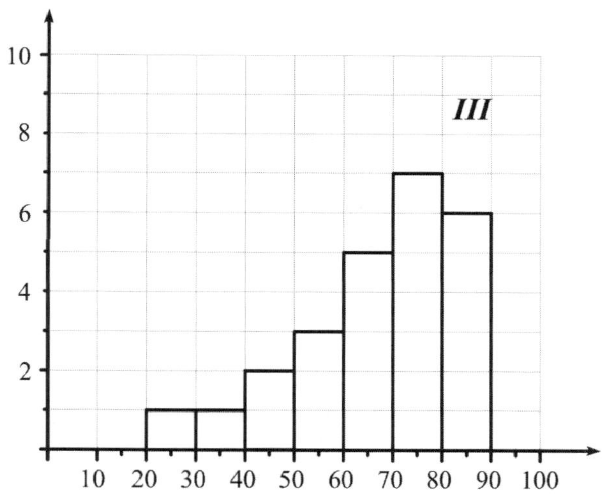

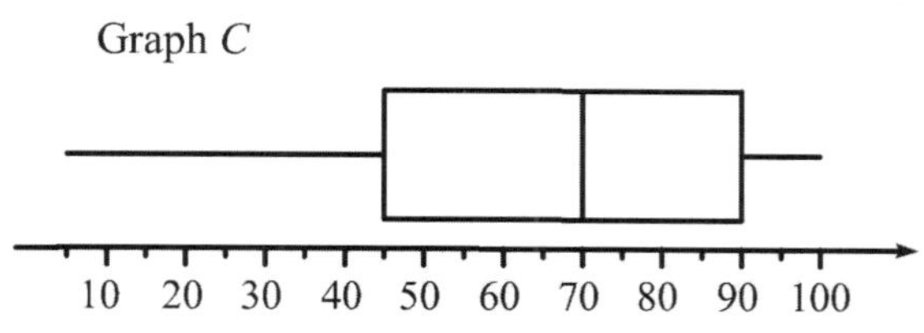

d. The dot plots below show the maths and science test results of a group of students. The results are out of a possible 10 marks in both subjects.

Maths test

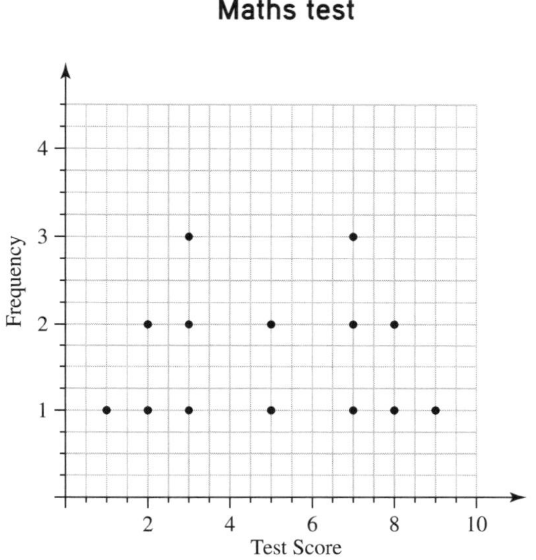

Science test

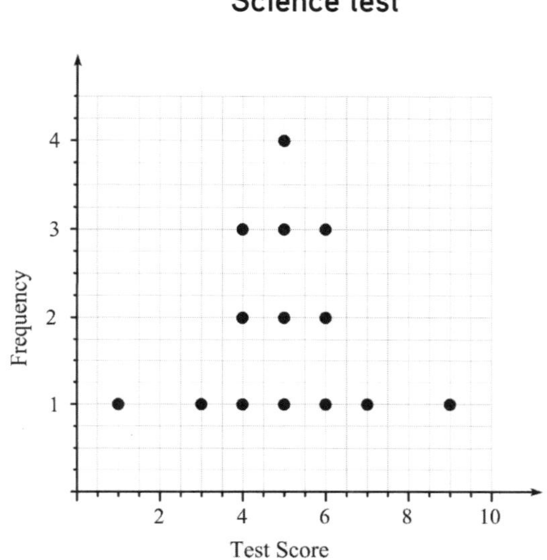

i. Construct parallel box plots for both the maths and science results.

ii. Comment on the similarities and differences between the two datasets.

11.7 Bivariate data

Bivariate data is data involving two variables that are usually collected together during observation. These variables can be numerical (e.g. height and weight) or categorical (e.g. hair colour and eye colour). By collecting the variables together, we can compare them and explore any relationship they might have.

Scatter plots

One way to display bivariate data is with a scatter plot. The data is displayed on a two-dimensional plane where:

- the horizontal axis (x-axis) represents one variable (e.g. studying hours)
- the vertical axis (y-axis) represents the other variable (e.g. exam scores).

The following terms describe the way variables are related.

Relationship	This term suggests that the variables are somehow interdependent, that is, that a change in one might influence the other. However, the term gives no indication of the strength or direction of that influence.
Correlation	This term refers to the strength and direction of a linear relationship between two quantitative variables (such as strong positive, weak negative or no correlation).
Association	This term indicates that two variables are not independent but have some connection. The association could be positive, negative, or even non-linear.

Types of correlation

The following scatter plots illustrate various types of correlation.

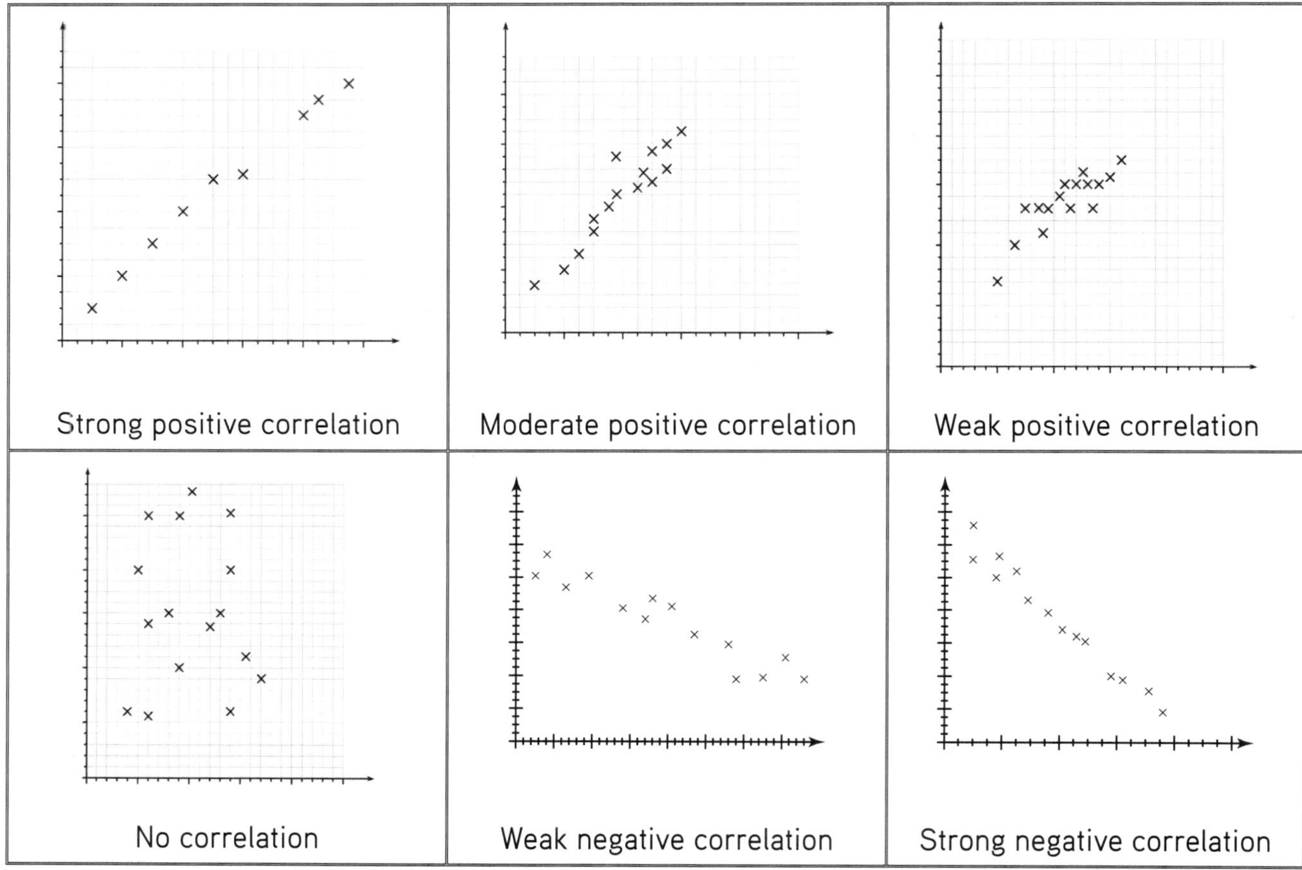

When commenting on a scatterplot, consider the following features.

- **Shape:** examine the shape of the distribution to see if the relationship between the variables looks linear or not linear.
- **Direction:** decide if the relationship is positive or negative.
- **Strength:** examine the distribution of the points and comment on the strength of their linear association.
- **Outliers:** check for any points that are located in an unusual position compared to the other points.

Association and causation

An **association** means that two variables tend to occur together more often than what might be expected by chance. This doesn't necessarily imply that one causes the other.

For example, a study shows a link between drinking coffee and living longer. This is an association. People who drink coffee might tend to live longer, but it doesn't mean coffee directly causes a longer lifespan. Other factors, such as coffee drinkers making healthier lifestyle decisions, could be the real reason.

Causation implies that one variable (the cause) directly influences another variable (the effect). A change in the cause leads to a change in the effect.

For example, a controlled experiment isolates a group of people who take a new medication and compares them to a control group who don't. If the medication group shows a significant improvement compared to the control group, this is strong evidence of causation: the medication caused the improvement.

Understanding the difference between association and causation is crucial for interpreting data and avoiding misleading conclusions. Two things might appear related, but this does not mean that one causes the other.

For instance, a news report might claim that a rise in ice cream sales causes more shark attacks. While there might be an association (both increase in summer), it is highly unlikely that ice cream sales directly cause shark attacks. There is likely to be a third factor, such as warmer water temperatures, that influences both.

Example

Draw a scatter plot for the following data and describe the correlation, identifying any outliers.

x	4	7	2	10	3	5	6	9	8	4
y	5	6	4	8	4	4	5	7	6	3

✓ *Solution*

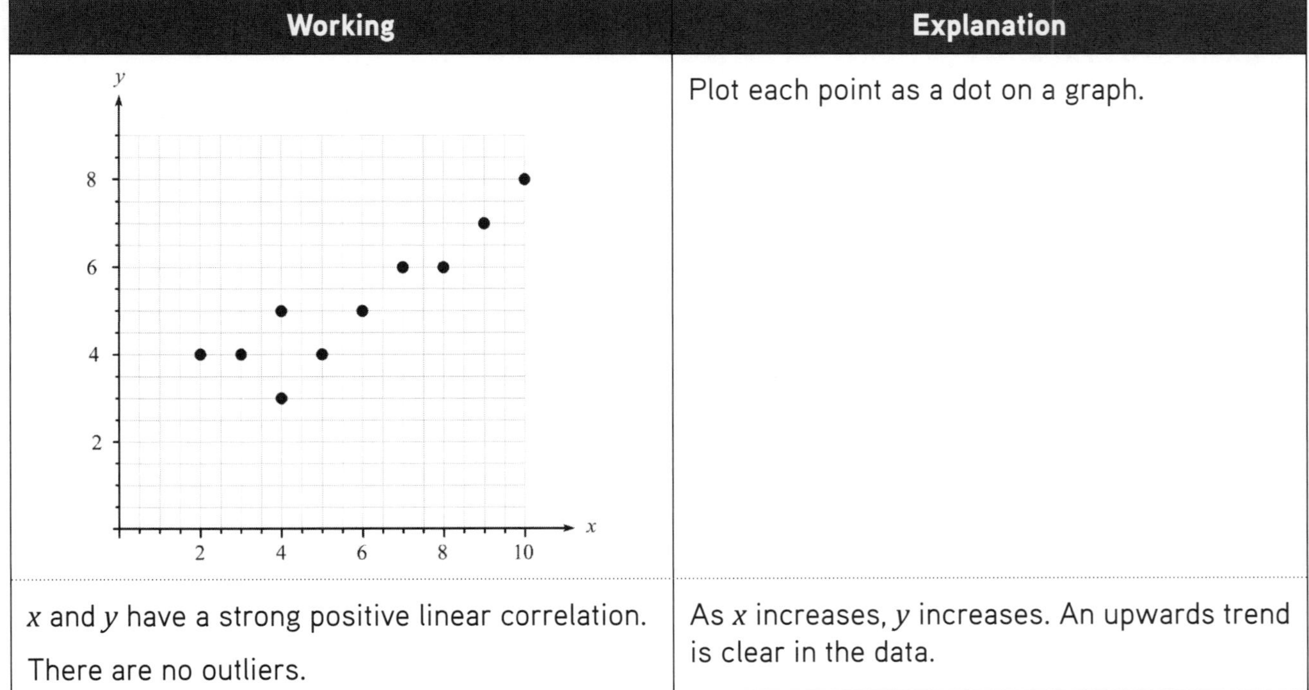

Working	Explanation
(scatter plot)	Plot each point as a dot on a graph.
x and y have a strong positive linear correlation. There are no outliers.	As x increases, y increases. An upwards trend is clear in the data.

Example

Draw a scatter plot for the following data and describe the correlation, identifying any outliers.

x	3	9	2	17	3	6	8	15	11
y	1.6	4	6.2	1.3	5.5	4.2	3.5	1.6	2.8

✓ Solution

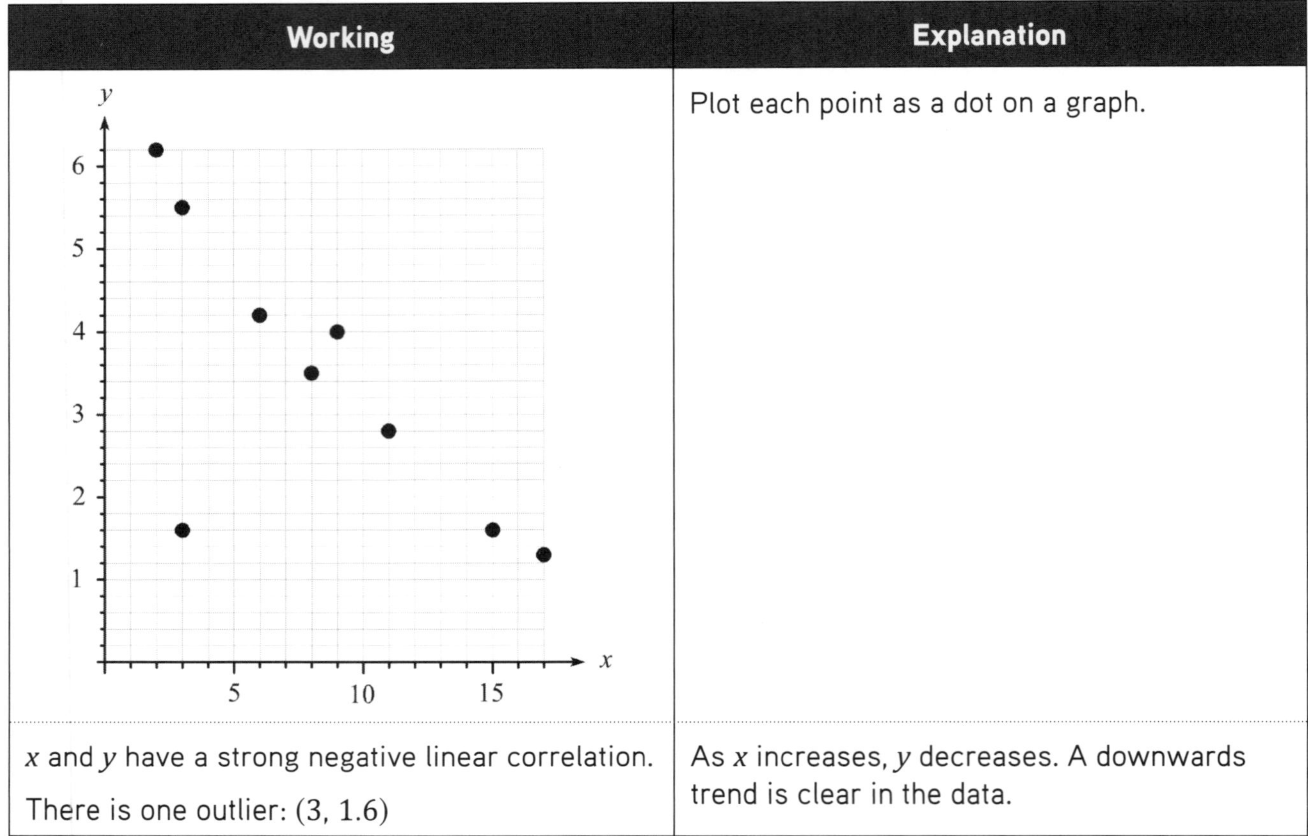

Working	Explanation
(scatter plot)	Plot each point as a dot on a graph.
x and y have a strong negative linear correlation. There is one outlier: (3, 1.6)	As x increases, y decreases. A downwards trend is clear in the data.

Exercise 11.7.1

a. Draw a scatter plot for each of the following datasets. Describe the correlation and identify any outliers.

i.

x	11	15	12	10	13	15	16	11	18	17
y	8	10	6	8	7	2	5	4	9	7

ii.

x	1	2	3	4	4	5	6	7	8	9
y	3	4	3	4	8	4	5	6	6	7

b. The risk of a motor vehicle accident is associated with a driver's blood alcohol level (*BAL*). The risk factor, *R*, is the number of times more likely it is that a driver who has alcohol in their bloodstream will have a crash than a driver with no alcohol in their bloodstream. The table below shows the relationship between *BAL* and *R*. Construct a scatter plot of the data and describe the correlation.

BAL	0	0.04	0.08	0.10	0.15	0.17	0.18	0.20
R	1	2	4	15	28	40	55	70

c. A group of 12-year-old children were given two fitness tests. The first test was to measure maximum lung capacity before exercise and the second was to measure heart rate one minute after strenuous exercise. The test results are tabled below.

Lung capacity	48	26	45	36	40	43	30	29	38	44	35	39	33
Heart rate	80	95	84	90	85	84	82	94	90	82	88	86	92

i. Construct a scatter plot of the data.

ii. Describe the correlation between the two variables and suggest what this might mean.

iii. Identify the child with the greatest variation from the main group.

Line of best fit

The line of best fit, also known as the trend line or regression line, is a straight line drawn through a scatter plot that attempts to represent the overall trend of the data points. We can draw a line of best fit by balancing the number of points above and below the line. Once we have drawn the line, we can find the equation of the line from the coordinates of two points on it.

The line of best fit can help us to understand relationships. By looking at the slope and direction of the line, we can get a sense of the direction (positive or negative) and strength of the relationship between two variables plotted on a scatter plot.

The line of best fit can also be used to make predictions. Once you have the equation of the line of best fit, you can use it to predict the value of one variable based on the value of the other variable, either through **interpolation** or **extrapolation**.

- Interpolation is predicting an unknown value that falls between existing data points.
- Extrapolation is predicting a value that extends beyond the range of the existing data points.

Example

A veterinary clinic keeps a record of the mass and height of the dogs it treats, shown in the table below.

Mass (kg)	10	15	20	20	30	35	40
Height (cm)	20	30	30	40	50	50	70

a. Construct a scatter plot of the data and describe the correlation between the two variables.

b. Draw a line of best fit on the scatter plot and determine the equation of the line.

c. Use the line of best fit to estimate a dog's height if its mass is 25 kg.

d. Use the line of best fit to estimate a dog's mass if its height is 80 cm.

e. Why might using the line of best fit to make predictions cause problems?

✓ *Solution*

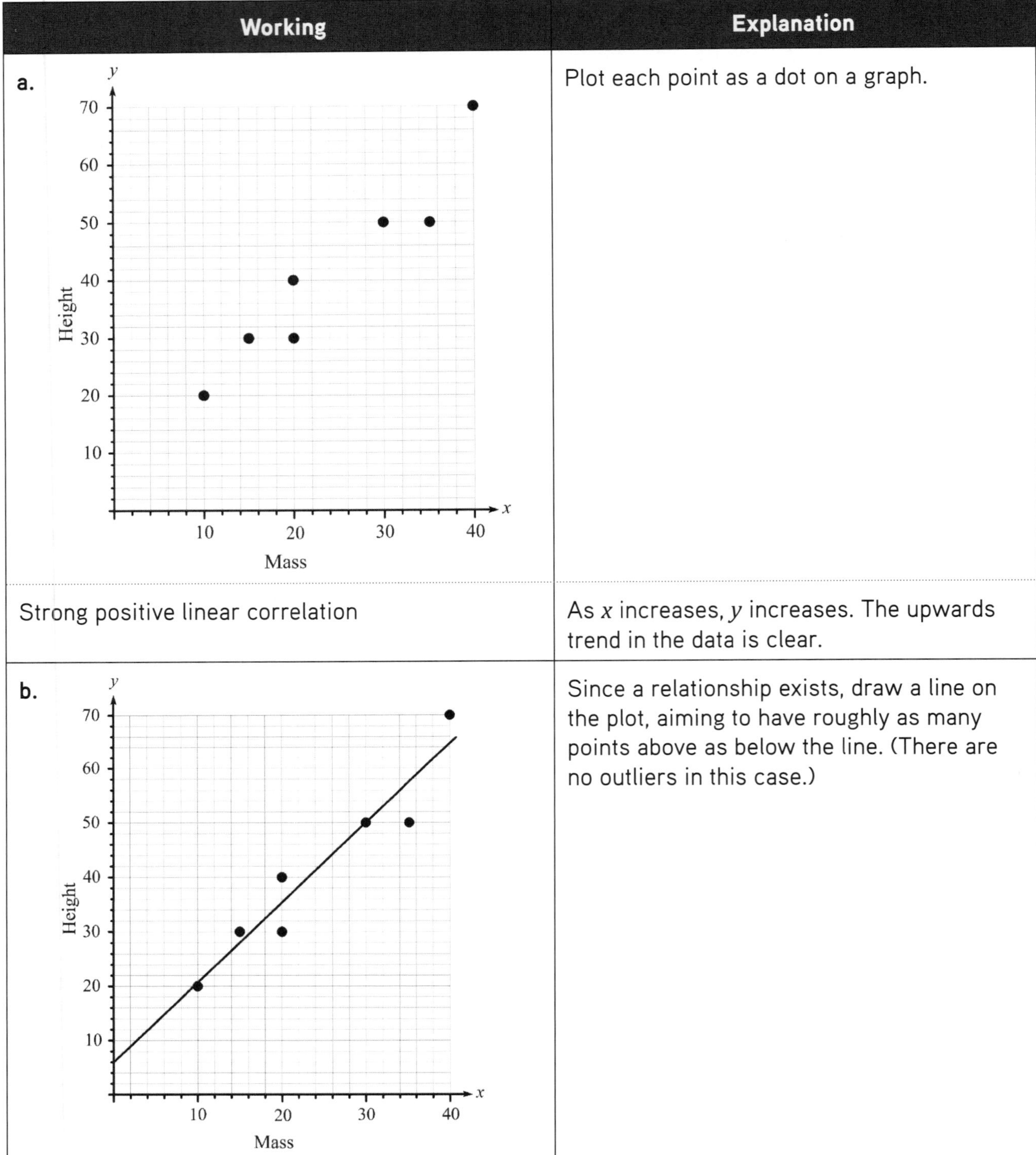

Working	Explanation
a. (scatter plot: Height against Mass)	Plot each point as a dot on a graph.
Strong positive linear correlation	As x increases, y increases. The upwards trend in the data is clear.
b. (scatter plot with line of best fit: Height against Mass)	Since a relationship exists, draw a line on the plot, aiming to have roughly as many points above as below the line. (There are no outliers in this case.)

Gradient $= \frac{50 - 20}{30 - 10} = \frac{3}{2}$ $(y - 20) = \frac{3}{2}(x - 10)$ $y = \frac{3}{2}x - 15 + 20$ $y = \frac{3}{2}x + 5$	Determine the gradient of the line by choosing 2 points on it: for example, $(10, 20)$ and $(30, 50)$. Substitute the gradient and the coordinates of one point into the point-slope form of a linear equation to determine the equation of the line.
c. Substitute $x = 25$. $y = 42.5$ cm The height of the dog is approximately 42.5 cm.	Substitute the mass, $x = 25$, into the equation to estimate the height.
d. Substitute $y = 80$. $80 = \frac{3}{2}x + 5$ $x = 50$ kg The weight of the dog is approximately 50 kg.	Substitute the height, $y = 80$, into the equation to estimate mass.
e. A dog of mass 1 kg would only have a height of 6.5 cm, which is unrealistic.	Test the equation for a mass beyond the values in the dataset.

Exercise 11.7.2

a. Consider the following dataset.

x	6	13	10	8	18	4	17	5	2	15	17	9
y	16	20	25	14	28	9	29	8	11	27	24	20

i. Construct a scatter plot of the data and draw a line of best fit by eye.

ii. Determine the equation that indicates a relationship between the two variables.

iii. Use the line of best fit to estimate y when $x = 7$.

iv. Use the line of best fit to estimate x when $y = 40$.

b. A survey conducted by the Chicken Meat Association compared the number of weeks a chicken has been on a special diet with the weight gained during that period. The data collected is tabled below.

No. of weeks on the diet (n)	5	15	18	9	20	7	20	30	15	25
Weight gain in grams (w)	80	200	220	150	260	100	240	300	180	280

i. Construct a scatter plot of the data and draw a line of best fit by eye.

ii. Determine the equation of the line of best fit.

iii. Use the line of best fit to estimate w when $n = 52$.

iv. Use the line of best fit to estimate n when $w = 250$.

v. Identify a problem that might arise from using the line of best fit to make predictions.

11.8 Statistical investigation process

It is important to understand the process by which statistical investigations are carried out. This process is represented in the diagram below.

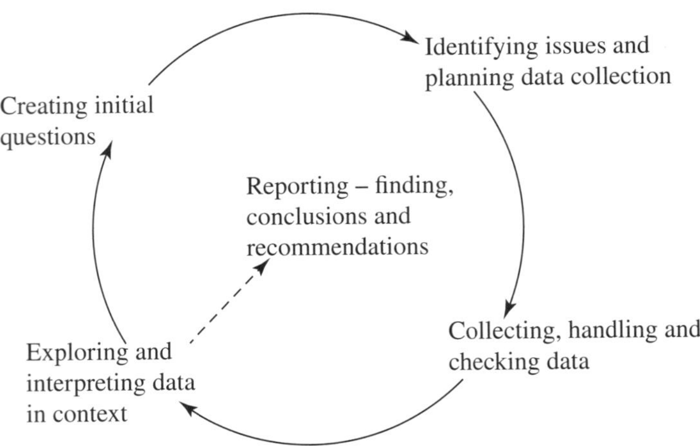

A statistical investigation typically begins by asking one or more relevant questions. For example, if the school canteen would like to know what type of specials they should feature in different months, their initial questions might include the following.

- Do the students prefer hot or cold meals?
- Do the students have any preferences for certain types of food depending on the weather (e.g. warm soups in colder weather, refreshing salads in warmer weather)?
- Are there any differences in purchasing habits between students from different year levels?

The next step is to think about the issues that need to be considered when planning a statistical investigation. Determining the sample size, identifying appropriate measures or variables, and deciding how to pick an appropriate sample are all important. In the example above, issues could include:

- How many students should be surveyed?
- Do we pick 10 students per year group to answer our questions?
- How do we carry out the survey: interview in person or with an online method such as a Google form?

The next step is to think about collecting and checking the data. It is very important to check for any obvious mistakes (for example, a Year 11 student might have entered their grade as 'Year 1').

Once the data has been received, it needs to be explored and interpreted. The data could be displayed visually – as a stem-and-leaf plot or histogram, for example – and analysed using the statistical descriptors discussed in this chapter (i.e. location, spread and shape). The results of the analysis can then be used to make recommendations and decisions.

Note that this can be a cyclical process. Analysing the data may prompt more questions which lead to another investigation. In fact, there may be numerous iterations until the findings support a satisfactory recommendation.

Chapter 12 – Networks

12.1 Introduction

A **network** is composed of a set of nodes or points (called **vertices**) which are connected by a set of lines (called **edges**). The areas enclosed by the edges are called **faces** (or regions).

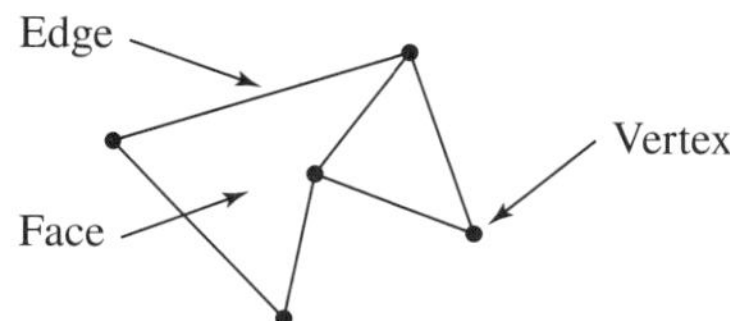

Networks are used to represent many real-life situations, such as railway systems, travel itineraries, and water and power connections.

For example, the network shown on the right represents certain ways of travelling by car from Melbourne to Shepparton.

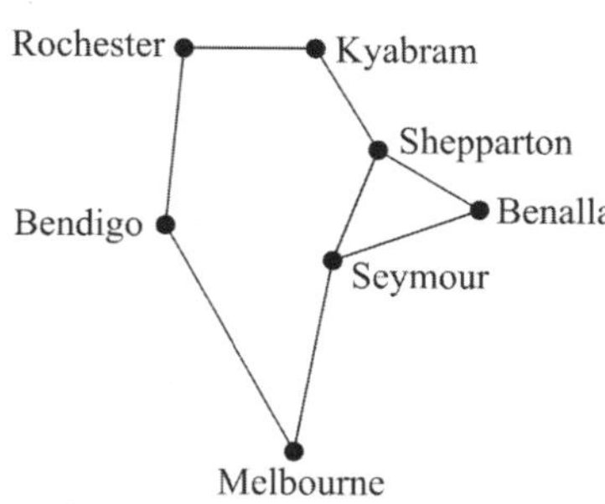

12.2 Properties of networks

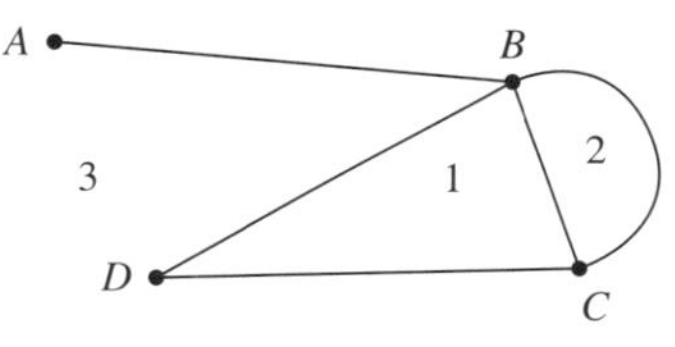

The network on the right has 4 vertices, 5 edges and 3 faces.

Vertices are usually labelled with capital letters.

Edges are labelled by joining the labels of the connecting vertices (e.g. the line between A and B is called edge AB).

Faces 1 and 2 are clearly bounded by edges. Face 3 is not bound by edges but it is still considered a face. (Faces are labelled in this diagram, but they are not usually labelled.)

Between vertices B and C there are two edges. These are called **multiple edges** (i.e. edges with the same start and end vertices).

This is a **connected** network because all vertices are connected.

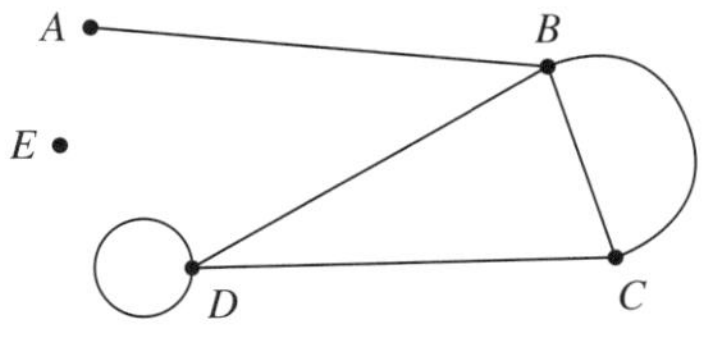

Consider the network on the left, where an additional vertex has been added (E). Vertex E is called an **isolated vertex** because it is not connected to any other vertex in the network. Since there is an isolated vertex, this network is **not connected**.

At vertex D there is an edge connecting to itself. This edge is called a **loop**.

Vertices A and B are **adjacent** vertices as they are connected by an edge. Vertices A and C are not adjacent because there is no edge connecting them.

Example

State the number of vertices, edges, faces, adjacent vertices and multiple edges in each network below.

a.

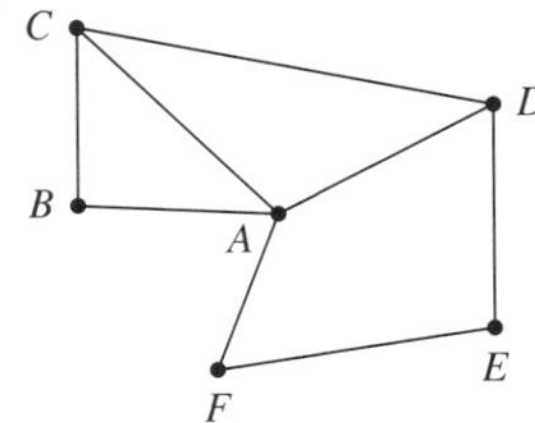

b.

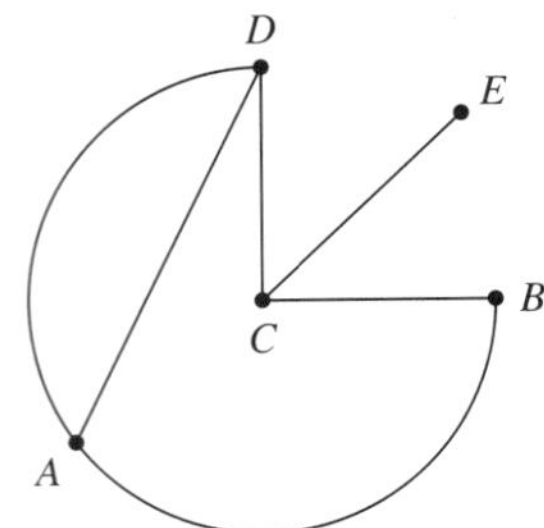

✓ Solution

	Working	Explanation
a.	6 vertices, 8 edges and 4 faces	Count the number of vertices, edges and faces. For the faces, you must include the area outside the network as one of the faces.
	Adjacent vertices: A and B, B and C, A and D, C and D, D and E, A and C, E and F, A and F	State all the adjacent vertices.
	No multiple edges	There are no multiple edges.
b.	5 vertices, 6 edges and 3 faces	Count the number of vertices, edges and faces.
	Adjacent vertices: A and D, D and C, C and E, B and C, A and B	State all the adjacent vertices.
	Multiple edges: AD, AD	State the multiple edges. Since there are two edges connecting A and D, state the edge twice.

Exercise 12.2

State the number of vertices, edges, faces, adjacent vertices, multiple edges, loops and isolated vertices in the networks below.

a.

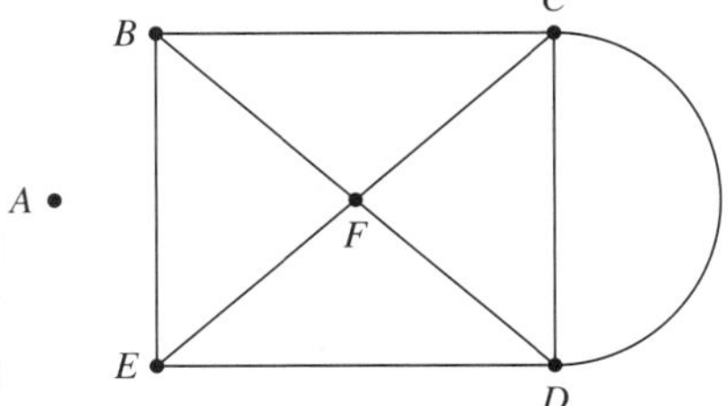

b.

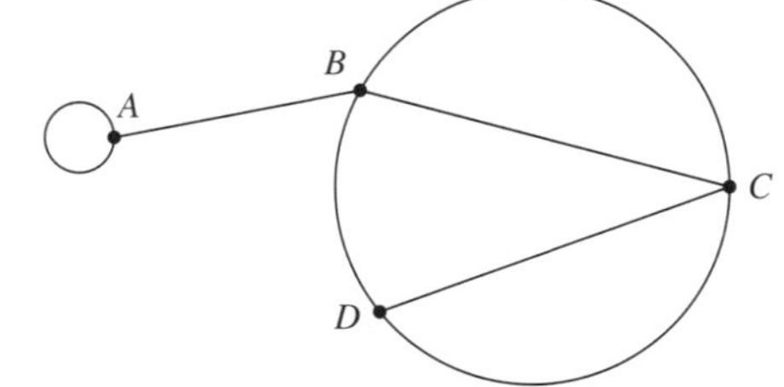

12.3 Weighted and directed networks

A network can have weights indicated on its edges. Weights might represent the distance between two points or the cost of installing a cable between two buildings.

A network can also have directions indicated on its edges. Directions might represent a one-way street or social network connections.

Weighted networks

The road network from Melbourne to Shepparton considered earlier in this chapter could be redrawn with the distance, in kilometres, between nodes added as labels to the edges, as shown in the diagram on the right.

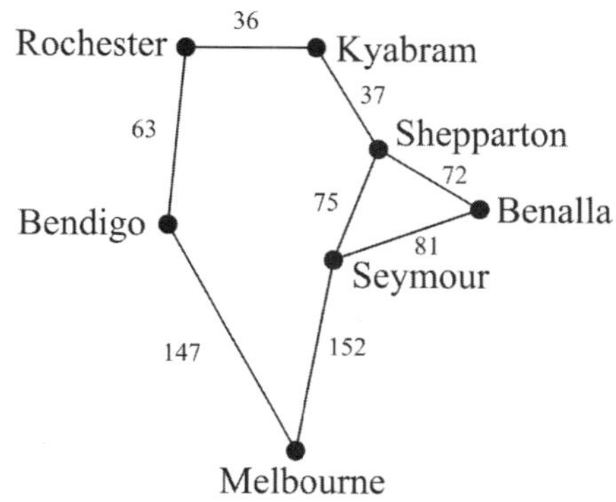

With this information, it is possible to determine the shortest distance between Melbourne and Shepparton (227 km). If the trip had to go via Benalla, we can determine that the shortest distance will now be 305 km. (Note that a network need not be drawn to scale.)

Example

A courier has to travel from A to C via B. The available routes between each node and the time in minutes it takes to travel between them are shown in the network diagram below.

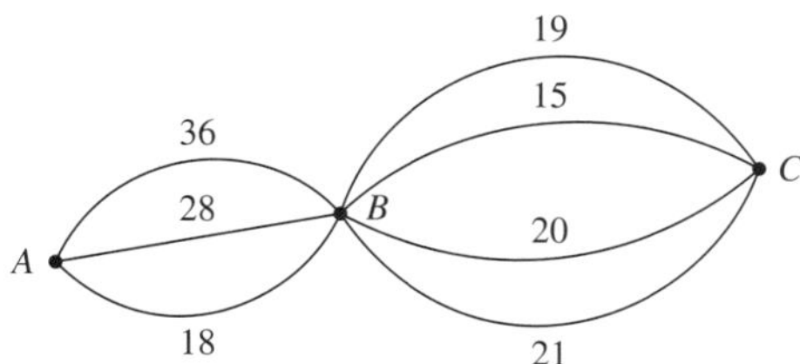

a. List the number of ways the courier can travel from A to B, B to C and A to C.

b. What is the shortest time it will take the courier to get from A to C?

✓ *Solution*

Working	Explanation
a. There are 3 ways to travel from A to B.	**1.** Count the number of edges from A to B: this is the number of possible routes between A and B.
There are 4 ways to travel from B to C.	**2.** Count the number of edges from B to C: this is the number of possible routes between B and C.
There are 12 ways to travel from A to C.	**3.** The number of routes between A and C via B is 3×4 (i.e. 3 possible ways from A to B and 4 possible ways from B to C).
b. The shortest time to travel from A to C is 33 minutes.	Determine the shortest travelling time between A and B, and between B and C. • The shortest time to travel from A to B is 18 minutes. • The shortest time to travel from B to C is 15 minutes. Add the two times together. This is the shortest travelling time from A to C.

Example

The network below shows the routes Ms Wade can take to drive to school (S) from her house (H).

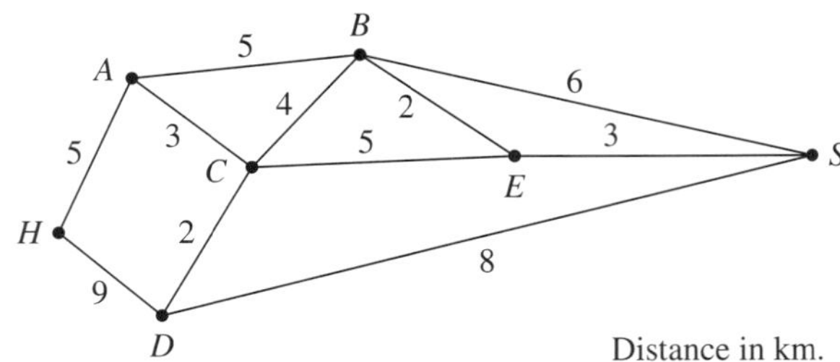

a. State the distance Ms Wade has to drive if she takes the route $HDCES$.

b. Determine the shortest route from Ms Wade's house to the school.

✓ *Solution*

Working	Explanation
a. $9 + 2 + 5 + 3 = 19$ km	Add up the distances from H to D, D to C, C to E and E to S.
b. Start by determining the shortest distance from H to each vertex and continue until you reach S. The shortest route from Ms Wade's home to the school is $HABES$ and the distance is 15 km.	From H to A there is only one way and therefore the shortest distance is 5 km. Write that distance beside vertex A. Similarly, the shortest distance from H to D is 9 km. From H to C, she can go via A or D. The shortest distance is via A, therefore the shortest distance from H to C is 8 km. From H to B, she can go via A or C. The shortest distance is via A, therefore the shortest distance from H to B is 10 km. From H to E, she has to go via A and then either B or C. The shortest distance is via B, therefore the shortest distance from H to E is 12 km. This leaves the distance from E to S. The shortest distance from E to S is 3 km. Hence the shortest distance between H and S is 15 km. The shortest route is $HABES$, shown on the diagram on the left.

Directed networks

Arrows on the edges of a network diagram show the allowable direction of travel from one vertex to another. If there is no arrow on an edge, you can assume that travel can occur along it in both ways.

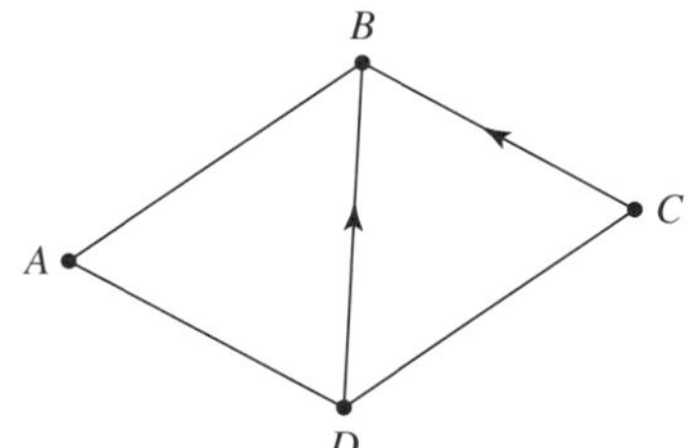

Consider the network diagram shown on the left. The arrow on edge BC indicates that you can travel from C to B but not from B to C. Similarly, you can travel directly from D to B but not vice versa.

Example

The network diagram to the right shows how six friends interact on a social network site.

a. Can M interact directly with L on the social network site?

b. List the pairs of friends who can interect with one another.

c. Who should J approach to pass a message to M?

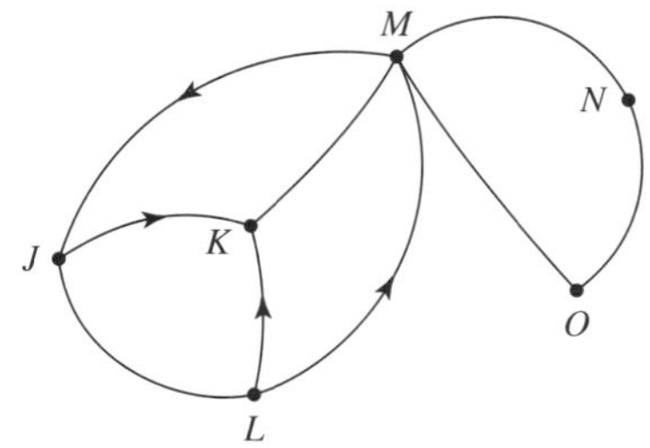

✓ *Solution*

Working	Explanation
a. No	The arrow on edge LM indicates that L can interact with M but not vice versa.
b. J and L, K and M, M and O, O and N, and M and N	The edges with no arrows show that the friends can interact with one another.
c. K or L	J cannot interact directly with M and has to go through L or K.

Example

A courier has to travel from A to C and back via B. The available routes between each node and the time it takes to travel between them are shown in the network diagram on the right.

Determine the shortest time for the courier to travel from A to C and back to A.

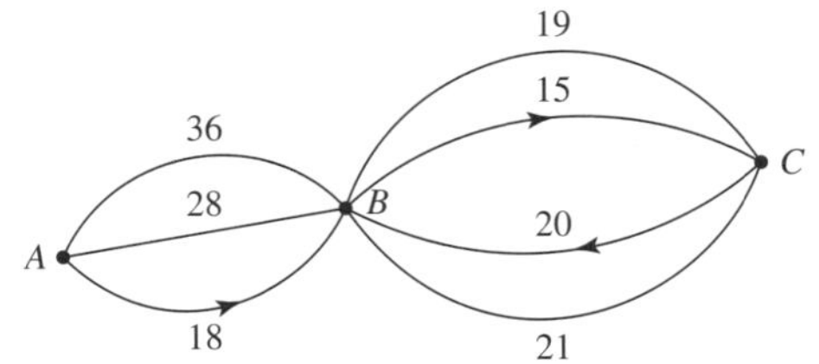

Travel times in minutes

✓ *Solution*

Working	Explanation
$18 + 15 + 19 + 28 = 80$ minutes	The shortest time to go from A to C is to go via the two shortest routes $(18 + 15)$. Going from C to A, the courier cannot go via the two shortest routes from A to C, so they have to use other routes $(19 + 28)$.

Exercise 12.3

a. The cost of replacing fibre optics cables between six buildings at a school is represented in the network diagram on the right.

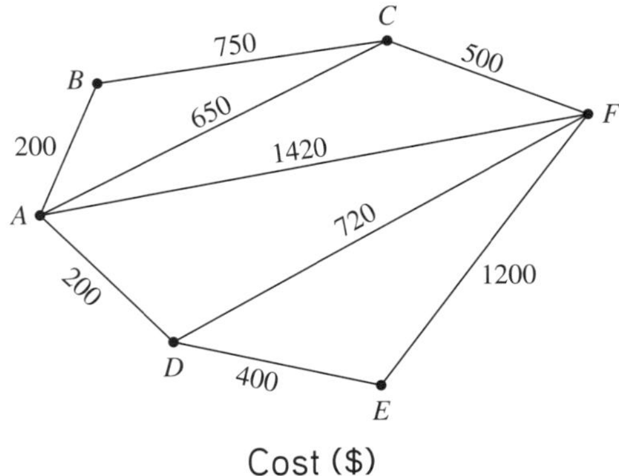

i. How much would it cost to replace the cables along route $ADFC$?

ii. Determine the cheapest route to replace the cables from A to F.

iii. It was found that the current fibre optics cable from E to F is still working properly and will not need to be replaced. What is the cheapest route and cost to replace the cable from A to F?

b. The network diagram on the right represents the ferry routes between islands at a tourist hotspot.

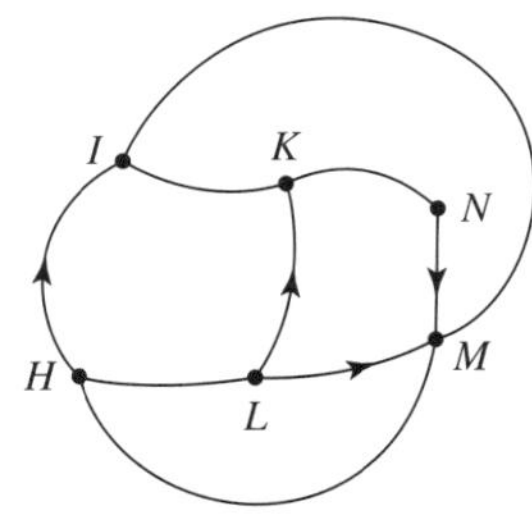

i. A group of tourists starts from L. What could be their first stop(s)?

ii. A tourist intends to start from H, travel directly to M and then directly to L. Is this route possible? Justify your answer.

iii. Another tourist starts from I and would like to visit every island once. (She is happy to finish her trip on a different island.) Determine the route she should take.

c. Hiking trails in a national park are represented in the network diagram on the right. Marcus starts his hike from P and walks to V and then back to P. Determine the route Marcus would need to take to walk the shortest distance, and state the distance he would walk.

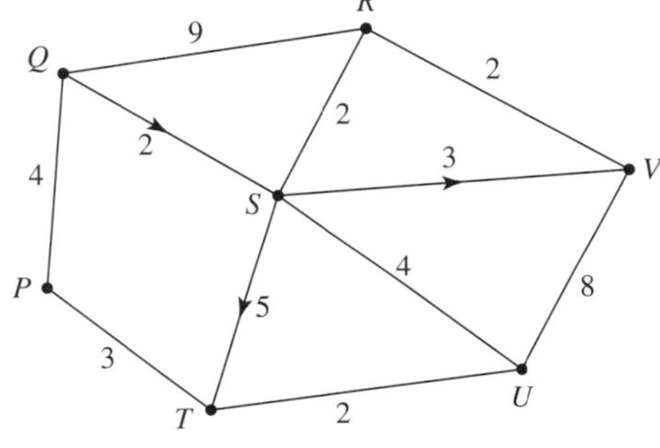

12.4 Euler's formula

It is possible to draw some undirected connected networks without any of the edges crossing. Such a network is known as a **planar network**. An example is shown in the diagram below on the right.

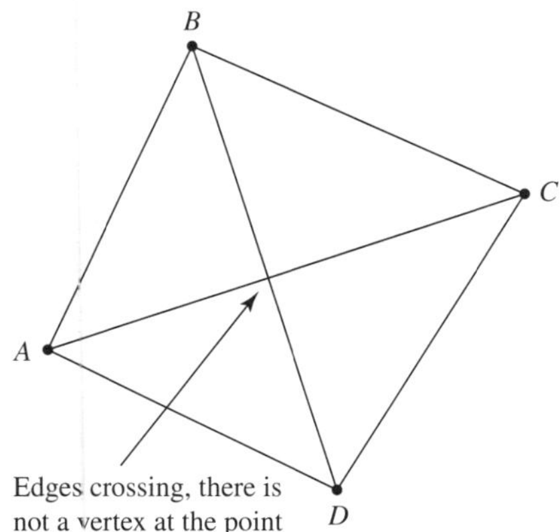

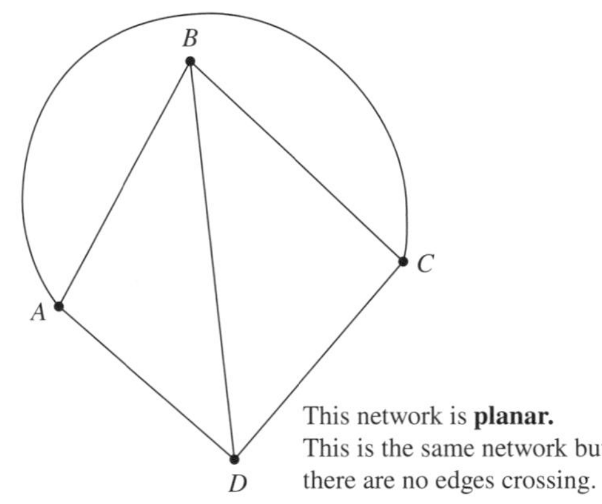

A connected network that is also planar satisfies Euler's formula:

$$V + F = E + 2$$

where V is the number of vertices, F is the number of faces and E is the number of edges.

Conversely, if a network satisifies Euler's formula, it must be planar.

Note: when you determine the number of faces, you must include both the interior faces (bounded by the edges) and the exterior face.

Example

Redraw the network diagram shown below as a planar network, if possible. Show that this new network satisfies Euler's formula.

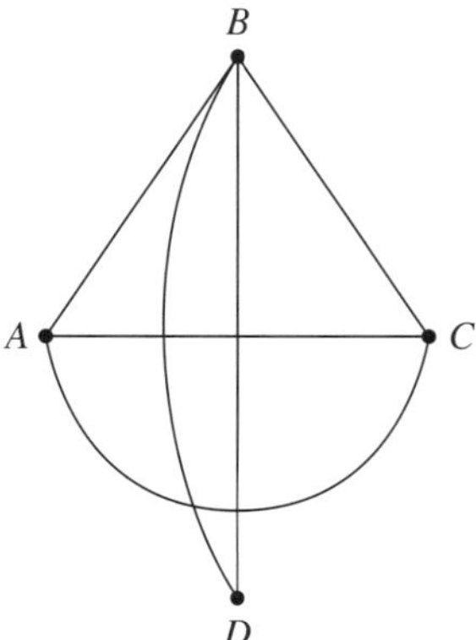

✓ *Solution*

Working	Explanation
	Redraw the network by moving vertex D to a different location. Redraw the two edges BD. The network is now planar.
$V = 4, E = 6, F = 4$	Determine the number of vertices, edges and faces.
$V + F = 8$ $E + 2 = 8$	Determine $V + F$ and $E + 2$.
Since $V + F = E + 2$, Euler's formula is satisfied.	State the conclusion.

Example

Redraw the network diagram shown below as a planar network, if possible. Show that this new network satisifes Euler's formula.

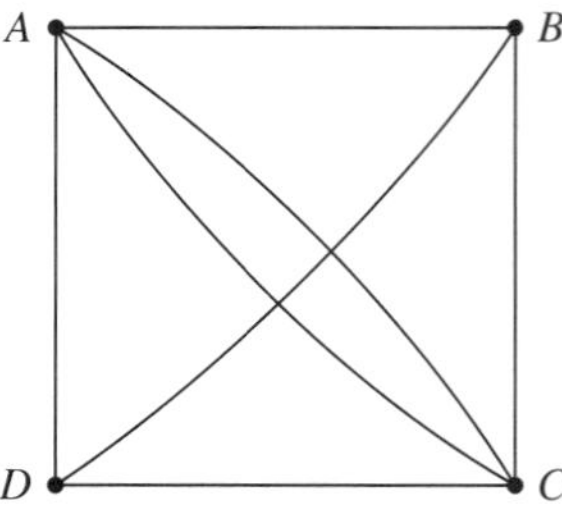

✓ ***Solution***

Working	Explanation
	Redraw the network by moving the two AC edges. The network is now planar.
$V = 4$, $E = 7$, $F = 5$	Determine the number of vertices, edges and faces.
$V + F = 9$ $E + 2 = 9$	Determine $V + F$ and $E + 2$.
Since $V + F = E + 2$, Euler's formula is satisfied.	State the conclusion.

Example

Redraw the network diagram shown below as a planar network, if possible. Show that this new network satisifes Euler's formula.

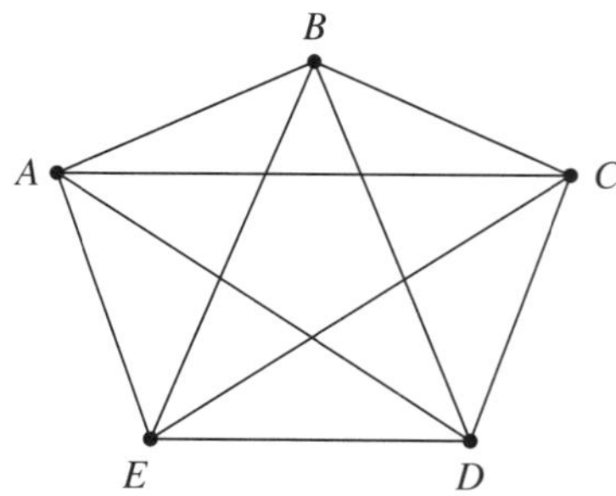

✓ ***Solution***

Working	Explanation
Is it not possible to redraw this network as planar. It is not possible to determine the number of faces and therefore we cannot test whether Euler's formula applies.	You might try by first redrawing two edges (e.g. BE and BD) as shown below. 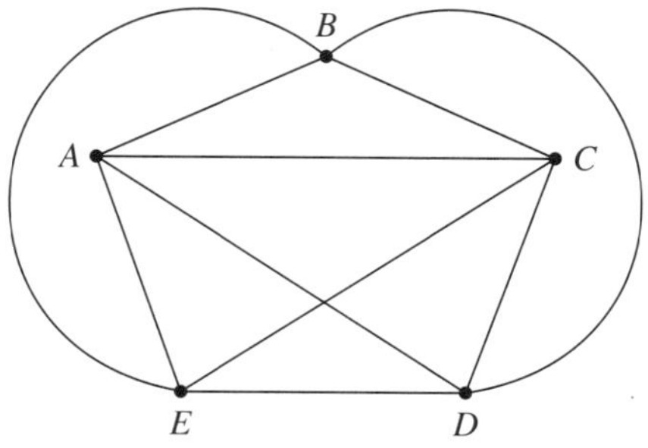 B A C E D To make the network planar, either CE or AD has to be redrawn. However, it is not possible to redraw either of these edges without crossing BE or BD. Therefore, this network cannot be made planar.

Some polyhedra (that is, solids with flat polygon faces) can be represented by a planar network. Two examples are shown in the table below.

Polyhedron	Network	Explanation
Cube 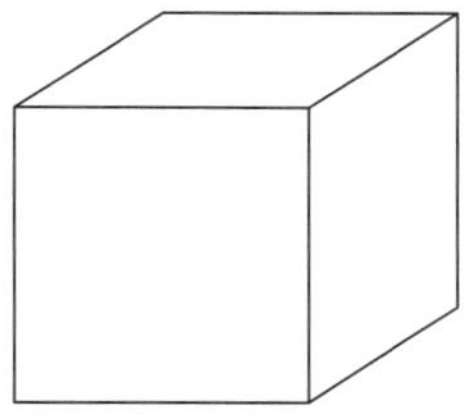	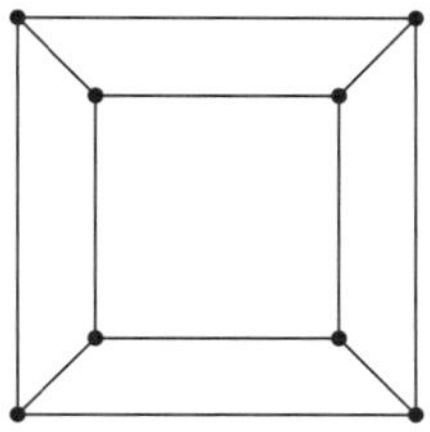	The network has 6 faces, 8 vertices and 12 edges. Each face of the network represents a square. Three edges meet at each vertex.
Tetrahedron 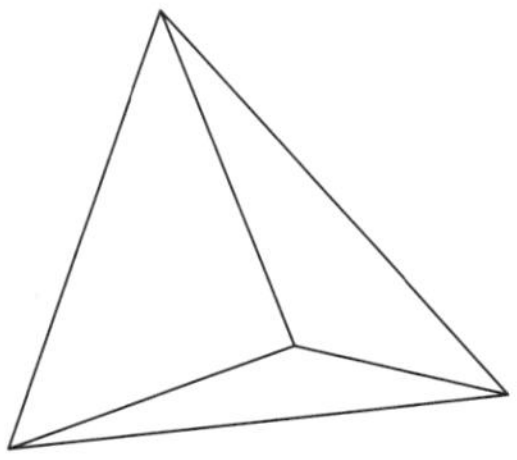	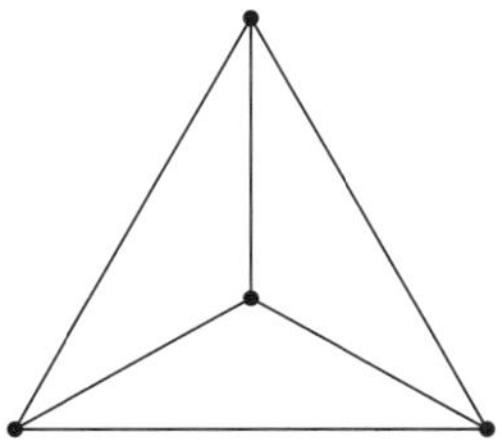	The network has 4 faces, 4 vertices and 6 edges. Each face of the network represents a triangle. Three edges meet at each vertex.

Exercise 12.4

a. Redraw the following network diagrams as planar, if possible. Show that each new network satisifes Euler's formula.

i.

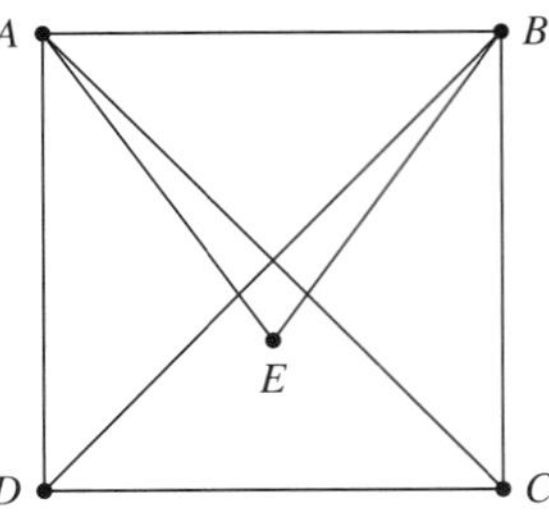

ii.

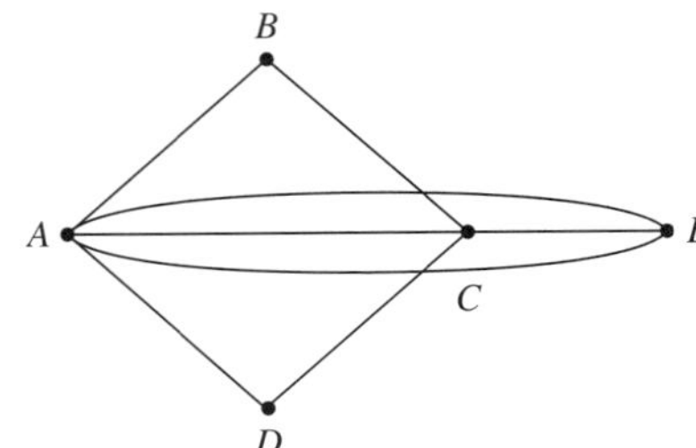

iii.

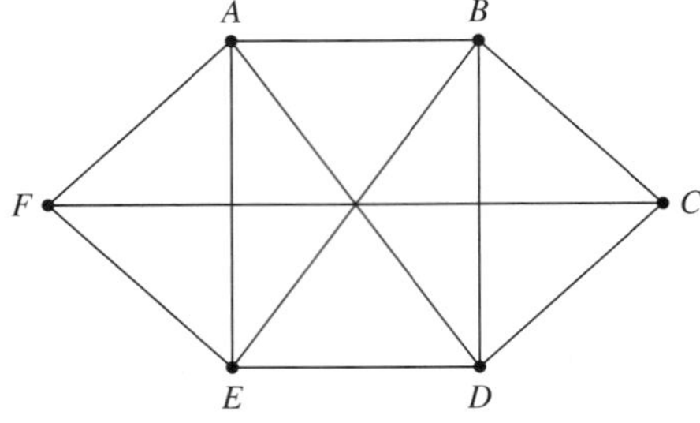

b. The diagram below is a hexagonal pyramid. Redraw it as a network and determine the number of faces, vertices and edges it has.

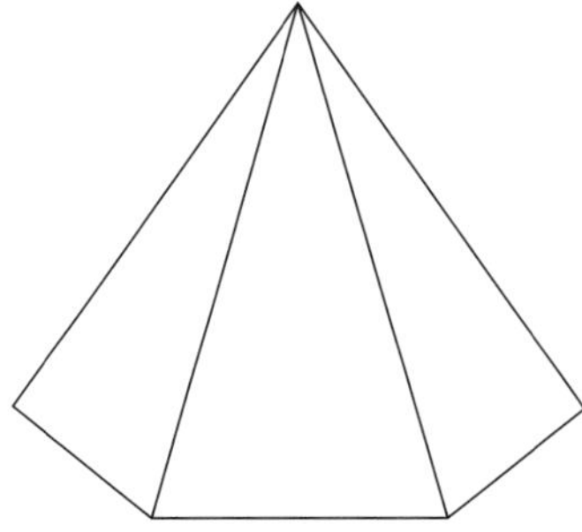

Answers

Scan the QR code below to access the answers to all the exercises in this book.